D0495159

Storm in the Desert

Storm in the Desert

Britain's Intervention in Libya
and the Arab Spring

MARK MULLER STUART

BIRLINN

First published in Great Britain in 2017 by
Birlinn Ltd

West Newington House
10 Newington Road
Edinburgh
EH9 1QS

www.birlinn.co.uk

ISBN: 978 1 78027 452 2

British Library Cataloguing-in-Publication Data
A catalogue record for this book is available on request from the British Library

Typeset by Biblichor Ltd, Edinburgh
Printed and bound in Britain by T. J. International, Padstow, Cornwall

To my son, Louis Muller Stuart, who aged eleven asked why it was necessary for me to go to Libya, after seeing violent images of the Libyan Revolution on television. This book is an attempt at an answer.

And to my daughters Charlotte, Isabella and my wife Catherine for allowing me to wonder afar without complaint.

And finally to my parents for being citizens of the world.

'They make a desert and call it peace.'

Gaius Cornelius Tacitus (Senator and Historian of the Roman Empire)
Ascribed to a speech by the Caledonian chieftain Calgacus addressing assembled
warriors about Rome's intervention into the affairs of other nations

Contents

Acknowledgements

This book could and would not have been written were it not for the support I received from a number of institutions and individuals who have assisted me and my work in relation to the Middle East North Africa (MENA) region over the last two decades.

Firstly, thanks to the Human Rights Programme at Harvard Law School and its former academic director, Mindy Rosen, who gave me valuable time and space in 2012 to capture and record my memories of Benghazi during the Libyan Revolution through the form of a Senior Fellowship.

Secondly, thanks to all my friends and colleagues at Beyond Borders Scotland (BB), the John Smith Memorial Trust (JSMT), the Delfina Foundation (DF), the Bar Human Rights Committee of the Bar Council of England and Wales (BHRC), the Centre for Humanitarian Dialogue (CHD), Beyond Conflict (BC), the Kurdish Human Rights Project (KHRP) and Democratic Progress Institute (DPI), Inter-Mediate (IM), Doughty Street Chambers (DSC) and Traquair House for their unstinting support throughout this period. They all know who they are. Certain other institutions and individuals have not been named for operational reasons.

However, it would be remiss of me if I let this opportunity pass without recording my particular thanks to Allan Marson, Jessica Forsythe, Professor Brian Brivati, Paul Doubleday, David Marshall, Kirsten Winterman, Jenny Munro, Georgia de Courcy Wheeler, Emily Gifford, Sarah Macdonald, David Packard, Elliot Campbell, Dave Barras, Dave Angus, Gary Moore, Anna Irvin and Isabella Scott, David Steel, Jeremy Purvis, Stephen Gethins, Malcolm Fleming, Sylvia Whitman, Andrew Brown, Mark McLeod, the late Stephanie Wolfe Murray and all the interns for their contribution towards the work of Beyond Borders Scotland; Elizabeth Smith, Catherine Smith and David Charters at JSMT; Delfina Entracanales and Aaron Cezar at DF; Catriona Vine and Mustafa Gündogdu at KHRP and DPI; Sir Kieran Prendergast, Staffan de Mistura, Martin Griffiths, David Harland, David Gorman, Jonathan Powell, Teresa Whitfield, Roelf Meyer, Tim Phillips and

Kerim Yildiz for their invaluable example and assistance in relation to my dialogue work with non-state organisations involved in the MENA region; Sydney Kentridge QC, Helena Kennedy QC, Michael Mansfield QC, Ben Emmerson QC, Kirsty Brimelow QC, Nick Stewart QC, Peter Carter QC, Michael Ivers QC, Sudhanshu Swaroop QC, Gareth Pierce, Louis Charalambous, Blinnie Ni Ghrálaigh, as well as all my former colleagues from the Chambers of Mark Muller, including Raj Rai, Edward Grieves, Ajanta Kaza, for their long-term support of my legal and human rights work in the MENA region; Jason McCue and McCue and Partners for their comradeship and company during a truly remarkable journey into the heart of the Libyan Revolution; Allan Little, William Dalrymple, Oscar Guadiola-Reveria, Jim Naughtie, Magnus Linklater, Robert MacDowell and all the other regular international BB participants and presenters who each year help bring to life the stories and tales of people from the MENA region at Beyond Borders' various culture festivals held during the Edinburgh Festival; and of course to my family, Catherine, Isabella, Louis, Charlotte, Maria and Christopher.

Finally, a special huge thanks must be given to my editor, Mairi Sutherland, for all her advice and patience in helping to edit this book, including putting up with my never-ending travels with the United Nations; Christine Gilmore, Peter Sacks, Tertia Bailey, Mark Gorman and my wife Catherine Maxwell Stuart for reading the text; and to Neville Moir, Hugh Andrew and their team at Birlinn, without whose support this book would not have seen the light of day.

Abbreviations

AFRICOM	United States of America African Command
AKP	Justice and Development Party (Turkey)
ANC	African National Congress
AQIM	Al-Qaeda in the Islamic Maghreb
AU	African Union
BDF	Bahrain Defence Force
BDP	Peace and Democracy Party (Turkey)
BHRC	Bar Human Rights Committee of England and Wales
BHRWS	Bahrain Human Rights Watch Society
BICI	Bahrain Independent Commission of Inquiry
BM	British Museum
BMC	Benghazi Medical Centre
BRIC	Brazil, Russia, India and China
CHD	Centre for Humanitarian Dialogue
CIA	Central Intelligence Agency
COS	Commandement des Opérations Spéciales
CP	Close Protection
CSO	Civil Society Organisation
DDR	Disarmament, Demobilisation and Reintegration
DFID	Department for International Development
DPI	Democratic Progress Institute
DS	Diplomatic Security
ECHR	European Court of Human Rights
EOCCS	Executive Office of Cultural Relations and Civil Society
FBI	Federal Bureau of Investigation
FCO	Foreign and Commonwealth Office
FJP	Freedom and Justice Party
FSU	Former Soviet Union
GAM	Free Aceh Movement (Indonesia)
GCC	Gulf Cooperation Council

GIA	Groupe Islamique Armé
GPA	Global Political Agreement
HDI	Human Development Index
HMG	Her Majesty's Government
ICC	International Criminal Court
ICISS	International Commission on Intervention and State Sovereignty
ICJ	International Court of Justice
IRA	Irish Republican Army
ISRT	International Stabilisation Response Team
JSMT	John Smith Memorial Trust
KADEK	Kurdistan Freedom and Democracy Congress
KHRP	Kurdish Human Rights Project
KRG	Kurdistan Regional Government
LAF	Legal Aid Forum
LCRA	Libya Claims Resolution Act
LIFG	Libyan Islamic Fighting Group
LSE	London School of Economics
MDC	Movement for Democratic Change
MECAS	Middle East Centre for Arabic Studies
MENA	Middle East and North Africa
MNLF	Moro National Liberation Front
MoU	Memorandum of Understanding
NATO	North Atlantic Treaty Organisation
NDP	National Democratic Party
NES	National Economic Strategy
NFSL	National Front for the Salvation of Libya
NGO	non-governmental organisation
NIO	Northern Ireland Office
NSC	National Security Council
NTC	National Transitional Council
NUG	National Unity Gathering
OIC	Organisation of the Islamic Conference
OSCE	Organisation of Security and Co-operation in Europe
PFLP-GC	Popular Front for the Liberation of Palestine – General Command
PFR	People's Resistance Forces
PKK	Kurdistan Workers Party
PMOI	People's Mujahedin of Iran
POAC	Proscribed Organisation Appeals Commission
PSD-10	Presidential Study Directive on Mass Atrocities
RAF	Royal Air Force

RARDE	Royal Armament Research and Development
RPG	Rocket-Propelled Grenade Launcher
R2P	Responsibility to Protect
SADC	Southern African Development Community
SAS	Special Air Service
SBS	Special Boat Service
SCAF	Supreme Council of the Armed Forces
SCCRC	Scottish Criminal Cases Review Commission
SCR	Security Council Resolution
SIAC	Special Immigration Appeals Commission
SRR	Special Reconnaissance Regiment
SRSG	Special Representative of the Secretary-General
SSC	Supreme Security Council
UAE	United Arab Emirates
UNDPA	United Nations Department for Political Affairs
UNHCR	United Nations High Commissioner for Refugees
UNSMIL	United Nations Support Mission in Libya
USDOS	United States Department of State
VTA	Victims of Terrorism in America
WGI	Worldwide Governance Indicator
WMD	Weapons of Mass Destruction
ZESN	Zimbabwe Election Support Network

Introduction: Benghazi or Bust

It was a classic breezy spring day in Benghazi as Qais Ahmad Hilal made his way towards Freedom Square by the quayside to finish yet another iconic image of the Libyan Revolution. 'Good, the paint will dry quicker today,' he thought to himself, as he added the last remaining touches to his most recent offering. Suddenly an unmistakable whistle rang out through the air. Qais only managed to turn his head before the sniper's bullet entered his chest. He immediately dropped to his knees as if in prayer while horrified bystanders began to scream out in panic. As his shattered torso hit the ground the image behind him came into view. It was of Colonel Muammar Gaddafi's vengeful figure cloaked in green, holding a black umbrella dripping with blood-red rain. Within seconds the 'Graffiti King of Benghazi', who for a few short weeks brought untold laughter to the people of his beloved city through his lampooning of the 'Great Leader', was dead. He was only twenty-nine years of age. Qais's summary execution could not have been more telling or poignant.

Gaddafi had elected to send an assassin into Benghazi to execute not a rebel leader, but rather an unknown artist whose work had laid bare his inner core. Both men recognised the danger that artistic ridicule posed for a ruler who depended on fear to exercise power. Both knew that it was laughter rather than dissent that broke the spell of political invincibility. And both knew that only one man would survive this portraiture. That is why Qais had to die. Yet if Gaddafi thought he could cow the young people of Benghazi into submission he was in for a shock. The next day dozens of them presented themselves at the little blackened office by the courthouse in central Benghazi, offering to paint the city afresh with biting new images of the 'Mad Dog' of Tripoli. These young people came not by chance but by moral choice. Within hours of his death Qais's image was to be found on the very walls he had sought to adorn. He joined a long line of honoured martyrs who gave their lives in defence of freedom and the so-called 17 February Revolution. The graffiti revolution had begun.

I first came across Qais's images in Benghazi in early April 2011, two weeks after he was executed following the UN Security Council's imposition of a no-fly zone in defence of the people of Benghazi against Gaddafi's advancing forces. I had just completed a madcap thousand-mile dash across the desert from Cairo to Benghazi with Jason McCue, the London-based solicitor who had harried Gaddafi for over twenty years on behalf of the British victims of the IRA Semtex and Lockerbie attacks. His purpose in travelling to Benghazi was to initiate a private dialogue with the newly established rebel National Transitional Council (NTC) on some of the most protracted legacy issues that haunted UK–Libyan relations, including the Lockerbie bombing incident.

As chairman of the Bar Human Rights Committee of England and Wales (BHRC), I too was interested in testing New Libya's stated commitment to the rule of law and to see how the BHRC might help it rebuild its shattered society. Yet these objectives quickly paled into insignificance after we encountered the brave people of revolutionary Benghazi. Their sense of defiance in the face of tyranny literally took one's breath away. It was as if Hegel's zeitgeist had infused itself into the soul of this ancient city as the hitherto repressed political aspirations of an entire continent suddenly, and miraculously, made themselves felt. Benghazi's faith in the redemptive power of democracy, despite everything it had experienced at the hands of Gaddafi and the West, was both exhilarating and troubling. It was difficult to know whether what was happening in Benghazi was indicative of real change and the cunning of reason or just an idealistic pipedream. It felt as if fact and fiction were locked together in an intoxicating revolutionary waltz across an entire region with little or no thought given to the outcome of such a deadly embrace.

After coming across this lacerating image of Gaddafi, I resolved to talk to some of the artists holed up in that blackened office by the side of the revolutionary courthouse, because I wanted to find out who had painted it. I soon discovered that – like so many other key moments associated with the early part of the Libyan Revolution – Qais's execution had passed from fact to fiction and into the stuff of myth and legend. Many of the young artists I met spoke of how Qais had died next to his artwork, while others closer to the family told of how he was shot in a car as he made his way to work. Whatever the real truth about the details of his execution, his personal act of defiance spoke to a city in the grip of a monumental struggle for freedom. Qais was an early legendary emblem of that struggle. Only time would tell whether his unquenchable belief in the power of democracy was misplaced or not. Yet it was increasingly evident that he was not alone in holding such a belief. All across the Middle East and North Africa (MENA) region a multitude of like-minded civil society activists were on the streets and taking inspiration from his and his comrades' actions.

As I contemplated the significance of Qais's sacrifice, I thought about an appropriate epitaph for Gaddafi's obscene attempt to erase Qais and his work from Benghazi's memory. 'Benghazi or Bust' came to mind. This was a throwaway quip I made to Jason McCue as we flew from London to Cairo on 1 April 2011. Yet it was also a phrase that continued to hang in my head as I tried to accustom myself to revolutionary Benghazi and get to grips with the deadly power struggle unfolding across the region. It was certainly 'Benghazi or Bust' for Gaddafi, the rebel leadership, and the ordinary people of the city. And for the embattled Mediterranean coastal town of Misrata, whose only hope of relief from Gaddafi's assault was through the port of Benghazi. It was also 'Benghazi or Bust' for all those governments and international institutions that either tacitly supported the Gaddafi regime or backed the imposition of a no-fly zone, which included the relatively new and inexperienced Cameron and Obama administrations. Not only were huge geo-political and economic interests at play in Libya, but the possibility of a wider democratic dispensation across the region hung in the balance, as did the efficacy of the humanitarian doctrine known as the 'Responsibility to Protect' (R2P).

The stakes could not have been higher, whether for Libya, the fate of the Arab Spring more generally, or the future conduct of multilateral diplomacy within the international community. Benghazi was fast becoming key for each of the principal players involved in this multi-dimensional drama, and whoever lost control of it was, to all intents and purposes, bust. Thus, as I stood transfixed amid the beflagged streets of revolutionary Benghazi on April Fools' Day 2011, it really did seem as if all roads in the Arab Spring, triumphant or treacherous, led inexorably to Benghazi. I realised then that whatever happened there over the course of the next few months, and possibly even years, was likely to change the West's relation to Libya and the Arab region forever, whether any of these players realised it or not.

Was the wind of change blowing through the region an ill one or was it capable of ushering in a new era of democratic reform and hope? This question would haunt NATO after it helped rebels push back loyalist forces from Benghazi and finally oust Gaddafi from Tripoli in late August 2011. It was a question that remained largely unanswered a year after the rebel victory, when the militias refused to give up their weapons and cede power to the new civilian government following Libya's first free and fair election in June 2012. And it was a question that became even more acute after another assassination on the streets of Benghazi on 11 September 2012, not far from where Qais fell. This time the assassin was not a Gaddafi loyalist but a radical Islamist who had helped bring down the former regime. More significantly, the victim was not a lowly artist but Chris Stevens, the US Ambassador to Libya, who had been instrumental in giving the rebels much needed support during the revolution. Stevens arrived in Benghazi the same week in April that I did but stayed, off and on, for the duration. He died in a hail of bullets and smoke on the anniversary of 9/11 in what later proved to be a pre-orchestrated jihadist attack on the US diplomatic compound in Benghazi.

Like Qais, Stevens passionately believed in the ability of ordinary Libyans to create a more stable, representative and constitutionally based government. He also believed the US needed to support the struggle for democratic reform in the region on a long-term basis. A few weeks later, President Barack Obama talked to the UN General Assembly about Stevens and the US's unbroken commitment to reform in Libya. He spoke of how Stevens had loved the streets of Benghazi, 'tasting the local food, meeting as many people as he could, speaking Arabic and listening with a broad smile'. Yet despite this unambiguous commitment to the 'New Libya', Stevens's death quickly raised questions in the back of every Western policymaker's mind. Was it really in the interests of the West to support largely unknown rebel movements against a set of aged, unrepresentative MENA elites, in the name of democratic reform? Or should it back the forces it knew in the name of regional stability, if only to head off the emergence of an altogether more hostile form of political Islam? Over the next five years this question, above all others, would bedevil the West's relations with Libya, Bahrain and, above all, Egypt.

It was somewhat unsurprising, then, that within a day of Stevens's tragic death the US Republican presidential nominee Mitt Romney used the circumstances of his execution to question the Obama administration's entire Middle East policy, claiming that the jihadist assault on the compound of the US consulate in Benghazi typified the weak disposition of the Obama administration towards countering Islamic fundamentalism and supporting the US's real allies in the region. Policy prescriptions in favour of democratic change, he implied, were nothing more than a dangerous delusion that put America, its officials and its allies in serious peril. Such sentiments chimed with the analysis of sceptical commentators like Robert Bradley, who believed the general liberal commitment to democratic change in the MENA region was delusional. What the West needed to do was work with its trusted allies and return to the tried and tested ways of traditional state diplomacy, based upon a clear-cut vision of geo-political and economic self-interest, backed up by the threat of military might. Any other approach was bound to lead to yet more chaos, in which Islamists would take advantage of the vacuum created by the West's misguided policy, just as they had done in Tunisia and Egypt in elections in 2011 and 2012.

One could not have devised two more different and compelling narratives about what was unfolding in Libya and across the wider MENA region. Each narrative called for radically different policy prescriptions about how to respond to the winds of change sweeping through the region. Stevens's view was based upon his long diplomatic experience in the region and of revolutionary Benghazi. Bradley's reflections were based upon his counter-terror experiences in Tunisia and Egypt in the aftermath of the Arab Spring. So who was right? Certainly each narrative was open to criticism. Yet each also contained more than a germ of truth. What was telling, however, was how each man felt impelled to nail his colours to the mast. Neither sought to hide or nuance his position. That they did so was because the nature of the Arab Spring made it virtually impossible for those involved to sit on the fence or conceal where their ultimate allegiance lay. The tumultuous uprisings in Tunisia, Yemen, Egypt, Libya, and Bahrain forced Western states and civil society not only to articulate the principles they believed in but also to take a stand in support of those principles. The demand for international solidarity was not just for words but deeds. Like President Bush after 9/11, the people of Cairo, Manama, and then Benghazi, demanded to know in unadulterated terms if the West was 'with us or against us'. The answer to this question would shape the future of the people of not only Benghazi but also the West, as the maelstrom that was the Arab Spring threw up profound questions about the West's identity, values and relationship to the MENA region in an increasingly inter-dependent world.

In fact, the debate about how the West should react to the conflict in Libya and the Arab Spring more generally would continue to rage well into the next decade. It came to haunt President Obama throughout his second term, as more and more questions began to be asked about his administration's decision to intervene in Libya. Then US Secretary of State Hillary Clinton's alleged failure to properly protect and secure the US compound in Benghazi on the night of 11 September 2012 was used as a battering ram by the Republicans to smash Obama's wider policy of engagement in the MENA region. It certainly formed the centrepiece of Donald Trump's acceptance speech at the Republican Convention in late July 2016 when he was officially declared the Republican presidential nominee. He used this platform to attack Hillary Clinton – the Democrats' presidential nominee – on her policy record in the Middle East in the most combative and unmistakable terms. 'In Libya, our consulate, the symbol of American prestige around the globe was brought down in flames,' he thundered, continuing:

America is far less safe and the world is far less stable than when Obama made the decision to put Hillary Clinton in charge of America's foreign policy. I am certain it is a decision he truly regrets. Her bad instincts and her bad judgment . . . are what caused so many of the disasters unfolding today. Let's review the record. In 2009, pre-Hillary, ISIS was not even on the map. Libya was stable. Egypt was peaceful. Iraq had seen a big reduction in violence. Iran was being choked by sanctions. Syria was somewhat under control. After four years of Hillary Clinton, what do we have? ISIS has spread across the region and the entire world. Libya is in ruins, and our ambassador and his staff were left helpless to die at the hands of savage killers. Egypt was turned over to the radical Muslim Brotherhood, forcing the military to retake control. Iraq is in chaos. Iran is on the path to nuclear weapons. Syria is engulfed in a civil war and a refugee crisis that now threatens the West. After fifteen years of wars in the Middle East, after trillions of dollars spent and thousands of lives lost, the situation is worse than it has ever been before. This is the legacy of Hillary Clinton: death, destruction and terrorism and weakness.

For Trump the lessons were clear: 'To protect us from terrorism we must have the best, absolutely the best, gathering of intelligence anywhere in the world. The best. And we must abandon the failed policy of nation-building and regime change that Hillary Clinton pushed in Iraq, Libya, in Egypt, and Syria.' For many observers, Trump certainly seemed to be right when he intimated that how the US chose to respond to the diplomatic, political, legal, security and moral challenges posed by the Arab Spring would define the political landscape in the MENA region for a generation to come. For many others, however, his historical account and political analysis were both unfair and widely off the mark.

This book seeks to explore the central policy dilemma that faces the UK and the West as a consequence of the Arab Spring and its interventions (and indeed, non-interventions) in the MENA region – namely whether it was and is wise to go out on a limb to back peoples seeking democratic reform at the expense of more immediate geo-political and security interests and concerns. It does this from an avowedly civil society perspective by drawing upon personal experiences of the Egyptian, Bahraini and Libyan protests and uprisings and by examining the UK intervention in Libya. The book is divided into three parts. Part One deals with the origins of the Arab Spring and the initial uprising in Benghazi. Part Two focuses on the UK's civil intervention and non-intervention in Libya during the conflict and after it ended. Part Three deals with the aftermath and examines some of the wider policy lessons to be learnt from the Coalition intervention.

In more concrete terms the text tells the story of how Jason McCue and I came to go to Benghazi to meet with the NTC in an effort to secure compensation agreements for Lockerbie and IRA Semtex and other victims affected by the Northern Ireland conflict, as well as to try to help New Libya rebuild the rule of law. It describes some of the extraordinary characters who went on to frame the Libyan Revolution and documents the murky relationship that existed between Gaddafi and Britain's political elite. More significantly, it sets out how the heroic people of Benghazi came to take on a ruthless tyrant in an effort to free their country from a corrupt government as part of a wider struggle for dignity and greater freedom across the region.

Elsewhere it charts how the debate over whether to impose a no-fly zone forced the UK to reconsider some of its more traditional diplomatic and political approaches towards the region and international security more generally. In particular, it reveals how the UK's intervention altered the international diplomatic and legal architecture concerning the resolution of conflict; the fight against terrorism; the right to resist; the promotion of democracy; and the right to self-determination in the twenty-first century. In doing so it examines the rise of non-state mediation, civil society and cultural diplomacy as means of resolving conflict, in comparison with conventional diplomacy. The book ends with a tentative answer to the question of whether the West should support the cause for reform in the MENA region at the expense of immediate political and economic interests.

Yet, to be clear, I only decided to publish this book in the summer of 2016 after reading some of the submissions made by the Foreign and Commonwealth Office (FCO) and certain former UK coalition government ministers to the Foreign Affairs Select Committee inquiry into Britain's intervention in Libya. Those submissions effectively claimed that the coalition government, through its stabilisation team, had done all it reasonably could to support the fledgling National Transitional Council in its efforts to stabilise and reconstruct Libya, both during and after the conflict. These are assertions with which I profoundly disagree. There are important lessons to be learnt from the UK's half-hearted intervention in Libyan affairs which have been glossed over.

As a senior UN mediation advisor to the Department of Political Affairs who has been involved in a number of sensitive conflict resolution processes over the years, I am disinclined to put pen to paper about my mediation work, as I believe it is important to keep professional and diplomatic confidences in life, and I disapprove of kiss-and-tell memoirs. I decided to make an exception in the case of my experiences of Libya and certain other parts of the MENA region during the Arab Spring in the course of 2011. Firstly, because the nature of the work I undertook there was in my capacity as a human rights lawyer for the BHRC and as a dialogue expert for more open non-state organisations like Beyond Conflict. Secondly, because I believe civil society also needs to share its experiences of the UK's intervention in Libya and the region if the UK is to successfully resolve fundamental policy dilemmas that it continues to face as a consequence of the Arab Spring.

Thirdly, and most importantly, because I believe that the world needs reminding that the people who rose up in Benghazi in 2011 were not Islamic fundamentalists but ordinary people like you and me. If Libya is now a place of lawless disruption and an incubator for jihadist terror, it is not as a result of their aims and endeavours. This appalling state of affairs happened for other reasons, for which the UK Foreign Affairs Select Committee has rightly called our policymakers to account.

Thus, although a definitive history of the Arab Spring has yet to be written, there are tentative lessons that can, and should, be learnt now. What follows is neither an annotated nor an authoritative history of the Libyan Revolution or the Arab Spring. Nor is it an insider's guide. None of what is conveyed here is based upon confidential archives or classified material. Rather it is a hastily compiled account written from the vantage point of a civil society activist who, like politicians and other policymakers involved in the Arab Spring, had to react to events as they happened. Some parts of the book are therefore autobiographical and read like a diary, while others are more akin to reportage, and the last part is more policy-orientated. In many ways it is a book that falls between all genres and professional stools. Nevertheless, I hope that it provides some useful initial insights into one of the most extraordinary political events of our time.

One matter, however, remains beyond contention. None of us involved in civil society could begin to explore what needs to be done were it not for the exploits of a remarkable group of journalists, film makers, photographers, artists, political activists, diplomats and lawyers who all put their lives on the line to bring out the truth about Gaddafi's Libya. The story of what happened to the people of Libya during a few unforgettable weeks in the spring of 2011 could not have been publicly told or examined were it not for their extraordinary efforts. Their dispatches and individual plights pepper the pages of this book. The book is dedicated to all those who lost their lives trying to convey the truth about the Libyan and Arab Spring uprisings to a wider audience – people such as Qais Ahmad Hilal and my friend Marie Colvin, a journalist whose death in Homs in February 2012 must not be forgotten either by those on whose plight she reported or the international community at large, whose institutions remain tasked with ensuring peace and security in this deeply troubled but beguiling region. For whatever the prevailing political circumstances or exigencies may be, the primary responsibility of those in power or seeking to gain it should remain the protection of the fundamental rights of their citizens.

If this book does nothing else then, I hope it reminds the public about the courage of such women and men, and of the international community's responsibility to protect not only civilians caught up in conflict but also civil society activists, human rights defenders and journalists who seek to report on their plight. When push comes to shove, it is not governments but civil society that invariably unearths the truth about conflict and the ill-treatment of civilians at the hand of state forces, as well as making peace and rebuilding shattered communities.

PART ONE: The Uprising

1. The Arabs Awaken

Like many people around the world I watched with something approaching awe as ordinary men, women and children took to the streets of the Arab world in the spring of 2011 to protest against a series of unrepresentative regimes across the MENA region including in Tunisia, Egypt and Yemen. By the time the protests erupted, many of the leaders of these regimes had ruled over the protesters' lives for the better part of two generations, without so much as a free or fair election. The original catalyst of the Arab Spring and the demonstrations that took place in Tunisia in December 2010 could not have involved a more heartrending and tragic story. Who could have been anything other than moved at the plight of the Tunisian street vendor Tarek el-Tayeb Mohamed Bouazizi, who, having suffered years of poverty, state corruption and personal humiliation at the hands of officialdom, set himself ablaze on 17 December 2010 in the nondescript town of Sidi Bouzid, in an act of total despair, and protest against a world of unrelenting hopelessness.

This lonely act of self-immolation somehow spoke to millions of ordinary Arabs and their own experience of unbridled corruption and unresponsive government. It was an act that unleashed a wave of unparalleled protests in Tunisia and Egypt before spreading like wildfire throughout the rest of the Arab world, confounding the world's politicians, diplomats, policymakers and spooks alike, all of whom had conspicuously failed to predict their occurrence. I can still recall the moment when I turned on my TV and watched wide-eyed as the tumultuous scenes from Tahrir Square beamed themselves from Cairo into my hotel room. It was late January 2011 and I was in New Delhi attending a legal symposium on the concept of equality with members of the Indian Supreme Court. Suddenly I was transported from the somewhat theoretical preoccupations of India's finest legal minds towards a real-life struggle for equality unfolding before my very eyes, with deadly consequences for all those that rose up if they failed to prevail.

The spontaneous and authentic nature of the demonstrations was there for all to see and utterly compelling. There was nothing stage-managed or politically orchestrated about them whatsoever. More significantly, they did not appear to be directed towards Israel or the United States, or initiated by radical Islamic groups who too often relied upon the poverty and misery of the masses to elicit support for their ongoing campaign against the West. Neither did they appear to have much to do with the so-called 'war on terror' which had come to define much of the West's relationship with the Middle East in the first decade of the twenty-first century. On the contrary, these protests appeared to be quintessentially Arab in terms of both their core focus and their demands, namely about corruption, democratic reform, equality and above all human dignity.

The fact that these protests came as a shock to the West says more about it than about what was unfolding in the Arab world. For those who had spent time working with civil society in the Middle East, however, the protests did not come as too much of a surprise. As chair of the BHRC and the Kurdish Human Rights Project (KHRP) as well as director of the Delfina Foundation, Beyond Borders Scotland, and the John Smith Memorial Trust (JSMT), I had worked for many years conducting numerous dialogue sessions, trial observations, training seminars and workshops in Syria, Iraq, Lebanon, Bahrain, Oman, Jordan, Egypt, Tunisia, Morocco, Israel and the Palestinian Occupied Territories. In doing so, I had noted the growing sense of frustration, hopelessness and lack of opportunity with which most ordinary Arabs had to deal. Many of the lawyers, human rights defenders, artists, writers and activists I met routinely evinced the same criticisms and calls for reform that were later voiced by the masses in the squares of 2011.

These calls for reform largely fell on deaf ears until, that is, Bouazizi voiced his criticism in fire. Even then Arab political elites resolutely failed to understand, let alone respond to, these calls for reform. The failure to grasp either the nature or extent of the outrage expressed by the masses was neither incidental nor without precedent. It formed part of a systemic failure on the part of Arab rulers and their Western allies to address the root causes of conflict in the Middle East or respond to the shifting tectonic plates within civil society that had been moving in favour of some sort of radical change for quite a time. The issue was not so much religion or political ideology, as some in the West would have the world believe, but rather, social justice. For these elites had forgotten the most elemental truth about any human society – and the truth that built America – namely that what most ordinary people want is simply the opportunity to live in peace with some prospect of personal happiness and prosperity for their children and themselves. The difference lies in the fact that whereas the American people were given the political tools by which to construct a law-abiding prosperous society the Arab people were not.

A Dangerous Lacuna

This was a truth that the Bush administration should have capitalised on in its response to 9/11. Instead it developed a counter-terrorism strategy that effectively designated half the Arab world as a threat to the security of the West and Israel. President Bush's ultimatum, delivered in late September 2001, that member states of the UN must decide whether they were 'with' or 'against' America did nothing to engage with the complaints of the ordinary Arab on the street. Instead, this simple binary corralled governments into a counter-terrorism paradigm and dangerous diplomatic lacuna in which conflict was allowed to prosper. Countering terror became more important than countering the societal injustice that often gave rise to terror. Over the course of the next eight years more and more communities in the Middle East became personae non gratae as a result of their loose affiliation with certain radical movements, who enticed the population with commitments to overcome corruption and injustice.

The Bush administration's heavy emphasis on proscription, which resulted in the exclusion of political movements that advocated radical change, locked it into a cycle of perpetual conflict. It made it virtually impossible for other Western leaders to advocate mediation as a tool for the resolution of conflict for the better part of a decade. As a consequence, no meaningful dialogue occurred with radical groups in the Middle East in the first decade of the twenty-first century. This, despite the evident support that movements like Hamas, Hezbollah, the Muslim Brotherhood and the Kurdistan Workers Party (PKK) enjoyed in the region. Unsurprisingly, new state actors like Turkey and Qatar soon emerged onto the scene to fill the mediation vacuum in a blatant attempt to extend their regional influence, something both would later try to do in 2011. The pendulum only began to swing back in favour of some form of dialogue and countering injustice after Barack Obama came to power in 2008, after Bush's security-driven strategies in Iraq and Afghanistan lost favour with an increasingly sceptical public. Yet for many seasoned observers, the decade-long refusal of Western governments to engage with grass roots constituencies in the Middle East, and the radical groups that claimed to represent them, constituted one of the gravest failures of conventional state-driven diplomacy in the twenty-first century.

In the end it would take the Arab Spring of 2011 to reveal how redundant Bush's counter-terror strategies were in addressing the underlying sources of political tensions in the Middle East. If Bush had paid more attention to the needs of ordinary Arabs earlier on he might have discovered that the Egyptian, Lebanese and Palestinian flirtation with resistance movements such as the Muslim Brotherhood, Hezbollah and Hamas had less to do with any ideological identification than with the social and economic support that these movements cleverly provided to ordinary people. The reason why Palestinians voted in droves for Hamas in 2006 was not out of religious fanaticism but because Fatah had conspicuously failed to improve the political or economic lot of the ordinary Palestinian. In reality, the supposed 'radicalisation' of sections of the Arab population did not rest with the innate pulling power of Al-Qaeda or global jihad. Rather, it reflected the failure of Arab and Western elites to provide the people of Palestine and Lebanon with a viable exit strategy after decades of repression, poverty and statelessness.

Thus it was not religion that brought ordinary Arabs onto the streets in the spring of 2011, but the refusal to countenance another decade of despair. What the Bush administration should have done was engage directly with those impoverished and marginalised communities rather than the state institutions that claimed to represent them. It should have diverted some of the billions of dollars ploughed into anti-radicalisation programmes in the UK and the MENA region into the economic and social infrastructure of MENA countries. The reason why it did not do so was because many of the state institutions it relied upon to further US strategic interests enjoyed little political legitimacy and were implacably opposed to any form of reform for fear of losing power. Thus, the cycle of despair for ordinary Arabs continued unabated for year after year without resolution in sight, despite occasional noises from the West about the need for democratic reform.

Ameliorating the 'War on Terror'

It was within this arid and prescriptive diplomatic climate that a number of new mediation and civil society organisations stepped into the breach to try to overcome the growing lack of understanding between the peoples and cultures of the West and the Middle East. These new mediators filled the space vacated by conventional state diplomacy, pre-eminent among which was the Centre for Humanitarian Dialogue (CHD) in Geneva, for which I worked from 2005. Founded in 2001 by the former UN diplomat Martin Griffiths, CHD was instrumental in helping forge the peace in Aceh in 2005 and providing crucial advice to peacemakers in places like Nepal, South Sudan and the Philippines. Elsewhere it helped Kofi Annan broker peace between the presidential contenders in the Kenyan elections in 2008, after widespread violence had broken out following the incumbent president's failure to accept the results. It also engaged in a number of confidential dialogue processes in the MENA region. It was one of only a handful of non-state organisations, along with Forward Thinking, the Berghof Foundation, Conciliation Resources and the Carter Centre, that actively sought to engage with radical and marginalised groups in the Middle East during this period. Today, CHD is involved in a quarter of the world's conflicts and has helped spawn a welter of other dialogue organisations.

These dialogue organisations were joined in their endeavour by cultural bodies like the British Council, the British Museum, the Tate and the Delfina Foundation which reached out to countries scorned by the West, such as Syria. Their efforts stood in marked contrast to the focus of domestic human rights advocacy organisations in the UK during these years, which remained largely directed towards domestic legal issues concerning the 'war on terror'. It was of course easy for cultural organisations to operate more freely in places like Syria, but this did not fully account for their presence. They had a deep-seated knowledge of the cultures of the Middle East and innately understood the pernicious effects that the debilitating language of the 'war on terror' was having on cultural relations. They understood the role that cultural diplomacy could play in healing misunderstanding between societies, if not governments. Yet there was an obvious limit to what these bodies could do in the Middle East without further support. Nevertheless, their experiences in the field meant they were altogether less surprised by what later occurred in 2011.

Take, for example, the Delfina Foundation, a small charity dedicated to promoting East–West understanding through the provision of artistic residencies that I helped co-found in 2006 with Delfina Entracanales. Delfina was an eighty-year-old Spanish millionaire who had previously provided studio spaces for some of the UK's most avant-garde artists in the 1990s, which were located in converted factories in the East End of London. In the summer of 2006 I convinced her to travel with me to the Middle East to experience first-hand just how different the Middle East was from the Bush administration's portrayal. My human rights work in Palestine, Syria and Iraq convinced me that more had to be done to ameliorate the growing cultural polarisation between the West and the civil societies of the Middle East, particularly after disturbing revelations came to light about Abu Ghraib, Guantanamo Bay, and the use of Central Intelligence Agency (CIA)-backed torture programmes at secret detention facilities. For me, this was not just a human rights story – it was a story about the alienation of cultures and peoples.

So, in the spring of 2006, Delfina and I travelled from Aleppo in the north of Syria across the Syrian Eastern Desert to Damascus, and from there on to Amman and Aqaba before traversing the Red Sea and carrying on to Cairo. As we did so, we witnessed how many young Arabs felt ostracised and marginalised from contemporary Western cultural discourse. Everywhere we went young artists also flocked to show us their work. Their sense of alienation and lack of opportunity was palpable but so too was their renewed hope as soon as new possibilities began to open up before them. They did not hate the West. They just wanted the West to stop hating them. I remember returning to Damascus a year later in 2007 after we set up the Foundation. We watched transfixed as dozens of young artists queued under a baking sun in the back streets of the old city to exhibit their wares, in the hope of securing one of just two residencies in London. I recall feeling embarrassed at being unable to offer more places, but as one young artist commented, 'just the existence of the opportunity' was enough to set their hearts alight.

These experiences taught me that what these young people wanted was not more ideology but the freedom to explore the world just like their counterparts were able to do in the West. They craved a different, fresher sort of discourse with the outside world. A discourse in which the reality of their existence was not expressed through sympathetic campaigners or human rights advocates from the West acting on their behalf, but through direct communication with the outside world via the liberating means of new media. As a consequence of these trips, the Delfina Foundation was formed. Over the next five years, Aaron Cezar, the Foundation's talented executive director, built a world-class residency programme, teaming up with new cultural houses from across the Middle East and North Africa. As a result, numerous Middle Eastern artists came to London. But, more significantly, they went back to their countries with new ideas and experiences, including a growing understanding of the power of new media. The sheer power and potential of this type of cultural dialogue contrasted neatly with the failure of conventional diplomacy or international law to provide people with any meaningful redress against societal injustice or to increase the prospect of greater personal freedom. In short, what these young people wanted most of all was to take control of their lives both as an act of personal self-determination and in order to reclaim some sense of human dignity.

New Social Discourses

As it turned out, the hopes and aspirations of the young people we encountered were indicative of a much wider spirit of adventure spreading throughout Arab civil society. It was not long before these types of cultural exchanges began to replicate themselves on the Internet on a massive scale and within all sorts of different contexts and communities. More and more people harnessed the power of new media to enter into profoundly empowering discourses with other peoples and cultures from around the world. Between 2009 and 2011, these communications multiplied by their millions as huge numbers of Arabs became socially networked. As new media and mobile smart phones flooded the markets of the Middle East, whole communities began to connect with the West in ways that were far less susceptible to traditional monitoring by the authorities. A fresh and powerful wave of freedom of expression spread across the Arab world, under the ageing noses of a set of authoritarian leaders incapable of fully understanding the power of these applications. In the course of a single year in Tunisia the number of Facebook accounts doubled from one million to two million in a population of eleven million, a higher proportion than in most European countries. Many of these new Facebook accounts enjoyed over 10,000 subscriptions and included the unpaid collators and editors of cultural and political events on the streets of numerous Arab towns. Suddenly, ordinary Tunisians were connected up to hundreds of thousands of other like-minded people. As a result, new ideas spread about how to protest and express oneself politically, as people sought to experience some of the greater freedoms that the World-Wide Web promised them. A book from a Bostonian professor about how to protest in new and unpredictable ways became an Internet sensation.

More significantly, these discourses were rapidly taken up by innovative satellite TV channels, such as Al Jazeera, which began to use 'citizen media reports' in its nightly news bulletins. Within a year Al Jazeera had started to train citizen journalists to report on events happening in their local districts. By integrating new media into its 24/7 news coverage of the whole region it pushed the boundaries in news reporting, particularly through its exploitation of cell phone coverage. This form of reporting brought a focus and unity to a whole series of seemingly disparate events that were happening across the region. Ordinary people and communities now shared their experience of government. Thus while the self-immolation of Mohamed Bouazizi spoke directly to the sense of hopelessness that lay within ordinary Arabs, the social networks that had arisen during the previous decade gave each Arab a hitherto unheard of opportunity to express their individual and collective horror at his death. So when Bouazizi's mother, Menobia, protested outside the Sidi Bouzid municipality her nephew uploaded images of the protest onto the Internet. It was the spark that lit a collective sense of outrage, mediated through millions of individual clicks on the Internet, which resulted in a multitude of people coming out onto the streets of the Middle East and North Africa in spontaneous gestures of defiance.

Many of these protesters were middle-class, well-educated and young, but with no jobs or housing opportunities to speak of. What they possessed, however, was an enhanced ability to organise politically and to express themselves through media such as Facebook, Twitter, the Internet, smartphones and satellite TV. Thus, as people in Tunis and Cairo experienced the intoxicating feeling of self-empowerment through spontaneous popular protest, a revolutionary spirit was born which bypassed all political elites and conventions. This wind of change quickly proceeded to blow in every direction. After finding expression on the streets of Tunisia, Egypt, Yemen and Bahrain, it finally turned once more towards the West and blew across the desert from Cairo towards Benghazi in Libya, a town and country I knew very little about.

2. The Libyan Uprising

The Rise of Muammar Gaddafi

Like many Westerners I was familiar with aspects of Libya's history. I knew Libya was another Arab state that had been ruled by the whims of one man for over forty years. I also knew of Gaddafi's support in the 1980s and 1990s of certain terrorist and left-wing causes around the world. But I knew precious little about Libya's internal political history, apart from Gaddafi's well-known hatred of Benghazi. I was aware that Muammar Gaddafi seized power on 1 September 1969 after he overthrew the British-orientated Senussi monarchy in a bloodless coup, with the assistance of twelve other young military officers. This after the ageing King Idris left the country for health reasons, following his failure to unite a fractious country. It is remarkable to consider that Gaddafi was just twenty-seven years old when he seized control of the fourth-largest country in Africa endowed with a strategic position on the Mediterranean and one of the highest oil reserves in the world. Gaddafi saw himself as an Arab nationalist and regarded Egypt's President Nasser as his 'loving father'. As a consequence, he quickly closed the United States Air Force Wheeler military base outside Tripoli and the British bases in Cyrenaica. He followed this up by calling the bluff of Western oil companies to win higher revenues for every barrel of oil exported, to massive popular acclaim. Yet Gaddafi proclaimed this was to be no ordinary military coup but a thorough-going revolution in which the masses would henceforth rule over Libya 'through popular will'. Fate may have appointed him the 'guide and master' of this revolution but it was the people who were to rule.

This narrative provided the ideological cover under which Gaddafi broke up the fledgling state structure that King Idris had created. Over the next ten years Gaddafi announced the suspension of all laws; the destruction of bureaucracy and the bourgeoisie; the dispossession of 40,000 merchants and shop owners; the abolition of most professional classes; and the arming of the people to defend 'their' revolution. Libya was henceforth to be ruled by 187 Basic People's Congresses and forty-seven Municipal People's Congresses. These in turn were to be guided by Maoist-style 'revolutionary committees' which would act to Gaddafi's order in accordance with the Third Universal Theory as set out in his infamous *Green Book* (1975). This claimed to combine religion and nationalism to form a new political front against Western state-run capitalism. The revolution reached its apex in March of 1977 when Gaddafi declared the establishment of the Great Socialist People's Libyan Arab Jamahiriya – a term which means 'State of the Masses'. By this time over 100,000 professional Libyans had fled the country.

Not content with revolution at home, Gaddafi now sought to become the father of revolution abroad. Throughout the 1970s and 1980s Gaddafi supported a bewildering array of terrorist and liberation groups, in an attempt to cast himself upon the world stage as some sort of latter-day Arab nationalist 'philosopher king'. In particular, Gaddafi bankrolled radical Palestinian groups, including the Popular Front for the Liberation of Palestine – General Command (PFLP-GC), which was later suspected of involvement in the Lockerbie bombing. After a series of IRA bombs went off in London in 1976, he declared in the newspaper *al-Fajr al-Jadid* ('New Dawn') that 'the bombs which are convulsing Britain and breaking its spirit are the bombs of the Libyan people [. . .] We have sent bombs to the Irish revolutionaries so that Britain will pay the price of her misdeeds'.

Beyond the IRA, Gaddafi also supported the Italian Red Brigade, the German Baader-Meinhof gang, the Armenian Secret Army, the Filipino Moro National Liberation Front (MNLF), and the Free Aceh Movement (GAM) in Indonesia. He also backed the vicious Abu Nidal Organisation, whose party trick against members suspected of disloyalty included burying them alive, feeding them through a tube for a few days, and then firing a bullet down the tube once guilt was deemed to have been established.[1] Gaddafi likewise developed close relations with a host of dictators including Nicolae Ceausescu in Romania, Imelda Marcos in the Philippines, Robert Mugabe in Zimbabwe and many more in Africa.

It was not long before the Jamahiriya found itself ostracised by the international community for bankrolling a number of terrorist attacks against Western interests and civilians. A range of targeted international sanctions was imposed on the regime, particularly in the aftermath of the Lockerbie bombing in 1988. This included a ban on air travel, trade, business contacts, foreign study and medical treatment. The UN sanctions had a huge impact. These measures soon began to cripple the economy and dent 'Brother Leader's' self-image as a lion of Arabia, although Western oil companies continued to do business with the regime throughout this period. Between 1992 and 1998 Libya lost $24 billion and experienced a 200 per cent increase in food prices. Foreign investment in infrastructure projects stopped overnight. George Tremlett captured the decline of Libya in the 1990s in his book *Gaddafi: The Desert Mystic*:

> Everywhere one goes in Libya, there is filth [. . .] rubbish is left wherever anyone chooses to leave it. There are vast piles of black plastic sacks, stinking with rotting garbage, abandoned furniture, beds, chairs, and old mattresses, and beside every highway, for miles on end, heaps of builder's rubble, burnt out cars, derelict trucks and other vehicles, and, wherever one looks, dead cats and dogs rotting in the sun.[2]

It was only a matter of time before something had to give and that something turned out to be 9/11. With the advent of the 'war on terror' and the fall of Saddam Hussein in Iraq in 2003, Gaddafi knew the game was up. Thus, in a carefully choreographed set of political manoeuvres, mapped out and agreed with the US and UK in advance, Gaddafi consented to the extradition of two Lockerbie suspects. He also promised to give up his weapons of mass destruction (WMD) and fully co-operate in the 'war on terror' against Islamic fundamentalism, which threatened his own regime.

Moussa Koussa and the UK

The principal architect behind these deals and rapprochement was Moussa Muhammad Koussa, Gaddafi's security chief, whom Jason McCue believed was behind the supply of Semtex to the IRA. He had issued a writ against him on behalf of IRA Semtex victims. Koussa was Western educated, attending Michigan State University where he read sociology before taking up a number of posts in various Libyan embassies across Europe. After a short stint at the Libyan Embassy in London he returned to Tripoli to become deputy head of the intelligence service by the late 1980s. He then served as deputy minister of foreign affairs from 1992 to 1994 before finally becoming head of intelligence between 1994 and 2009. It was Koussa who negotiated away Libya's nuclear programme with MI6 officials in the Travellers Club in Pall Mall, London, following meetings between him, the CIA and Mark Allen, a top counter-terror MI6 agent, in the unlikely setting of the Bay Tree Hotel, Burford, in the sleepy Cotswold hills. At the Cotswolds meeting Koussa was played a ninety-minute covert recording of a meeting held between a Libyan scientist and the renegade Pakistani nuclear scientist, Abdul Qadeer Khan, in Casablanca in February 2002. That meeting was held with a view to Libya acquiring nuclear weapons. After hearing the tape

Koussa was given an ultimatum from President Bush and Tony Blair. Either give up the nuclear, chemical and biological programme and come in from the cold or face the wrath of the US and the UN. Unsurprisingly, the meeting was accompanied by positive overtures towards Gaddafi as recorded in minutes later disclosed to *The Times* newspaper after the fall of Tripoli. These state: 'The British Prime Minister is very interested and he wants the initiative to be successful. Its success and the success of our work together has a great benefit for all of us, for the world, for Europe.' Moussa Koussa knew what he had to do. He soon forged even closer links with the CIA, particularly in relation to the hunt for Islamic terrorists, receiving glowing assessments in US diplomatic cables as 'a strong supporter of re-engagement with the West'.[3]

Gaddafi's rehabilitation was nowhere better exemplified than in that memorable moment when Gaddafi and Tony Blair shook hands in Gaddafi's desert tent in 2004. The choreographed nature of these exchanges was ultimately revealed when documents were found in Moussa Koussa's office after the fall of Tripoli in August 2011. These confirmed that it had been Blair's people rather than Gaddafi who had insisted on the handshake in the desert tent. As Jonathan Powell later told an audience at the Beyond Borders International Festival in the Scottish Borders in the summer of 2011, it had been the No. 10 Press office that had requested the presence of some camels so as to add to the 'authenticity' of the occasion. This, as widely predicted, opened the way for billions of pounds of trade with the UK.

The relationship deepened and even blossomed over the next six years. Western companies and intelligence services alike scrambled to cash in on the political dividend created by Tony Blair's 2004 'handshake in the desert'. The process of international rehabilitation was finally sealed when Gaddafi agreed a $1.68 billion deal with the Bush administration to compensate US victims of terrorism through a Humanitarian Fund, in what was widely regarded as a mealy-mouthed ill-defined apology for unspecified acts. It later transpired that the money paid into the Fund had come from companies connected with oil extraction in Libya. Koussa was also intimately involved in negotiations over the return of the Lockerbie suspect, Abdelbaset al-Megrahi, to face trial before a Scottish court for the Lockerbie bombing. He was also instrumental in securing the release of Abdelbaset after meeting officials from the UK government and the Scottish Executive in 2008. These gestures precipitated a remarkable about-turn in both Gaddafi's personal fortune and Libya's dealings with the West.

Yet by 2008 a little of the shine was coming off Gaddafi's international rehabilitation. Massive public outrage greeted the release of al-Megrahi on 'compassionate grounds', particularly in the US. In an unprecedented move, US Senators opposed to the UK's mollycoddling of Gaddafi demanded that the Scottish First Minister Alex Salmond and his Justice Minister Kenny MacAskill attend the US Congress to justify the decision. Predictably, the nationalist Salmond declined this intemperate invitation. For a while the SNP government was castigated from all sides until further documents came to light which indicated that the then Prime Minister, Gordon Brown, actively supported the release of al-Megrahi, while hiding behind the fig leaf of devolution. The earlier prison exchange agreement thrashed out between Libya and the UK a year or two previously now appeared to be a barely disguised device to achieve what everyone in power desired. In the words of Gordon Brown 'Al-Megrahi should not die in prison.'

For David Cameron and the Conservative Party the whole process smacked of shabby, unprincipled deal-making, hence Cameron's sustained support for the victims of Gaddafi's sponsored acts of terrorism and violence overseas. This, however, didn't stop a succession of European governments allowing Gaddafi to pitch his Bedouin tent in the centre of their capitals, as he and his sons bestrode the international stage like pop stars on a world tour. Thus, by the time protesters massed in Cairo's Tahrir Square on 25 January 2011, Gaddafi had ruled Libya for a total of forty-two years. He was, by any standards, at the height of his influence. Until, that is, the sudden revolutionary wind that swirled up in Tahrir Square blew in across the desert from Cairo to Midan al-Shajara in central Benghazi.

The Revolt in Benghazi

On the day that the Libyan uprising began, 17 February 2011, I was in the Court of Appeal in London representing Moloud Sihali, an Algerian asylum seeker, in an appeal against a deportation order granted by the Special Immigration Appeals Commission (SIAC). SIAC was a secretive immigration tribunal that dealt with national security immigration cases, including ones relating to Libya and North Africa. I therefore had both a professional and legal interest in how the Arab Spring might affect certain cases. After completing a set of submissions about the nature of the Algerian regime, I returned to chambers and turned on the television to see what was happening in Bahrain, where protests had erupted three days earlier. Instead of scenes from the Pearl Roundabout in Manama, I was greeted by reports of an uprising in Libya. I watched intently as a group of rebel Libyan lawyers in Benghazi protested against Gaddafi's excesses and proclaimed their commitment to the rule of law. They did so not from inside, but outside, the central courthouse in Benghazi. I became transfixed as over the next few days more and more judges, lawyers, professionals, students and ordinary people took to the barricades in Benghazi to declare the start of an uprising against the regime.

For the next two weeks this courthouse became the epicentre of the Arab Spring. It was from the rooftop of this infamous palace of injustice that lawyers proclaimed the establishment of a new transitional council for New Libya. These scenes reminded me of the overthrow of President Musharraf in Pakistan three years earlier. That revolt likewise began when judges and lawyers openly protested against constitutional dictatorship, corruption and injustice, after Musharraf deposed the Chief Justice for challenging his constitutional coup d'état. I joined forces with UN Special Rapporteur and leading Pakistani human rights lawyer, Hina Jilani, to lead an international coalition of NGOs in support of the Pakistani lawyers and the detained Chief Justice.

A similar process was now unfolding in Libya. On 5 February 2011, Khaled al-Saji, the previous chairman of the Libyan Bar Association, who later became a member of the rebel judicial sub-committee, drove to Tripoli to see Gaddafi in his desert tent. He demanded that newly elected Bar Association officials be allowed to take office to replace Gaddafi loyalists who had unlawfully clung to power. Saji told Gaddafi that the time had come to embrace democratic reform in the wake of the Tunisian Revolution. Gaddafi was deeply suspicious and, on 15 February, arrested the lawyer Fathi Tirbil in Benghazi, who was famous for having brought a lawsuit against Gaddafi's security forces for the murder of 1,200 inmates of the infamous Abu Salim prison in Tripoli in 1996. It was a classic sign of Gaddafi's political intent towards those agitating in favour of reform from the city that he had come to hate.

Benghazi was the second largest city in Libya and capital of the Cyrenaica region, with a history of rebellion and repression which didn't go unnoticed by the regime. It was in Benghazi in 1911 that Omar Mukhtar, supported by half the local population of Cyrenaica, resisted the Italian occupation of the country before succumbing to reprisals. The repression reached its height under the fascist dictator Mussolini, when over 100,000 Libyans were forced into concentration camps. Yet Benghazi's spirit of resistance remained undiminished. And it was here that King Idris al-Senussi declared independence, to create the capital city of the Emirate of Cyrenaica, which lasted from 1949 until 1951, when, under American pressure, Cyrenaica merged with Tripolitania and Fezzan to form the independent Kingdom of Libya.

Benghazi would eventually lose its status as the capital after Gaddafi came to power through a coup d'état in 1969 and moved all government institutions to Tripoli. Thereafter, he deliberately perpetuated a constant atmosphere of rivalry between Benghazi and Tripoli, which replicated the wider historical animosity between the two historical regions of Cyrenaica and Tripolitania. Predictably, support for the old Senussi dynasty remained strong in Cyrenaica where Benghazi functioned as a kernel of opposition throughout the 1980s and 1990s, until Gaddafi brutally exterminated opposition figures in the Abu Salim prison massacre of 1996. It can be no coincidence, then, that the Libyan uprising began in Benghazi.

The catalyst for the uprising occurred just after sunset on 15 February 2011, when Khaled al-Saji and another Benghazian lawyer, Salwa al-Dighaili, demonstrated in front of the courthouse near Benghazi's main square in support of those lawyers arrested by Gaddafi. Salwa would later become a prominent leader of the National Transitional Council. As the protest continued, the lawyers were joined by more and more people from Benghazi, including relatives of the murdered 1,200 prisoners of Abu Salim prison and some of its former inmates, including Mahmoud Matar, 56. He had survived the 1996 massacre and spent twenty-one years in Abu Salim for his involvement in the National Front for the Salvation of Libya (NFSL), an underground movement dedicated to overthrowing Gaddafi.

Matar was beaten, electrocuted, threatened with dogs, and then left for dead in a windowless cell crawling with cockroaches and rats, in which he saw the sun only four times in twelve years. By some miracle, on 29 June 1996 he was accidentally removed from the prison just forty minutes before soldiers opened fire, killing 1,200 prisoners, including 120 sick prisoners who lay defenceless on their stretchers in an adjoining courtyard. Matar was finally hauled before a court in 2008 and given a life sentence after Gaddafi's playboy son Saif al-Islam tried to revive Libya's external image with the international community. Matar was eventually released from custody on 2 February 2011; the first demonstrations erupted in Benghazi thirteen days later. Like many other dissidents who had resisted Gaddafi's tyranny, Matar remained unbowed and determined to use all means at his disposal to bring down Gaddafi once and for all.

As Matar and other unarmed protesters marched through Benghazi, government forces attacked them with batons, bottles and water cannon; thirty-eight were injured. This sparked a chain of secondary events that added fuel to the protesters' fire. The novelist Idris al-Mesmari was arrested hours after giving an interview to Al Jazeera about the police reaction to the protests. Meanwhile, in the cities of Bayda and Zintan, hundreds of protesters called for an end to the Gaddafi regime and set fire to police and security buildings, setting up tents in the town centres. The next day more protesters gathered in Midan al-Shajara, later renamed Freedom Square, just outside the police headquarters next to the Benghazi courthouse, to demand the release of Fathi Tirbil. Suddenly shots rang out as officers opened fire on the unarmed civilians. The display of unbridled state force against defenceless people sparked a further wave of anti-government protests in Benghazi and several other eastern towns. Protests then erupted in Derna and Bayda, leading to four deaths and three injuries.

As more and more Libyans began to believe that 'enough was enough', leading Libyan opposition figures announced a 'Day of Rage' to be held on 17 February 2011. The National Conference for the Libyan Opposition asked all groups opposed to the Gaddafi regime to protest in memory of earlier demonstrators in Benghazi. It was a day that would not simply incur the rage of the people but also of the regime. The protesters knew that Gaddafi would show them no mercy if they did not prevail. Yet on this occasion, as police turned the water cannons on them once again, the outraged protesters set fire to Gaddafi's palace and stormed the secret police building next to the court-house, where dissidents were routinely tortured. The circumstances of 2011 were altogether different from 1996. This time opposition figures knew they were not alone. The whole world was watching as another Arab city became engulfed in the Arab Spring.

Fuelled with adrenalin, the rebels marched in procession to the hated Katiba military barracks on the outskirts of Benghazi, where Gaddafi's soldiers once again opened fire indiscriminately. The next day, the protesters commandeered bulldozers and tried to breach the Katiba compound, but were met by a firestorm of bullets and artillery. They responded by throwing stones and crude bombs made of tin cans stuffed with gunpowder. As the fighting continued, rebels attacked an army base on the outskirts of Benghazi and disarmed the soldiers. Among the equipment seized were three small tanks, which were then rammed into the compound. On 20 February the gates were finally blown apart by a Benghazi resident who blew himself up in a self-made car bomb.

The following day, the Libyan Interior Minister Abdul Fatah Younis arrived with a squad of special forces to relieve the defence of the compound. However, instead of taking on the rebels, he defected and announced safe passage for loyalists out of the city. Gaddafi's response was unequivocal, and he executed 130 soldiers who had refused to fire on the rebels. But by then it was too late. Benghazi was in rebel hands and the Libyan revolt had begun, sending shock waves around the region and certain Western capitals, where a number of corporate executives, security experts, diplomats and academics were reaching for their shredders to destroy documents detailing their dubious transactions with the Libyan dictator.

The Spread of Dissent

The fight for the rest of the country now began in earnest. The Benghazi protests quickly spread to Misrata and then the capital. On 21 February, the *New York Times* reported that Gaddafi had tried to impose a general black-out on information across Libya.[4] Several residents reported that the mobile phone service was down, while even landline connections became sporadic.

Gaddafi loyalists started to strafe demonstrators in Tripoli with anti-aircraft weapons. 'For days, you could not sleep; they drive in front of your house and you find empty bullets in your garden. If you went out you would have been executed,' recalled Walid Danna who would later join the resistance in Zintan. Then on 23 February 2011, the Warfallah tribal leaders declared that they no longer supported the regime. One day later, the 17 February Coalition formed a Benghazi local council. However, it quickly saw the need to co-ordinate resistance between different towns in rebel control and present a united front to the world. In Misrata a respected judge, Khalifa al-Zawawi, had been elected to lead a new local council. On 26 February a consensus was reached to bring the local councils under a national council to run rebel areas in the east.

Meanwhile a number of diplomats began to take up the rebels' cause. On 25 February, Libya's permanent representative to the UN, Abdel-Rahman Shalgham, gave an emotional speech to the Security Council associating Gaddafi with Hitler. According to Shalgham's deputy, Ibrahim Dabbashi, the incident was instrumental in convincing Russia and China to support UN Security Council Resolution 1970 which referred Libya to the International Criminal Court (ICC) and imposed an arms embargo, travel ban and asset freeze on Gaddafi and senior regime officials.[5] This encouraged other elements of the regime, who had worked with Gaddafi's son Saif al-Islam on his polit-ical and economic reforms in the 2000s, to switch sides, including Mahmoud Jibril, a US-educated economist who was chair of the National Economic Board based in Abu Dhabi. Jibril arrived in Benghazi on 28 February and helped structure the council, which was given the name the National Transitional Council (NTC), and comprised thirty-three members allegedly representing all segments of Libyan society. The first act of the Council was to appoint the former Justice Minister, Mustafa Abdul Jalil, as its leader. He immediately called for a no-fly zone and air strikes against the Jamahiriya and set up a Crisis Management Committee, led by Jibril, who was given the foreign affairs brief to negotiate international recognition of the Council.

All of this led more sailors from the naval base in Benghazi and soldiers in Zawiya to switch sides and join the rebellion, as did the air force cadets in Misrata after Gaddafi's security forces shot and fired rocket-propelled grenades at protesters. Gaddafi responded by shutting down all Internet communications and arresting Libyans who had given phone interviews to the media. International journalists were banned from reporting from Libya except by invitation of the Gaddafi government. During this period a young Libyan law student named Iman al-Obeidi came to prominence when she was forcibly silenced and detained after bursting into the restaurant of the Rixos Hotel in Tripoli and attempting to tell the international press corps of her gang rape by Gaddafi's troops.

Meanwhile, journalists who attempted to cover the events now came under attack by Gaddafi's forces. A BBC News crew was beaten and then lined up against a wall by Gaddafi's soldiers, who shot next to a journalist's ear and laughed. As the protests and funeral processions multiplied, Gaddafi employed snipers, artillery, helicopter gunships, warplanes, anti-aircraft weaponry, warships and Tuareg mercenaries from Mali to quell the demonstrations. Military commanders summarily executed soldiers who refused to fire on protesters. More disturbingly, a Scottish doctor claimed security forces were deliberately targeting children, while Amnesty International reported that the security forces had targeted paramedics helping injured protesters. The government also banned giving blood transfusions to people who had taken part in the demonstrations.

Members of Gaddafi's Revolutionary Committees stormed hospitals in Tripoli and summarily executed injured protesters. They then confiscated the bodies, possibly for cremation. Elsewhere injured demonstrators were denied access to hospitals and ambulance transport. Numerous writers, intellectuals and other prominent opposition sympathisers disappeared during the early days of the conflict, in cities controlled by Gaddafi. Rebels held off Gaddafi forces in Zawiya on 1 March and went on to take Ghademes and Nalut on 2 March and Bin Jawad on 5 March. This resulted in Gaddafi launching a massive counter-offensive on 6 March, during which he retook the coastal towns of Ras Lanuf and Brega. As he pushed towards Ajdabiya, the last remaining town before Benghazi, Gaddafi vowed to deal with the opposition without mercy, thereby precipitating a global diplomatic crisis. As the prospects of a massive humanitarian catastrophe in Benghazi began to dawn on the international community, the question of Britain's relationship with Gaddafi became more acute and the subject of contentious debate.

The LSE Debacle

Back in London, it wasn't too long before disturbing evidence emerged of how the previous Labour government had sought to ingratiate itself with the Gaddafi regime. While certain government officials and ministers talked up Algeria's and Libya's quick march to democracy in tribunals like the SIAC, other individuals and institutions closely associated with the New Labour government had been quietly seeking oil and government contracts. Revelations quickly surfaced about how the London School of Economics (LSE) had been used to secure favour from the Gaddafi family. It transpired that Gaddafi's son, Saif al-Islam, had been awarded an MA in global governance at the same time as he endowed the LSE with £1.5 million and its director, Howard Davies, accepted a personal invitation from Tony Blair to become a government business advisor to a UK–Libyan trade organisation.

Born in 1972, Saif al-Islam was the eldest of seven children that Gaddafi had with his second wife, Safia, and was his heir apparent. He affected a dapper, westernised image, with his shaved head, fashionable suits, rimless glasses and two Bengal tigers called Freddo and Barney, which he kept at his home in Tripoli. He was instrumental in repositioning his father's regime with the West, often acting as an envoy during the negotiations which took place in 2003 and 2004 over the dismantling of Libya's WMD programme. In all of this Saif presented himself as an arch-moderniser, buying a £10 million house in Hampstead and welcoming a succession of world leaders and Western intellectuals to Tripoli. His contact list famously included the Duke of York, Lord Mandelson and Nat Rothschild. His control over the Libyan Investment Authority and the Sovereign Wealth Fund gave him huge influence. This he used as leverage in negotiations over Lockerbie, during which he made clear that if al-Megrahi, the only man convicted for the bombing of Pan Am Flight 103, died of cancer in a British jail, all business deals with the UK would be cancelled. Saif was the one who facilitated talks in Britain that eventually led to al-Megrahi's release in 2009.

Yet, despite this carefully cultivated urbane image, Saif al-Islam Gaddafi would prove to be every inch his father's son. Five days after protests broke out in Benghazi, I watched incredulously as he threatened to unleash all hell against anyone in Libya who dared oppose his father's regime. This news piece was preceded by previously unseen footage of Colonel Gaddafi giving a 'closed' lecture at the LSE via video link from Tripoli, where he was introduced as 'Brother Leader' by a female LSE professor, who then proceeded to shower him with praise for a rambling and incoherent speech. A minute later the news piece switched to Saif's infamous 'rivers of blood' address of 20 February, which told you all you needed to know about his belief in democratic reform. Saif seemed bewitched as he delivered a forty-minute long rant, laced with menacing invective, to an increasingly apprehensive nation. His disjointed treatise on loyalty and vengeance bordered on the deranged, as he wagged his finger at the TV and sought to brand all opponents of his father's regime a rag-tag bunch of Islamic fundamentalists, corrupt tribal leaders and Western-backed crusaders' lackeys. 'We will fight until the last man, the last women, the last bullet,' he said. 'We will not lose Libya.' The news piece ended with the unedifying spectacle of the LSE professor giving Gaddafi a LSE baseball cap – the same present the LSE had given to Nelson Mandela. The professor later claimed she was forced to introduce Gaddafi after the director, Howard Davies, found himself indisposed.

This was the same Saif al-Islam Gaddafi who had allegedly written so eloquently about democracy in his thesis, at least according to his LSE tutor, the co-director of the Centre for Global Governance, Professor David Held. It later emerged that Saif received advice on his thesis from Tony Blair, who wrote a letter that began 'Engineer Saif' and ended with Tony's 'warmest wishes'. Saif's speech was followed on 22 February 2011 by even more blood-curdling warnings of unrestrained bloodshed from his father, who talked of the unremitting revenge he would exact on all those who rebelled. Those who opposed him were 'rats' to be hunted down and exterminated in the streets of Benghazi since those that did not 'love' him did not 'deserve to live'. According to Gaddafi, these 'rats' had been variously influenced by hallucinogenic drugs put in milk, coffee and Nescafé distributed by Bin Laden and Al-Qaeda or were part of a sinister colonial plot by France and the UK.

The ensuing controversy concerning the LSE only served to increase my interest in what was unfolding in Libya. My wife, my father and I had all studied at the LSE, while my grandfather-in-law, Sir Alexander Carr-Saunders, had been its director for twenty years. What was the LSE about if not good governance, transparency and the development of sustainable international relationships predicated on respect for human rights and the rule of law?

It was a mystery to me why LSE governors had not forcefully enquired into what was going on, especially after Professor Fred Halliday raised the alarm about the LSE's relationship with Gaddafi. In his book *Political Journeys* (2011) he wrote: '[T]he outside world may be compelled by considerations of security, energy and investment to deal with this state: there is no reason, however, to indulge its fantasies or the fictions that are constantly promoted within the country and abroad about its political and social character. The Jamahiriya is not a "state of the masses": it is a state of robbers, in formal terms a "kleptocracy".'[6]

It was perhaps not too surprising that a number of UK oil and gas companies made a headlong, government-backed dash to cash in on potential economic rewards in Libya – but the London School of Economics? It would take just a day for the otherwise astute LSE director, Howard Davies, to suddenly identify 'two failures of judgment' and resign after the furore broke over Saif's award. Perhaps Davies and his academic colleagues really did think that the Gaddafi regime had turned the corner and become a trusted democratic reform partner. But if they thought this they didn't say it. It was difficult to believe that such an obvious conflict of interest was not identifiable from the outset.

Yet, to be fair, the approach adopted by Davies towards Gaddafi was hardly peculiar to the LSE. For sceptics it was indicative of a broader instrumental attitude evinced by Western power elites towards Libya and the Middle East more generally. These were countries where you could acquire money and influence fast. As a result, the ordinary Arab's desire for good governance didn't count for very much. What mattered most in this world of easy business and realpolitik was the cultivation of a set of Arab elites who had been allowed to rule without the burden of real democracy since the mandate era of the mid-twentieth century. For the better part of sixty years both Western governments and the international business community had conveniently come to regard ordinary Arabs as either incapable of or uninterested in aspiring towards the democratic values of the West.

The failure to have any regard for the ordinary people of the Middle East was exemplified by the Sykes–Picot Pact signed by France and Great Britain in 1917, in which the Great Powers took a pen to the map of the Middle East to delineate their respective zones of influence without regard to any ethnic or tribal fault lines. It would take another twenty-five years before the mandate system gave way to decolonization, by which time Palestine had become a political melting pot. This dismissive attitude towards the Arabs continued during the Palestinian–Israeli conflict in which Western politicians made erroneous and deeply offensive distinctions between Israelis and Arabs. Israel was deemed to be closer to the West not just in terms of its politics, culture and morals, but also in terms of the individual aspirations of its people. The Arabs, on the other hand, were considered altogether more bovine and less responsive to individual aspirations and incentives. Such a phenomenon was nowhere better illustrated than in Raphael Patai's book *The Arab Mind* published in 1973, which claimed the Arabs were incapable of understanding Enlightenment values.

This approach reached its nadir just before protests swept across Tunisia, Yemen, Egypt, Bahrain and Libya in 2011. It drove the Harvard-based Nobel Prize winning economist Amartya Sen to make the following observation in his book *The Idea of Justice*, published just two years before the Arab Spring: 'There is an often-articulated belief that this block of countries [in the Middle East] has always been hostile to democracy. That constant repeated conviction is exasperating for fighters for democracy in the Arab world, but as a piece of historical generalisation it is basically nonsense.' Sen reminded the West that the Middle East was historically much more tolerant of different views and faiths than Inquisition-ridden Europe. He went on to remark that 'the illusion of an inescapably non-democratic destiny of the Middle East is both confused and very seriously misleading – perniciously so – as a way of thinking about either world politics or global justice today'.[7]

It would take another six months before LSE Professor David Held eventually resigned for 'academic' reasons. He would do so a few days before the publication of an inquiry into whether Saif al-Islam had plagiarised others in writing his thesis. In his report, Lord Woolf, the former Lord Chief Justice, found that the LSE had been used by British businesses to promote links with

Gaddafi. Professor Held had written to Saif a month before he was awarded a doctorate, requesting that he 'establish a business connection' with a man thought to be Imran Khand, a prominent Labour supporter from Glasgow. Professor Held subsequently took Mr Khand to Libya to meet Gaddafi, later telling Sir Howard Davies that the 'meetings went very well and [AB] is confident of business opportunities in Libya'. Mr Khand thereafter pledged £187,000 to the LSE with a further £250,000 a year for the next three to five years, although it later transpired that he donated only £32,500. Lord Woolf found that 'the obtaining of business in Libya by AB and AB providing a gift to Professor Held's Centre could give rise to an unfortunate perception'.[8] Lord Woolf's report gave credence to the view that there was a network of elites in Britain content to secure favours from and for the Gaddafi regime.

It was not without significance that other prominent establishment figures connected to the UK government also enjoyed close relations with the LSE. For example, Sir Mark Allen, the former head of counter-intelligence, who conducted many of the earlier negotiations with the Libyan regime, and who later became an advisor to BP on Libya, enjoyed a relationship with the LSE through its foreign policy think-tank LSE IDEAS. Cherie Blair, the former Prime Minister's wife, was also an LSE governor during this period in which her husband made at least six visits to Libya for commercial reasons. This included one on behalf of JP Morgan Bank, which he joined in 2008 following his resignation from office. Other commentators pointed to a former FCO junior minister who acquired positions at the LSE while enjoying an appointment on the Libyan National Economic Development Board.

For its part, the *Daily Mail* revealed that the Foreign and Commonwealth Office (FCO) had in fact unsuccessfully tried to pressurise Oxford University into giving Saif al-Islam a place on a LLM course in 2002. It reported that the head of the Department of International Development at Oxford had told LSE administrators that: 'the FCO would appreciate help in this case since Libya was opening up to the West again'.[9]

There was then little surprise when two months after the fall of Tripoli a whole cache of correspondence emerged documenting Western cosseting of Gaddafi and his family. On 25 October 2011 *The Times* newspaper published a somewhat cringe-making letter from Tony Blair to Muammar Gaddafi. Yet such sycophancy was hardly unique. Information now surfaced detailing how the US Boston-based consultancy firm Monitor had accepted substantial sums of money from Gaddafi in order to send a succession of Western intellectuals to Tripoli in an attempt to cast Gaddafi as some pre-eminent reformer with deep intellectual interests. Suddenly the likes of Francis Fukayama, Joseph Nye and Richard Perle found themselves being flown to Tripoli in order for the Great Leader to converse with intellectual luminaries of his own purported stature. They included former LSE director Lord Giddens, who flew to Tripoli to have in-depth philosophical conversations with Gaddafi over The Third Way.

Monitor had previously been hired and charged with responsibility for drafting the National Economic Strategy (NES) for Libya after Saif approached the legendary Harvard management academic Michael Porter, in 2004, to help him implement economic reform. The result was the creation of the NES, which many regarded as big on jargon but light on substance. The strategy that was subsequently developed failed resolutely to tackle head-on any issues relating to political reform in Libya. Instead, it described the country as 'the only functioning example of direct democracy' in which the People's Congresses provided for 'a meaningful forum for Libyan citizens to participate in law-making'. Ethan Chorin, an official who served in the US Liaison Office in Tripoli between 2004 and 2006, later observed: 'within a short time, Monitor had gone from being the author of competitiveness reports and holding training seminars to steering a good part of Saif's agenda and "selling" of the Gaddafis to the Western intellectual and political elite'.[10]

I later talked to Monitor founder, Mark Fuller, about Libya while doing a fellowship at Harvard Law School in 2012. It became clear that Monitor's engagement, just like that of the LSE's, was part of a much greater transatlantic neo-liberal accommodation with the regime. Fuller had been initially cautious about developing relations with the Libyan regime until intelligence agencies made it clear that it was consistent with the national security interests of the US government.

The LSE and Monitor controversies graphically illustrated just how insidious the Western relationship with Gaddafi's Libya had become. It was a relationship that went far beyond the moral and professional failings of a handful of individuals, to include crucial elements of the UK's security, foreign policy and political establishment. A debate still rages as to whether the Blair government was right to re-engage with Gaddafi in the aftermath of 9/11, including over the issue of weapons of mass destruction (WMD). It was a difficult and complex call for which the UK Foreign Affairs Select Committee would rightly give credit to Blair. Imagine what Gaddafi might have done had he had access to WMD in 2011? But there was nothing particularly complex or creditworthy about the manner in which certain Western elites sought to cash in on the UK government's successful rapprochement with Libya in 2004.

By early March 2011, this relationship was becoming more toxic with each passing day as Gaddafi became ever more bellicose in his outbursts towards the rebels. These outbursts stood in marked contrast to the moderate tone coming from the fledgling opposition in Benghazi, whose spokespeople talked of human rights, democracy and the restoration of the rule of law in terms that one might ordinarily have expected to feature in an LSE classroom on global governance. Thus, as the violence of the regime spiralled out of control, and certain LSE administrators began to run for the hills, the issue of the UK's political response to the impending humanitarian disaster in eastern Libya suddenly came to the fore. It was within this deeply murky political context that President Sarkozy's and David Cameron's demand for an internationally backed no-fly zone over Libyan airspace hit the UK's political, security and business elite on 28 February 2011 like a thunderbolt.

3. Memorandum of Misunderstandings

The events unfolding in Benghazi and the wider region were not without import for the Court of Appeal case I was dealing with on the day that the Libyan uprising began. Gaddafi's response was to brand all rebels 'terrorists'. This was the same Gaddafi with whom the Blair government had concluded a Memorandum of Understanding (MoU), in which it agreed to send foreign national security suspects back to Libya to what on any view was a deeply uncertain fate. This included dissidents whose organisations had been proscribed by Blair after his rapprochement with Gaddafi. Blair negotiated similar security compacts with other regimes in the region, including Algeria, a country to which the authorities now proposed to send back my client, Moloud Sihali.

Blair was nothing if not determined to rid the UK of foreign nationals whom the authorities suspected of being involved in terrorism, but could not try or convict for one evidential reason or another. The problem was how to send them back without breaching rights protected under the Human Rights Act of 1988. The answer lay in a set of security compacts with MENA governments, which could include specific individual diplomatic assurances as to how suspects would be treated upon their return by the host authorities. This, argued Blair, enabled the government to legally deport foreign national security suspects back to countries with bad human rights records without ostensibly breaching obligations under the Human Rights Act. Such assurances allowed the UK authorities to side-step earlier factual rulings made in asylum cases concerning the incidence of torture/unfair trials in those countries.

Yet, by entering into these compacts Blair ensured that a whole set of diplomatic, political, business, security and legal interests became dangerously intertwined. For example, the Algerian government only agreed to sign its 2006 compact after the UK consented to drop its insistence on an enforceable monitoring system of the treatment of suspects who were to be returned. Blair was so insistent on securing this compact that the Home Secretary was made to do an astonishing evidential about-turn in which, over the space of two months, he concluded that democratic developments in Algeria had progressed so far that there was no longer a demonstrable need for a detailed monitoring regime, despite FCO legal advice and a welter of independent expert evidence to the contrary.

Former UK Ambassador to Libya and Morocco, Anthony Layden, was repeatedly wheeled out in a series of SIAC security cases to give evidence about how the Algerian government had embraced democratic reform and was emphatically moving away from its brutal past now that the threat from Islamic fundamentalism had been dealt with. For good measure he also denied there was any diplomatic link between these compacts and the Libyan and Algerian governments' repeated threats to withdraw from security co-operation if the UK did not agree to extradite or send back opposition figures or prisoners. These included the likes of al-Megrahi (who Saif al-Islam later admitted was 'always on the negotiating table' concerning 'all commercial contracts for oil and gas with Britain') and a prominent Algerian businessman called Abdelmoumen Khalifa who had dared criticise the regime of President Bouteflika.

More significantly, Layden also told the tribunal there were no 'behind the scenes' dirty dealings between the UK and Arab governments that would result in the watering down of the UK's stated policy of zero tolerance of torture. For sceptics, however, these security compacts shone a worrying light on the nature of the UK's relationships with these regimes, and the nature of its fight against terror both at home and abroad. Many wondered how the then Conservative Home Secretary Theresa May could consider these diplomatic assurances reliable over the long-term, given the evident turmoil in the area. The new coalition government's attitude towards these compacts and diplomatic assurances went to the heart and integrity of the UK's overall strategy towards the region. Would it continue to instruct its officials to maintain before SIAC that the governments of Libya and Algeria had already embraced democracy and respected human rights or recognise the import of the events now unfolding in the region?

The problem for the government was that my client Moloud Sihali was one of those touchstone individuals it was intent on deporting. His original national security designation was made as a result of his association with a number of Algerian radicals with whom he had shared a flat. The authorities alleged they were all involved in the infamous ricin plot of 2002 to commit mass murder by releasing poison on the London Underground. The Blair government used this allegation to help justify its case for invading Iraq. In 2003, Colin Powell held up a vial of the ricin before the Security Council to demonstrate how Iraq was in possession of chemical weapons after intelligence agencies claimed that the ricin had emanated from Iraq, where it was thereafter distributed to jihadist groups operating in North Africa.

This claim was later found to be false after the lone Iraqi intelligence source that proffered the evidence confessed he had made it up. Sihali was eventually tried and acquitted of the allegation by a jury sitting in the Old Bailey. This did not stop the Home Secretary from continuing to designate Sihali a national security threat, a designation which took a further two-year battle to overturn when SIAC accepted that Sihali did not, in fact, constitute such a threat. Despite this, the then Home Secretary reordered his deportation, reliant upon the diplomatic Algerian assurance acquired under the security compact, even though Sihali no longer fell within its strict terms.

In the event, SIAC ruled that Sihali could be returned to Algeria, notwithstanding credible evidence from Amnesty International and Human Rights Watch that the authorities routinely tortured national security suspects held in detention. It did this after considering 'secret evidence' about the reliability of a diplomatic assurance. Such consideration was only possible after the Labour government introduced legislation to ensure that such evidence remained secret and could only be considered in closed hearings from which the applicant's representatives were excluded. Blair recognised that justice demanded that the applicant be able to evidentially test the basis of the government's belief in the reliability of the assurances, so the legislation provided for the appointment of security-cleared 'special advocates' to look after an applicant's interests. The problem was these advocates could not talk to, let alone take instructions from, the applicant. Unsurprisingly the use of such bilateral assurances became the subject of considerable criticism by the human rights community and a number of UN bodies, including the then UN Rapporteur on Torture, Manfred Novak. The difficulties they created for the principle of open justice was obvious to all and sundry.

The result of this legislative approach was that SIAC was required to delve into complicated diplomatic and political matters in deciding whether the assurances given could be relied upon or not. Much rested upon the integrity and ability of individual SIAC members to sift, scrutinise and weigh the significance and reliability of partially recorded diplomatic exchanges between governments. This was an extremely difficult task given the Commission members' limited diplomatic experience and lack of expertise in the region about which they were asked to judge. State diplomats were skilled in constructing official minutes and cables to ensure that sensitive quid pro quos were not officially linked together. If the disclosures about the existence of a secret CIA extraordinary rendition programme involving secret detention facilities had taught the international community anything, it was that officials involved in counter-terror operations and sensitive diplomatic exchanges rarely reduced their exact activities to paper.

It was somewhat predictable when SIAC elected to give 'due deference' to the 'expertise' of the government 'in foreign policy matters'. Any other approach would have probably resulted in a massive car crash between the judiciary and the executive. Whether this approach was sustainable, post Arab Spring, was to my mind a live issue. The long-term stability and reliability of the Algerian and Libyan regimes now looked altogether less assured, as did their purported commitment towards democratic reform, which the Home Secretary's lawyers consistently relied upon and trumpeted before SIAC. In short, there was a demonstrable historical tendency within these regimes to suppress all popular democratic protest when faced with a political crisis that threatened their very existence.

As the Appeal Court judges pored over SIAC's decision, I raised the issue of how the current revolutionary fever sweeping across North Africa might affect matters. How could the Home Secretary reassure the courts of the long-term reliability of such assurances? The Home Secretary's lawyers once again emphasised Algeria's demonstrable commitment to democratic reform. Mr Layden, they submitted, had given cogent evidence that Algeria had dealt with its extremist problem and was well on the road to societal reconciliation. The government's confidence in its bilateral relationship, as documented in secret diplomatic exchanges, was enough to demonstrate the assurance's reliability. Both governments remained steadfastly committed to the rule of law and good governance. Accordingly, the oft-repeated suggestion that these assurances were in any way linked to other diplomatic negotiations between the two governments was without foundation.

Yet the problem with the government submission was that much of the evidence it relied upon pre-dated the Arab Spring, and the political calculations that were likely to govern the treatment of critics in this highly volatile situation. The government lawyers need not have worried. I can still recall the scorn with which one appeal judge dealt with my question. He looked down from the Gods to make the obvious but startling point that matters concerning the Arab Spring had not been before SIAC six months earlier when it had come to the decision it had. This was not a matter for this court although it might be for the Home Secretary at some point in the future. Myriad new procedural and substantive points and appeals began to appear on the horizon. As I met the judge's eye I could not shake off my absolute disquiet at this legal fiction. Rule of law this may have been, but speedy justice it was not. The sheer futility of the litigation in which I was involved, with its never-ending merry-go-round of appeals, was beginning to tell. By the time Sihali appeared before the Court of Appeal in 2011 he had spent ten long years in litigation with the UK government, all largely successful, but with no hope of an end to it in sight.

It was particularly disturbing to watch so-called 'cogent' assessments being made about the nature of certain MENA regimes and their diplomatic reliability without any reference to the extraordinary political events unfolding before our eyes. I was appalled to see how much reliance government lawyers continued to place on the undertakings of leaders such as Gaddafi, given their abject record of resorting to violence when threatened with an internal political crisis. In reality not a single government MENA country expert that appeared before SIAC ever foresaw the popular protests that later engulfed the region. It seemed to me that we were all living in an artificial legal 'war on terror' bubble – dominated by diplomatic and legal elites who paid little heed to the real experiences of real people in real Arab communities. A bubble in which the democratic aspirations of the Libyan people were neglected in the face of the West's desire to combat Islamic fundamentalism and prosecute a wider 'war on terror'.

Most disturbing of all, however, was the coalition government's position concerning allegations relating to the UK's facilitation of torture. At the centre of the Home Secretary's submissions to SIAC stood her oft-repeated commitment regarding the government's zero tolerance of torture. No administration in Britain would ever facilitate torture given its commitment to the rule of law and good governance. SIAC placed great store by these statements and often scoffed at submissions that questioned their veracity. Yet Mr Layden's undiluted claims would soon become sorely tested, at least in the court of public opinion, when evidence emerged following the downfall of the Gaddafi regime that UK security officials had helped render back to Tripoli certain Libyan dissidents whom they must have known Gaddafi's feared security apparatus would ill-treat.

The Libyan expert Ethan Chorin probably got it about right when he later commented:

> It is unclear whether specific individuals were targeted for rendition because the West had reason to believe they had information, or whether the Libyans, as the Egyptians were thought to have done before them, simply drew up a list of people they wanted for their own purposes (dissidents for example) with the cover that their interrogation would produce information pertinent to the war on terror. Former State Department officials said these arrangements mirrored those Washington had carried out a few years before with the Algerian regime. That regime had also attempted to exploit Washington's obsession with Al-Qaeda to have members of the military arm of the principal opposition, the Islamic Salvation Front (FIS), delivered to Algeria. In the case of Libya, the fact that the Bush Administration had

declared the Libyan Islamic Fighting Group (LIFG) – whose primary target was Gaddafi – a terrorist organisation in 2003, assisted in justifying renditions of LIFG-affiliated members back to Libya.[1]

Chorin's comments were offered with the benefit of hindsight but they dovetailed with admissions made by former CIA agent Robert Baer who was reported by the American Civil Liberties Union back in 2005 as saying: '[I]f you want a serious interrogation, you send a prisoner to Jordan. If you want them to be tortured, you send them to Syria. If you want someone to disappear – never to see them again – you send them to Egypt.' It was startling how much faith UK government lawyers publicly placed in the reliability and long-term stability of these regimes. There appeared to be an implicit and unspoken compact in these MoUs, whereby certain authoritarian regimes had agreed to co-operate with the UK in combating terrorism in exchange for little or no diplomatic criticism about the lack of serious democratic reform in their countries.

Three things became clear to me that day. Firstly, I knew that none of the lawyers or judges in these cases would have ever countenanced sending trusted agents of the British state back to these states on the basis of such flimsy assurances without at least a viable monitoring regime being in place. Secondly, it was extremely unlikely that Sihali would be sent back any time soon given the interminable system of appeals. By the time Sihali appeared in the Court of Appeal in February 2011 not a single national security suspect subject to a bilateral assurance had been sent back by court order to any Middle East country in over ten years of constant litigation. It would take a further three years before even a *convicted* foreign security national, Abu Qatada, was returned under such a compact. Even then he gave up his last rights of appeal voluntarily. In reality the system of appeals acted as a de facto detention system for those that the authorities suspected of terrorism but could not charge with a criminal offence due to a lack of admissible evidence.

Thirdly, and most importantly, it was time for me to stop pretending that justice, as I knew it in the ordinary courts, could be dispensed in such a Kafkaesque system. SIAC and the Appeal Courts sought to apply the ordinary rules of administrative law without any regard to the extraordinary political and legal context in which they operated. It rather reminded me of those German positivist judges of the Nazi era who applied the law without regard to the surrounding political circumstances that clothed their learned judgments. The Commission's so-called 'deference' to the executive's expertise in foreign policy matters was just another device by which SIAC members absolved themselves of the need to peer too closely into the obscure politics that lay behind the litigation. It was an approach that had nothing in common with the ordinary ancient principles of open justice that governed the practice of our normal criminal and civil courts. As I walked out of the Court of Appeal I knew there had to be better ways to promote the rule of law than litigating in secretive courtrooms where the eventual outcome was so far in the future as to make any result totally redundant by the passage of time and politics. It was time to re-engage with the real world out there. Thus, as the humanitarian crisis unfolded in Benghazi, and the idea of the no-fly zone began to be debated across the Atlantic, I turned my attention to what the BHRC might do in respect of Libya to help promote the rule of law.

A Unique Opportunity for the BHRC

Like other human rights organisations, the BHRC had received and issued numerous statements of concern about government attacks on unarmed protesters in a number of different countries. Yet I remained plagued by the thought that there was something more we could do. The fact that the leaders of the Libyan uprising were all lawyers set something off in me. I became captivated by the emerging story of revolution and law in Libya, just as I had with Pakistan. In Benghazi lawyers and retired judges continued to direct and shape the uprising against Gaddafi. They now proclaimed that this was a revolution in support of the rule of law. But was this true? Were the carefully packaged proclamations indicative of a genuine revolution based upon principle? Some journalists believed that the statements of the rebel council were real. Others thought they were a convenient political fig-leaf behind which a motley group of former loyalists sought to retain and justify power.

If they were indicative of the democratic aspirations of the Libyan people what, I wondered, should be the response of civil society to the rebels' pleas for military and political support, now that Gaddafi had turned his brutal regime on the ordinary people of Benghazi? It was within this somewhat febrile context that a unique opportunity presented itself during the course of a conversation I had with a solicitor, Jason McCue, who had instructed me to advise imprisoned Belarusian opposition leaders about various UN human rights mechanisms that might be open to them following their unlawful detention after a recent presidential election. McCue told me that he had managed to establish a channel of contact with Mustafa Abdul Jalil, the leader of the rebels in Benghazi, with a view to visiting Libya. He was interested in pursuing compensation and an apology from New Libya on behalf of the 150 IRA victims he represented, and against whom Libyan-supplied Semtex explosives had been used.

McCue had fought a nineteen-year campaign for redress on behalf of these victims, bullying Gordon Brown along the way into establishing a Northern Ireland–Libya Reconciliation Unit in the FCO. The unit was set up after the UK government failed to convince the US to include UK victims in the $1.68 billion compensation package brokered between Gaddafi and Bush for past acts of Libyan-sponsored terrorism. As a consequence, on the afternoon of 6 September 2009, Mr Brown made the following televised statement from Berlin:

> I desperately care what has happened to those people who have been victims of IRA terrorism. When I met with the families and the supporters and lawyers [. . .] I assured them of our support and our sympathy for their cause. Our judgment has been that the cause most likely to succeed and bring result is to support the families themselves in their legal representations through their lawyers to the Libyan authorities [. . .] by establishing dedicated foreign office support to the victims' campaign. We'll appoint dedicated officers in the foreign office and our embassy in Tripoli will accompany the families and their representatives to meetings with the Libyan government to negotiate compensation.

Following the creation of this Unit, McCue communicated with the Libyan government, initially through the then Libyan Ambassador to the UK, Omar Jelban. This led to an unofficial cross-party parliamentary delegation visiting Tripoli between 31 October and 2 November 2009 on behalf of UK victims. It was drawn from both houses and included Lord Daniel Brennan (Lab.), Lord Paul Bew (Crossbench), Mr Mackinlay (a former MP), Jeffrey Donaldson MP (DUP), and Mr Nigel Dodds MP (DUP). They met with Libyan ministers to negotiate the UK victims' position. Although the visit to Tripoli was self-funded, Mr Brown announced that it was to be fully facilitated by the FCO. In order to encourage the Libyan government to enter into discussions on the matter of compensation, the delegation presented a proposal for Libya to participate in a wider humanitarian programme that was emphasised as a new and innovative means of giving closure to the past and promoting peace and reconciliation for the benefit of all affected in the UK, particularly in Northern Ireland. This included substantial business and infrastructure investment projects and wide-ranging community development projects.

The Unit's remit was further extended across Whitehall after David Cameron came to power, when he publicly declared his own moral support for the victims and McCue's campaign. In a letter dated 22 October 2010, Cameron wrote to McCue in the following terms: 'The Government will be unequivocal in its attitude to Libya's past sponsorship of terrorism while welcoming the progress that Libya continues to make in reintegrating into the international community. As you know, I am hugely sympathetic to the sufferings of the victims and their legitimate attempts to seek redress.' The official letter was accompanied by a note handwritten by Mr Cameron which I later saw and which read: 'I am extremely enthusiastic about what you are doing and really want to see it progress and come to fruition. If there is anything I can do to help make it happen, let me know.' On 24 February 2011, as a consequence of the popular uprising in Libya, McCue formally terminated his initiative with the Libyan government until such time as a new government could be formed.

Pursuant to this move, on 2 March 2011, the Prime Minister was then specifically asked by Northern Irish MP Nigel Dodds about his commitment to the victims now that Libya was heading for an outright civil war. He asked: 'Given our campaign for compensation for the victims of Libyan state-sponsored IRA terrorism, will the Prime Minister give an assurance that before the normalisation of relations with Libya under any new regime, the outstanding matter of compensation will be addressed by the Government, not least through the use of Gaddafi assets seized in Britain?' The Prime Minister's reply was instructive: 'An FCO-led unit is still working on that issue and it is vital that it continues to go on doing that. It is an ingenious idea to use the frozen assets in that way. Having sought advice, those assets really belong to the Libyan people. The whole problem with Libya is that it is a rich country with poor people. We can see that in the extensive assets that have been frozen. Those assets belong to the Libyan people first and foremost.'

It was within this context that McCue asked whether the BHRC wanted to open up its own line of communication with the rebel leader Mustafa Abdul Jalil, and travel with him to Benghazi. 'Yes,' I replied. A plan was quickly drawn up to give the new National Transitional Council the opportunity to demonstrate in practice its publicly stated commitment to democracy and the rule of law. It would be invited to move forward on a number of legacy issues, particularly the open sore of the Lockerbie bombing, that continued to haunt UK–Libyan relations, while the UK would help the NTC to strengthen the rule of law in New Libya.

The Lockerbie Case

McCue now told me that he had also received instructions from a number of Lockerbie victims to open up a channel of communication with Mustafa Abdul Jalil, who had made informal voluntary public statements claiming that he was in possession of documents that proved Gaddafi's criminal involvement in the Lockerbie bombing of 1988. Abdul Jalil was an interesting character. He had quit as Gaddafi's Justice Minister on 21 February 2011 in protest at 'the excessive use of violence against unarmed protesters', and was the first member of the General People's Committee to resign. He was originally brought into the regime in 2007 as Justice Minister by Gaddafi's son Saif al-Islam to help cast the regime in a more reform-minded light. But Abdul Jalil was to prove to be no Gaddafi acolyte. He later won recognition from international human rights bodies for his attempt to reform the criminal code.

Born in the eastern city of Bayda, home of the Senussi dynasty and one of the first cities to rebel against Gaddafi, Abdul Jalil went on to study law at the University of Libya in 1952. He thereafter worked as a lawyer, before becoming a judge in 1978 and then president of the Court of Appeal in 2002, a post he retained until his appointment as Justice Minister. During his judicial career he was one of the few judges known for ruling against the government. In 2010 he publicly criticised Gaddafi, in an unprecedented address to the General People's Congress, over the failure to comply with court rulings concerning the release of over 300 detainees. Gaddafi refused to accept his resignation. Abdul Jalil finally resigned in mid-February 2011 after witnessing the shooting of peaceful demonstrators, declaring 'We want a democratic government, a fair constitution, and we don't want to be isolated from the world anymore.' Two weeks later he became chairman of the NTC. Heba Morayef of Human Rights Watch noted that she had 'never seen an Arab minister of justice who will publicly criticise the most powerful security agencies in the country [. . .] It is as if he just wouldn't lie.'

Both McCue and I were interested in whether Abdul Jalil would permit the UK authorities to interview him. I had no basis for knowing whether his claims were credible or capable of corroboration. Like many other human rights lawyers, I had grave doubts about the Lockerbie trial process and the conviction of al-Megrahi before the Scottish courts. I did not believe that sufficient admissible evidence existed in the public domain either to justify the conviction of al-Megrahi or to establish the Libyan link to the bombing to the requisite criminal standard and burden of proof. I was aware that other credible evidence pointed to the involvement of a radical Palestinian group, the PFLP-GC, backed by Iran. After all it was known that the PFLP-GC leader, Ahmad Jibril, had met with Iranian government officials in Iran the year before the Lockerbie bombing. He offered his services to Iran after the US battleship *Vincennes* shot down Iran Flight 655 over the Persian Gulf, with the loss of 290 innocent passengers, many of whom were on their way to Mecca, leading Tehran Radio to vow to avenge the attack 'in blood-splattered skies'.

More significantly, Jibril's right-hand man, Hafez Dalkamoni, had been arrested in Germany on an unrelated matter along with the Jordanian bomb-maker Marwan Khreesat. He was carrying a Toshiba cassette recorder laced with Semtex and a barometric time-delay switch of the type found at the Lockerbie crash site. According to the *Sunday Times*, another member of the

Dalkamoni group, an Egyptian named Mohammed Abu Talb, was identified by Maltese shopkeeper, Tony Gauci, as the purchaser of clothes later found in the suitcase in which police believed the bomb had been planted. Thus, for the first two years of the Lockerbie investigation, everything seemingly pointed to the involvement of the PFLP-GC and Iran. Until, that is, the summer of 1990 when, following the invasion of Kuwait by Iraq, the West needed the help of Syria and other Middle Eastern states in relation to its conflict with Saddam Hussein.

It was within this wider political context that the CIA and Scottish investigators changed track and began to finger Libya as the sole culprit behind the bombing. Suddenly, a fragment of an entirely different type of timer was discovered on a shirt collar emanating from the suitcase that had been placed in the aeroplane's hold in Malta. The fragment was found by Thomas Hayes of the Royal Armament Research and Development (RARDE), and Thomas Thurman of the Federal Bureau of Investigation (FBI). According to Lockerbie prosecutors, this fragment allegedly matched circuit boards produced by a manufacturer from Switzerland whose owner, one Edwin Bollier, claimed had been sold exclusively to Libya. Moreover, al-Megrahi, who had worked for Libyan Airlines and Libyan intelligence in Malta at the time, was now identified by Tony Gauci as the true purchaser of the clothes, after he retracted his previous identification of Abu Talb. Al-Megrahi was subsequently extradited, convicted, sentenced and imprisoned.

Predictably, the proposed second appeal against conviction rested upon doubts about both the scientific evidence and the quality of the identification evidence. Tony Gauci had originally described a six-foot, hefty, fifty-year-old man, whereas al-Megrahi was only five feet eight inches tall and thirty-seven years old. His purported identification was riddled with inaccuracies. Under Scottish law, this identification had to be corroborated with an independent piece of evidence. The prosecution relied upon the scientific evidence concerning the timer. Yet, within a year or so of the trial, huge concerns began to emerge in relation to the continuity of this scientific evidence. The logging, bagging and transfer of the relevant shirt fragment were irregular to say the least. The fragment was unaccompanied by the type of proper labels, notes and diagrams that one would ordinarily expect in such an important criminal investigation, especially where the integrity of circumstantial evidence was everything to the prosecution. Moreover, the credibility of those who found the fragment was now in doubt. FBI agent Thurman's work as an investigator was discredited by ABC news network. He was subsequently barred from FBI labs after it transpired that he had lied about his qualifications.

During this period, RARDE scientists were also found by the English Court of Appeal to have provided the basis for wrongful convictions in a number of high profile political cases, such as the Maguire Seven. More significantly, the evidence of Edwin Bollier, the Swiss manufacturer of the timer boards, was shown to be inconsistent, after it was discovered that identical circuit boards to the one allegedly used in the Lockerbie bombing were sold to non-Libyan clients elsewhere in the world. Bollier later admitted that he was offered $4 million to connect the timer to Libya. And then there was the evidence of his former employee, Ulrich Lumpert, a Swiss electronics engineer, who signed an affidavit after the trial confirming that in 1989 he had stolen a circuit board and handed it to 'a person officially investigating in the Lockerbie case'. Taken together, this called into doubt both the identification and scientific basis of the prosecution case as advanced by the Crown. In short, it destroyed any irresistible inference of guilt in what was always a thin and circumstantial case.

Yet all of this evidence did not rule out the possibility of Libyan complicity in a wider conspiracy involving Gaddafi, with or without Iran's connivance. After all Gaddafi had in the past assisted a variety of radical groups and governments both within and outside of the Middle East to commit atrocities against Western interests. The provision of Semtex to the IRA in the 1980s was just one example. There was also clear-cut evidence of his direct involvement in a range of other terrorist attacks perpetrated in Europe during this period in the late 1980s. It was at least possible that while al-Megrahi may not have been the person who purchased the clothes or placed the device in the suitcase, he may have had knowledge of a wider conspiracy in which Gaddafi had sanctioned the bombing. It was an open secret that Libyan agents operated all over Malta, including at the airport where al-Megrahi was employed and had acted as a Libyan intelligence agent, and it was entirely likely that if Gaddafi had been involved, then al-Megrahi may have known about it. Why else did Gaddafi agree to extradite al-Megrahi and pay hundreds of millions of pounds in compensation, albeit on a without prejudice basis? Why do this if he was completely innocent of any involvement in the atrocity?

As a member of the Faculty of Advocates in Edinburgh who lives a few miles from Lockerbie in the Scottish Borders, and whose sponsor, Bill Taylor QC, had defended al-Megrahi, I was fascinated by the case. I was more than a little interested to see what could be teased out of Abdul Jalil by way of real evidence concerning Gaddafi's wider involvement. Although he had every reason to denounce Gaddafi as a rebel leader, Abdul Jalil was not a man given to hyperbole or legal recklessness. Jalil had been Justice Minister during the period when Gaddafi and his son had sought and negotiated al-Megrahi's return from Scotland and the UK. He knew about these crucial negotiations. There were rumours that al-Megrahi, whose family had over the years received handsome compensation from Gaddafi, had threatened to spill the beans about Libyan complicity if he was not permitted to return to Tripoli now that he had been diagnosed with terminal cancer. Why was Gaddafi so concerned to effect al-Megrahi's return given his rehabilitation in the international community? After all there was an imminent second appeal that was due to come before a Scottish appeal court. Were Saif al-Islam's unrelenting diplomatic efforts to get al-Megrahi back to Tripoli simply humanitarian, or were they indicative of something more sinister? Some thought so.

Yet, to my mind, despite all the conjecture, the sparseness of the evidence before the Scottish court remained telling. The evidence was certainly not capable of supporting a conviction of individual guilt against al-Megrahi as presently charged. Little did I know that Kenny MacAskill, the SNP Justice Minister, had secretly offered al-Megrahi a deal to let him out on compassionate grounds if he desisted with his appeal, this at least according to his defence team. The celebrated civil rights lawyer Gareth Peirce probably got it about right when she commented that, 'the idea of their individual responsibility was anyway bizarre. As agents of the state, where not a mouse speaks without the say-so of Gaddafi, al-Megrahi and Lamin Fhimah [al-Megrahi's co-defendant and alleged co-conspirator, who was acquitted] were either ordered to do what it was said they did, in which case dealing with Gaddafi as a statesman then and now has been beyond hypocrisy – or the thesis was wrong'.[2] Well, now that a mouse had spoken it seemed only right to see whether he was prepared to stand by what he had said and allow the prosecuting authorities to test his new evidence.

Making Contact with the Rebels and Mustafa Abdul Jalil

On 1 March 2011 I wrote to Abdul Jalil to see if he wanted to establish a dialogue with the BHRC about such legacy issues and how the Bar might help the NTC strengthen the rule of law in Libya, in line with his published declarations. On the same day McCue flew to Dubai to meet a number of other exiled Libyans there, to see if they would help lobby the newly formed transitional council in Benghazi to meet with us. One of the exiles came from a prominent Benghazi family. His father was a hugely respected leader who had acted as a mediator for the Benghazi tribes. Having initially trained at British Military Academy in Iraq and served under King Idris, he went on to teach Gaddafi and other military officers. Interestingly, he elected not to take part in Gaddafi's revolution in 1969 but retained his rank. He eventually retired as a colonel in charge of recruitment and supplies for the Libyan Air Force, before leaving Libya on 21 February 2011, after his son fell out with Saif al-Islam.

The son, on the other hand, was a multi-millionaire commercial trader in his own right. He fled to Dubai, leaving his estranged wife and young children in Benghazi after disagreeing with Gaddafi's approach towards the uprising. He had grown up on Gragour Street in the Military Controlled Zone in Tripoli, where he and his family were neighbours of the Gaddafi family. He became a close personal friend of Saif al-Islam, who later used him as an intermediary with the Benghazi tribes. On 7 February 2011 he was told to go and see Gaddafi. Thereafter he met with Saif and his father on a daily basis up until 22 February 2011. The exile claimed he had strongly tried to persuade Gaddafi not to shoot at the Libyan people after protests began on 16 February 2011, but to no avail. When Gaddafi crossed that line he decided to defect and was shot at as he left the protected compound in Tripoli. He secretly pledged his support to the rebels in Benghazi on the same day Saif delivered his blood-curdling, finger wagging speech on Libyan TV.

It was rumoured that Saif had, at one stage, intended to deliver a different speech emphasising the rule of law, which had allegedly been written with the assistance of some Swiss-based professors, and that he had also decided to confront his father that day to demand he be allowed to take over. In the event Saif and his father talked for two hours. How much weight should be given to the rumour is debatable. Tapes of Gaddafi's meetings during this period can be found for as little as fifty pence in the markets of Tripoli. It transpired the security forces recorded everything, but nothing emerged to suggest that Saif confronted Gaddafi with this ultimatum. In any case it is extremely doubtful that he would have succeeded had he done so. Many of his attempts at reform during the 2008–10 period were routinely scuppered by regime hardliners who saw him as nothing more than a playboy with international pretensions rather than as a leader capable of ruling over and uniting Libya's complex polity. Lord Hague would later tell the UK Foreign Affairs Select Committee that Saif had called him 'as the trouble began'. He rejected the idea that Saif could have facilitated the abdication and a negotiated solution to the conflict. 'It would have been unwise for the British Foreign Secretary to suggest an internal coup within the Gaddafi Administration, particularly as the succeessor might have been no better than the predecessor,' he told the Committee.[3] According to Hague Saif did not call back again.

Also at the meeting with the exiles in Dubai was a former cavalry officer called Peter Marks. He was a small-time trader of goods and services to Libya who was intent on recouping his losses in Libya with the new Council after the UN imposed sanctions on Libya. Marks had extensive knowledge of Libya and had helped with the evacuation of British subjects from remote locations. He had left Libya through Tripoli Airport on a flight to Malta with officials from the British Embassy, on 26 February 2011, after the Embassy's closure. He now agreed to carry our letters to Benghazi on his next journey. On 6 March Marks flew to Cairo and travelled overland to join a convoy of 300 tonnes of food and medical aid at the Egyptian border. The convoy was partly arranged by Abdul Karim Khalil, head of the Islamic Association in the UK, and Yousef, the son of Azzat Magarief, who had been kidnapped from Egypt and assumed killed by Gaddafi's external Intelligence Service in 1990.

At around 7pm on 9 March 2011, Marks finally got to meet rebel leader Mustafa Abdul Jalil and three of his staff for about half an hour in Benghazi, where he handed over the letters. After reading them, Abdul Jalil told Marks to convey the message that the new Council was indeed different from the Gaddafi regime. It intended to establish a democratic government based on social justice, the rule of law and a fair distribution of wealth for all the people of Libya. Furthermore, the Council was minded to recognise all relevant international treaties and was committed to resolving all outstanding legacy issues, including recent human rights atrocities perpetrated by Gaddafi, as a mark of New Libya's commitment to the rule of law. The Council stood ready to meet us and invited us to come to Benghazi.

During the trip Marks also met with Dr Ahmad Gaweidhi, through Ramadan Addressi, the Cabinet Secretary to the Council. Gaweidhi was a surgeon who spoke perfect English and worked for thirteen years in Berne. He had established a NGO in Libya dedicated to the promotion of social justice, civic society and human rights, linked to the Humanitarian Rights Solidarity Group based in Geneva. He was passionate about social justice and also keen to ensure that the new regime dealt with all outstanding historical matters. He remained in contact with the new Council on these items, including with Fathi Tirbil, the lawyer who had risked his life by representing the families of the 1,200 prisoners killed in the Abu Salim prison massacre. Tirbil was now responsible for youth and civic matters on the Council, but agreed to send any letters from us on to Mustafa Abdul Jalil and the NTC. On 10 March 2011 Marks returned overland to Cairo and flew to Dubai to meet with McCue, Lord Brennan, counsel to the IRA victims, and the exiles, to communicate Abdul Jalil's invitation.

Abdul Jalil's positive response was consistent with the NTC's public statements. On 5 March 2011 it had issued the following concerning the fundamental choice that confronted Libya: 'At this important historical juncture which Libya is passing through right now, we find ourselves at a turning point with only two solutions. Either we achieve freedom and race to catch up with humanity and world developments, or we are shackled and enslaved under the feet of the tyrant Mu'ammar Gaddafi where we shall live in the midst of history.' The Council claimed to derive its legitimacy from the city councils set up by the revolutionary people of Libya on 17 February to run the liberated cities. It then went on to list its revolutionary and democratic objectives. These statements cemented my desire to meet with Abdul Jalil. Thus I immediately wrote another letter on behalf of the BHRC welcoming his invitation to visit Benghazi.

The Debacle in the Desert

On his return to the UK, McCue communicated our intention to travel to Libya to the FCO Northern Ireland–Libya Reconciliation Unit. However, he was strongly advised by the FCO to delay any trip. The situation was extremely dangerous and very volatile. Its concerns about conditions on the ground in Libya became a little clearer two days later when William Hague, then the Foreign Secretary, revealed to a stunned public that a 'small British diplomatic team' consisting of six Special Air Service (SAS) soldiers and two British diplomats (aka MI6 officials), had 'experienced difficulties' after they went to Libya 'to initiate contacts with the opposition' in an attempt to help the revolution. The 'junior FCO team' had flown unannounced into Eastern Libya, dressed in plain clothes, only to be unceremoniously detained in the desert, with their communications compromised, to the desperate embarrassment of the British government.

The six SAS soldiers belonged to E Squadron. It had been formed five years earlier, with a mandate to work closely with the intelligence service, MI6, on missions that required 'maximum discretion' in places that were off the radar or considered dangerous. The Squadron was a composite organisation formed from selected SAS, Special Boat Service (SBS) and Special Reconnaissance Regiment (SRR) operators. It was not technically part of the SAS or SBS but at the disposal of the director of Special Forces and MI6. E Squadron often operated in plain clothes, with the full range of national support, such as false identities, at its disposal. The purpose of this particular mission was to cement MI6's contacts with the opposition by flying in two MI6 agents in a Chinook helicopter to meet a Libyan intermediary in a town near Benghazi, who had thereafter promised to fix them up with a meeting with the NTC.

The six SAS commandos, part of Tier One units, carried bags containing arms, ammunition, explosives, computers, maps and passports from at least four nationalities. But despite all this technical back-up the team entered Libyan territory without any prior agreement with the rebel leadership. The plan fell to bits as soon as the helicopter landed, as locals became suspicious about possible foreign mercenaries and spies. The whole episode read like a scene out of the comic spoof film, *Johnny English*. After being placed under arrest the men were taken to a military base in Benghazi where they were hauled before a senior rebel leader. The team told him that they were in Libya to find out more about the rebels' needs and to offer assistance. However, the discovery of British troops on the ground enraged the rebels, who were fearful that Gaddafi would use such evidence to destroy the credibility of the NTC. Negotiations between senior rebel leaders and British officials in London finally led to the eight Britons being released, and they were thereafter allowed to board HMS *Cumberland* which had been stationed off the Libyan coast.

The debacle became even more embarrassing after the Gaddafi regime released a tape on Libyan TV of an intercepted call in which Richard Northern, the exiled British Ambassador to Libya, was heard pleading with the NTC for the team's release. The *Sunday Times* later reported that the junior diplomats had been intending to pave the way for more senior colleagues to arrive and build relations with the rebels. 'They have now left Libya. We intend, in consultation with the opposition, to send a further team to strengthen our dialogue in due course. This diplomatic effort is part of the UK's wider work on Libya, including our ongoing humanitarian support,' explained a clearly embarrassed Hague.

It was, by any standards, a severe public humiliation for the FCO. According to a later report by Mark Urban of BBC Newsnight in January 2012, those who advocated the use of special forces and MI6 to topple the regime and turn some key figures in Gaddafi's inner circle were sidelined for months as a consequence of this debacle. Little wonder, then, that the FCO was so jumpy about us going to Benghazi, especially when no UK diplomatic presence existed in the city. The advice of the FCO was unambiguously reinforced a week later by the Prime Minister who told McCue directly – and in no uncertain terms – not to venture into Libya while the no-fly zone was being negotiated. By then all our correspondence with Abdul Jalil had been copied in to David Cameron at Downing Street and the FCO Northern Ireland–Libya Reconciliation Unit. We therefore reluctantly agreed to delay our trip, as Britain and France embarked upon an intense round of diplomatic lobbying to get the UN Security Council to agree to Resolution 1973 concerning the establishment of a no-fly zone for humanitarian protection.

4. Libya, Bahrain and the 'Responsibility to Protect'

As we waited for the no-fly negotiations to start, my attention switched back to the deteriorating situation in Bahrain. For many of us who had dealt with Bahrain previously, it was not too much of a surprise when mass demonstrations broke out in Manama in the wake of the tumultuous protests in Tunisia and Egypt. These protests were just the latest instalment of a struggle that dated back to Bahrain's independence in 1971 and followed years of simmering unrest, detentions and allegations of human rights abuses. The underlying source of all this political tension was the social and political discrimination meted out to the majority Shia community, who allegedly made up 70 per cent of the indigenous population.

Since independence, the al-Khalifa monarchy had maintained political power with only a modicum of democracy. Although there were regular elections, and a functioning opposition in Bahrain, executive power rested almost exclusively with the King who appointed the government and controlled the army and security forces. The bicameral parliament had a lower house with a built-in majority favouring the minority Sunni community, and an appointed upper chamber. Yet, for many dissenters, the real source of tension was the power of the Prime Minister, the King's brother, who had ruled Bahrain for forty-one years, ever since independence.

What happened in Bahrain was of immense significance to the stability of the entire region. It held a strategic position in the Persian Gulf. Yet it was small enough for a mediator to count the political power players in the country on two hands. The UK enjoyed a particularly close relationship with Bahrain as a former colonial power. It had provided security to the ruling al-Khalifa family ever since the eighteenth century when they first acquired control of the island. The US Sixth Fleet was also stationed there. The situation was further complicated by the fact that both Iran and Saudi Arabia considered Bahrain to be in their strategic backyard.

Bahrain, more than any other Arab state, was likely to test the West's stated commitment of support for democratic reform in the region, post Arab Spring. The question was whether diplomatic and political pressure should be brought to bear to institute a meaningful dialogue about sustainable reform.

Bahrain held a particular interest for me as I had dealt with the human rights situation in the country for some seventeen years and knew many of the actors on both sides of the political divide. In 1998 I wrote a report on the state security tribunals and incidence of torture in Bahrain. This helped lead to the abolition of the tribunals after the new King adopted a national charter of reform following a referendum in 2001. The reforms were an attempt to stem years of instability that followed the suspension of parliament in the early seventies. In the event, the constitutional reforms were seen not to go far enough in implementing the terms of the charter, and tensions continued, at least as far as the opposition was concerned. Throughout this period the BHRC continued to observe numerous trials involving Shia leaders and human rights activists, including two cases in 2010 when twenty-four opposition and human rights campaigners were taken into custody and prosecuted for agitating in favour of greater political freedoms. These trials were still live when the protests in Tunisia and Egypt erupted. As a consequence of this work, I had established relations with most opposition figures as well with figures from the government who remained particularly sensitive to UK criticism given its historical links to the country.

As a non-state mediator with experience of the region, I was interested in whether a dialogue could be established between the parties to lessen the prospect of violence. Such a dialogue seemed possible in late February/early March 2011, despite tensions over the Prime Minister's tenure, as there was nothing homogeneous about the early demands of the protesters. Some called for modest reforms to the system, others for the establishment of a constitutional monarchy, while others still insisted on the establishment of a republic. There was everything to play for. Yet within a few days of the start of the protests the authorities reacted with lethal force, which led to a number of demonstrators being killed. I watched these developments with increasing alarm. Mass protests quickly turned into an occupation of Pearl Roundabout in the capital, Manama. Then on 17 February 2011, the roundabout was violently cleared of protesters for the first time. The treatment of the protesters resulted in yet more international criticism and caused considerable concern amongst more moderate members of the ruling family, who were all too conscious of what happened in Egypt when Mubarak tried to snuff out dissent through sheer force.

For the next couple of weeks, the King's son and heir, the Crown Prince, and moderate opposition groups, spoke conciliatory words and urged restraint. A number of opposition leaders who had been on trial for an alleged earlier plot against the state, which the BHRC had been observing, were pardoned and set free. During this period other dissidents in exile abroad were given the green light to return. For a few magical days everything seemed possible as the young people of Bahrain danced to the uplifting chants and music of the Arab Spring. Yet all was not as it seemed.

At this time, I met with opposition leaders, including the exiled leader of radical Haq Movement for Liberty and Democracy (Al-Haq) Saeed al-Shehabi, who was based in London. He told me how the FCO and the British Ambassador in Bahrain, Jamie Bowden, had rung him directly on his mobile to ask him to delay sending his radical colleague, Hassan Mushaima, back to Bahrain after the King announced that all dissidents could return home safely. 'Give us two weeks and we will ensure the twenty-three other detainees arrested last year will be released but we need more time,' he allegedly pleaded. An FCO official now requested an immediate meeting, something Saeed had been asking for for the last fifteen years. He refused to meet them. Saeed then explained how he got another call from a frantic official at the Foreign Office in King Charles Street, London, as he and Hassan Mushaima made their way to Heathrow Airport. 'The official was literally pleading with us to turn back,' recalled Shehabi. Both men once again refused and the next day the twenty-three detainees were released without condition.

Hassan Mushaima flew to Beirut where he was detained for ten days en-route to Bahrain. Sunni loyalists later alleged he went there to meet Hezbollah leaders to discuss tactics. When he arrived in Bahrain he went straight to the Pearl Roundabout to agitate in favour of the creation of a republic. Emboldened by the protests and the increasing international attention, Saeed sought to apply maximum pressure on the kingdom from London. 'We will not accept mediation or dialogue,' he told me. 'Not until the royal family has stood down and there is a real prospect of democracy.' 'You should at least consider a back channel,' I replied, somewhat alarmed at his inflexible stance and total confidence in the success of the street protests. 'Let us see,' he replied. I had little doubt that his hardline attitude would place even greater pressure on Al-Wefaq National Islamic Society (Al-Wefaq), the more moderate parliamentary-based Shia political party, to hold out for more in its tentative discussions with the Crown Prince.

At this point, I was also in contact with government representatives. On 4 March I met with the Bahraini Ambassador in London and the Social Development Minister, Dr Fatima Bouloshi, who was a hardliner in the

Bahraini administration, to see whether a private dialogue could be established with moderate elements. By that time, I was aware of the work being done by the Crown Prince, who was in favour of limited constitutional reform. He had spent a lot of time considering how to mitigate the demands of the protesters and the main opposition party, with the assistance of a Boston-based consulting firm, which was helping advise on negotiations along with Harvard guru and former Ecuadorean Prime Minister Jamil Mahuad. The Boston team spent eleven days in the country mapping out the interests of the various factions in readiness for real talks. The Crown Prince also received the assistance of the British Ambassador, Jamie Bowden. Meanwhile the protesters' sense of power and confidence continued to grow, particularly after 13 March 2011, when rumours spread through Manama that the Crown Prince had entered into semi-secret talks about democratic reform with Al-Wefaq. It was said that the Crown Prince had put forward seven guiding principles of reform.

But it was not to be. Within a day of the Crown Prince offering talks based upon these seven principles, all hope of a dialogue evaporated. The failure of Al-Wefaq to respond immediately to the Crown Prince's overtures on 13 March proved fatal. Whether the pressure exerted by Al-Haq had a hand in Al-Wefaq's failure to respond remains a hotly contested point. But whatever the reason for it, the failure to get 'the street' to send an appropriate signal to the ruling family fundamentally undermined the Crown Prince's initiative in what later proved to have been a race against time. As it turned out the machinations over the Crown Prince's negotiations, together with renewed demands for the creation of a republic by radical Shia groups from Al-Haq, was the last straw for the Prime Minister and, more importantly, the Saudis. They had been watching events in Manama with increasing alarm, as small Shia protests began to erupt along the eastern seaboard of Saudi Arabia. Seen from the vantage point of today, the seven principles of reform offered by the Crown Prince to Al-Wefaq look like a present from heaven. Unfortunately for the opposition, on 14 March Saudi troops, assisted by soldiers from other Gulf Cooperation Council (GCC) states, crossed the causeway to crush the protest once and for all.

Matters were put beyond doubt one day later, when the King issued Royal Decree 18, which declared a state of national safety, one of the two forms of state of emergency allowed in the constitution. The next day the Pearl Roundabout was brutally cleared of protesters for a second time. Bahraini security personnel fought pitched battles with Shia youth. Immediately, many opposition leaders were detained. These included Hassan Mushaima, Dr Abdul Jalil al-Singace, Abdulwahab Hussain, Ibrahim Sherif and others, many of whom had only been released from detention following the King's pardon in February. Protests were banned. State media talked of a terrorist plot and hinted at the involvement of Iran. As a consequence of these events relations between ordinary Shias and Sunnis began to plummet and polarise on all levels. Subsequently, fourteen opposition leaders were convicted by a military court and sentenced to long terms of imprisonment, including life in several cases.

When I next met Saeed al-Shehabi he looked ashen-faced, after reports of the ill-treatment of Hassan Mushaima in custody began to surface. At least thirty-five people had died as a result of the troubles in February and March 2011, of whom five were police officers or members of the Bahrain Defence Force (BDF) personnel. Thousands were detained and hundreds brought before National Safety Courts established under Royal Decree No. 18 of 2011. These included opposition leaders; lawyers who had acted for the protesters; medics who had treated protesters and spoken to the international media; and teachers, journalists, trade unionists and sportsmen and women who had supported the protests. Detainees were held without access to their families or lawyers for long periods, and allegations of torture and mistreatment were widespread. At least two men were sentenced to death, and many to life imprisonment or lengthy terms. Thousands of workers were sacked for supporting the protests, and the Formula 1 Grand Prix was cancelled for the year. Al-Wefaq quickly resigned its parliamentary seats en masse, as the government started legal moves to disband it.

Unsurprisingly, international condemnation of the Bahrain government's reaction to the protests swiftly followed, with calls for investigations into the legality of the detentions and the allegations of torture and indiscriminate killing of civilian protesters by members of the security forces. On any view, what transpired in Bahrain during March of 2011 was deeply disturbing. The polarisation and radicalisation of the Sunni and Shia communities had real ramifications for the Arab Spring on national, regional and geopolitical levels. In many ways it prefigured the conflict between the two communities that would later be stoked in Syria. Who knows today what might have transpired had the Crown Prince been allowed to negotiate a non-violent constitutional solution with the moderate Shia opposition. The decision to crush the protesters, it was alleged, came not so much from the King but the Prime Minister, whose court was unable to countenance reform as a consequence of insurrection. Neither he nor the octogenarian King Abdullah of Saudi Arabia was willing to permit what happened to Mubarak in Egypt to happen to them. I remember being told by a friend of the Clintons that King Abdullah had refused to take even a personal call from President Obama during this period. As the hardliners exerted control in Manama, almost overnight the British and US Ambassadors in Bahrain became personae non gratae for their involvement in supporting dialogue and acting as the thin edge of the wedge for unwanted reform.

The No-Fly Zone Debate

As Bahraini security forces began to regain control of the streets of Manama my attention switched back towards Libya and the issue of the no-fly zone. It was clear that the intervention in Bahrain would have consequences for the cause of democratic reform across the MENA region. Protesters and civil society activists alike began to weigh up how much real support they could expect to receive from the West in their own struggles for democracy. The muted response of the UK and the US governments to the crackdown in Bahrain graphically illustrated the perceived double standards that the West often applied towards supporting its allies in the Middle East when its own strategic interests were affected. Yet, if anything, the developments in Bahrain heaped yet more public pressure on Cameron and Obama to do something for the people of Benghazi. While it was arguable that the UK could have done very little to stop the crackdown in Bahrain once the Saudis had decided to intervene, Libya was an altogether different story. Unlike the Al-Khalifa family, Gaddafi did not enjoy the fulsome support of powerful neighbours. The King of Saudi Arabia had detested Gaddafi ever since he publicly humiliated him. Saudi animosity runs deep. In 2004, Colonel Gaddafi was accused of being directly involved in a plot to assassinate King Abdullah, who was then the Crown Prince. Then in 2009, Colonel Gaddafi embarrassed the Emir of Qatar, Sheikh Hamad bin Khalifa al-Thani, and infuriated King Abdullah, during an Arab summit meeting in Doha, Qatar. Colonel Gaddafi first denounced King Abdullah 'as a British product and American ally', concluding by calling him a 'liar'. When Sheikh Hamad tried to quiet him, he said, 'I am an international leader, the dean of Arab rulers, the king of kings of Africa and imam of Muslims, and my international status does not allow me to descend to a lower level.'

Furthermore, unlike in Syria, it was the West rather than Russia and China that enjoyed close relations with the Gaddafi regime. Gaddafi was a maverick rather than a reliable long-term ally. The political decision about whether to ditch Gaddafi as an ally in the 'war on terror' and impose a no-fly zone in favour of the civilian population and the rebels was one that was open for Downing Street and the White House to take, though it was not without risk.

The diplomatic landscape across the region was shifting at breakneck speed. The world wanted to know whether the US and the UK were prepared to let Gaddafi commit crimes against humanity when they had the military means and political space to do something about it. Were they prepared to come to the rescue of the civilian population of Benghazi or not? And if they were prepared to intervene, were they also prepared to deal with the diplomatic, geo-political, legal and economic consequences that came with any military intervention into the internal affairs of a sovereign country, particularly after Iraq? That was certainly what a number of French intellectuals with connections to rebel leaders urged French President Sarkozy to do. Gaddafi's threat to annihilate Benghazi had crystallised the issue on the international stage. It was as yet unclear if Cameron and Sarkozy had the diplomatic nous to construct a sufficient international consensus in favour of military intervention. Although Cameron and Sarkozy had floated the idea of a no-fly zone no one quite knew how serious each was, particularly given Sarkozy's previous flirtation with Gaddafi. Either way, the next few days would have huge consequences for Obama and Cameron's leadership and the struggle for democracy, as well as for the conduct of international relations more generally. The stakes could not have been higher.

Like a lot of people, I initially felt torn about whether the West should risk becoming embroiled in yet another potentially intractable conflict or instead ignore the pitiful calls for help and permit a massacre to occur? For the Left, intervention in Libya was just a pretext for imperialist adventure and a convenient cover by which to obtain strategic control over oil supplies from an unreliable ally. A cursory glance at the articles of John Pilger told you all you needed to know about the possible hidden motives and objectives behind a UK military intervention in Libya. Pilger, a self-proclaimed 'world citizen', told *New Statesman* readers that: 'The Euro-American attack on Libya has nothing to do with protecting anyone; only the terminally naïve believes such nonsense. It is the West's response to popular uprisings in strategic, resource-rich regions of the world and the beginnings of a war of attrition against new imperial rival, China. President Barack Obama's historical distinction is now guaranteed. He is the first black president to invade Africa.'[1]

As for Gaddafi's alleged vicious assault on his own people, Pilger observed: 'Statements by western officials and media that a "deranged and criminal Colonel Gaddafi" is planning "genocide" against his own people still await evidence.' Despite his overblown rhetoric about Obama's invasion of Africa, Pilger expressed many of the deep-seated fears of the Left. Yet Pilger failed to notice that many on the Right also regarded intervention as a recipe for disaster. For them the UK could ill afford to get bogged down in another doomed attempt at democratic nation-building as it had in Afghanistan and Iraq. What neither set of critics seemed to understand was that while the West had sought to impose an alien democratic settlement in both Afghanistan and Iraq from above, the call for a democratic revolution in Libya came from the Libyans themselves.

And then there were those like Rory Stewart MP. He argued that the West should reluctantly agree to provide some humanitarian assistance but studiously avoid being caught up in a full-blown military intervention, through careful diplomatic tap dancing. Just how humanitarian assistance was to be practically provided without the threat or use of force was not explained by the otherwise erudite Mr Stewart. 'I am in favour of having a UN-backed no-fly zone in Libya to protect civilians. But anxious about what happens next,' he opined in an article about the limits of intervention in the *New Statesman*.[2]

Much of the problem with foreign policy institutions stems from new obsessions, rooted in a new corporate culture [. . .] A culture of country experts has been replaced by a culture of consultants [. . .] Lack of knowledge may make us more, not less, likely to over-intervene [. . .] Given the frailties of twenty-first century institutions we should be far more wary of intervention. At the moment in Libya, we can resist putting boots on the ground because of the language of the UN resolution. If Colonel Gaddafi were still in place in three-months' time, or there was a humanitarian catastrophe despite our no-fly zone, or opponents were crying for help, how would we respond?

A vital question you might think.

According to Rory Stewart, the answer lay in the rapid deployment of a group of technical country experts.

These are scenarios that are best imagined and understood by people who know the place and have known it over many years. We need people who understand the Italian colonial history, the past ten years in Benghazi and the sorts of networks Gaddafi still possesses. They would need to be able to judge whether the power of tribal groups is fading and how much emphasis to put on Islamist parties and how far to trust them.

Wise words, but was that how governments operated when time was of the essence and a humanitarian catastrophe imminent? Even HMG's finest Arabist ambassadors all failed to predict the social and revolutionary forces that swept across the continent.

Ethan Chorin later observed in his book *Exit Gaddafi: The Hidden History of the Libyan Revolution*: '[I]n the late 1990s and early 2000s, the amount and quality of information the US and other Western governments had on events in Libya were poor at best [. . .] Once the extremist-orientated intelligence-gathering collaborations between the US and UK clandestine services were underway, there appeared to be an added incentive not to know exactly what was happening within the country.' A supreme example of this phenomenon was the Control Risk Group analysis on the eve of the revolution: 'politically, Libya is a stable country. There is currently no viable challenge to Gaddafi's leadership. The security risk to business is very low [. . .]' As the former UK Ambassador to Libya, Sir Dominic Asquith, would later admit to the UK Foreign Affairs Select Committee, with characteristic understatement, 'the database of knowledge in terms of people, actors and the tribal structure – the modern database, not the inherited historical knowledge – might well have been less than ideal'.[3]

This was a fast-moving situation that cried out for resolute action not prolonged analysis. Even if Western leaders had been given expert information about Libya, the crucial issue remained political will and the moral resolve of leaders who were elected to lead. You didn't need a group of Libyan experts to identify a demonstrable urgent humanitarian need. The real issue was what to do about it politically. I, like Rory Stewart, was against another errant Western military adventure in the Muslim world. Yet when push came to shove, I could not but support David Cameron's unambiguous call for a no-fly zone. It was simply unconscionable to stand by and permit a bloodbath of ordinary civilians, whatever others said of the hidden intentions of the West.

The threat of mission creep was an issue in all interventions but not one that, in and of itself, justified non-intervention. Ordinary people were battling for their lives against an unforgiving dictator in an attempt to establish a better future for themselves and their country. Britain was one of the permanent members of the Security Council charged with the responsibility of helping to secure both the security and peace of the region, based upon respect for fundamental freedoms and the rule of law. It could not just sit back and wash its hands of its historic responsibility towards Libya or the wider region. The fact that the international community did not apply the same diplomatic vigour to countries like Bahrain was irrelevant. Thus, despite the issue of double standards, the case for intervention in Libya remained compelling in my view.

Throughout early March I watched as distinguished former senior diplomats floundered about what Britain's appropriate response should be. Stung by criticism of past interventions, many advised extreme caution about creating a no-fly zone. It is often said that military commanders end up fighting new wars with the tactics of the last one – so too diplomats. Yet within three weeks, and despite the US Defence Secretary Robert Gates describing the suggestion of a no-fly zone by David Cameron as 'loose talk', the option became the principal way forward for the international community. On 14 March 2011 Cameron set out his position with admirable clarity in a statement to the House of Commons:

Every day Gaddafi is brutalising his own people. Time is of the essence. There should be no let-up in the pressure we put on this regime. I am clear where British national interest lies. It is in our interests to see the growth of open societies and the building blocks of democracy in North Africa and the Middle East. And when it comes to Libya we should be clear about what is happening. We have seen the uprising of a people against a brutal dictator, and it will send a dreadful signal if their legitimate aspirations are crushed, not least to others striving for democracy across the region. To those who say it is nothing to do with us, I would simply respond: Do we want a situation where a failed pariah state festers on Europe's southern border, potentially threatening our security, pushing people across the Mediterranean and creating a more dangerous and uncertain world for Britain and for all our allies as well as for the people of Libya? My answer is clear: this is not in Britain's interests. And that is why Britain will remain at the forefront of Europe in leading the response to this crisis.

On the same day that Cameron addressed Parliament, Dr Mahmoud Jibril met Hillary Clinton at a G8 and NATO leaders' meeting in Paris to press the case for intervention. He had a profound effect on her. His Western orientation helped convince Clinton about the reliability of the National Transitional Council. Jibril was the head of a successful consultancy that trained Arab businessmen in leadership skills. He had a PhD in strategic planning from the University of Pittsburgh and also ran a profitable asset-management company whose clients included the Emir of Qatar. Used by Saif al-Islam to promote his reformist agenda, he knew the system inside out. But American policy was still on a knife-edge. Against intervention, and worried about mission creep were the Secretary of Defense Robert Gates, Mike McFaul, Tom Donilon, Dennis McDonough at the National Security Council (NSC) and John Brennan, Obama's counter-terrorism chief. In favour of intervention were Samantha Power, Jeremy Weinstein, Gayle Smith, all the other NSC advisors, and the UN Ambassador Susan Rice.

Sceptics suspected Power was intent on using Libya to bed down the principle of the 'Responsibility to Protect' (R2P). She was the Pulitzer-Prize-winning author of *A Problem from Hell: America and the Age of Genocide* (2002) and had famously criticised America for 'promoting a narrowly defined set of economic and security interests'. The failure of the international community to intervene in Bosnia had turned Power into an outspoken advocate in favour of humanitarian intervention in defence of human rights. Susan Rice felt a similar moral imperative towards intervening as a result of her experiences in Rwanda. The following day Hillary Clinton rang in to a highly contentious NSC meeting from Paris. By then she had made up her mind and, critically, had convinced the Russian Foreign Minister Sergey Lavrov and her Chinese counterpart Yang Jiechi to abstain on any UN vote authorising the no-fly zone. It was now up to Obama to take the final decision. With increasing pressure from the Saudis, Obama finally announced on 16 March that 'the words of the international community would be rendered hollow' if nothing was done to stop Gaddafi. All eyes now turned towards the United Nations.

The 'Responsibility to Protect'

Questions concerning the international community's right to intervene in the internal affairs of a state had dominated many of the contentious Chapter VII debates within the Security Council of the United Nations over the last twenty years, most notoriously in relation to Iraq. Much of the controversy revolved around the 'Responsibility to Protect' or R2P doctrine, which had been quietly cultivated as an international norm since the end of the Cold War and the rise in prominence of humanitarian law. Any UN decision adopted on Libya would ultimately be based upon this new doctrine. R2P rested on a reconceptualisation of sovereignty based on the idea that individual subjects had rights whereas states had responsibilities, the first and foremost of which was the responsibility to protect subjects from mass atrocities. Where a state was unable or unwilling to carry out this responsibility, it did not fall into abeyance but instead passed by default to the international community. Although it was the primary responsibility of governments to protect their populations against gross violations of human rights, the promotion and protection of human rights was also a legitimate concern of the international community. This new conception of sovereignty and the role of the international community sat uncomfortably with the established rules that had traditionally governed relations between states. Ever since the Peace of Westphalia put an end to the Thirty Years War in Europe in 1648, non-interference in the internal affairs of states had been the golden rule of international diplomacy, a principle of non-intervention which survived well into the twentieth century.

Thus, Article 2(7) of the UN Charter proceeds upon the assumption that there is no right to 'intervene in matters which are essentially within the domestic jurisdiction of any state'. Yet the UN was also established to avoid the internecine violence that characterised the first half of the twentieth century. Accordingly, the UN Charter created a treaty-based system in which international peace and security was the first priority. In this system the UN Security Council was given the task of ensuring peace and security amongst nations. States therefore accepted limits on their right to use force in order to benefit from collective action. Article 2(4) of the

Charter states: 'All members shall refrain in their international relations from the threat or use of force against the territorial integrity or political independence of any state, or in any other manner inconsistent with the purposes of the United Nations.'

There is, then, a limit placed on the Westphalian notion of sovereignty. Other limits include the Charter's recognition of the right of self-determination for all peoples of the world as well as the inviolability of the dignity of the individual. The 1948 Universal Declaration of Human Rights recognises that all people, irrespective of which state they live in, are endowed with the same basic rights and fundamental freedoms. This Declaration led to the enactment of over eighty international human rights treaties, including one making genocide a crime with universal jurisdiction, and another creating an International Criminal Court (ICC) which sought to hold state leaders accountable for the security of individuals when they committed egregious human rights abuses. Yet it would take the collapse of the Cold War before R2P and new ideas of international security began to take hold.

This was because the UN system was originally designed to stop interstate wars rather than internal armed or civil conflicts. However, as the latter half of the twentieth century progressed a new conception of security began to emerge as the world was ravaged by genocide, internal armed conflict, terrorism and pandemics, all of which transcended state boundaries. As the then UN Secretary-General Kofi Annan observed, in an increasingly globalised world threats to security had become 'problems without passports'. As a result, new concepts of 'human security' became pre-eminent as the new security agenda became the focus of the foreign policy of a number of liberal states such as Canada and Norway, particularly after the genocide in Rwanda in 1994 which Paul Heinbecker, the former Canadian Ambassador to the UN, characterised as 'the worst single failure of the UN'.

These states managed to expand the definition of a 'threat to international peace and security' under Chapter VII of the UN Charter to include humanitarian concerns. It was partly upon this basis that the Security Council authorised UN interventions in Somalia, Liberia, Rwanda, Haiti, Sierra Leone and Kosovo during the 1990s. Yet despite the atrocities of the 1990s, numerous other states remained deeply suspicious of this extension of powers, viewing such interventions at best an inadvertent incitement to armed uprising and at worst a 'Trojan Horse' of Western imperialism. They argued that no right to intervene existed in international law and it was politically impossible to put into practice an equitable intervention given the biased international system. For them the interventions of the 1990s lacked consistency and coherence such as to justify an infringement of sovereignty in each case.

It was within this context that Kofi Annan sought to confront the tension between traditional concepts of sovereignty and the increasing need to protect civilians head on. In his Millennium Report Annan asked: 'If humanitarian intervention is, indeed, an unacceptable assault on sovereignty, how should we respond to a Rwanda, to Srebrenica – to gross and systematic violations of human rights that offend every precept of our common humanity?'. The answer came from a 2001 report on R2P written by the International Commission on Intervention and State Sovereignty (ICISS), which claimed that R2P constituted a comprehensive approach to humanitarian crises. It defined intervention as a continuum spanning diplomatic and economic sanctions to military intervention, including both a 'responsibility to prevent' and a 'responsibility to rebuild'.

The Report identified six principles that needed to be satisfied before a military intervention could be justified: (1) Just cause – To warrant military intervention there must be an extraordinary level of human suffering, evidenced by either a large scale loss of life 'actual or anticipated, with genocidal intent or not', or by large-scale ethnic cleansing 'actual or anticipated, whether carried out by killing, forced expulsion, acts of terror, or rape'; (2) Right intention – The primary purpose must be to prevent or stop human suffering; (3) Proportional means – The intervention should be the minimum necessary to prevent or stop human suffering; (4) Last resort – Military intervention can only be employed if all non-military options have been considered; (5) Reasonable prospects – Military intervention should not go forward unless there is a reasonable likelihood of success; (6) Right authority – Security Council authorisation should be sought prior to military intervention. Underlying the Commission's report was a redefinition of sovereignty, in which a state only acquired full sovereign powers provided it discharged its primary responsibility to protect its citizens.

Unsurprisingly, R2P continued to cause deep disquiet amongst a number of states because of its inherent challenge to state sovereignty as enshrined in the UN Charter. Opponents of the norm argued that the illegal use of force in Iraq in 2003, and the early attempt by Bush and Blair to justify the intervention as serving humanitarian purposes, was an example of the potential danger and misuse of R2P. Other observers contended that the invasion of Iraq did not in any way represent a proper R2P case and should not be held up as an example of a response under the R2P framework. R2P was finally approved at a world summit in 2005 after the UN unanimously accepted the findings of the 2001 Report.

In the event, the summit narrowed 'responsibility to protect' to cases of genocide, war crimes, ethnic cleansing and crimes against humanity, but deepened it by agreeing that the international community should assist states in exercising this responsibility and in building their protection capacities. It also confirmed that the international community was prepared to take collective action in a timely and decisive manner when a state manifestly failed in protecting its populations from these four mass atrocities and, even more so, when it committed such atrocities against its own population. The authority to intervene was, however, henceforth to be vested exclusively in the Security Council. Thus, when Gaddafi threatened to unleash the forces of hell against his own people the issue of humanitarian intervention and R2P came to the fore. Cameron, who was acutely aware of how Tony Blair came unstuck through his failure to get a second UN resolution authorising force in Iraq, stuck rigorously to the six precepts of the doctrine of R2P. All his speeches reflected this adherence. Yet in the end Libya was very different from Iraq, both internally and externally, and as a consequence Cameron got his resolutions through. R2P became the moral and legal basis of the military intervention in Libya but it also became the framework through which military intervention in Libya would be later judged.

The UN Security Council Resolutions

Over the course of a few breathtaking days between 15 and 18 March 2011, the UK and France managed to bully and cajole a war-weary world to pass Security Council Resolution 1973. It was the French Foreign Minister Alain Juppé who introduced the Resolution, claiming that 'the situation on the ground is more alarming than ever, marked by the violent re-conquest of cities'. He argued that time was of the essence and that the Council had 'perhaps only a matter of hours' to come to its decision. The resultant Security Council Resolution imposed a no-fly zone in Libyan airspace. But it also ordered member states 'to take all necessary measures to protect civilians under threat of attack in the country, including Benghazi, while excluding a foreign occupation of Libyan territory' after the Obama administration concluded that a no-fly zone was not enough. This effectively imposed a no-drive zone and gave tacit authority for the US, UK and France to attack the Libyan government's command and communications network.

However, the Resolution neither formally authorised the deployment of ground forces nor addressed the question of regime change or reconstruction. It did, however, build upon UN Security Resolution 1970 adopted on 26 February 2011, again at British instigation, which condemned the use of lethal force by the regime of Muammar Gaddafi against protesters participating in the Libyan uprising. That Resolution imposed a series of international sanctions in response, including the implementation of a series of non-military measures, an arms embargo, a travel-ban for individuals, an asset freeze and a referral to the International Criminal Court for the first time. Cameron achieved in forty-eight hours what Blair had failed to achieve in over nine months of intensive lobbying at the UN regarding Iraq.

It was the first time that the international community had formally invoked the doctrine of R2P in a Security Council Resolution. Both Resolutions 1970 and 1973 were based on the grave concern of the Security Council at the violence and use of force employed by the Libyan government against civilians. Each resolution recalled the Libyan authorities' responsibility to protect its population. The biographer Anthony Seldon later described Cameron's thought processes during this period:

> The moral and national interests were intertwined: he was led as much by his heart as his head. The pivotal day for him was Saturday March 12, when he feared Benghazi might fall. On the train to Paris, he debated the consequences of acting and not acting, before deciding that the risks of the latter were greater. His fear was that it could become the North African equivalent of Srebrenica, the Bosnian town where many inhabitants were massacred in July 1995. It was a personal and lonely decision.

Liam Fox, the former Defence Secretary, confirmed as much when he later told the UK Foreign Affairs Selection Committee that 'a fear [. . .] of another Srebrenica on our hands [. . .] was very much a driving factor in the decision-making at the time'.[4]

Cameron put his case succinctly after the UN Resolution on 18 March 2011 was passed:

> Gaddafi's regime has ignored the demand of the UN Security Council in Resolution 1970, that it stop the violence against the Libyan people. His forces have attacked peaceful protesters, and are now preparing for a violent assault on a city of a million people that has a history dating back 2,500 years. They have begun air strikes in anticipation of what we expect to be a brutal attack using air, land and sea forces. Gaddafi has publicly promised that every home will be searched and that there will be no mercy and no pity shown. If we want any sense of what that might mean, we only have to look at what happened in Zawiyah where tanks and heavy weaponry were used to smash through a heavily populated town with heavy loss of life. And we don't have to guess what happens when he has subdued a population. Human Rights Watch have catalogued the appalling human rights abuses that are being committed in Tripoli. Now the people of Eastern Libya are faced with the same treatment. Mr Speaker, that is the demonstrable need.[5]

On 21 March 2011 he assured the House of Commons that the object of the intervention was not regime change.[6]

From a civil society perspective, there was now a full UN Resolution in support of humanitarian intervention, backed by the Arab League and secured in accordance with the very rules of international law that critics of Bush and Blair had used to condemn their ill-judged unilateral interventions in Iraq. Given the settled will of the international community, how, I wondered, could civil society stand by and watch a bloodbath ensue? Imagine how it might have judged the coalition government had it not sought to intervene, given the value of the UK's economic interests in Libya and its previous ties with the Gaddafi regime, as exemplified by the LSE debacle. How could Western civil society leaders call for the protection of protesters in Tahrir Square and Pearl Roundabout and not for those in Freedom Square in Benghazi? Had they not heeded the same non-violent call to democratic arms? Was Gaddafi going to be permitted to run amok by default because of our reservations about the past misdeeds of the West?

The fate of the Arab Spring hinged in part on how the West reacted to Benghazi. But as one Tripoli-based blogger known by the pseudonym 'Muhammad min Libya' warned in *The Guardian* on 1 March 2011, some two and a half weeks before the no-fly zone was imposed, the opportunities it presented ran both ways: would it be a first step towards Western military intervention or provide much-needed cover for the Libyan people to wrest back control of the country themselves? He wrote: 'I'd like to send a message to western leaders: Obama, Cameron, Sarkozy. This is a priceless opportunity that has fallen into your laps. It's a chance for you to improve your image in the eyes of Arabs and Muslims. Don't mess it up. All of your previous programmes to bring the east and west closer have failed, and some of them have made things even worse. Don't start something you cannot finish, don't turn a people's pure revolution into some curse that will befall everyone.'[7]

Deciding to Go to Benghazi

In the end, the US, the UK, France and Qatar decided to go ahead with military action and on 19 March 2011 Libyan air defences were continually attacked until NATO assumed command of all coalition military operations as part of NATO Operation Unified Protector on 31 March 2011. It then launched Operation Odyssey Dawn, a six-week bombing campaign designed to take out a series of air force and military bases, energy plants, TV and radio stations. Qatar immediately deployed its Mirage jets, C-17 Globemasters and Special Forces as well as flying Libyan rebels to Doha for training, a city which also became the base for Libya Ahrar TV and radio stations. McCue and I were now itching to get to Libya. But by the time the UN Resolution passed I was engaged on another mediation matter in Iraq, while McCue was in Liberia on behalf of the charity GREAT. We were dumbfounded at the speed with which the British and French governments had navigated the Resolution through the United Nations, without a veto from either China or Russia. It was, on any view, a diplomatic triumph for David Cameron and President Sarkozy. I finally got back to London on 30 March 2011 just after the Council issued its comprehensive Vision Statement for a New Libya at the London conference.

The Vision Statement was written by Fathi al-Ba'ja, who led its political advisory committee. It built upon an earlier statement issued on 22 March 2011, which stated that the ultimate goal of the revolution was 'to build a constitutional democratic civil state based upon the rule of law, respect for human rights and the guarantee of equal rights and opportunities for all its citizens including full political participation by all citizens and equal opportunities between men and women and the promotion of women's empowerment'. 'Libya,' it proclaimed, 'will become a state, which respects universal core values that are embedded in the rich cultural diversities around the globe, which includes justice, freedom, human rights, and non-violence. A state that is responsive to its citizens' needs, delivers basic services effectively, and creates an enabling environment for a thriving private sector in an open economy to other markets around the world.' This statement went on to affirm that Libya's foreign policy would be based on 'both mutual respect and common interests' including respect for international law and international declarations on human rights. It endorsed an earlier declaration issued on 19 March 2011 in which it agreed: 'to urgently prepare a file on the referral of Gaddafi, his gang and his associates involved in the killing of Libyans, to the International Criminal Court and entrusting a technical and legal team to complete the procedures'.

Any remaining doubts about the NTC's position concerning legacy issues were resolved on 29 March 2011 at the London conference when it stated its 'strong condemnation commitment to combat terrorism in all its forms and manifestations, committed by whomever, whenever and for whatever purposes, as it constitutes the most serious threats to international peace and security'. It obligated itself to implement all relevant Security Council resolutions on counter-terrorism, including sanctions concerning Al-Qaeda. The Vision Statement also crowned the NTC's democratic credentials by committing it to an eight-point plan to restore democracy and the rule of law, building on its earlier declarations, with detailed commitments to draft a new national constitution based upon the separation of powers; provide for the creation of plural political and civil society entities; guarantee the right to vote in free and fair elections; protect freedom of expression and association;

create effective economic institutions and so on. All of these statements simply reinforced our desire to pursue an immediate dialogue on legacy issues and the rule of law.

At the end of the London Conference the international participants agreed to the creation of a Libyan Contact Group to enable the NTC to meet with the Arab League, Organisation of the Islamic Conference (OIC), European Union (EU) and NATO on a monthly basis with an initial meeting pencilled in for 13 April in Doha followed by 5 May in Rome. While the UN Secretary-General Ban Ki-moon agreed that the UN would coordinate international assistance after the conflict.

After this Conference and declaration I wrote to the FCO Northern Ireland–Libya Reconciliation Unit for a meeting to discuss the way forward:

> We are looking to develop work in Libya with the Transitional Council re strengthening the rule of law and respect for fundamental freedoms, including (1) strengthening independence of the judiciary and capacity of local bar/legal associations; (2) increasing understanding/training on international HR standards; (3) advising re democratic legal reform; (4) assisting re legacy issues re the preservation/collation of evidence re human rights atrocities and crimes against humanity etc. I will meet the council on the weekend and wanted to brainstorm and get your views on the above issues including what support the FCO may be able to give over the medium term when developments become clearer.

On the afternoon of 31 March I met with FCO officials from the Northern Ireland–Libya Reconciliation Unit, the Arab Partnership Fund and the Embassy to talk through the aims and objectives of our trip. I was told that the travel advice remained unequivocal and that we should not attempt to go to Benghazi. HMG did not even have diplomatic representation in the city. Officials did indicate that the Prime Minister continued to support the overall objectives of McCue's campaign and regarded the BHRC's objectives as being wholly consistent with the Council's Vision Statement endorsed by the UK government at the London conference.

Whether we went was in the end a matter entirely for us. One legacy issue that HMG emphatically did not wish us to deal with was the murder of WPC Fletcher, who was shot outside the Libyan Embassy in London in 1986. That was a matter for the Metropolitan Police. The police wanted to ensure that any evidence-gathering procedure was not tainted by the intervention of a third party. I concurred. Little did I know that under the previous Labour administration the FCO had secretly agreed with Gaddafi not to pursue the murder inquiry with any vigour. I spoke to McCue and we decided to ignore the FCO travel advice. We had received the green light from a Libyan intermediary to proceed to Benghazi. McCue sent a message to Abdul Jalil to say we would only come to Libya if we had a personal invitation from him. We didn't need much convincing that a golden opportunity had presented itself to establish a unique dialogue on crucial legacy issues with New Libya at a time when the NTC was more likely than not to be willing to listen and respond to offers of support from civil society in furtherance of its stated democratic goals. After the meeting the Arab Partnership Fund wrote to me to say that 'Rule of Law was one of the 6 priorities and Libya was one of the eligible countries', noting that the deadline for bids was 27 April. It added, '[W]e are some way off an environment in which to tackle some of these longer term reform goals. But we wouldn't discourage you from submitting a bid if there was work that fitted our strategic priorities and looked doable in the next 12 months.'

Having obtained further assurances we agreed to go, and set about organising our route. The problem was that by March 2011 all commercial airports in the country were closed. We quickly turned down an offer of a twenty-four-hour speedboat ride across the Mediterranean from Malta to Benghazi and chose instead to take the land route from Cairo to Benghazi through the Eastern desert. Within an hour or so the ever-resourceful McCue had secured a Libyan driver with a vehicle and a private close-protection (CP) team. We also obtained further financial support from Victoria Cummock, a prominent US citizen and friend of President Obama, who had refused Lockerbie compensation for the death of her husband under the US-brokered agreement between George Bush and Colonel Gaddafi. She and the Victims of Terrorism in America organisation remained intent on securing more information about who really perpetrated the Lockerbie bombing. The speed with which McCue and I acted clearly surprised officials in King Charles Street. I can still recall the startled look on their faces when I told them we were going to Benghazi the next morning. They had been given next to no time to fully consider the implications of the trip, both in terms of our security and the FCO policy towards the resolution of legacy issues with New Libya. Had this been a government-funded trip it would have involved interminable discussions about terms of reference, the duty of care and such like.

Gone were the days of the nineteenth century when political officers were permitted to criss-cross the farthest reaches of globe unmolested by London, in search of imperial glory and adventure for king and country. It was increasingly obvious that non-state initiatives enjoyed distinct advantages over government ones in the twenty-first-century conflict environment. The BHRC was much more flexible and able to seize opportunities in the moment than a government-directed stabilisation unit. The BHRC and non-state mediators were used to operating in hostile places without the type of support that the FCO was legally obliged to offer its officials. We were neither plagued by inflexible policy and security protocols nor the ever-present requirement to constantly brief London concerning the progress of a mission. More importantly, the consequences of failure were altogether different for a non-government initiative. Quite simply we could afford to fail. And so it was that with barely five hours' sleep between us, and a host of unanswered questions racing through our minds, we found ourselves on a flight bound to Cairo.

5. Passing Through the Egyptian Revolution

Cairo to Benghazi

McCue and I landed at Cairo International Airport on the afternoon of April Fools' Day 2011 with a sense of adventure running through our veins. I had known McCue since 2009 when he asked me to become part of a Darfur civil society initiative sponsored by the Mo Ibrahim Foundation. Mandate Darfur enjoyed the support of a whole clutch of world leaders and celebrities including Kofi Annan, Mary Robinson and George Clooney. It built upon a UN Declaration which urged mediators to take account of civil society when negotiating peace with armed groups and governments. I was asked to help draft the Mandate. In the event the conference was suspended after President Bashir of Sudan stopped flights carrying members of civil society organisations from taking off from Khartoum to the Ethiopian capital.

Through Darfur we got to know each other, spending time together, along with his wife, Mariella Frostrup, at the Hay Festival, from where her book show for Sky Arts was broadcast. Yet in some ways McCue and I made strange bedfellows. McCue disliked terrorist movements and wasn't scared of saying so. In the 1990s he had operated in Northern Ireland and run a campaign against the Real IRA. I, on the other hand, was more sympathetic to some of the claims of historical injustices perpetrated against the Catholic community that helped create and fuel the conflict. I also belonged to the Jonathan Powell School of diplomacy which maintains that there is not a single terrorist or liberation movement that we should not talk with when it comes to the business of securing peace and saving civilian lives.

As an international facilitator involved in a number of secret negotiations between governments and armed groups, I was convinced of the ability of certain broad-based liberation movements to come in from the cold, given the right political and diplomatic conditions. Yet despite our different professional backgrounds and associations there was a palpable easiness to my relationship with McCue. As we sat back, dead tired, in our seats on the plane taking us to Cairo, McCue asked how I would sum up the trip. I thought for a short while and said: 'Benghazi or Bust'. He was about to ask another question when I intervened: 'Jason, just do the crossword. I'm trying to sleep.' McCue kept shuffling about looking for something. 'You got a pen?' he asked me. 'No,' I replied. 'Did you bring any notepaper?', I asked. 'What about a Dictaphone?' 'No,' he replied. 'For heaven's sake, you are supposed to be conducting a set of negotiations,' I lamented. A minute later, as I was dropping off to sleep, he started up again. 'How do you spell Baccalaureate?' Slowly I came to. 'You are really something special, aren't you? I spell it like this. F.U.C.K. O.F.F. McCue.' We looked at each other and laughed. 'Forget Benghazi or Bust, it's more like Dumb and Dumber,' he said, not entirely in jest, as we both drifted off back to our different worlds.

After landing at Cairo International Airport we proceeded to the outskirts of Cairo to a pre-arranged meeting point, where a two-man private close-protection team and driver were waiting for us. Charlie and Bob were both ex-SAS. Bob was a fluent Arabic speaker and had an extensive history of operating undercover in the Middle East. He was responsible for all security issues on the trip. Tight-lipped and eagle-eyed, it was immediately obvious that it was not a good idea to ask where he had been or what he had done in the past. Charlie was an Ulsterman, with a background in Northern Ireland Federal Intelligence. He was equally hard-headed but had a more easy-going manner and an irrepressible sense of humour. Yet like Bob, he was not a man to cross.

Having acquired $10,000 at Cairo International Airport, we caught a taxi to a nearby airport hotel where we met our Libyan driver and another intermediary. He gave us an immediate de-brief about the potential hazards we might face regarding the journey across Libyan territory, including the thirty-six makeshift check-points that were strung out across eastern Libya. For his part the Libyan driver looked like he had stepped out of a scene from *Indiana Jones*. Sporting a gold tooth, Tuareg scarf, khaki flak jacket and a cigarette always dangling from his lips, together with a regulation mad glint in his eye, you could not have made it up. 'All we need is a cheery fat Egyptian with a red Ottoman hat and we're set,' quipped McCue.

The Case of Khaled Said

After picking up some additional supplies we decided to set off for Alexandria via Cairo, where we would spend a night recovering from our previous travels. Alexandria was where the student Khaled Said was murdered in 2010, leading to the first countrywide protests against the Mubarak regime in decades.

Khaled was dragged out of an Internet café and beaten in the hallway of a nearby apartment block by plain-clothed policemen, for dissent. He was subsequently taken away in a police car and was never seen alive again. But unlike many victims of Egyptian police brutality, Khaled came from a middle-class family who were much less afraid to raise complaints publicly against the authorities. Khaled's elder brother Ahmad managed to get himself into the morgue and use his mobile phone to take pictures of his brother's condition to post onto the Internet. This sparked off widespread protest across Egypt.

These protests built upon the earlier Kefaya ('Enough is Enough') campaign, one of whose founders was the journalist and writer, Alaa al-Aswany, author of the international bestseller *The Yacoubian Building* (2002), which told the story of Cairo's pitiful descent from being the cultural and political capital of the Arab world into a hopelessly over-crowded, stench-filled, polluted city where financial and sexual corruption reigned supreme behind a thin veneer of religious conservatism. As a journalist he wrote under the strapline 'Democracy is the Answer'.

As complaints about Khaled's treatment at the hands of the authorities became more vocal, liberal celebrities such as the former head of the UN Atomic Energy Commission, Mohamed ElBaradei, joined the protests. For the first time in a generation the regime began to bend a little to the will of an outraged public. It set an important precedent. This campaign mirrored in a small, but significant, way the anger and power of the masses who would eventually pour out into the streets of Alexandria and Cairo during the Arab Spring of 2011. It was instructive to note that the young Google Internet executive, Wael Ghonim, who many credit for precipitating the revolution in Egypt in 2011, used an anonymous Facebook page entitled 'We are all Khaled Said' as the medium to call the original protest in Cairo's Midan al-Tahrir (Tahrir Square) on 25 January 2011. In the event, over 60,000 subscribers clicked they were attending that day and by the time Khaled's mother arrived hundreds of thousands of people were there to greet her as a national hero, holding images of her smiling son. Khaled's early death was an important moment in Egyptian political history. It was the start of a process that would result in Mubarak's decades-long reign finally coming to an end.

Memories of the Pyramids of Saqqara

As we drove through the outskirts of Cairo and passed by the blazing auburn and red pyramids of Saqqara glistening in the distance, I thought of my last visit to Cairo in February of 2010, with the Scottish landscape artist Joseph Maxwell Stuart, when we had travelled to Egypt to produce a book entitled *The Enduring Middle East: In the Footsteps of David Roberts* (2012). Between 2008 and 2010 Joseph and I traversed the Middle East to retrace the steps of Scottish artist David Roberts, who captured the Holy Land, Egypt and Nubia in over 300 iconic lithographs between 1838 and 1842. These images went on to frame the West's vision of the Middle East in the nineteenth century. We wanted to see whether the landscapes of Roberts had survived the ravages of the twentieth century. It had been fascinating to lose oneself in the mists of time, whether at Saqqara, Giza or in the Sinai Desert. I remember being entranced by the sheer history and architectural splendour of the Middle East as we toured Baalbek in Lebanon, Palmyra in Syria and Petra in Jordan.

We also came across unvarnished places like Sebastia near Nablus in Palestine, where we encountered lost Roman ruins with vistas of breathtaking splendour, diminished only by the network of twenty-first-century Israeli checkpoints that had sliced up the blanket of ancient, rolling Palestinian hilltop villages. In embarking on the project I was conscious that Roberts's lithographs sat uneasily with the modern realities of the Middle East. To many, the Middle East was a place of unending conflict, where dysfunctional governments, rampant unchecked urban growth, torture and brutality reigned supreme. For them the landscapes of Roberts were irrevocably scarred by the pillbox, minefield, refugee camp, but, above all, by border checkpoints and invidious security walls behind which communities which had once lived side by side in relative peace were now separated by fear and loathing. What relevance did Roberts's Victorian images have for us today? Were his lithographs just a stylised glimpse of a largely idealised bygone age or were they indicative of a more enduring culture that still informed the Middle East and its people?

As Joseph and I traversed across Egypt, the Sinai and Jordan, it became clear that much of the old Middle East remained intact beyond its ancient monuments. Whether among the Felucca boatmen in Aswan, the teeming crowds in old Cairo, or the ever-hospitable Bedouin of Wadi Rum, it was still possible to immerse oneself in the timeless ways of the past. As we toured the Pyramids and floated down the Nile in search of Roberts it didn't seem that much was likely to change in Egypt any time soon. A sense of historical perpetuity often pervades ancient sites, but this can be a deeply deceptive sentiment. Change can come quickly and brutally in the Middle East, and when it does it is no respecter of antiquity, as the war in Iraq demonstrated.

When we were in Egypt in 2010 all the talk was of President Mubarak's son Gamal assuming power. Yet within a year both men were facing criminal prosecution for corruption. I recall talking about the future of Egypt with my friend Josey as we sipped lemonade at her idyllic farm in the fertile valley of Saqqara, with the Red Pyramid in the distance. She was the widow of a former Culture Minister of Egypt in the 1980s, whose father had served as

Prime Minister. Josey had an encyclopaedic knowledge of the country. She formed part of a well-to-do set that inhabited Cairo's Garden City, an area packed with prominent Egyptian figures who predated Mubarak's regime, many of whom could have come straight out of an Agatha Christie novel. Urbane, multilingual and utterly charming, these octogenarians inhabited the old world of the Egyptian saloon. As a consequence, they had acquired a treasure trove of knowledge, not to say gossip, about a deeply evocative era when Britain ruled Egypt and a fifth of the world.

For people of my age and younger, it was barely conceivable that Britain had exercised so much power in Egypt just a couple of generations ago. As we sipped lemonade in the sun, Josey recounted tales of life in Cairo during the Second World War. Her stories mirrored Olivia Manning's account of the period which was later fictionalised in the *Levant Trilogy*. Manning also lived in Garden City, with her husband Reggie, who worked for the British Council. She captured perfectly the erudite and cultured atmosphere of the place, including the tradition of taking late afternoon tea on the banks of the Nile, where the diplomatic set had their wartime retreats. Cairo during the war years was full of political intrigue and romance. It was here in Cairo where the British recognised Idris al-Senussi (the future King of Libya who had fled the country following his resistance to the Italian occupation) as the Emir of Cyrenaica.

Josey talked of how the square formerly known as Midan al-Ismailiyya came to be known as 'Tahrir' or 'Liberation' Square after King Farouk celebrated the departure of British troops from their headquarters there in 1949. It was also in Midan al-Tahrir that she witnessed Gamal Abdel Nasser salute numerous military parades demonstrating Egypt's new-found prowess to the world, in the wake of his successful victory over Britain, France and Israel in the Suez Crisis of 1956. It was a prowess that deeply affected the young Muammar Gaddafi who, like Josey, had watched the rise of Arab nationalism with wonder. Little did Josey and I realise as she reminisced about this bygone era full of international intrigue that we were in fact living through the dying days of yet another Egyptian regime. Neither of us imagined that within a year a clutch of Middle Eastern and North African leaders would be consigned to the history books.

Yet if one looked closely enough, the signs of impending change were there. By 2010 social media had connected people together in scarcely imaginable ways that proved just too difficult for governments to control. Artists and writers across the region were becoming more adventurous in their criticism of the status quo. Cultural commentators I met were pushing back the boundaries of dissent more each passing year. Although no one quite countenanced the scale of political change that eventually occurred in the spring of 2011, certain activists felt Egypt was rumbling towards some sort of political dénouement. After all Mubarak was in his eighties and could not go on forever, and few on the streets were willing to accept his son as successor.

There was a growing body of young, well-educated people, with no jobs or housing. They had greater expectations and aspirations than their parents. Even in provincial backwaters like Aswan I met people who were open in their criticism of Mubarak in ways that would have seemed unimaginable just a couple of years before. Some complained about the economy and lack of tourists. Others railed at police corruption and the murder of innocent people like Khaled Said. Others spoke of kick-starting another 'Enough is Enough' campaign, or of how the Muslim Brotherhood should boycott the parliamentary elections set for the end of 2010. Hilarious reports did the rounds of an eighty-year old President manically daubing his head with more and more black dye in a vain effort to beat back the years.

As McCue and I drove towards central Cairo I wondered what the ancient rulers of Egypt might have made of Mubarak's rule. It was extremely doubtful that he would be remembered by history for anything other than presiding over decades of corruption and the manner of his downfall. What did he have to show for his twenty-four years of rule other than a gridlocked capital city choked with fumes and a collection of five star hotels and shopping malls slung around Giza and the resort of Sharm el-Sheikh? Yet Mubarak was hardly alone in the pantheon of recent Egyptian leaders who sought comfort in fake royal opulence. In 2010 Joseph and I stayed at the Marriott Hotel at Zamalek in Cairo which was formerly a palace built on the Nile for the Khedive Ismail Pasha in 1869 and constituted a vainglorious attempt by the Khedive to invest himself with a sense of European regal splendour.[1] Ironically, the palace provided the backdrop for the eventual dismemberment of the Middle East in 1921. It was here, in the ornate surroundings of the Khedive's fantasy playhouse, that General Allenby, Gertrude Bell, Winston Churchill and T. E. Lawrence had billeted themselves, and the imperial spoils of the Middle East were divided in the aftermath of the First World War, leading to a further ninety years of continuous turmoil as the Mandate Powers gave way to a set of weak Arab states.

What, I wondered, would Churchill or Lawrence have made of this latest political crisis? For the first time in a century it was the people, rather than the politicians that ruled over them, who were attempting to redraw the polit-ical lines of the Middle East. Would Churchill's vision of the Middle East as a set of dependent peoples and states essentially controlled by Western powers win out? Or would T. E. Lawrence's romantic vision of an unencum-bered Arab people – free of the yoke of imperial dominance – finally win the day? Only time would tell. Either way it seemed that war, revolution and the machinations of great power politics were never far from this ancient and endlessly fascinating country.

The Muslim Brotherhood

And then of course there was the perennial elephant in the room – the Muslim Brotherhood, also known as al-Ikhwan (The Brotherhood). It was a ready-made opposition in waiting. Largely unknown and distrusted by both the UK and the US, it had a history in Egypt as long as the Mandate Powers. Over the course of eighty years it had acquired legitimacy for its consistent defiance of secular government and from 1981 the Mubarak regime. Founded in 1928 by the Sufi scholar Hassan al-Banna in Ismailiyya, it sought to combine anti-colonial struggle against British occupation in Egypt with a new form of religious and spiritual regeneration. According to al-Banna, Islam was the solution to virtually all of society's ills. The way to liberation, both personal and societal, he argued, lay in jihad, whereby greater jihad constituted the fight against evil both within and outside the soul, while minor jihad constituted the fight against 'infidel' aggression, including colonial occupation. This was, and remains, a toxic combination for the West.

The ensuing repression of the Muslim Brotherhood in Egypt by the British during the inter-war years caused its membership to increase to over half a million in Egypt and the spread of its influence to Syria, Jordan and Palestine. Al-Banna was finally shot dead in 1949 after a Brother attempted to assassinate the Egyptian Prime Minister Mahmoud al-Nuqrashi for his failure to defeat Israel in its war of independence. The Brotherhood was subjected to further repression under Nasser's nationalist regime from 1952 onwards, leading many Brothers to take up refuge in Saudi Arabia, Nasser's chief rival in the region. They returned to Egypt after Nasser's death in 1970 to build a network of social and economic links within the community, having renounced the idea of violent struggle, particularly after President Hafez al-Assad of Syria smashed a Brotherhood-led Islamic revival in Hama and Homs in March 1982.

However, the abandonment of the military struggle antagonised other more radical Islamic groups such as Islamic Jihad, which went on to assassinate Anwar Sadat in 1981. The Brotherhood's non-violent stance also led Ayman al-Zawahiri and Osama Bin Laden to create Al-Qaeda (The Base) in 1989 after the Brotherhood refused to give the Mujahedin in Afghanistan anything more than political and financial support. There was little love lost between the Muslim Brotherhood and other jihadist groups such as Al-Qaeda. Indeed, Bin Laden's second-in-command, Ayman al-Zawahiri, bitterly criticised its participation in politics and failure to take up violent jihad, in his book *Al-Hisad al-Murr* ('The Bitter Harvest', 1991). That is why Saudi-born Bin Laden consistently denounced the Brotherhood in his global fight against the infidel and also lashed out at Hamas for agreeing to cease-fires with Israel, who in turn suppressed Al-Qaeda operatives in the Gaza Strip. Yet the abandonment of violence also precipitated the Brotherhood's increasing influence across the region, after they teamed up with Wahhabis from Saudi Arabia to create a network of new chapters in the Gulf, the Levant and the Maghreb. This alliance came to an abrupt end when the Brotherhood refused to support the US-Saudi invasion of Kuwait in August of 1990, in deference to the sensitivities of local constituencies, creating a schism with the Salafists that continues to this day. By the early 1990s vicious jihadist struggles had erupted in Algeria and Tunisia where the Brotherhood found itself caught in the middle.

Many of these nuances were utterly lost on the Bush administration, which tended to conveniently lump all these groups together even though, as Jean-Pierre Filiu noted in his book *The Arab Revolution* (2011),[2] each of these movements had its own complex ideological and religious roots:

America had taken sides, giving priority to regional stability and the subsequent peace deals with Israel, endorsed by Egypt in 1979 and by Jordan in 1994. The political rights of the Arab people were to be addressed only in that respect. And this subordination became even more pressing after 9/11, when the 'Global War on Terror' divided the world between the 'Axis of Evil' and its challengers. The Arab regimes were quick to designate all their critics, even the secular ones, as playing into the hands of *Al-Qaeda* and its allies. This line of talk was adapted perfectly to the counter-terrorism discourse that became dominant worldwide[. . .] No matter how gross the amalgam could appear, it repeatedly allowed various Arab security services to reap US rewards and help for the repression in which they had long been engaged against their local activists. The rendition programmes made the whole matter even more incestuous, especially in Egypt, one of the main destinations for interrogation (and torture) by proxy.

The existential threat posed by jihadism to the West meant that the right of ordinary Muslims to forcibly resist oppression or struggle in favour of democracy through Islamic opposition movements could not be countenanced. The Bush and Blair administrations quickly proscribed most of these organisations while fully aware of how the terror label affected the legitimacy of certain struggles. Post 9/11 proscription regimes were used to delegitimise Egypt's Islamic movement which found itself subjected to continual repression by state authorities, even though it had tried to advance its interests through participating in parliamentary elections, as had Hamas in Palestine in 2006. Mubarak was all too happy to grasp the opportunity presented by 9/11 to repress the Muslim Brotherhood, the only well-organised political opposition capable of replacing him.

The association of Islamic groups such as the Brotherhood with proscribed terror groups such as Al-Qaeda provided regimes across the region with a golden opportunity to involve the West in their own internal struggles for power. That is why many deliberately made little distinction between them. It is also why they were at pains to stop any direct contact from being established between Western envoys and the Muslim Brotherhood. This connivance was only possible if Western counter-terror officials bought the thesis that these Islamic groups were all essentially subversive and interconnected which, for many of these officials, was an all-too-attractive offer given the bewildering array of Islamic groups operating in the Middle East. Proscription then was not just a legal tool but an ideological one as well, designed and deployed not just to combat criminality but to de-legitimise organisations and their attendant struggles and to communicate the international community's profound disapproval of them.

The Libyan Islamic Fighting Group

Take for example the position of the Libyan Islamic Fighting Group (LIFG). It was proscribed in October 2005 after the Gaddafi regime made its peace with the West and the UK Labour government. The proscription of the LIFG constituted a classic example of how the UK Labour government used the concept of terrorism for foreign policy purposes. Historically speaking, the LIFG was one of the few organised resistance movements that had managed to rise up against Gaddafi. It used Islam as an early symbol of opposition to Gaddafi. At the time Islam was the only alternative value system that was allowed to exist alongside Gaddafi's Universal Third Theory in Libya. However, Gaddafi mercilessly repressed all Islamic dissidents after Islamic movements, whether fundamentalist or not, became a potent source of resistance. Gaddafi quickly stripped the religious community of much of its authority, curtailing the role of the Sunni clerics or *ulama*, and elevating his own position over religious life.

During this early period many Islamic dissidents escaped Libya and went to fight in Afghanistan for the CIA-backed Mujahedin against the Soviet occupation. These dissidents went on to found the LIFG in the 1990s. Many later settled in Britain in the aftermath of the US invasion of Afghanistan, with the full knowledge of the British security agencies, which occasionally visited them. Some were given full asylum status while others were simply monitored. Other members were even allowed to raise funds. At that stage they were not considered a serious threat to the UK national interest. There were even reports – officially denied – from renegade MI5 officer David Shayler that MI6 had encouraged the LIFG in an unsuccessful attempt on Gaddafi's life.

Meanwhile, Gaddafi launched a series of ground and air strikes against LIFG bases and arrested hundreds of suspected sympathisers of both the LIFG and the Libyan Islamic Group, the Libyan branch of the Muslim Brotherhood. Many of these suspects were subsequently detained and murdered during the Abu Salim prison massacre of 1996, and their relatives later helped spark the protests in February of 2011. It was said that it was only after Gaddafi managed to decapitate the leadership of the LIFG that some rank and file members flirted with the Groupe Islamique Armé (GIA) in Algeria and through the GIA with Al-Qaeda. In marked contrast, the leadership in detention in Libya kept its focus resolutely on overthrowing Gaddafi.

The legal status of the LIFG and its membership, however, changed in 2002 after Blair and Bush decided to court Gaddafi, to get him to give up his weapons of mass destruction. Suddenly, London was no longer a safe haven for the LIFG. In November 2002 the UK authorities detained a thirty-six-year-old LIFG member at Heathrow airport as he tried to board a flight, under the provisions of the Crime and Security Act 2001, an anti-terrorism measure that allowed the authorities to detain international terror suspects without trial. 'M', as he later became known, suddenly found himself incarcerated in Belmarsh, the high-security prison; and he appeared in front of SIAC, the immigration commission that allowed the government to give evidence in secret. Despite being anonymised by SIAC, M's full name, date of birth and membership of the LIFG were passed to the head of Libyan intelligence, Moussa Koussa, in a briefing that breached the order of the tribunal. For his part M told the tribunal that he had informed the authorities that he was a member of the LIFG when he entered the country eight years earlier and that he had no connection with Al-Qaeda, being concerned solely about the removal of Gaddafi. In March 2004, M became the only person detained under the Act to win an appeal before SIAC, which accepted that there was no evidence of any organised affiliation between the LIFG and Al-Qaeda. Indeed, it went on to criticise the authorities for its 'consistent exaggeration' of M's alleged connections to Al-Qaeda.

Thus, in 2004, the LIFG suddenly found itself proscribed by the UK, despite having been in existence for years. Libyan and British intelligence services immediately began to swap intelligence on the LIFG and terrorist suspects. A number of other members of the LIFG were now arrested. The

Home Office justified the arrest on the basis that the group was 'part of the wider global Islamist extremist movement, as inspired by *Al-Qaeda*'. Within a few months the British government had entered into a Memorandum of Understanding with Gaddafi to send Libyan dissidents exiled in London, whom it now classified as national security threats and Al-Qaeda affiliates, back to Tripoli. For his part General William Ward, head of the US's Africa Command (AFRICOM), wrote in a memo in 2009 that 'Libya is a top partner in combatting transnational terrorism'. Yet even the secretive SIAC tribunal couldn't find the stomach to send these dissidents back to what would be certain torture. It was a reflection of the lengths to which the British government was prepared to go in order to improve relations with Gaddafi that it sent its lawyers into an English court to argue that it was safe to rely upon the word of this whimsical tyrant – despite his abject record of torture, assassination and sponsorship of terrorist acts including the Lockerbie bombing, which the UK's own courts had deemed to be the work of a Libyan intelligence agent.

The proscription of the LIFG said a lot about the legal efficacy of the UK proscription regime under the former Labour government. It was arguable that such proscription actually promoted jihadism, as young adherents became increasingly angry at their discriminatory treatment at the hands of the West. This was borne out by a leaked memo from a US embassy official who managed to get to Derna on his own in 2008 and filed the following analysis:

> Frustration at the inability of eastern Libyans to effectively challenge the Gaddafi regime, together with a concerted ideological campaign by returned Libyan fighters from earlier conflicts, have played an important role in Derna's history as a locus of fierce opposition to occupation, and economic disenfranchisement among the town's young men. Depictions on satellite television of events in Iraq and Palestine fuel the widespread view that resistance to coalition forces is justified and necessary. One Libyan interlocutor likened young men in Derna to Bruce Willis' character in the action picture *Die Hard*, who stubbornly refused to die quietly. For them, resistance against coalition forces in Iraq is an important act of 'jihad' and a last act of defiance against the Gaddafi regime.[3]

If the failure to differentiate between Al-Qaeda, the Muslim Brotherhood and other Islamic groups was sustainable pre-Arab Spring, it was not afterwards. Many of the less violent Islamic groups played an instrumental role in the uprisings, particularly in Tunisia, Egypt and Libya. Thus, although the Muslim Brotherhood and the LIFG remained technically subject to a range of criminal sanctions, the political and legal climate in which all these movements operated changed fundamentally in 2011. This created a headache for Western governments, whose foreign policy establishments were still scrambling to catch up with events.

The lumping together of disparate Islamic groups without distinction became even more of an acute problem after two Islamic political parties, Ennahda and the Muslim Brotherhood, romped to victory in democratic elections in Tunisia and Egypt in 2011 and 2012 respectively. The over-reliance on blunt counter-terror strategies not only hindered efforts to democratise and stabilise the region, it also stifled the development of more nuanced and targeted counter-terror strategies against groups like Al-Qaeda, whose tactics included indiscriminate violence against civilians. Consequently, the classification of all Islamic movements as subversive was revealed to be deeply counter-productive to Western security interests.

In fact, the only country where a brand of political Islam was able to take hold in the first decade of the twenty-first century with the grudging support of the West was in secular Turkey. Here, remnants of the Brotherhood went into coalition with other moderate Islamists in 2001, to found the Party for Justice and Development (AKP), under the leadership of Recep Tayyip Erdogan. The AKP would go on to secure three general election victories and begin fundamental political and economic reform in Turkey, under an EU accession process. In doing so it became the pre-eminent Islamic party in the wider region, despite the overt opposition of the Turkish military. It was this 'Turkish model' that led to the creation of the Brotherhood's newly formed Freedom and Justice Party (FJP) in Egypt in the spring of 2011, after Mubarak stood down, which also advocated a free market economic policy alongside conservative social policies.

More than any other opposition group, the Muslim Brotherhood understood the need to create a viable political entity with an appealing political programme. Although it did not initiate the Egyptian uprising it knew how to capitalise on it, and was adept at building short-term alliances with Egypt's more secular and youthful protesters and using the language of democracy and reform, while all the time quietly building its own political force for future electoral battles. It was obvious to many veteran observers that victory for the Brotherhood in the November 2011 parliamentary election was likely, given it was much better organised and politically disciplined than its rivals. In the event it won by a landslide, securing around 40 per cent of the popular vote.

However, elections were just one part of a larger and deeper process of transition that had been put in train. The demonstrations on the streets of Cairo that we were now witnessing in April 2011, just months after the 25 January revolution were part of this greater transition and deeper democratic struggle. No one here assumed that once you took the lid off the political pressure cooker that the Middle East would suddenly reorder itself into a set of neat, secular, democratic, Western-leaning political parties. There was always going to be a longer-term struggle for democracy. What was unfolding in Cairo before our eyes was a multi-dimensional fight for the soul of the revolution and the political future of Egypt, not to say the region. It was a struggle in which what was happening in Benghazi held as much relevance to the people of Egypt as events in Cairo.

Tahrir Square and Central Cairo

Approaching central Cairo in the twilight such broad reflections came to an abrupt end as we heard the rumble of gunfire ringing in our ears. This meant only one thing – people were once again converging on Tahrir Square. As we drew nearer to the square it became abundantly clear that things were heating up. The initial euphoria generated by the revolution was being replaced by mounting concern that reform was being hijacked by the military. More and more protesters flooded onto the streets after Friday prayers chanting democratic slogans, as the call to prayer was followed by calls for the people to openly voice their frustration in Tahrir Square at the lack of democratic progress and the failure of the Supreme Council of the Armed Forces (SCAF) to implement promised reforms. For its part, the army was taking no chances – hence the warning gunfire. The tension in Cairo was palpable.

There was a substantial military presence on the streets, particularly as we drove past the former headquarters of Mubarak's ruling National Democratic Party (NDP), with its blackened windows and burnt out and gutted interior. The ransacking of these headquarters by outraged protesters some two months earlier on 28 February 2011 constituted one of the pivotal moments in the emergence of people power.

As we ventured further into the capital, more and more people continued to stream out of the alleyways and onto the streets and bridges of downtown Cairo. Within seconds of getting to the outskirts of Tahrir Square we became engulfed in a sea of banners, placards and fists of defiance. As we passed the terracotta-coloured Egyptian Museum, I called William Wells, the director of the Town House Gallery, the Egyptian partner of the Delfina Foundation. His gallery was situated a stone's throw from the Museum and Tahrir Square, in a leafy working-class district of the city. Ten years earlier William had taken over some derelict nineteenth-century buildings, turning them into a set of unique cultural spaces where young Egyptians mingled with their counterparts from abroad who came to Cairo on international artistic residencies, and rubbed shoulders with local car mechanics and workers. The mix generated a unique, tranquil and contemplative atmosphere in the heart of the capital.

William managed to fight off the unwanted attention of the Egyptian security forces and political establishment, who were initially deeply sceptical of his activities. In doing so, Town House became one of the few independent powerhouses of contemporary art in the capital. Within a decade many establishment figures that once sought to censor Town House attended its private viewings as part of the new social swirl of Cairo. Its success in galvanising Egypt's artistic youth, and rebutting the efforts of the state censor, was indicative of Mubarak's increasing inability to control a globalising world that Cairo's youth were intent on exploring, despite his clumsy efforts at cultural repression. Unsurprisingly, Town House played a significant role in nurturing artists and musicians involved in the protests in Tahrir Square, and helped strengthen the resolve of many protesters during the revolution's darkest moments. Musicians like the rapper Ramy Essam, whose song 'Irhal' ('Get Out')went on to become the anthem of the revolution. Ramy would later be joined by other Arab singers from the region, like my friend Reem Gilani, a hugely talented Palestinian singer, whose enormous presence helped galvanise the crowd just as she did in a series of master classes that she gave at Traquair House during the Beyond Borders Festival of 2013.

As gunshots rang out across the capital, my mind's eye returned to perhaps the lowest point of the protests when, on 1 February 2011, Mubarak let loose his Baltagiya (thugs) in Tahrir Square in a last-ditch effort to recapture the initiative and stop mounting international concern over the regime's inability to deal with the situation. By then, Mubarak had already tried to close down all social media platforms only to discover that more and more people had emerged into the open to find out what was going on. He had also withdrawn the police from the streets in a vain attempt to give his regime a pretext to quell expected social disorder. The anticipated riots and looting failed to occur, after protest leaders called upon the people to remain peaceful. And so it was that, in one last desperate throw of the dice Mubarak sent his goons, riding on camels and brandishing swords and batons, to spread fear throughout the Square and clear it of the defenceless protesters, who tried to flee or stood their ground in abject terror. It was an extraordinary sight and one that laid bare the true nature of his regime. Had Mubarak succeeded that day in clearing the Square, which had become the nation's symbolic centre of defiance, it is doubtful whether the protesters would have been able to retake it. One need look no further than Tiananmen Square in Beijing in 1989 to recognise how close the Egyptian uprising had come to defeat.

In the event, these agents were less organised and, unlike the protesters at Pearl Roundabout in Bahrain, sections in Tahrir Square fought back with stones and anything else they could find. These elements were principally led by the Muslim Brotherhood. Paradoxically this limited use of defensive violence saved the essentially non-violent and secular nature of the revolution. The action of the Brotherhood, together with the deft tactics of the protesters in creating divides between the regime and the army, with slogans such as 'the army and people are one', eventually won the day. On 10 February 2011 SCAF issued Communiqué No. 1, which committed the army to protecting the legitimate demands of the people. This was quickly followed by a last effort by Mubarak to appeal for national unity, in an ill-judged speech where he once more promised limited reforms provided he could stay on till the next presidential election in seven months' time.

The reaction in Tahrir Square was emphatic. A visceral wave of anger about his speech put paid to any notion of Mubarak clinging on to power. Soon afterwards the US crystallised its position, with Obama commenting: 'The Egyptian government must put forward a credible, concrete and unequivocal path toward genuine democracy and they have not seized that opportunity.' Within a day SCAF announced Mubarak had gone and that the military had taken over in order to oversee democratic elections leading to the formation of a new civilian government. Defence Minister, Mohamed Hussein Tantawi, quickly announced the dissolution of parliament and the establishment of a committee to draft an interim constitution that was ratified in March 2011, in a largely free, if somewhat ramshackle, referendum.

Egyptians subsequently learned that on 9 February 2011 the Saudi King had told the US that if it stopped Egypt's billion-dollar aid programme to punish Mubarak, his country would step in to provide in order to shore up the Mubarak regime. Writing in his diary the following day, the Palestinian lawyer and writer Raja Shehadeh commented on these events as follows:

> Of course he would. Naturally he does not want to see a popular revolution, just as he did not want to see the victory of the Palestinian experiment in liberation and democracy and spoiled it by showering our leaders with money [. . .] A new age has begun. It was astounding: the joyful celebration, the euphoria of those who had struggled and won. 'Long live Egypt,' they cried when he left. Next will be Libya, Yemen and Syria. Something great has happened. Israel and the Saudi rulers must be trembling and wondering, in the case of Israel, whether the peace it made with the tyrant regime will hold. All the assumptions they bet on have proved false. The people have had their say.

Yet the euphoria of the protesters' victory was relatively short-lived. While Mubarak had gone, the reforms promised by his military successors were nowhere to be seen. Two months on it was the army who were firing warning shots in the air to disperse the very same people it had stood aside for in order to bring an end to the Mubarak regime. The Arab Spring seemed to be veering towards a precipice. Rumours abounded that the Muslim Brotherhood was on the verge of concluding a private deal with the army, at the expense of the people and protesters. True or not, it made what was happening in Benghazi even more critical to the wider struggle for freedom and democracy in Egypt and the Middle East, as Egyptian demonstrators looked to their Libyan brothers and sisters to keep the democratic momentum going.

Thus, as McCue and I left Cairo and hit the open road for Alexandria it dawned on me that the Arab Spring was not an event but rather a historical process that was unlikely to disappear from our TV screens anytime soon. Its tsunami-like impact was just too big for it just to be archived like any other news story. For most ordinary Egyptians concerned about the safety and security of their families, it was a non-stop anxiety trip. Cairo taught me that the outcome of the Arab Spring remained extremely uncertain. The Egyptian revolution would continue to be affected by events occurring across the region, from the Gulf to the Maghreb, which in turn were likely to be affected by decisions taken in the West. The biggest question for Western policymakers was whether they should intervene to support the struggle for democracy or prevent civilian massacres if and when the authorities tried to put the protests down violently. It was the same question that has haunted the UN in a series of conflicts and civil wars ever since the collapse of the Cold War order. All of this made me recall an earlier visit to Cairo in 2008 when I had occasion to dine with former UN Secretary General Boutros Boutros-Ghali at his home on the banks of the Nile. He was a friend and patron of the Delfina Foundation but, more importantly, the UN Secretary General at the time of the genocide in Rwanda in 1994. After talking about the state of Egyptian politics I asked him about the civilian massacres in Rwanda.

I was struck by just how haunted he had become about the failure of the UN to intervene to stop the genocide. Despite his erudition, he carried with him the unmistakable whiff of moral failure. As he talked me through the difficult political machinations that he had faced, he appeared more intent on convincing himself than me as to why the UN was unable to intervene to save a million lives. His experiences demonstrated that sheer political resolve, bravery and nerve count for a lot in times of international crisis. This was as true for the Arab Spring as it was for Bosnia and Rwanda. The stakes could not have been higher for Sarkozy and Cameron, whom many believed had already stuck out their necks too far.

As I took leave of Cairo to head towards Alexandria, it seemed to me that unless the West supported the people's struggle for freedom in places like Benghazi, it was likely to face the wrath of the MENA people for another generation. This generation knew what Western double standards meant in reality. They were not about to be taken in by mere warm words. What these people wanted was action, and nowhere more so than in the skies over Benghazi where the next phase of the Arab Spring would almost certainly work itself out. We finally got to our Alexandria hotel just before midnight, and I collapsed in exhaustion in a room overlooking the Corniche. As I drifted into a deep sleep I wondered where, or if at all, Gaddafi and I might be sleeping in six months' time.

6. Entering Rebel-Held Libya

2 April 2011

The next morning, we drove the remaining 600 or so kilometres across a barren desert from Alexandria to the border with Libya. As we hurtled along Alexandria's famous late-nineteenth-century corniche built by Khedive Ismail Pasha, past the old citadel of Qaitbay, I thought of the brave young demonstrators who had stood along its side six months earlier looking out across the sea in a silent protest against the torture of Khaled Said by the Egyptian police. On we drove along the coastal road and into a sparse and monotonous desert landscape. As we passed the British Second World War memorial at El Alamein glistening in the morning light I wondered how many more lives might once again be lost in these deserts if the UK we were to embark on another campaign to liberate this continent from the yoke of oppression. Was it worth it? Hadn't history taught the UK anything about trying to impose order on a seemingly ungovernable region?

After all how much knowledge did we have about the rebels? Apart from the lawyers and judges like Fathi Tirbil and Mustafa Abdul Jalil, who had spearheaded the initial revolt, relatively little was known of the other members of the NTC. There were, of course, Western-orientated members like Mahmoud Jibril, Ali Tarhouni and Muhammad al-Alagi. Jibril would later become the interim Prime Minister of New Libya while Tarhouni would take the oil and finance ministry and al-Alagi the justice ministry. These were Western-educated men who spoke the language of democratic governance. Luckily for the NTC, over the course of the next few months, they undertook numerous missions to Western capitals to press the case for recognition and support. Their presence at the International Contact Group, convened by states involved in the conflict, steadied many a diplomatic nerve. But was it wise to risk lives on such a relatively unknown entity?

One thing was certain as we bade farewell to El Alamein – the only way we were going to find out was to go to Benghazi and see for ourselves what the NTC was all about.

Diplomatic Recognition

As we drove the last remaining 80 kilometres towards the Libyan border I took a call from Sir Kieran Prendergast, the former head of the United Nations Department of Political Affairs (UNDPA) and former UK Ambassador to Turkey, Kenya, Zimbabwe and Israel, with whom I had worked closely at CHD where he was also a senior advisor. I spoke with Kieran about the issue of diplomatic recognition concerning the NTC. The UK government had adopted the EU position of only recognising states rather than governments. This appeared to be a holding position that was unlikely to be sustained if the rebels made substantial gains. There were rumours that recognition had not been granted because British citizens were still trapped in Gaddafi's Libya. There were also legal opinions flying around 10 Downing Street advising caution in relation to directly arming the rebels. I had heard from friends of David Cameron how irritated he was by some of these legal strictures and how badly he wanted to release the 90 million dinars that had been printed in the UK but were subsequently impounded by the authorities after the UN resolutions were passed. He eventually succumbed to government advice.

The issue of diplomatic recognition was an important one because without it the rebel leadership could not unfreeze Libyan funds held by the international community. It also constrained the ability of the NTC to enter into agreements with individual governments and private institutions to raise money and acquire other much-needed items for the revolution. I asked Kieran whether any alternative diplomatic status could be conferred, that fell short of full diplomatic recognition, but gave the NTC the ability to unblock these funds. As the intense desert light pierced through the darkened windows of our people carrier, Kieran talked about 'acknowledgment' of an insurgency, and a putative government seeking recognition, and how it could acquire greater legitimacy and eventual recognition as its authority spread over a greater landmass of the state. This provided little comfort to the NTC which was in a perilous situation due to its lack of resources.

Time was of the essence. That morning we had received reports that Gaddafi forces had driven across the eastern desert, avoiding the coastal roads, to disable the only remaining functioning oil field in rebel hands with a pipeline to the rebel-controlled port of Brega. The rebels had just succeeded in filling their first ship of oil for sale in the international markets. As a stopgap measure to alleviate its dire financial position, Qatar had agreed to buy oil from the rebels in advance. It was a generous gesture which threw the rebels a lifeline while they tried to remedy the diplomatic situation concerning international recognition. It was also indicative of Qatar's growing influence in the region. None of us could quite believe that the rebels had failed to protect the eastern oil fields from attack from the desert. It was an extremely costly lesson and one that reinforced how makeshift the strategic leadership of the NTC was in reality.

Certain quarters in London had talked about the possible creation of a new Libyan Peoples Freedom Foundation, with Libyan and international trustees, through which the NTC could trade and acquire vital resources and international donors could pledge funds in accordance with the principles of due diligence. Such a vehicle could also be used in time to disperse funds in relation to legacy and other human rights claims. Kieran recommended that I speak to ex-UK diplomat Carne Ross, executive director of the New York-based organisation Independent Diplomat (ID), of which Kieran was a board member, since he had heard that Ross might be about to advise the NTC on diplomatic matters relating to the UN. ID promoted justice and conflict resolution by enabling governments and political groups who were marginalised by lack of diplomatic capacity to engage effectively in diplomatic processes, providing them with independent and confidential advice and assistance on diplomatic technique and strategy. Carne Ross had been at the UK government's permanent mission at the United Nations in New York until he resigned after Blair failed to obtain a second vital Security Council Resolution in 2001 authorising the direct use of force in Iraq.

I finally spoke to him at about 8.30 am New York time, as I stood in the baking desert. It soon became clear that Independent Diplomat did not have a contract to advise the Council but had had some preliminary discussions with people connected to it. I was later told by the FCO that the people who had talked to Ross in New York did not enjoy the full confidence of the NTC. In fact, the Council had set up a committee to consider all international offers of advice and assistance but had yet to appoint any external advisors. It plainly needed both internal and external strategic advice about communications, including how to handle matters at the UN in New York where a number of states were increasingly nervous about how Resolution 1973 was being used to justify NATO targets. The call from Ross was instructive for as we left El Alamein we now knew that the field remained open with the NTC concerning non-governmental advice on recognition, legacy, human rights and legal reform issues. After burning some confidential documents amongst the discarded remains of munitions from the Second World War that still littered the desert near El Alamein, we set off to cover the last ten kilometres to the border with renewed vigour.

Entering Rebel-Held Libya

We finally reached the Salloum Land Border Port between Egypt and Libya after passing a dozen or so badly camouflaged Soviet-made Egyptian armoured vehicles and tanks lying around adjacent sand dunes. It didn't take long to get a sense of some of the intractable problems that New Libya faced. On entering the dusty, drab and dirty stretch of no-man's land between Egypt and Libya we were confronted by a sea of humanity squashed into every corner, including in the Egyptian visa compound, where hundreds queued for permission to enter. The whole of the Maghreb and sub-Saharan Africa seemed to be there. Some had fled war, others famine and poverty, while others still had escaped the impending chaos now engulfing Libya. I saw numerous black Africans who looked terrified. It was difficult to discern whether these were migrant workers or mercenaries seeking to escape the wrath of rebel fighters.

As we drove slowly through, I watched with increasing horror the plight of hundreds of men, women and children corralled into makeshift, open areas, with only cardboard boxes or soiled blankets to serve as shelters. A few lucky ones had the benefit of faded blue plastic United Nations High Commissioner for Refugees (UNHCR) cover sheets. God only knew how many destitute families slept underneath them. Inside the collection of desolate buildings that made up the border facility were even more groups of bedraggled women and children. They slept collectively under dirty blankets cruelly surrounded by departure signs for 'foreigners', although none looked like they were going anywhere soon. There was little obvious humanitarian assistance in place. I spotted just one solitary UNHCR vehicle. Yet there must have been tens of thousands camped out at the desolate border post. Many children were encrusted with dirt, and looked dazed and hopeless. Elsewhere hustlers, pimps, drug dealers and fixers went about their daily work.

One fixer set us up with Libyan phones, as Gaddafi had cut all international access. Unless you had a satellite phone there was virtually no way of phoning out of Libya. Unfortunately the satellite phone McCue had with him was a Thuruya and not an Iridium, the only model that Tripoli could not track. After being herded through a succession of filthy rooms, replete with bloodshot-eyed disconsolate Egyptian officials, we finally got to the other side and experienced our first taste of rebel-held Libya. By then it was nearly dusk. Unsurprisingly, we needed no visa. As we crossed the border we were met by a motley collection of rebel guards, half-clad in civilian clothes and an assortment of military fatigues and makeshift insignia, who waved us through with what appeared to be euphoric smiles on their faces, as the emblem of New Libya – the red, green and black flag with the white star and crescent first adopted following Libyan Independence in 1951 – flapped in the wind around us.

Memories filled my mind of another border crossing I had undertaken in Czechoslovakia in 1989 just after a series of popular revolutions had swept across Soviet-controlled Eastern Europe. I was greeted by a group of ecstatic but drunken Czech border guards whose broad grins encapsulated the new hope that Czechs had about their future. The parallel didn't last long. Within seconds, a rebel Libyan border guard appeared in front of the car brandishing an AK-47, manically shouting at a group of black African male refugees intent on crossing the border. As he stepped back from them, wildly swinging his weapon in all directions, he let off a round of gunfire. People instantly ducked for cover as the trail of bullets moved in our direction. The momentary image of the rebel with his scarf and AK-47 seared itself into my memory. I knew then that it was extremely unlikely that Libya's revolution would be a velvet one.

Thankfully, our driver spotted an opening in the swirling crowd, immediately pressed the accelerator, and shot forward out of the compound without looking back. The easy banter between Jason and me that had characterised our journey through Egypt was quickly replaced by a contemplative silence, as we began to think about the thirty-odd checkpoints that littered the 500-kilometre road to Benghazi. We had heard stories from Peter Marks, who had undertaken the hazardous journey a few weeks before, about fake checkpoints where bandits dressed in rebel attire tried to relieve travellers of their valuables at gunpoint. Our security experts, Bob and Charlie, now took us through our security procedure. In case of being split up in Benghazi our first rendezvous point was to be the El Fadeel Hotel where we hoped to stay. If no one appeared there we were to make our way to Midan al-Tahrir or Freedom Square, where we should wait for two hours. If that was unsuccessful we were to travel by whatever means to a location they now identified on the Libyan side of the border, where we would be required to wait for each other for twenty-four hours. If no one appeared, then we would attempt to cross the border alone. Bob and Charlie now checked whether we had burnt all compromising documents. As for the wodge of dollars we had acquired at Cairo Airport, it was carefully hidden in rolled-up toilet paper. 'Let's hope,' said Bob, 'that any bandits we come across don't fancy taking a dump.'

From Salloum we headed toward Tobruk. We had heard disturbing stories of how smugglers and criminal gangs dominated the local economy. In the event, we did not encounter any false check posts and there was to be no hostage-taking. Instead, we passed through a succession of dimly lit points manned by teams of teenagers with only the odd adult soldier for support. These boys were decked out in makeshift semi-military attire. All acted older than their age. It was as if the last few weeks had become a rite of passage, as indeed they probably had. All exhibited the strange vitality that comes with the assumption of power. These elemental days they were experiencing were unlikely to repeat themselves again in their lifetimes. It would have been nigh-on impossible for these young guards to contemplate exercising such power over the towns and villages of eastern Libya just a few short weeks before. How, I wondered, could they ever be assimilated back into Gaddafi's regime after experiencing such freedom and responsibility? There seemed to be no way back but death.

As we passed one checkpoint in the shivering dead of night, I thought of my eleven-year-old son, Louis, who was safely tucked up in his bed back in Scotland. He was just a couple of years younger than many of these guards. Alarmed at my going to Libya, he had remarked, somewhat caustically, that I should come back via Japan for good measure since it had just suffered an earthquake. Why did I have to go to Libya, he asked, after seeing the images of the conflict on television? It was a good question and difficult to give him an adequate answer. The truth was that I was unaccountably attracted to uncovering what was going on. If half the statements I had read coming out of the NTC in Benghazi were accurate, then we were witnessing another 1989. This time I wanted to offer my practical support to those fighting in defence of freedom and the rule of law in a way that I could not do twenty years earlier. Back then I was a mere observer, but now I had some capacity to act.

The Katiba Barracks

As we tore down the long desert road towards the frontline town of Ajdabiya, after changing some dollars with a money-dealer near Tobruk, we came across the first of many rebels returning from the frontline. They were in their distinctive Toyota pick-up vehicles, bedecked with revolutionary graffiti and improvised gun emplacements on the back. Although these scenes were familiar to anyone who watched the international news, there was simply no denying the awesome power of these images in real life. It was rather like the difference between seeing a lion in a magazine and seeing one in the wild in the splendour of its natural habitat. I became captivated by these untrained young men, some no more than twenty years old, who were willing to put their lives on the line for an ideal they didn't even know they revered until a month or two ago. I felt then that I had made the right choice to come and see for myself what was going on in Libya. Interspersed between the rebel vehicles were trucks from the port of Tobruk loaded with new Toyotas gleaming in the moonlight. Who, I wondered, had paid for all these vehicles? Qatar perhaps. A frisson of excitement ran through me as we passed the last checkpoint before arriving in Benghazi in convoy, as a succession of rebels, high on the naturally-induced adrenalin that war often produces, swapped Churchillian two-fingered victory signs.

After sixteen hours of manic driving, we entered the outskirts of Benghazi just after midnight. Almost immediately we passed by the infamous and much feared Katiba military barracks, where, just six weeks before, the revolution had effectively begun. This was where, for over four decades, Gaddafi's security forces brought people from Benghazi for questioning and torture. There, for all to see, were the twisted concrete remains of the gates blown apart on 20 February, after Mahdi Ziu, a forty-eight-year-old oil worker with no political history to speak of, deliberately smashed his car filled with propane gas into the barracks. It was the first of a series of supreme sacrifices made by ordinary people in support of the uprising.

We drove by the ghostly remains of burnt-out cars, and the interior of the white and green tinged buildings of the scarred barracks flickered momentarily into our vision, as the rays of the few remaining street lights shone through the shattered outer walls of the compound. It felt and smelt like a place of death. A few days later McCue and I visited the barracks with Tim Whewell and Maria Polachowska from the BBC's *Newsnight* programme. The entire interior of the buildings had been torched and ransacked. Most of the windows bore the markings of black soot from the engulfing inferno, as the residents of Benghazi exacted their long-awaited revenge. The soldiers inside had fired indiscriminately, strafing many of the civilians massing beyond the perimeter walls, leading to an orgy of violence, in which some of the rebels' exacted justice, revolutionary style. Later reports alleged some of Gaddafi's soldiers were lynched and beheaded.

The whole scene reminded me of another infamous bombed-out place of death I had come across in the disputed Syrian border town of Quneitra in the Golan Heights in December 2010. There was an eerie similarity between the barracks and the hospital in that town that had been strafed and blown to smithereens by occupying Israeli forces during the Six-Day War in 1967. The town was left derelict to stand as a permanent monument to the brutality of the Israeli occupation, by the Assad regime. All around the Katiba buildings lay the abandoned carcasses of similarly burnt-out vehicles, reminiscent of those that had been blown to bits by NATO forces along the road of death towards Baghdad in the first Iraq War, some twenty years before. The smell of death and destruction was overwhelming. Yet the graffiti left by those that liberated the place from Gaddafi's forces told their own unmistakeable story. 'Freedom for all Libyan Peepol!' read one message. 'Leave forever!' said another. 'Free4ever!' screamed out yet another. Only time would tell whether these clarion calls and declarations of freedom would last the test of time and were worth the apocalypse that had evidently occurred here.

The El Fadeel Hotel

As we passed the last remnants of the Katiba barracks Benghazi was shrouded in semi-darkness. There were few people on the streets. A few minutes later we pulled into the grounds of the El Fadeel Hotel, which lay just outside the centre of town, by the entrance to the new harbour. After we had parked up in the gated and patrolled courtyard, we encountered fighters in fatigues, journalists and a retinue of unidentified international advisors, all mingling and relaxing in the hotel's dilapidated foyer. It was a scene that I had encountered many times before in places like Iraq and Afghanistan, yet this time it seemed to bubble with cautious optimism. We had not booked any rooms in advance for fear of notifying hostile elements of our arrival, but were confident that the hotel's owner, who was a close friend of our Libyan intermediary, would find us some. As we suspected the hotel was full, but he said that yes, he could, at some expense, make available rooms in another building behind the hotel which were reserved for VIPs. Exhausted, we retreated to the hotel restaurant with its single drab light, where we ate a meal of warm rice and watery lamb, or at least that is what we were told it was. I have never seen such gristle and fat on just one bone. 'Gaddafi never let us build any new hotels,' said the waiter, who felt obliged to apologise for the state of things. 'He always hated Benghazi,' he added.

As I surveyed the scene in the outer foyer, I spotted a tall silver-haired man with the classic deportment of a senior British official, who arrived just after we did. Who, I wondered, was that? We later learnt it was the interim British Envoy, Christopher Prentice, sent into Libya that night from Rome where he was Ambassador. Prentice had previously served as Ambassador in Iraq and had had dealings with Gaddafi's Libya. Although the FCO had mooted in London that some lower level officials might arrive in Benghazi later on in the week, it had said nothing the previous day in London about Prentice's arrival. We felt more than a little let down about not being told of his arrival. He had been flown into Tobruk on a government plane, a fact that would not have been lost on the FCO Northern Ireland–Libya Reconciliation Unit when we had talked to them about how to get to Benghazi. Prentice would be the first diplomatic envoy to officially present his credentials to the NTC. He had with him other unspecified military personnel.

I later learnt that these men belonged to a small advisory team tasked with setting up a 'train and equip' programme that would take three months to implement. The go-ahead for the deployment was given at the end of March 2011 by the NSC in a meeting involving Liam Fox, William Hague, the Chief of the General Staff General Richards and David Cameron. This happened after key figures in Downing Street, particularly Ed Llewellyn, Cameron's Chief of Staff, became convinced that air strikes alone would not achieve the desired result. The NSC had to struggle with legal advice that raised doubts about arming the NTC or targeting Gaddafi. UN SCR 1973 authorised force 'to protect civilians and civilian populated areas under threat of attack' but noted that the measures used to achieve this aim excluded 'a foreign occupation force of any form on any part of Libyan territory'. Some government lawyers argued that any presence on the ground was extremely problematic.

In the end, the NSC authorised steps to be taken in order to develop the NTC's embryonic ground forces. A later investigation conducted by Mark Urban, the BBC *Newsnight* correspondent, in January 2012 confirmed what I had been told. He reported that: 'when half a dozen British officers arrived at a seaside hotel in Benghazi at the beginning of April, they were unarmed and their role was strictly limited'.[1] They were instructed to help the NTC set up a nascent ministry of defence which was to be located in a commandeered factory on the outskirts of the city. 'The first and most basic task of the advisory team was to get the various bands of Libyan fighters roaring around in armed pickup trucks under some sort of central co-ordination. As reporters had discovered, most of these men had little idea of what they were doing, and soon panicked if they thought Colonel Gaddafi's forces were attacking or outflanking them,' he reported.

The hotel owner finally took us to a suite of palatial rooms in a different building at the back of the hotel, where both Berlusconi and Gaddafi had stayed and entertained themselves in God knows what manner. The suites were ludicrous in terms of their size, fake opulence and cost, but we had little choice but to take them. Unbeknownst to us, this was the building where the UK Envoy would stay and where the rebel leadership would later meet. We retired to our rooms around 2 am, only to be awoken an hour later by a huge explosion which shook the foundations of the building. Almost immediately a swarm of close-protection officers tore out of their rooms to investigate what had happened. I just stayed in bed, too dog-tired to venture out. That didn't stop a series of questions from circulating in my head about who and what had triggered the explosion. Were Gaddafi's ground forces that close – surely not? Was it the work of a sleeper cell in Benghazi – possibly? Was it NATO? But if so, what was the target?

The next morning the post mortem began in earnest, as journalists in the El Fadeel swapped notes over breakfast and tried to piece the evidence together. In fact, the most likely explanation I heard came from a local man who told me that it was probably bored rebel forces firing heavy TNT bombs into the sea to catch fish. It provided a classic example of how Western minds often over-interpreted situations and joined up dots that had no relation to each other.

3 April 2011

The next morning, we set about making contact with the rebel leadership. Numerous messages were sent through a variety of sources. The most direct line was via McCue's Libyan intermediaries in exile. We hung around our suites, drafting various documents and memoranda while waiting for a response from the Council. Every couple of hours we received a message that the meeting would happen, but not until later. New intermediaries with new phone numbers were passed on to us, but still we waited for a substantive response about when, where and with whom we would meet. Someone from the Council would be with us by late afternoon, we were told, as late afternoon came and went. The gathering frustration began to tell on both McCue and me. It was difficult to discern whether we were being given the cold shoulder or if the Council was merely engaged in more important matters. After all recent news from the front was not good. That afternoon CNN, the BBC and Al Jazeera reported that the rebels had been forced out of the strategically important oil town of Brega and were now embarking on a mad dash to Ajdabiya in order to secure cover. The exuberant optimism of the previous day had disappeared. Now there was mounting anger towards NATO for failing to provide air cover in contrast to the French and the British military-led operations that preceded it.

The Special Envoy

There were other complicating factors militating against an early meeting, not least the arrival of new diplomats from various NATO countries. Earlier that morning we had been ambushed by Martin Fletcher of *The Times*, who managed to smuggle himself into the back of our building. 'Are you the new FCO team sent in from London?' he pressed. I now became convinced that the silver-haired man I had seen the previous night was indeed FCO. In what seemed like a comedy of errors both teams twice passed each other on the stairs without so much as speaking to each other. Two hours later Christopher Prentice's close-protection (CP) team finally initiated contact. A muscle-bound CP officer who looked like Christopher Reeves on steroids approached our CP team and said, somewhat conspiratorially, 'My summary wants to meet your summary.' And so it was that the two British teams finally met up.

We met Prentice in his equally lavish suite just down the corridor from ours. He confirmed that he too had driven across the desert the night before and would be here for the next three weeks. During this time the size of the British team would increase from eight to sixteen and would include a person from the stabilisation unit to work on post-regime stabilisation and reconstruction, whom Prentice recommended we meet.

Prentice informed us that he had briefly met with Mustafa Abdul Jalil and established reasonable relations with him two weeks beforehand, after bobbing about in the Mediterranean on HMS *Cumberland* for about ten days. Apparently there was a high degree of risk aversion on the part of the British government about tying up *Cumberland* on the quayside at Benghazi, especially after the FCO debacle in the desert in early March 2011. When asked, Prentice claimed he had no knowledge of our mission, although he did recall reading a copy of an e-mail he had received aboard the *Cumberland* in which he was informed that a person called Peter Marks, the English intermediary who carried some of our letters into Libya, had been emphatically told by the FCO not to go to Benghazi.

Both McCue and I briefed the Ambassador on our respective missions. In turn Prentice, who had dealt with both the Yvonne Fletcher murder and Al-Megrahi case in his previous postings, informed us that he had had two quick conversations with Abdul Jalil on legacy issues when he had met the rebel leader two weeks before. Prentice had been sent 'priority instructions' from London to engage with Abdul Jalil on these issues. He confirmed what we knew already about Abdul Jalil:

I saw him as soon as I came. He actually mentioned all the legacy issues they were trying to get rid of in his opening remarks. He said there was an absolute rejection of Gaddafi and all his ways. So when I mentioned that this was also a priority of the British government he immediately said he understood and that they would give us their fullest possible co-operation. The new Libya was going to be a state of law. I thought that Abdul Jalil was personally quite sincere about his intentions. So I was immediately able to report to London that that had been his commitment from the start.[2]

Prentice had been in Benghazi for about one and a half days and saw a lot of other people on the Council. At the end of his visit he talked briefly to Abdul Jalil again who repeated the oral commitment he had given to us that he intended to co-operate with all investigative bodies to clear up all legacy issues on the basis of proper statements and evidence.

We talked for an hour or so. Prentice appeared very much taken by the BHRC mission to strengthen the rule of law and confirmed that the Deputy Foreign Minister of the Council had emphasised the need to build up civil society in Libya. He also expressed interest in the idea of a new humanitarian foundation for New Libya through which the NTC could access international funds, without necessarily being granted full diplomatic recognition by the UK. He told us that he would communicate the idea back to London and advised us to raise the idea with Abdul Karim Bazawa, the Secretary General of the Council, who, along with Salwa al-Dighaili, had drafted the NTC's impressive Vision Statement. Prentice also confirmed that he was interested in exploring with the Council the provision of an advisor on constitutional issues. Apparently, the NTC was looking at amending the previous 1951 constitution. There was, in addition, talk of resuscitating the tripartite federal structure of the Idris period, before US oil interests had pressurised Libya into introducing a unitary system in the 1950s.

The Envoy detected 'an absolutely fundamental difference' between the situation in Libya and that in Iraq, where he had just served. 'Seven years on, Iraqi officials are still struggling to convince any of their many thousands of able Iraqi professionals to re-invest into Iraq, whereas in Libya, officials are attracting able ex-pat Libyans to come back immediately. They want to become part of Libya's future and it is hugely encouraging,' he confided. 'The Libyan Revolution is a cross between the Velvet Revolution in Prague, and Paris before the Bastille fell. We have to make sure it doesn't end up with the Directoire and the Terror but I don't think these guys are going to produce either,' he concluded. We ended the meeting after Prentice indicated that he would raise our presence with members of the Council with whom he was meeting that night. The Council were still in session and the French were due to present their diplomatic credentials at 5 pm. All we could do was wait and watch more news dispatches about rebels retreating from the front. However, when Prentice returned from his meeting that evening he reported, in somewhat cursory fashion, that he hadn't managed to find the right opportunity to talk about our presence in Benghazi.

Moussa Koussa and IRA Semtex

By the time Prentice returned we had received an assurance from a Libyan intermediary that we would be seen the next morning. There had been a delay in meeting Abdul Jalil because of a shooting that had occurred at a funeral. Notwithstanding the assurance, McCue decided to up the ante by making his presence in Benghazi known to the international media. If Abdul Jalil's invitation was given in good faith, then any media coverage was unlikely to prejudice the mission. Time was running out as I was due in Zimbabwe the following week and McCue in India. That evening Matt Jury, a solicitor at McCue's firm, let it be known to the media that McCue was in Benghazi seeking an apology and compensation for IRA victims. The media response was immediate. Just a week earlier, dissident members of the Real IRA had killed a Catholic policeman in the town of Omagh in Northern Ireland, with a car bomb laced with Semtex. It was more than possible that it was the same Semtex that had originally been supplied to the IRA by Libya. McCue had credible evidence that Semtex had found its way to the Real IRA, as the Quartermaster of the IRA at the time of the Libyan shipment later defected to the Real IRA. This, after the British government and Sinn Fein were embarking on the Northern Ireland peace process. The international media were interested in both the domestic angle and the attitude of the new National Transitional Council towards the alleged crimes of the Gaddafi regime.

There was also the issue of Moussa Koussa, the former Libyan Foreign Minister and intelligence chief, who, just a day before we got to Benghazi, spectacularly defected from the Gaddafi regime. He had surreptitiously flown from Tunis to London via the Ras Ejder border after fooling Gaddafi into thinking that he was embarking on a private diplomatic mission to Tunisia on behalf of the regime. Reports suggested that Gaddafi was beginning to finger Koussa for his present political plight, as he was personally responsible for convincing Gaddafi to give up his weapons of mass destruction and to come in from the diplomatic cold. He was met by the welcoming, not to say protective, arms of MI6 at Farnborough Airport. With the defection of Koussa, Cameron now faced his own acute ethical dilemmas. What journalists wanted to know was whether Koussa would spill the beans on Lockerbie after being whisked away from Farnborough airport to a MI6 safe house for immediate de-briefing. They wanted to know whether he would be investigated or prosecuted for terrorism and other crimes against humanity, or offered immunity from prosecution in exchange for cogent evidence of Gaddafi's involvement in the commission of such crimes. In fact, the full extent of Koussa's co-operation with the British government, including its alleged complicity in torture, would only emerge after the fall of Tripoli. But even back in April 2011 there was enough public knowledge to cause concern.

As head of the Libyan intelligence services, Koussa undoubtedly knew where all the bodies lay. As Libya's Ambassador to Britain in 1980, he had advocated the killing of Libyan dissidents on British soil from the steps of the Embassy in St James's Square in London, a full four years before WPC Fletcher was shot from behind an Embassy curtain as she helped to police a demonstration. He told *The Times* newspaper: 'The revolutionary committees have decided to kill two more people in the UK. I approve of this.' The threat followed the assassination of two Libyan exiles earlier in the year. Not content with this declaration of murderous intent, he went on to indicate Libya's possible co-operation with the IRA, which he praised for its war against English colonialism. He was quickly expelled, whereupon he returned to Libya to rise up the greasy ladder to become head of intelligence.

According to some Western intelligence agencies he was involved in the Lockerbie bombing which killed 270 people, as well as the destruction of a French airliner over Niger in 1989, and the bombing of a disco in a Berlin nightclub that killed two US soldiers and a Turkish women and injured 230 more, including fifty US troops. A classified profile drawn up by British intelligence in December 1995 described him as the head of an institution 'which has been responsible for supporting organisations and for perpetrating state-sponsored acts of terrorism'. It cited him as the handler of the Libyan agent Khalifa Bazelya who was implicated in the murder of dissidents in the UK and the supply of weapons and training to the IRA. Mahmoud Shamman, head of information for the NTC in Benghazi, has stated Koussa was responsible for killing more than twelve people in Europe and the US: 'He was involved in terrorism and I was one of his targets,' the long-time political dissident and journalist told Tom Coghlan of *The Times*. This dovetailed with the account of another alleged victim, Muftah al-Thawadi, who told the BBC *Panorama* programme that he was tortured personally by Koussa at Tripoli's Abu Salim prison in 1996. 'While I was being questioned Moussa Koussa was electrocuting me in my neck with the electric rod,' he said of the interrogation.

Despite his gruesome curriculum vitae, Koussa was allowed to develop very close contacts with the UK intelligence services after Gaddafi came in from the diplomatic cold after 2004. The true extent of his involvement in the CIA rendition programme would only be revealed after the fall of Tripoli to the rebels, when letters sent by then head of British counter-terrorism Mark Allen to his friend 'Moussa' were found by Human Rights Watch in his office. Those letters documented Britain's crucial role in the extraordinary rendition of certain Islamist radicals opposed to Gaddafi, with links to Al-Qaeda, back to Libya. These so-called radicals were subsequently tortured by Gaddafi, both for their dissent and to obtain intelligence for use in the 'war on terror'. But whatever the machinations of New Labour's time in office, it rapidly became clear that the new coalition government also saw Koussa's defection and potential co-operation as crucial to breaking the resolve of Gaddafi's other senior acolytes. Before I left for Libya I had a number of conversations with FCO officials about Koussa's defection. The FCO claimed it was none the wiser about his legal status as he was literally in the process of being de-briefed by MI6. However, it was clear he was viewed as a major intelligence asset and that his defection was capable of hastening the process of defections, as it provided other high value assets facing the same dilemma with tangible evidence of how they were likely to be received by the Coalition.

The possible issuance of further legal writs against Koussa at such a crucial time was an unwelcome diversion for Britain and its NATO allies. It was no coincidence that five Libyan diplomats were expelled from the UK on national security grounds the day before Koussa arrived in the country, given Gaddafi's penchant for using diplomatic assets to assassinate turncoats. In the event, the Foreign Secretary William Hague issued a statement that Koussa would not be given immunity from criminal prosecution by the UK government but would receive protection if his life was in danger. The Foreign

Secretary's statement was rather disingenuous since under devolved power arrangements he had no power to stop Scottish investigators from offering immunity in exchange for giving evidence. As to prosecution, all Hague would say was that 'ministers shouldn't decide', although somewhat unusually both the FCO and Downing Street went on to suggest that Moussa Koussa was not 'a prime suspect' in the Lockerbie bombing and did not have a case to answer. Indeed, Hague felt obliged to tell the world how 'helpful' Koussa had been in securing the release of captured Britons since the crisis. It was reported that he assisted NATO in its targeting of military sites and identification of potential defectors. Koussa was eventually allowed to slip out of the UK in mid-April 2011, ostensibly to attend a meeting on Libya in Qatar, to the fury of the victims of Lockerbie and IRA Semtex. The government continue, at least theoretically, to await his return.

It was within this context that the media spotlight turned towards McCue and his pursuance of Koussa in the civil courts. Koussa was specifically cited in the civil writ for damages issued on behalf of IRA victims for the exporting by Libya of IRA Semtex. Journalists wanted to know whether any new writs would fly against Koussa. Back in London Lord Brennan, counsel for the IRA victims, intimated that fresh writs might indeed be issued. However, sitting in Benghazi, McCue felt that such an announcement was premature, given the events unfolding in London and Tripoli. He judged that it was in the interests of his clients that the Gaddafi regime fell apart as quickly as possible, and therefore held back on further legal moves against Koussa, at least for the time being.

7. Experiencing Rebel-Held Benghazi

The Press Conference

We rose early the next morning, 4 April, for a press conference. A blue sky set against the beige war-worn buildings of Benghazi greeted us as we stepped onto our balcony overlooking the new harbour. By then the presidential suite where we were staying was a hive of activity, as protection teams rolled up with their precious diplomatic cargo, intent on presenting their credentials to the NTC, which had moved its operations to our building for the day. Someone mentioned that the French had arrived. As we walked the short distance across the garden square to the makeshift press tent at the back of the El Fadeel Hotel I spotted a few familiar British faces, including Tim Whewell of BBC *Newsnight* and Lindsey Hilsum of Channel 4 News, Martin Fletcher of *The Times* and Ben Farmer of *The Telegraph*. As we sat down in a sea of wicker chairs, the journalists began to circle us like a pack of hounds. It was both fascinating and amusing to observe a crowd of journalists in search of a story. Stuck in Benghazi away from the front line, I sensed a certain creeping desperation in some of them, as they sought to find and file a new story for each day – a task that grew more arduous with each passing week. There was something unappetising about the collective competitive foray for information. Yet these journalists were hugely impressive individuals when separated from the amorphous pack. Their unerring search for the truth about the Libyan uprising was there for all to see.

The press conference began by each of us explaining the purpose of our visit. Almost immediately the focus turned to IRA Semtex and the search for an apology from the NTC. Yes, McCue explained, Libyan-exported Semtex could have been used in the recent Omagh bombing. It had its own unique chemical DNA that could be traced back to the bill of lading documents concerning the shipment of Semtex from a Czech manufacturer to Libya. Yes, the victims were looking for apologies from the NTC to help bring some form of closure and to draw a line under the past. And yes, both of us were still waiting to see the Council but a meeting with Abdul Jalil was imminent. No, McCue was not at present minded to issue new writs against Moussa Koussa and had no wish to assist the Gaddafi regime by making it more difficult for potential defectors to switch sides at this crucial time in the conflict. And so it went on.

About half an hour later Chris McGreal of *The Guardian* wandered in and pointedly asked why the NTC should apologise for crimes committed by a different regime. It seemed a reasonable enough question, but I detected a slight element of animosity towards McCue. It wasn't difficult to see why McCue's credo might rankle with some on the liberal left. He had been much lauded by the right-wing press for his legal case and campaign against the Real IRA in relation to the Omagh bombing. For some in government he was considered to be a legal irritant to the peace process. Others took a swipe at his alleged celebrity lifestyle. Certainly he was not one of those black letter lawyers so beloved by the liberal media and legal establishment. Shorn of much of the pretension that some at the English Bar exhibit, there was an element of the swashbuckling legal entrepreneur about him. Yet McCue had his own distinct charm and had got things done in very difficult circumstances. He literally bullied Gordon Brown into creating the Northern Ireland–Libya Reconciliation Unit in the FCO through his dogged pursuit of his clients' interests. The ever-affable McCue repeated why an apology from the Council was important for the victims and how it might engender a new era of friendship and co-operation between Britain and New Libya. McGreal didn't buy it. I countered that if the NTC won the day it would have to deal with legacy issues in any event, given its recent Vision Statement.

Experiencing the Libyan Revolution

I was now determined to get into central Benghazi to see what was happening on the ground and meet elements of civil society. Around mid-day we drove out of the gated compound and headed towards the city centre past an assortment of abandoned upturned boats, whose yellow skeletal remains resembled the carcasses of pre-historic creatures that had been left to bake in the sun for centuries. It made for an eerie and surreal atmosphere. The next thing we saw was a dozen or so revolutionary green, black and red flags with bold white star and crescent, blowing wildly in the wind in the middle distance. The flags had been strategically placed on top of most of the prominent buildings that flanked the approach to the heart of the city. As we got to the outskirts of the city centre, we came across numerous emphatic declarations of defiance scrawled on the walls of the outer ring of the centre in both Arabic and English: '42 years of Dictatorship.' 'Go to Hell.' 'Fuck Muammar.'

Any doubts about Benghazi being the central redoubt of the rebels vanished when we hit the last big crossroads before the old town. There, standing in the centre, dressed in full attire, was one of Baden Powell's finest. The Scouts had been charged with directing the traffic. We looked on in total amazement as we were stopped and then waved through by a twelve-year-old boy dressed in pristine Scout kit, complete with woggle. His shirt, shorts and socks were immaculately pressed and made for an absurd contrast with the ramshackle vehicles that surrounded him, which were now under his sole authority and direction. We watched transfixed as old men sat patiently in their broken down cars waiting for the boy to give the order to move on. Were these the Islamic fundamentalists that Saif al-Islam was talking about? What clearer sign could there be that this was a people's revolution?

I later learnt that there were over 3,500 Cubs and Scouts in Benghazi and 18,000 across Libya, mostly aged between eight and eighteen. The movement had been around in Libya since about 1954 and had managed to prosper under the Gaddafi regime by keeping a very low profile, thereby providing ordinary families with a non-ideological alternative to the youth wings of the revolutionary committees. The Scouts and Girl Guides were the only well-organised, disciplined, uniformed force left in eastern Libya after the police had been disbanded in the immediate aftermath of the uprising. By that time, most basic public services had collapsed, after thousands of foreign and Egyptian workers had fled the country. The Scouts were tasked not only with directing traffic but cleaning the streets, distributing food and medicine, assisting in hospitals, providing first aid to the injured, giving blood, finding homes for refugees, picking vegetables, unloading aid shipments, clearing shrapnel from the airport runway, making meals for the fighters, cleaning weapons, and washing and burying dozens of casualties daily. It gave a new meaning to the motto 'Be Prepared'. According to one report, three Scouts had been captured by government forces while working in an ambulance near the front line on 24 March and were still missing. I was dumbfounded by the courage and civic consciousness these young people exhibited and will never forget the image of the brave, pristine Scout standing resolutely at the edge of Benghazi.

We pressed on towards Midan al-Tahrir and the courthouse. The graffiti on the walls increased in number and intensity. Huge cartoons of Gaddafi and his cohorts appeared on the side of buildings, lampooning him and them in every conceivable way, including on the walls of the largest colonial building from the Italian period, the former Catholic cathedral in Midan al-Catadraya (Cathedral Square) with its two magisterial domes, built in the 1920s. I came across the mesmerising image of Gaddafi in green holding a black umbrella dripping with red blood, which I later learnt had been painted by Qais Ahmad Hilal. There appeared to be 100 Arab Banksys in Benghazi.

The free-flowing nature of the imagery and quips accompanying the cartoons indicated the existence of a new and profound freedom of expression in Libya, which any oppressive state would find hard to contain, for there was nothing centrally orchestrated about these images and declarations. Their random authenticity was there for all to see. I figured it would take a year to power-wash these images from the streets of Benghazi. Even then it would take an eternity for Gaddafi and his henchmen to wash them from the minds of Libya's people. Once freedom of expression is tasted in this way, there is little way back for a despotic regime intent on cultural control.

Freedom Square was festooned with revolutionary paraphernalia; I thought about how a triumphant Gaddafi might have entered Benghazi surrounded by all these images. I had no doubt that a vengeful bloodbath would have ensued, starting with the public execution of all revolutionary artists. I recalled how a Libyan university student of mine in Cyprus, where I taught Middle East Studies in the mid-1980s, once told me how he was forced to watch the public hanging of a young man by Gaddafi's revolutionary councils for ridiculing 'Brother Leader'. This student was also present during the horrific execution of a number of rebels in Benghazi in the 1980s when, in an act of devotion and subservience to Gaddafi, a woman rushed toward a condemned man hanging from the gallows to pull down on the legs to ensure his death and public humiliation. She was later rewarded with the mayorship of Benghazi for her efforts. It seemed to me that all those sceptical about intervention should have been made to take a trip through downtown Benghazi to witness the remarkable flowering of freedom of expression and human solidarity that was occurring.

Disembarking into Freedom Square made me feel giddy. It seems trite to say it, but it was like stepping into a Hollywood blockbuster. Midan al-Tahrir was rectangular and stood across from the promenade and the old harbour, whose white walls on the far side protected it from the sea. In the harbour lay a series of rusty and faded pastel-coloured fishing vessels that made for a vibrant backdrop. A crisp breeze blew through the square as if auguring the arrival of freedom itself. The other side of the square was flanked by a succession of official-looking nineteenth-century Italian colonial buildings resplendent with formal facades and balconies, which looked outward across the Mediterranean towards Europe, all drenched in the black, red and green colours of the New Libya. To the right stood a 1930s art-deco-style building more evocative of the fascist architectural period. I could also see the facade of the municipal palace built in 1924, which combined Moorish arches with Italianate motifs. The lower walls of these buildings were draped in revolutionary literature, posters and personal messages of defiance and thanks, including many to Britain and France. One huge canvas message read: 'Great thanks from the Libyan people to Qatar, Emirates, France, USA, Britain, Italy and the Security Council.' Elsewhere, walls were pasted with the portraits and photographs of young martyrs who had died at the front, during the Abu Salim prison massacre, and during previous episodes of dissent. Hundreds of faces of dead martyrs stared down from the walls, some in posters, some in wooden frames. Little icons to the dead and injured were placed at the foot of the buildings.

Freedom Square heaved with revolutionary and political activity. All around its sides stood improvised tents. Some were filled with more cartoons of the 'Mad Dog' from Tripoli. Others contained practical political declarations, public messages, while others still included personal poems and laments from the front. One child's depiction of Gaddafi had the single word 'Killer' next to it. Another said 'He'll fall soon.' Others just mocked Gaddafi in pictures. Slung around the square were a couple of captured desert-camouflaged tanks daubed in revolutionary colours, that sat motionless in the mid-day sun like sleeping lions. Children played boisterously on their turrets while below them a phalanx of older teenage Guides and Scouts dressed in white medical coats swept the square of debris and litter, in what appeared to be a collective civil homage to the new people's order. This mirrored the volunteers who had cleaned Cairo's Tahrir Square so assiduously just one month earlier.

On the far side lay a series of larger tented encampments where residents and refugees from the war congregated to rest and talk. I saw an old man bend and tenderly blow up a revolutionary balloon for a little girl. One tent doubled up as an art installation consisting of a series of ever-greater shell encasements, dud missiles and shrapnel-shaped objects. Somewhat surreally at the centre of the display lay a small girl-doll with a milk bottle and a gas mask with a flower display, guarded by an utterly dishevelled middle-aged man with encrusted Rastafarian hair and a mad stare. He was dressed in unidentifiable torn military fatigues and looked straight out of a scene from the film *Mad Max*. It was hard to take it all in.

It dawned on me that everywhere I looked were images of defiance. Memories of my experiences of the revolutions of 1989 came flooding back. In particular, the scene reminded me of the walls of the Romanian Embassy in Prague which, in December 1989, had been daubed in dark red wax in honour of the ordinary mortals who had fallen in defence of the people's revolution against Ceausescu in the squares of Bucharest and Timisoara. How devastating the power of art can be, especially for brutal and repressive regimes in cultures unused to seeing anything like it in the political sphere. But Benghazi was on an altogether different scale. Quite simply, I had never seen anything like this in the Arab world.

It was also telling that the square was filled not just with the cadres of the revolution but also the ordinary people of Benghazi. It was in every sense a

People's Square. I watched intently as men, women and schoolchildren gathered to look at the notice boards or chat amongst themselves to catch up on the latest news from the front. Suddenly an impromptu demonstration of about 200 citizens of Free Benghazi emerged from a side road carrying a huge revolutionary banner. They marched around the square to the tumultuous applause of the locals. These demonstrations were part of the ebb and flow of the radical fever that gripped the town. Later I watched another demonstration, this time exclusively of women, some dressed in civilian clothes, others in military costume, as they made their way to the steps of the courthouse to proclaim their own defence of the revolution. The cacophony was deafening as more and more onlookers took up their chants. It was obvious that these women felt empowered in a way they probably never had before. One looked intently into my eyes and thrust yet another banner towards me. It read: 'We'll fight to the bitter end.'

The Media Centre and the Siege of Misrata

From the square I made my way to the makeshift media centre where the daily press conferences of the Council were given. In the outer hall we came across this message: 'We need all the world to see what Mummer do to the innocent people he killed, children, women, all innocent people. Libya one Nation.' To the left was written: 'Human Dignity. Human Rights.' We passed through a blackened corridor, burnt to a cinder by the original protest that had ushered in the revolution, into an inner hall surrounded by large graffiti images and posters mocking Gaddafi. Another banner read: 'To Cameron, Obama, and Sarkozy. We are neither extremists nor Al-Qaeda. We want Liberty,' while another added for good measure: 'China and Russia never care about Libyan blood.' In the interior rooms were to be found the artists themselves hard at work creating new images of derision. One poster detailed the daily health requirements of the revolution against Gaddafi: '20 milligrams of freedom of speech, 20 milligrams of democracy, 20 milligrams of an independent judiciary' and so on. McCue was later given this poster as a present by the rebels. As we walked through the otherwise soiled and darkened rooms, it rapidly became apparent that the whole building was plastered with graffiti art. It had become a sort of ministry of revolutionary art.

We pressed on to the first floor where we came across the official press room with a solitary podium, with the official flag of the revolution and a couple of decaying flowers beside it. The backdrop read: 'Free Libya with Tripoli its Capital.' Someone had evidently tried to ape the White House press room. The attempt at state building almost brought a tear to the eye. It could easily have been a memorial to the revolution given the news that began to filter in from the front suggesting that things were not going at all well. In the corner of the room I found the prominent Benghazi lawyer Salwa al-Dighaili who was active in the Benghazi Bar Association and whose uncle was imprisoned for opposing the regime. Salwa, together with other younger Association lawyers, such as Fathi Tirbil, had played an active part in campaigning for reform and orchestrating the early anti-government protests in Benghazi. Salwa had been intimately involved in organising the peaceful demonstration on 15 February by the relatives of the 1,200 inmates murdered by Libyan security forces in 1996, and was considered to be a rising star within the NTC. She had a kind face and evinced a calm demeanour as she negotiated a bevy of photographers who had crowded round her intent on taking her picture.

I spoke to her about her work and role in a daring rescue attempt to evacuate civilians from Misrata. The previous night a Turkish relief ship called *The Ankara* had finally managed to dock in Benghazi. It had heroically sailed to the beleaguered rebel-controlled town to rescue 230 of the sick and wounded. The grief-stricken and frightened faces of the women and children aboard the ship told their own story. Gaddafi's forces had turned Misrata into Dante's Inferno. For over a month, just a hundred or so rebels had held out in the town centre against a ferocious bombardment as well as indiscriminate artillery and sniper fire. Civilians were dying by the dozens daily. No Western journalists had made it into the town and reliable news was extremely scarce. Very occasionally satellite news channels broadcasted snippets of mobile phone video coverage of Gaddafi's snipers shooting and injuring civilians. But no one really knew just how bad things were until the boat from Misrata finally docked in Benghazi. The sheer number and nature of the injuries sustained by those on board confirmed people's worst fears of what Gaddafi was capable of if left to his own murderous devices. Most of the maimed and disfigured victims appeared to have been hit by tanks, artillery and sniper fire. I listened intently as Salwa spoke eloquently of the plight of the people of Misrata.

The Docking of The Ankara

In fact, we had all heard the horns of the surrounding ships the previous night as *The Ankara* finally entered Benghazi harbour and the first few walking wounded came off the ship to be hugged by a spellbound and ecstatic Benghazi crowd intent on giving their compatriots an emotional heroes' welcome. Yet even those scenes did not reflect the whole story. Unlike the bystanders on the quayside, Martin Fletcher of *The Times* managed to get on board the ship to witness the full truth of what had been happening in Misrata. He later filed the following report: 'We noticed that some of those at the railings had bandages around their heads, or arms in slings, but nothing prepared us for what we found when we were let on board. The windowless steel car deck was carpeted with men, young and old, lying on blankets and flimsy mattresses. On the upper decks every cabin was similarly filled. There were people with amputated limbs, on crutches and in wheelchairs. There were people with faces grotesquely scarred by shrapnel, with heavily bandaged heads and limbs and torsos, with legs and arms in splints to hold broken bones in place. Some were barely conscious.'[1]

The patients on board were all seriously injured but they were not by any means the worst to be found in Misrata. The ship could not relieve the city's hospital of their most critically injured cases because it did not have the facilities on board to keep them alive. Other wounded could not be taken because they had been sent home. Thousands of other people had begged to leave but *The Ankara* was forced to turn them away. The victims all gave uniformly grave accounts of life in Libya's third city, which Colonel Gaddafi's forces had spent the past six weeks trying to capture. 'It's a disaster. It's hell,' said Muad Shetwan, whose thighbone had been shattered by a bullet. 'There are snipers everywhere, in every building. They don't make any difference between men, women and children – even animals. They're killing everything.' Said Sharif, whose legs had shellfire wounds, said: 'It's terrible . . . There's no place you can say you are safe, not even your home. There are tanks everywhere. They're firing on Misrata from all directions.' Several begged the coalition to step up its air strikes to save their city. 'Gaddafi is like an animal. Please help. Please help Misrata. Don't let him destroy my city', said Mustafa Abdulla, who had lost his lower left leg to a shell seven days ago. But while many of the patients' bodies were broken, their spirit was not. 'I want to go back. I want to fight again. I want to kill Gaddafi,' Sharif said vehemently, as he lay prone and disabled on the floor of *The Ankara*. Even the battle-weary people of Benghazi could not compute what they were witnessing, when images of the scene below deck were broadcast. If ever anyone needed confirmation of Gaddafi's contempt for the laws of war and of civilian life, well here it was.

Over the next few days the people of Benghazi became increasingly angry at the failure of the newly installed NATO command to come to the aid of Misrata and those rebels who were trying desperately to hold the strategically important oil town of Brega. Reports from the front line consistently noted the lack of discipline and co-ordination among the rebels and the scarcity of basic battlefield communications such as two-way radios. There was also little basic training of new recruits about how to use the few weapons they had at their disposal. These problems were exacerbated when, just as we arrived in Benghazi, NATO explicitly ruled out supplying weapons to the rebels under a NATO flag. Tensions further deepened after the Turkish Prime Minister Erdogan warned NATO members that arming the rebels might feed terrorism and fracture the coalition. No one quite knew what would happen next but the scenes emanating from *The Ankara* were hardly reassuring for the civilian population of Benghazi.

The Courthouse

After taking my leave of Salwa I crossed over to the courthouse, where McCue and I talked to another high-ranking NTC official about seeing Abdul Jalil. It was a hive of civic activity. Many rooms were filled with ordinary residents lodging written and oral petitions for all manner of things. Most of the petitioners were extremely concerned about family members living in the west of Libya under Gaddafi's regime. I was far more concerned about the lax security at the grimy entrance to the courthouse. A broken body scanner and a couple of inattentive guards who seemingly waved anyone through who wanted to come in hardly seemed likely to deter any would-be suicide bomber. But such was the make-do nature of the revolution that we just had to cross our fingers. As we left the building, we immediately ducked into an alcove as another round of revolutionary gunfire ricocheted off the street walls. Although a tentative governing structure was slowly emerging in Benghazi, it was evident that there was very little professional co-ordination or discipline either at the front or back at the governmental hub in Freedom Square. Rudimentary organs of state had been set up, like a press and media centre, but in reality there was little central control or command structure. The situation was not helped by the appalling lack of telecommunications. What there was, however, was an untold amount of goodwill.

As we took our leave of the swirling activity in the courthouse I couldn't help thinking of the stirring first-hand account of the Bolshevik revolution of 1917 in Russia written by John Reed, the radical American journalist, who had come across similar scenes of chaos and hope. In his book *Ten Days that Shook the World* (1919), Reed described in minute detail the course of the Bolshevik revolution over a number of days. This included the trials and tribulations at the front and the organisational chaos at the rear that attended the Bolsheviks' early attempts to impose order from within. What, I wondered, would finally emerge from all this revolutionary activity here in Benghazi? Would it, too, veer towards authoritarianism as ruled and rulers alike tired of the chaos of revolutionary freedom and flirted once again with the advantages of certain order? Would it, like the French and Russian revolutions before it, devour its children and turn inward on its own people in order to stamp its revolutionary authority on the country? Or would the leaders of this revolution be different and keep their promises of a new democratic opening and ride the tide of chaos towards a better, more open, future? It was impossible to tell. What was clear, however, was that without outside moral and practical assistance there was every danger that non-democratic spoilers, including jihadists, would exploit such chaos to promote their own brand of the rule of law. As I walked around Freedom Square that late spring afternoon, inspired and awe-struck at the capacity of ordinary people to try to heal their shattered society, I knew it had been the right decision to come to Benghazi.

The Art of Resistance

From Midan al-Tahrir I drove with Tim Whewell and the wonderfully effi-cient Maria Polachowska of BBC *Newsnight* to the Katiba barracks to see where it had all started. The footage taken of us walking through the charred remains of a now bygone era told its own story of the torture and final venge-ance that had been exacted at this forbidding place. As the BBC filmed us for a piece about IRA Semtex, my mind wandered back to Midan al-Tahrir. Somehow I sensed that there was something else going on that I should witness. So I decided to double back into Benghazi on my own to try to meet other elements of Benghazi civil society. As I reached the side streets near the courthouse a man with an AK-47 started to fire rounds in all directions. It was difficult to know whether he was a rebel or not and whether he was firing in celebration or anger. Either way, I didn't hang around to find out.

I quickly ducked into the hallway of an adjacent building, only to come across a beautiful young woman with long dark hair sporting a Che Guevara cap, who spoke perfect English. 'Where can I meet artists?' I enquired, osten-sibly on behalf of the Delfina Foundation. She smiled and said: 'Come with me. I'll take you.' The woman took me to another building, this time modern, to meet Tarek Moustafa Ben Omran, the chief of the Writers and Drawers Centre. I still marvel at the sheer romance of that title. Tarek introduced me to all the main graffiti artists and showed me their work. The whole place was covered from top to bottom in their cultural endeavours. Even Tarek expressed surprise at the sheer versatility of the artists, their work, and range of ironic humour, which seemingly covered both Arab and Western tastes. It was here that the graffiti artist Qais Ahmad Hilal had worked. Qais was one of the most gifted of all the graffiti artists in Benghazi. He had inspired the whole town with his deeply cutting portrayals of Gaddafi in the first few weeks of the uprising.

As previously noted, after a month of challenging and undermining the Great Brother Leader's vain self-image, Qais was finally shot dead by a sniper as he painted yet more images of defiance in the streets of the old town of his beloved Benghazi. The power of art to move and offend people in equal meas-ure was nowhere better illustrated than in his murder. No dictator can withstand laughter and ridicule for too long, so Qais's death was perhaps inevitable. Yet overnight he became an emblem of resistance, as more and more students and young people flocked to the fledgling Writers and Drawers Centre to sign up to work for the revolution. Thus began Benghazi's own Warholesque factory of art. As I took in the portrait of Qais above the door and looked at Kimo and other artists hard at work I asked Kimo whether he was scared of being killed, given what had happened to his friend Qais. He smiled shyly, shook his head gently and then raised his hand in a V sign. Like Qais, he was only twenty-nine.

The Social Networkers

Tarek took to me to another office where I met a different group of young people who had volunteered to put out material in support of the uprising on the web and on other social networking sites. On the wall of the one-room office was inscribed '42 years of slavery. We don't give up. We win or Die.' These teenagers sat me down and played me videos and photo packages of stories from the revolution. Extraordinary images of life at the front, accompanied by stirring music, flooded the screen. What was remarkable was their sense of teamwork and solidarity. They worked with each other, rather than under the direction of adult managers. Their creative audio and visual output came from their unique youthful perspective of the struggle. They all seemed shorn of ego or rivalry. It felt like a commune motivated by higher ideals that went beyond the individual self.

In that moment I thought of how the Delfina Foundation and Beyond Borders might be able to help them. Perhaps the FCO Arab Partnership Fund could assist. 'Write down in English what you need,' I told them. They seemed transfixed by the idea that there already existed civil society organisations in the world that had somehow prefigured their activities and were willing to help them. Unlike in Egypt and Tunisia, the Internet was not widely available here, and Libya's youth had not already immersed itself in the ways of Facebook, YouTube and Flickr. It was a travesty to suggest that the uprising in Benghazi was a Facebook uprising. It was no such thing, but that didn't stop the young people of Benghazi quickly harnessing the potential and power of new social media in defence of the revolution as soon as they had the ability to access it.

The Musicians and Radio Free Libya

Even more remarkable than the graffiti artists and social networking group I encountered was the small group of Arab rap artists I found hard at work in a small room in the backstreets just behind the courthouse. Like the graffiti artists, these musicians wrote and produced songs in both Arab and English.

They had constructed a studio consisting of a couple of old computers, a mixing board, and an odd assortment of instruments. Their commitment to their music was truly inspiring. They learnt on the job, infusing traditional Arab tunes and poems with rap and the music of the ghetto. Although they mimicked much of the demeanour and teenage angst of Western contemporary rap artists, there was nothing derivative about their musical output. It had an authentic revolutionary flavour, with an elemental anger against state and dictatorial repression. By engaging in real political struggle, these young Arabs had discovered a new and powerful voice that elevated their songs beyond the youthful indignation and sham rejection of society exhibited by many young Western artists.

They took their inspiration from a number of revolutionary sources. In Tunisia, one of the most powerful voices was Hamada Ben Amor, otherwise known as the 'General', a twenty-one-year-old rapper from the southern city of Sfax. Amor put out a remarkable riposte on behalf of the Tunisian people to President Zine El Abidine Ben Ali entitled 'Rais Lebled' ('Head of State'). 'Mister President,' the lyrics thunder, 'your people are dead. So many eat from garbage. Look at the country. So much misery and no place to sleep. I am speaking on behalf of the people. Who are suffering under your boot.' His other songs included 'Tunisia is our Country'. Elsewhere, the Tunisian group Armada Bizerta released the album *Music of the Revolution* with some other artists. Tahrir Square in Cairo also gave rise to a number of revolutionary anthems, including 'Sawt al-hurriya' ('Voice of Freedom') by Adel and Amir Eid of the Egyptian rock band Cairokee and the Arabian Knights' version of 'Rebel'.

Within a month, the Benghazian rapper performing under the pseudonym of Ibn Thabit had released 'A Call to the Youth of Libya'. He had been demanding the overthrow of Gaddafi since 2008. But by far the most important inspiration came from Radio Free Libya, which broadcast from rebel-controlled Misrata every day. It had added an AM channel so that on clear days the station could be heard as far away as Lebanon and southern Europe. The station was originally seized from Gaddafi's forces in February, when the rebels took the centre of Misrata. Back then, it was a hated mouthpiece for Gaddafi and was said not to play a single record or news item that did not have at least some reference to the great man. Then on 21 February, four days after the uprising in Benghazi, there was an announcement: 'This is Free Misrata and we now own the radio.' For the first time in a generation, the people of Misrata heard traditional Arab songs, rap songs about the revolution, as well as daily digests of world news about Libya. Even more remarkably they heard other ordinary people discuss the affairs of their nation for the first time in forty-two years. The station regularly warned residents where Gaddafi forces were attacking each day, with daily reports from the frontline, while all the time taunting government forces about how they were being manipulated.

In a very real sense the station had become the people's pulse and constituted a supreme act of civic and cultural defiance. One rebel soldier spoke of how he had come across a dead government soldier crouching with his chin resting on his rifle and half his head blown off. A damaged radio tuned into Radio Free Libya lay next to him. As Ahmad Hadia, the station manager, later told *Guardian* journalist Xan Rice: 'It's driving Gaddafi crazy that we are still on air. We want to make him even crazier.'[2] Hadia told of how Gaddafi's forces had shot up the original studio, made three unsuccessful attacks on the broadcast tower, and ordered snipers to prowl the entrance to the studio to shoot anyone who entered. In response the radio set up in a ship container and then in an abandoned school, as shells rained down unremittingly on the people's beacon of freedom of expression. But as producer Ali Almani exclaimed: 'When you hear the taste of freedom there is no going back. No one is going to make me obtain permission any longer for the songs I play.'

As I listened to the stories of the musicians and their compatriots in Misrata, I realised just how vibrant the uprising was for the youth of Benghazi. It had awakened them from an enforced cultural slumber that had shrouded Libya in monotony. Their encounter with the arts and new media galvanised the political revolution and gave them a unique role to play in entrenching democratic aspirations in the minds of the Libyan people, and indeed the world at large. How could any of these youths meekly return to the status quo now that they had tasted the fruits of their own independent cultural endeavours? The answer was, they couldn't.

Berenice and the Young Journalists

The impression that Libya had reached a point of no return was reinforced by yet another group of inspiring young people I met, who were responsible for the creation of Benghazi's first weekly independent newspaper of the revolution. Although amateurish in output and design, its content was heartrending in effect. They called it the *Berenice Post* with a strap line of 'Towards a Better Tomorrow!' 'Berenice is the ancient Macedonian form of Attic Greek [Pherenike]. It means "bearer of victory" and was the name the Greeks gave to the city of Benghazi,' explained one young journalist called Ali.

This is the labour of Libyan youth. These are great times for Libya. We are making history. For forty-eight days the tyrant has not quenched his thirst for the blood and lives of the innocent. He is the same tyrant who many prominent figures in the West have been dealing with, along with his offspring and clan of terror, all for the sake of money and greed. But this is history and bygones are bygones. The *Berenice Post* is part of the rebirth of the Libyan Nation and Benghazi has been victorious throughout history.

The young journalist went on to explain how a group of youths became inspired by the words of a local fifty-three-year-old mechanical engineer from Benghazi, who had become famous after being interviewed by the world's press at the beginning of the uprising. 'Libya,' he declared, 'will inspire the world!' 'These words resonated with many of us, as did the deeds of other ordinary Libyans, and so *Berenice* was born,' recounted Ali.

Another inspiration for the paper was Mohamed Nablous, a twenty-eight-year-old man, who was one of the first Libyans to speak on television about the truth of the situation without concealing his identity. 'It was he who started encouraging people through Facebook to go out and demonstrate for their rights. He helped secure an Internet connection to connect Libyans with the outside world to make sure everyone knew what was happening in Libya. He even started his own TV channel "Libya al Hurra" and broadcasted interviews on the Internet by live streaming,' said another aspiring journalist. Yet Nablous had never been political or a rebel before the uprising. He was later shot dead by one of Gaddafi's snipers while trying to cover the shelling of a civilian district on the outskirts of Benghazi. 'Before he died he told his friends, "I'm not afraid to die. I'm afraid to lose the battle." *The Berenice Post* is our contribution to that battle,' explained Ali.

In fact, the impact of Nablous's work was felt not just in Libya but also around the world. Nablous managed to team up with a number of innovative Internet-based journalists from different countries in different continents, such as Andy Carvin, a senior strategist at Public National Radio in the United States. Carvin later told me at a lecture in Harvard how he would rebroadcast Nablous's feeds and tweets around the world to his own followers. Ever since the start of the Tunisian uprising in December 2010, Carvin had been ignoring his day job and serving as a one-man broadcast channel-cum-newswire on events in the Middle East. Carvin had spoken with Nablous just four hours before he died, just before he went to bed. When he got up the next morning he could not believe that his colleague was dead. Carvin listened in horror at Nablous's last news feed as he reported the shelling of civilian homes in Benghazi. 'You can literally hear the shells exploding all around him. Then suddenly without notice the feed goes dead as the bullet hits and kills him', he told me. Carvin spoke of how Nablous's pregnant wife continued to file reports on his feed right up until the day she gave birth to their first child in June 2011, exorting the world never to forget either her beloved husband or country. It was yet another graphic example of a personal act of bravery on the part of the ordinary people of Benghazi in defence of their revolution.

The Professionals of Benghazi

Yet it wasn't just the youth of Benghazi that etched itself into my memory that day. It was all the people of Benghazi. Throughout our time there we met and talked with a range of different people. Everyone wanted to tell their story and establish relations with us. I particularly recall a businessman called Hassan who, on meeting us, immediately rang up his uncle, who had been a senior player in the Libyan Bar Association. He wanted to arrange a meeting between us all, after he had heard about the BHRC mission. His uncle later brought legal books to our hotel as if in homage to the rule of law, urging us in no uncertain terms to conclude the BHRC Memorandum of Understanding with the Council. He too used his own relations with the National Transitional Council to get just such an agreement. He talked eloquently about how the Benghazi law faculty had been starved of resources and outside contacts, except for one International Bar Association seminar a couple of years ago. New Libya needed all the help it could get.

Other Libyans urged me to come with them to see for myself how Gaddafi had deliberately failed to invest in physical infrastructure. Some buildings were left half constructed, after Gaddafi changed his mind over what projects to back. They wanted to show me evidence of his wanton abandonment of the city, from the potholed roads, to the outdated sewage plant, to the lack of municipal parks. It seemed as if Gaddafi literally hated Benghazi. He had made all the shopkeepers paint their shutters green in honour of his rambling philosophy. One account from an engineer took my breath away. Apparently, for the last twenty years, Gaddafi had not allowed cinemas to operate in Benghazi. The ordinary people of the city weren't even given the opportunity to escape the tyranny and hopelessness of their lives by going to the pictures.

As to education, a Benghazi teacher told me: 'Libyan income per capita is $10,000 but Libyan people live on a dollar a day. Teachers only get paid one month every six months. In Benghazi alone we have 300 private schools and I'm talking about living room schools. Yes, teachers' living rooms are being used as a school.' Before the revolution began in February 2011, school-teachers and children were forced to endure mandatory weekly lessons of 'Mushtama' and 'Fikr al-Jamahiri', based on the teachings of Gaddafi contained in his infamous Green Book. These included 'Brother Leader's' unique insights into human nature which included lines like: 'Women menstruate every month or so, while men, being male, do not.' 'It was really shameful that you had to memorise and repeat all the things it said as if you were convinced of it,' Brayka Tarhouni told a Reuters journalist. She was a doctor who was made to repeat her second year of university after passing all her medical subjects but failing Fikr al-Jamahiri. In fact, Gaddafi's thoughts and ideas permeated all aspects of the syllabus except for history, where the regime preferred the children of Benghazi to study the Stone Age rather than contemporary history in case the heroic deeds of others inspired them to stand up for their rights. 'History was completely distorted. The system needs a complete overhaul,' said Hana el-Gallal, whose responsibility was education for the local council in Benghazi.

The People's Spokesperson

I talked about many of these issues at length with Mustafa Gheriani, the NTC's media spokesman, who had become a familiar face on the international news channels. Mustafa was a dentist by trade and had never been actively involved in politics before. Yet when the uprising began, he, like many other professionals, took to the barricades. It was people like Mustafa that obliterated the lies and fictions put about by Saif al-Islam that the rebels were just a front for Al-Qaeda. Mustafa Gheriani was not a radical Islamist agent provocateur at all. He was a peaceful, gentle, thoughtful character who felt compelled to dedicate all his time and energies to the uprising in order to ensure that the outside world understood what was happening in Benghazi. 'I haven't been home in three weeks,' he confided to me. We spoke of the need to strengthen the rule of law and to build mutual relations between lawyers from our respective countries. He agreed to collect a wider assortment of lawyers for my next visit and confirmed that he had heard about our arrival, as had the NTC. He would communicate our desire to meet them soon, given our need to depart within twenty-four hours. We then talked about the young people I had just encountered. 'Not many journalists focus on these stories,' he told me. 'Most of the time I am inundated with questions about Al-Qaeda and terrorism,' he sighed quietly.

It certainly appeared to me that what most journalists, or at least their editors, were obsessed with was the issue of Islamic fundamentalism and whether the West was unwittingly supporting a radical religious revolution by intervening in Libya. The international news media was full of this stuff. I watched as yet another journalist approached Gheriani and before long asked: 'What of Al-Qaeda and the LIFG?' 'We are Sunni and have a moderate form of Islam,' replied Gheriani.

> We do not have a sect. This country is very much unified as far as religion goes. When we look at Afghanistan and Iraq, we want nothing of that – the suicide bomber – the assassinations that are taking place – the struggle that

is taking place between the Kurds, Sunni and Shia. Thank goodness we don't have any of this, it is much easier to deal with the storm in Libya. Gaddafi is trying to scare the international community with talk of Al-Qaeda extremists. I can tell you one thing. Libya is free. Who will Gaddafi use to work against us? They do not have Sunni against Shia. They have no platform with which to work against us. Libyan society is very integrated. People know each other. There is no room for suicide bombers and we don't fear them. In a democracy you do not fear a political view. They cannot take the radical steps that have been taken in Iraq or Afghanistan because the Libyan people will not permit it. They are not ready to embrace something like that. The radicals have no room here.

Such questions, Gheriani later suggested to me, rested on a fundamental misconception of what Libyans and Libyan society was all about.

The Libyan People do not regard the West as our enemy, Israel as our enemy, or the Arab nations as our enemy. In reality there is nothing that makes them feel threatened by the outside world. It is Gaddafi who arrested them, tortured them, broke their homes, and finally now that they have tasted freedom I don't think they are going to go back. They have rejected, overnight, forty-two years of brainwashing in which the West was cast as our enemy. Once we build a new freedom not imposed by a military coup the people will not go back. So there is no room for extremism in this country whatsoever and I'm not worried and I don't think others here are worried about such extremism. If need be we will terminate these kind of people before the rest of the world says you have extremism. People in Libya love Libya and Libya comes first. We have a modern political programme for Libya. In America they have the KKK. Should I be worried about American being a white supremacist country? No I should not. Because I know America has a constitution, democracy, and viable political authorities. The existence of different political parties is healthy for the country but I repeat people are not ready to entertain extremism. Once we have a constitution that works, and people have decent jobs that pay, I believe we can solve our problems. What we have is an opportunity.

According to Gheriani, it was not religion that drove ordinary people to revolt in Benghazi, but the chance for a better life.

The Regime has not done anything good for this country. Two thirds of the population are below the age of thirty-five. That means they have only known the regime of Gaddafi. They have no idea how to go about these things. They only know one thing – they lived through the 1980s – with the worst of something that resembled a communist like system, when people had to stand in long lines to get food and clothing. They don't want that anymore. We understand that. What is it that these young people see when they see a little success in the national media – they see the West! They want nothing less than what the West has. America has the American dream. I believe we will soon have something called the Libyan dream – a dream to own the roof over your head, to have a good education, a proper diet, and healthcare. People should be entitled to the basic necessities as well as the right to do business as they wish within a free enterprise system. We should have freedom of thought enshrined in a constitution that guarantees the separation of powers.

Gheriani went on to set out his vision:

What we need to do is write a constitution where all political parties will develop. We hope people work together to become a democratic country. We don't have to reinvent the wheel. There are a lot of constitutions out there. There's the Egyptian constitution. We know the type of articles that need to be discussed. I think we will have a national forum. People from all over Libya will be involved in it. I don't think it is going to take too long. But if it does we are prepared: democracy and freedom are not cheap. We have shed a lot of blood for it and we are prepared to shed some more. We are looking at the West, and specifically the Arab League, and the Arab people to help us achieve democracy as fast as possible. Otherwise time brings despair, people can start losing hope, and then the area does become fertile ground for extremist groups, but we don't want to get to that level. We need Western countries to help us enhance the democratic process. We have been proactive and progressive but we do not have the luxury of time.

But what, I wondered, did he say to those analysts who predicted that Libya might divide into two states or spheres of influence? 'Gaddafi's regime is crumbling within,' explained Gheriani.

There is a misconception that Colonel Gaddafi controls the west part of the country. He *rules* the west part of the country with the mighty machine that he has. He has no loyalty whatsoever. In fact, the demonstrations that he stages are dwindling down to a hundred. How can you have a hundred people support you in Tripoli with a population of 2.5 million people? In conclusion, I think we have a lot of talented people to help run this country. We have a lot of young men and women who are starved of education but who want to contribute to this country. You can see how they have taken their place in the liberated areas. I am quite optimistic about the future. I think Libya can be a modern state, and play its part in a wider world, that can be used as an example in the third world as to how democracy can benefit the people.

It was exhilarating stuff to listen to but I had to get back to McCue. As dusk fell, and I attempted to make my way back to the El Fadeel Hotel through the revolutionary throng outside the media centre, I wondered how, in fact, it would all end for these brave people. There was something deeply endearing and possibly even tragic about Gheriani's optimism and vision of democracy, especially given the latest news that was seeping back into Benghazi.

Protesting against NATO

Throughout the day the news from the front was not good. Exhausted rebels came back into the city dispirited at the lack of NATO air support. Not only had the rebels lost Brega, they were now in danger of losing Ajdabiya, the last town before Benghazi. Furthermore, the situation in Misrata was desperate. The NTC needed all the support that NATO could muster to hold the front line and alleviate the mounting humanitarian disaster in Misrata, yet for some reason NATO had gone quiet. Reports started to reach Benghazi that the Turks and other member countries, who were less hawkish than Britain and France, had deliberately begun to drag their feet within NATO in order to change the facts on the ground to the advantage of the Gaddafi regime, in anticipation of internationally orchestrated mediation talks. The Turks, it was said, were particularly keen to lever themselves in as potential mediators, as part of a more independent dynamic foreign policy they were developing in the region which looked beyond its alliance with the West.

The next day it was reported that the Gaddafi regime had sent its diplomats to Athens to talk to the Greek government about a potential cease-fire, but many suspected the real destination was Ankara. The Turks had urged NATO to take control of operations concerning the no-fly zone, not because they were enthusiastic supporters of the no-fly zone but so they could influence the course of events both militarily and diplomatically in a way that was detrimental to the rebels. The Turks were on record expressing grave concerns about the NATO intervention, in the hope that Gaddafi would choose the Turks, aided by the African Union, as the main mediators to any negotiated cease-fire. This was leading to increasing concerns within the NTC about the extent of NATO's commitment.

The growing sense of despondency over NATO's role was consistent with the mood I encountered in Freedom Square as I made my way out of town to return to the El Fadeel Hotel. 'Stop here,' I told my driver as I was confronted by a huge demonstration that had come together in front of the courthouse to express support for Misrata and the fighters on the eastern front. I got out of the car and immersed myself in the throng. Thousands of ordinary Benghazians had gathered to express their disappointment in peaceful protest. People lined up to sign petitions to plead for greater Western support. The mood was pensive. In fact, a tense atmosphere descended upon the whole of Benghazi as it waited with bated breath for further news and developments from the front. Confusion reigned among the crowd as to why NATO was no longer providing the type of air cover that the French, British and Americans had previously provided.

Although some of the placards hoisted high above a sea of arms still thanked the French and the British, others were less complimentary. A multitude of other placards told their own story. 'Where is NATO force?' one asked. 'To NATO. Please help the civilians of Misrata, Zintan, Nalot, Zawiya and Tripoli. They are suffering by Gaddafi,' read another. Elements of the crowd seemed aware of the alleged internal machinations swirling around NATO. One placard thanked the people of Italy for recognising the NTC as the legitimate government of Libya, a massive symbolic step in the campaign to get the Council diplomatically recognised internationally. Yet other messages expressed suspicion at what was occurring on the wider international plane: 'Erdogan in Gaza – 1200 Martyrs. But in Libya more than 10,000!' read one, while another reminded the West and NATO: 'We are not Al-Qaeda. We want Freedom!' One of the most moving moments I witnessed that evening was of some children at the head of a demonstration, which walked into Freedom Square to join the main rally where members of the Council were listing their demands. These children solemnly walked in front of a huge makeshift banner held up by adults behind them asking: 'Where is the NATO to protect the people of Misrata?' The five-year-old little girl who walked at the apex of the column, holding the hand of her bigger sister, carried her own message. It read: 'Save our children from Gaddafi the Kriminal.' The misspelling made it all the more poignant.

By the time I got back to the El Fadeel Hotel, McCue had been told by our main intermediary that we would meet Abdul Jalil at around 9.30 am the next day in the same building that we were staying in. Not content with that assurance, we approached the UK Special Envoy Christopher Prentice and showed him the letter McCue had received from Cameron early on in his premiership. Later that evening Prentice also urged Abdul Jalil's right hand man Dr Said Ali to use his best endeavours to ensure the Council met with us the following morning. One hour later he confirmed to us directly that the meeting was definitely on. We were relieved, but by then it was far from obvious that we would have enough time with the NTC to get everything done.

As we ordered in cheap pizza and some illicit hooch for a late dinner we sat down to watch the international news for the latest developments about the situation at the front. It rapidly became clear that the NTC had much more immediate concerns than our meeting. Firstly, matters had definitely taken a further turn for the worse on the battlefield. Secondly, it was likely that over the next twenty-four hours the Council would be deluged with new international diplomatic delegations arriving in Benghazi from different countries. That night, McCue and I worked through a series of questions that Victoria Commeck's US attorneys had sent us to ask Abdul Jalil concerning the Lockerbie bombing and Gaddafi's involvement in it. It was now extremely unlikely that we would have enough time to formally interrogate Abdul Jalil about Lockerbie given his mounting diplomatic commitments. Each of us had to reach agreement with the Council on the other matters before dealing with Abdul Jalil's personal connection with Lockerbie. That night I went to bed with my mind full of the images of Benghazi that I had witnessed that day. I thought of the Council upon which all the hopes of everyone I had met had fallen. Would it match the endeavour and vigour of the people it claimed to represent or fall short? We would soon have our opportunity to find out.

8.   Misrata and Negotiating with the NTC

5 April 2011

I awoke the next morning around 7 am, with McCue sleeping like a cherub next to me. We had run out of money to pay for the four suites the team had taken, and as a result McCue had been forced to move into my room the night before. Images of Steve Martin from the film *Planes, Trains and Automobiles* came to mind, as McCue and I gingerly got out of the huge purple bed in which we were obliged to sleep together. After a shower and shave I left the bathroom free for McCue while I got dressed. Within seconds, however, I found myself bursting back through the bathroom door as McCue watched in utter bemusement while, half dressed, I dashed towards the wash basin, where a sustained projectile of vomit burst out of my mouth. It is in moments like these that the bonds of friendship are established. 'You twat. How the fuck am I supposed to brush my teeth now,' intoned McCue.

As we emerged into the diplomatic milieu, the trip began to feel more and more like a comic movie with each passing day.

The Arrival of the National Transitional Council

The building was now a hive of activity, as teams of NTC security officials swept the building before its members arrived. Outside the building, US and UK close-protection units scoured the perimeter. I could see journalists sniffing around near the back of the hotel. We were asked to vacate our rooms in readiness for the Council's imminent appearance and our own departure for Cairo later on that day. It was clear to all concerned that one of the major issues was going to be the general position of NATO and the plight of Misrata. We watched the French Envoy take up a similar position to ours on the upstairs sofa as he too waited for the call to meet Abdul Jalil and present his credentials. Every so often, the UK Ambassador and his officials would pass by purposefully. By that stage the Ambassador's close-protection team had warmed to ours as they began to realise why McCue was here. Both teams had served in Northern Ireland and respected what McCue was doing. This was useful in different ways, as it made for a more informal process of communication between the two teams throughout the day. Outside, numerous diplomats walked the gardens with their satellite phones sending their latest dispatch back to their foreign ministers. If it was going to happen for us it had to be today and in the midst of an emerging crisis.

Meeting Mustafa Abdul Jalil and the NTC

At about 9.30 am we met Dr Said Ali. Luckily, he spoke fluent English and we talked extensively about the respective agreements we wanted to conclude. 'Give us the documents,' he said, 'and we will work through them and let you know whether we agree with them or need to change their contents.' We then took him through the material that had been hastily cobbled together by us the previous night. I had drafted a short MoU on behalf of the BHRC, which put forward seven areas in which the two parties could work together to strengthen the rule of law, subject to obtaining requisite funding. McCue put forward a separate document on behalf of IRA Semtex victims as well as other victims caught up in the conflict. On Lockerbie we had concluded that we were unlikely to be able to have the time to adequately probe Abdul Jalil about Gaddafi's involvement. I was a little sceptical about what direct evidence Abdul Jalil had to implicate Gaddafi.

We decided to obtain a short statement from Abdul Jalil confirming in broad terms what he had said, plus a commitment to submit himself to detailed questioning at some appropriate point. He would be asked firstly to confirm whether or not he was willing to give a sworn statement that admissions made previously to journalists concerning Gaddafi's involvement in Lockerbie were true; secondly, that he stood by a commitment to deal with legacy issues, including giving requisite oral and documentary evidence on Lockerbie to relevant investigators in the not-too-distant future; thirdly, to confirm rumours that were already swirling in the press that he had documentary evidence concerning the payment of monies to al-Megrahi by Gaddafi to keep him quiet about Gaddafi's involvement in the sanctioning of the bombing. A series of propositions were drafted for Abdul Jalil to consider. Dr Said Ali now took the documents away for examination and translation.

An hour or so later we were ushered into another suite to meet Mustafa Abdul Jalil who sat on an ornate gold-crested French sofa flanked by his interpreter. A bevy of aides fussed around us as we were guided in. We both took up seats next to Abdul Jalil after he gestured to us to sit down. McCue took Abdul Jalil through the various issues concerning the IRA and Lockerbie victims and also the contents of the relevant documents. Abdul Jalil was told that the proposed agreements would enable New Libya to draw a line in the sand about legacy issues that had plagued relations with the UK in a way that was consistent with the NTC's statements on the rule of law. Furthermore, Abdul Jalil already knew that David Cameron supported the victims' campaign, and had a unit in the FCO to deal with these questions. His consent to these agreements could only assist the Council in its wider relations with the West. We therefore urged Abdul Jalil to sign all the agreements, telling him that we needed to leave by early evening in order to make our connection at Cairo Airport the following afternoon. None of this came as a surprise to Abdul Jalil, as he understood how important these acts of reconciliation were for sections of the British and US public.

I then specifically recalled my original correspondence and took him quickly through the BHRC Memorandum of Understanding and the suggested areas of work. He indicated from the outset his support of the proposals. As a lawyer and former judge this was very much his territory. The issue of inter-militia dialogue was also raised. I briefly talked about the work of the Centre for Humanitarian Dialogue based in Geneva. We then discussed at some length the creation of a new Libyan Peoples Freedom Foundation and the issue of diplomatic recognition. Abdul Jalil and Dr Said Ali ended the audience by telling us that the Council's staff would consider the proposals and let us know whether they were acceptable, including the propositions that had been put to them about Lockerbie. Abdul Jalil was not flamboyant or charismatic. Nor was he much given to Arab gesticulation or small talk. Instead, like the former appeal court judge he was, he sat motionless and listened intently to what we had to say. He was neither an arrogant nor an insignificant man, but came across as a convincing caretaker leader of the Transitional Council that he was elected to serve.

Abdul Jalil then asked how matters should be handled with regard to the outside world, if agreement was reached. McCue was emphatic in stating that although he intended to hold his own press conference in the UK, any apologies issued by New Libya and agreements reached over compensation should be announced by Abdul Jalil at the Council's press conference in Benghazi, after which we would say a few words of thanks. It was important for the Council to take ownership of the agreements and tell the world themselves what they had agreed to do, and why. Abdul Jalil indicated his agreement and confirmed that either he or his deputy, Abdul Hafiz Ghoga, would make an announcement about any agreements reached at the Council's evening press conference. As to evidence concerning Lockerbie, which was a personal matter, it was agreed that any statement made by him would be given to the lawyers of Mrs Victoria Cummock. Abdul Jalil thanked us for coming to

Benghazi. We in turn thanked him for the invitation and finally asked if he might sign a few revolutionary flags for both of us and, indeed, a third for the Prime Minister, David Cameron. Abdul Jalil finally indicated his consent to the remaining requests with a slight nod and with that we left him.

Enter the Diplomats

We now spent a number of hours waiting for the NTC to come back to us. Throughout this period, we had conversations with Said Ali about the contents of the documents and other matters. We took up residence on the corner sofas. From this vantage point we watched as various diplomatic missions came and went. All other personnel and journalists were relegated to the outer confines of the El Fadeel Hotel. It was fascinating to observe the body language and demeanour of the different members of the Council and their entourage. General Younis was particularly striking in his military fatigues. He had an undoubted physical and psychological charisma and was surrounded by fawning underlings. Physically, if not mentally, he reminded me of General Mladić from the Bosnian war, with his big barrel chest, and large frame and forehead. You could tell that he was used to, and comfortable with, the trappings of power and influence, whether under Gaddafi's regime or the new rebel Council, whose members seemed to treat him with a degree of caution and respect.

I also watched as newly appointed US Envoy Chris Stevens, who had served at the US Embassy in Tripoli until it was shut down, strode purposefully into the building followed by a retinue of US advisors to hold a series of emergency talks. He had just arrived in the city courtesy of a Greek freighter which had sailed across from Valletta, Malta. Stevens was asked to go to Benghazi as a special envoy by the Secretary of State Hillary Clinton. It was to be his second tour of duty in Libya and he jumped at the chance. Stevens was a true Arabist who would not have looked out of place in the FCO's Camel Corps. Born in California, he acquired his abiding passion for the Arab world while working for the Peace Corps in Morocco during the 1980s. A graduate of Berkeley, Stevens read law and initially practised as a trade lawyer before joining the State Department in 1991. As a junior political officer at the US consulate in Jerusalem, he gained an in-depth understanding of the situation in the West Bank and Gaza. Further postings in Damascus, Riyadh and Tripoli gave him unparalleled experience of the wider region. Between 2007 and 2009 Stevens served as the Deputy Chief of Mission in Tripoli where he developed relations with all the principal players. He became known in the State Department as the Subject Matter Expert for Libya and quickly came to believe in the power of US diplomacy to change the world for the better. More to the point, he believed that such diplomacy depended on the development of interpersonal relationships based upon a deep understanding of the local culture.

According to Stevens, his initial mandate was 'to go out and meet as many members of the leadership as I could in the National Transitional Council'. That morning he met both the Council and the British Ambassador to talk about NATO and the frozen $30 billion-worth of Libyan assets held by the US. These talks continued long into the afternoon. His ability to disarm and build relations with men from widely different backgrounds was immediately obvious to all, switching conversation effortlessly between the UK Special Envoy Christopher Prentice and General Younis and the younger advisors who surrounded Abdul Jalil. He did it with the same ease and openness as Bill Clinton, despite the tense and insecure circumstances. As Fred Burton and Samuel M. Katz later observed in their book *Benghazi under Fire: The Untold Story of the Attack in Benghazi* (2013), when the uprising erupted, that's where Stevens needed to be: 'Establishing a rapport with the many militias that battled Gaddafi loyalists required a deft hand and a talent for breaking bread with men in camouflage fatigues who talked about long-standing relationships while a walkie-talkie stood on the table next to their plate of hummus and an AK-47 was nestled by their feet.'

Burton and Katz's description of Stevens certainly chimed with my own experiences. Ambassador Stevens was accompanied by a small security team from the US State Department. They came replete with several armoured SUVs, weapons and communication equipment and were tasked with getting a diplomatic location up and running. The Special Mission in Benghazi they set up on 21 June 2011 was a temporary facility that did not meet the normal security standards of US consulates, but this was no normal situation. As one Diplomatic Security (DS) agent later told Burton and Katz, 'The crackle of gunfire in the dark is not the sound a Bureau of Diplomatic Security agent longs to hear, but [. . .] in Benghazi it was all too common as exuberant fighters celebrated the day's revolutionary successes with rounds dispatched into the night sky.' But these diplomats were here to meet people, establish connections, and do a difficult job. Comfort and security was not high up on their agenda in early April of 2011.

I continued to watch as these diplomats, including Christopher Prentice, appeared and disappeared into different rooms. Every so often Prentice would leave the building with his satellite phone to speak to London in the garden. It was clear that he was under considerable pressure. At one point we exchanged notes. He told us that a serious issue had arisen within NATO. A rebel ship laden with supplies, including much-needed weapons, had left Benghazi bound for Misrata. It had sailed into international waters on the understanding that NATO would permit it to dock in Misrata. However,

NATO was bound by Security Council Resolution 1970, which imposed an embargo on the supply of military equipment to all of Libya. Some lawyers interpreted this obligation as applying not just to Gaddafi's regime but to all the opposition forces as well. This legal opinion was extremely useful to those NATO countries that were deeply sceptical about political intervention in Libya's affairs. The fissures between NATO members now came to the surface in spectacular fashion.

During this tense day of NATO-focused talks, Dr Said Ali returned every so often to talk with us about the contents of the draft agreements and obtain the views of Christopher Prentice on our meeting with Abdul Jalil. Prentice communicated how progress on these legacy issues would be seen in a positive light in London.

Protecting Misrata

That afternoon, the NTC was finally informed that a Canadian NATO naval vessel, tasked with policing the Libyan coast, had indeed blocked a relief ship's re-entry into Libyan waters around Misrata. Council members went berserk, and Christopher Prentice now felt the full force of their anger. He was one of only a few NATO member ambassadors operating out of Benghazi. The situation in Misrata was so awful that the supplies on the rebel ship might make or break the dire military and humanitarian situation. Ambassador Prentice was now engaged in a full-scale diplomatic fight to 'knock NATO heads together', as one source put it. He had already advised the Council to pull the ship back towards Benghazi and sail it through Libyan waters to Misrata, as the diplomatic row bounced around the ministries of NATO countries. The Council were furious at the conduct of NATO, and indeed Prentice's temporary solution, which effectively delayed the ship's passage by at least a day, but they had little choice in the matter until a solution could be hammered out. The British and French launched a rearguard action to open up the sea lanes for the ship to get back into Libyan waters.

In fact, none of the world's press in Benghazi had the slightest inkling of this unfolding story, except for the two intrepid *Sunday Times* reporters Hala Jaber and Nick Cornish, who had boarded the embattled ship, but were unable to get a word out until it was finally permitted to dock in Misrata a few days later, after NATO allowed it to sail along the coast in Libyan waters, as suggested by Christopher Prentice. Hala Jaber reported that she had travelled on 'a gun running trawler',[1] packed with AK-47s, rocket-propelled grenade launchers (RPGs) and mortars. She confirmed that 'weapons had been sent by rebels in the opposition stronghold of Benghazi to help comrades in Misrata face up to Gaddafi's snipers, artillery and tanks'. She went on:

When our trawler left Benghazi last Monday with 24 passengers on board, the skipper contacted a NATO vessel by radio with details of our 36-hour voyage. 'Okay, NATO is informed, protection provided,' came the reply. Half an hour later a Canadian warship came alongside. All seemed well. On Tuesday morning, however, the Canadians instructed us to deviate our course and then asked were there any weapons on board. 'Yes some,' said the skipper's assistant. 'Most for personal protection.' This was only partly true. Apart from three doctors and the journalists all the passengers were carrying machine guns. Some had RPGs, too, and one had brought some sort of anti-aircraft gun. Boxes of ammunition had been piled up in the skipper's storeroom and under a blue plastic sheet were the mortars. The Canadians boarded, found the weapons and ordered us back to Benghazi.

Jaber's report further confirmed that a Greek ship had joined the Canadian NATO vessel to block the rebel ship's passage. It was then that the skipper of the relief ship pointed out that it was perfectly legitimate to transport arms from one part of Libya to another and that he had only strayed into international waters and in breach of sanctions on account of the Canadians. He stood his ground, stating: 'Gaddafi is killing women and children and you only seem to be imposing a no-fly zone and a sea blockade. But who protects Misrata? I cannot obey your order to head back.' This is what sparked off the street protests in Benghazi that I witnessed later that day, as well as the ensuing diplomatic standoff the next morning in the Council building between Ambassador Prentice and the rebel leadership, until the ship was eventually given permission to go on its way and dock in Misrata to the shouts of 'Allahu Akbar' ('God is Great').

Hala Jaber went on to send a heartrending dispatch from inside the besieged city of Misrata, where Colonel Gaddafi's forces had unleashed a pitiless assault on the civilian population, leaving unarmed men, women and children to die. 'What I found was a city in desperate need of help, not only military but also humanitarian,' she wrote. It was by any standard an astonishing account of the abject cruelty of a state's hatred towards its own civilian population. She described in gruesome detail how children were dying in the arms of their parents as a torrent of bullets and artillery shells rained down upon them. One such instance involved Dr Ali Abu Fannas and his wife, who watched helplessly as two sons and two daughters were blown to bits in the back of their car as they were driving in search of refuge. The conflict in Misrata was fought quite without mercy.

What was clear was that if Gaddafi did go, some sort of process of societal reconciliation and transitional justice mechanism would quickly have to be put in place, if Libyans were to have any prospect of healing the wounds of their shattered society after the conflict ended. After reading Hala's and other reports of a similar nature, I resolved to raise the issue of reconciliation initiatives with the FCO immediately upon my return to London.

The Deaths of Tim Hetherington and Chris Hondros

In fact, the indiscriminate firing that Hala Jaber witnessed would rain down on Misrata for at least another two months. It would result in the deaths of two award-winning photographers, Tim Hetherington and Chris Hondros, on 20 April 2011, as they were caught in a bombardment. Hetherington and Hondros worked for the Getty Agency and had gone to Misrata to document Gaddafi's attempts to crush the uprising in the city. Hetherington, who was only forty years old and an Oscar-nominated photojournalist and film maker, was renowned for his intimate portrayals about how war affects ordinary people and the human psyche. 'War is intimate. The very things war brings out in persons are very intimate emotions – love, killing and friendship. Those are the emotions that we don't normally see,'[2] he once said. In 2009 Hetherington released the documentary *Restrepo*, an extraordinary story about how ordinary men coped with fear, pain and the suffering of war in Afghanistan. He went to Misrata to document a similar elemental struggle for freedom and survival that was being waged by the civilian inhabitants of the city. Hetherington, like Hala Jaber, travelled to Misrata by boat along with Chris Hondros and Guy Martin, a British photographer, whom he met in Benghazi.

On 20 April, the three men were following a rebel unit as they fought room to room near Tripoli Street, where rebels and soldiers were struggling for control of a bridge at a crucial intersection. Suddenly mortar shells began to rain down upon them. 'The nature of the fighting was so violent, close quarter and brutal, while the random shelling was terrifying. I remember rebels firing between the trees but I didn't hear the rocket. The next thing I remember was waking up in the Misrata Hospital with intestinal injuries and shrapnel in the right side of my pelvis,' recalled Martin. His life was saved after an extraordinary vascular surgeon constructed an artificial vein for his leg. Martin was evacuated a week later with 50 per cent of his intestines gone, after a fisherman who had sailed from Malta to drop off medical supplies picked him up. Hetherington was also hit in the rocket attack but his leg was so badly wounded that it resulted in his femoral artery being severed. 'Help me, I'm hit,' he said as he was loaded onto a pickup truck, bleeding profusely. According to Margarette Driscoll of *The Sunday Times*, his last message complained of 'indiscriminate shelling by

Gaddafi's forces, with no sign of air cover from NATO'. In fact, Hetherington's last words, contained in a Tweet sent from the city, simply stated: 'No NATO.' 'Why not?' It was a question that people in Benghazi had been asking for some weeks.

The full truth about the crimes against humanity being perpetrated by Gaddafi's forces in Misrata had yet to emerge as Hetherington lay dying in the back of his pickup truck. A small glimpse of the depth of depravity that occurred in Misrata later emerged through the dispatches of the truly inspirational *Sunday Times* correspondent, Marie Colvin. She spent seven weeks holed up in an abandoned hospital in Misrata documenting the plight of the people, particularly the women. After rebel forces finally managed to break through Gaddafi's lines and take some prisoners the horror and brutality of what they had been up to began to come to light. One captured soldier, Abu Bakr, a recruit to the elite Khamis Brigade, named after Gaddafi's son, told Colvin how he had been promised £100,000 to kill as many people as possible, payable on victory for Colonel Gaddafi. He gave a graphic account of how his officers had given orders to engage in 'an orgy of rapes' of all girls and young women in Misrata 'that mirrored their destruction of the city's homes and buildings'.[3]

Many of these rapes were allegedly recorded on mobile phones in a deliberate act of further humiliation. According to Colvin,

> A video seen by *The Sunday Times* showed a group of Gaddafi's soldiers in camouflage uniform breaking down a door and confronting a frightened family – a man, women, five girls whose ages ranged from about five to their early twenties, and a boy aged about seven. The soldiers, shouting and waving their guns, stripped the four older girls in front of the family and took them into the next room, where they raped them. The girls cried for mercy, calling on Allah. A soldier, at one point yells, 'Gaddafi is our Allah.' The video was found on the phone of a loyalist soldier.

The purpose of such rapes was to purposely lower morale and split families apart through shame, abortions and the transmission of sexual diseases. The European Court rightly describes such actions as constituting a gross form of torture. I had virtually no doubt that what had occurred in Misrata was a war crime of dreadful cruelty that would ultimately lead to a plethora of female suicides if medical help and some sort of justice were not forthcoming. As Colvin noted, these stories mirrored the experience of Iman al-Obeidi, who had earlier burst into the Tripoli Hotel at the start of the revolution claiming to have been gang-raped by Gaddafi loyalists. All of this formed a consistent pattern of abuse, which was plainly contrary to the statutes of the ICC.

Marie later wrote to me about her time in Misrata in the following terms:

My notebook from two months in Misrata, Libya, is stranger than any I have ever filled in 20 years of covering wars. There are pages of macabre diagrams. I had no time to ask for the names of the dead and wounded rebels who were hauled out of the pickup trucks and into a white triage tent in front of the hospital. I drew the gurneys and young men on them with pen marks for injuries and notes like 'chest and brain, shrapnel' and their clothing. One diagram has 22 gurneys at helter skelter angles. I felt the injured and dead should be documented, but in retrospect it was obsessive. There were no machines. To start a heart, doctors cut open the side of the chest and reached in halfway up their bloodied forearm and pumped the heart with a bare hand. Few survived. I could tell the rhythm of the fighting on the front from numbers carried in to the tent. I slept on the hospital floor and lived on cans of tuna fish. Most days I went up to one of the three fronts ringing the besieged port city. It was a very different war, more like the Spanish Civil war than a modern war of smart bombs and drones. I would hitch a ride in a rebel pickup truck to the sand berms that hid the rebels from the bullets and missiles of Gaddafi's men, so close that if you poked your head over you could see them in their own emplacements. I didn't really have to look. I could tell how close were Gaddafi's troops by the sound of the weapons – a hornet snap for a Kalashnikov bullet too close, the malevolent whine of a Grad rocket coming in and the comfort and guilt that came with the relief when it crashed in to a different part of the line. I knew I had probably stayed too long when a rebel on his break ambled over and said conversationally, 'Want to shoot the mortar?' Everyone was so young.

Many of these stories were only just beginning to surface in early April as we waited for the NTC to come back to us, but I was convinced that such crimes were being committed by Gaddafi's forces and that the Council would shortly be in need of sustained assistance in relation to the collation and preservation of evidence of crimes against humanity, as well as advice as to what appropriate transitional justice arrangements should be created, should it finally win the day.

The Agreements

And so after a tense day of diplomatic broadsides and discussion Said Ali finally emerged to confirm that the NTC had decided to enter into a number of agreements. He carried with him signed copies of them, which he handed over. The first agreement was with the BHRC regarding future efforts to strengthen of the rule of law in New Libya. The second concerned IRA

Semtex victims and the provision, in principle, of compensation for other victims of human rights abuses. The third agreement covered Lockerbie and included a personal statement signed by Mustafa Abdul Jalil regarding Gaddafi's alleged involvement, which would be given to Victoria Commeck's lawyers. Said Ali also told us that the Council intended to give a press conference at about 8 pm that evening for the purpose of announcing the apologies and the compensation agreements. Proceedings were to be conducted by the NTC vice-chairman Abdul Hafiz Ghoga, as Abdul Jalil was likely to be busy with other pressing matters. We could then respond with our own remarks. McCue looked at his watch as we ruminated on what was bound to be an even more manic midnight drive across the eastern Libyan desert than the one that got us here. It was leaving it tight to get out of Benghazi and back to Cairo to catch next day's afternoon's flight, but what could we do? McCue turned to me and gave me a huge smile. For him, it was beginning of the end of a twenty-year-long campaign on behalf of IRA victims, and the start of an interesting dialogue on Lockerbie and transitional justice issues with the New Libya, or so he hoped. As we checked through the last of the text, thoughts of a glass of pinot noir in the BMI business lounge of Cairo Airport flickered through my mind. It was time to go.

The MoU between the NTC and the BHRC built on the Vision Statement and involved a seven-point plan to help strengthen the rule of law. On IRA Semtex, the Council agreed upon a statement of reconciliation to be issued to the victims of Gaddafi-sponsored IRA terrorism. The Council also reiterated its gratitude to the UK government for its assistance in securing UN Resolution 1973 and issued the following declaration:

(1) As an act of friendship towards the British people, and in recognition of the pain suffered by British victims as a consequence of IRA acts of violence, which were actively supported by the Gaddafi Regime in contravention of international law, the Council hereby issues a voluntary and sincere apology on behalf of the Free People of Libya for the previous conduct of the Gaddafi Regime in supplying Semtex explosives and other support to the Provisional IRA for the purposes of committing such acts of violence; (2) The Council further declares that, within a reasonable time frame that acknowledges the difficult situation currently on the ground in Libya, it is its sincere desire to reach a morally just and appropriate settlement of the existing UK claimants in McDonald et al v Gaddafi US Case legal claim, on a parity basis, in line with other US victim claimants in the same action who have already received compensation pursuant to the principles of the Libyan Claims Settlement Act in the USA which has been brought about by Bush and Gaddafi; (3) In recognition of the wider class of similar UK IRA/Gaddafi victims that are not claimants in the case, their

sincere desire to enter discussions to consider an appropriately resourced humanitarian fund to be set up to recognise the pain and suffering of such victims and the wider society in the UK, and in particular Northern Ireland.

It concluded by stating that the 'Free People of Libya feel great compassion and sorrow towards those victims that have suffered at the hands of the Gaddafi Regime and wish to offer a hand of friendship to ease their pain'.

On Lockerbie, the Council agreed on another statement of reconciliation to the Lockerbie victims as a voluntary act of friendship towards the victims of the tragedy, and in recognition of the pain suffered by them as a consequence of the gross act of terrorism committed, organised and directly sanctioned by the Gaddafi regime, in contravention of morality as well as international law. In that statement, the Council issued 'a voluntary and sincere apology on behalf of the Free People of Libya for the previous conduct of the Gaddafi Regime in sanctioning and facilitating such a despicable and direct act of terrorism against the victims'. It also declared 'its willingness and desire to facilitate all investigations into the Lockerbie bombing by using its best endeavours to secure all records and evidence including the securing of witness statements from those who have relevant knowledge or records in order to bring closure to the remaining historical legacy issues'. The council went on to make clear its sincere desire 'to facilitate inquiries by the Lockerbie victims to discover the truth surrounding the Lockerbie tragedy, in particular the culpability of Gaddafi in sanctioning and conspiring in the act of terrorism against innocent people [. . .] The Free People of Libya feel great compassion and sorrow towards the victims that have suffered at the hands of the Gaddafi regime and wish to offer a hand of friendship to ease their pain'.

The Lockerbie Statement

We also took receipt of the following signed statement:

STATEMENT OF MUSTAFA MOHAMMED ABDUL JALIL,
CHAIRMAN OF THE NATIONAL TRANSITIONAL COUNCIL

I, Mustafa Mohammed Abdul Jalil, Chairman of the National Transitional Council and formerly Minister of Justice during the Gaddafi Regime swear to tell the truth, the whole truth, and nothing but the truth herein.

I make this statement on behalf of the families of Pan Am 103/Lockerbie victims regarding the planting of an explosive device upon a US flagged aircraft that resulted in the explosion and crash of Pan Am 103 on December 21st, 1988 over Lockerbie, Scotland.

I am the former Justice Minister that made statements to the media regarding Muammer Gaddafi ('Gaddafi') ordering the bombing of Pan Am 103/Lockerbie. I can confirm that the following article recorded accurately what I said: February 24th, 2011 Mail Online by Gerri Peev: 'Gaddafi personally gave the order for Lockerbie bombing and I have proof, claims dictator's former justice minister'. I repeat herein that 'I have information that is one hundred percent sure, that Gaddafi is behind the tragedy at Lockerbie' as is accurately reported in: Swedish interview dated February 24th, 2011, Minister: Jag såg djävulen I Khadaffi, Expressen (Minister: I saw the devil in Gaddafi) by Kassem Hamadé.

I have personally seen official documents of the Gaddafi regime that directly implicate Gaddafi in the ordering, sanctioning and implementation of the Lockerbie terrorist incident and its subsequent cover up. In due course, I will provide all such evidence to the proper investigating authorities and representatives charged with carrying out investigations in order that the victims may discover the truth about how Gaddafi directly murdered their loved ones.

It was common knowledge within the closed circles of the regime that Gaddafi ordered the act of terrorism that occurred at Lockerbie.

I can confirm that through his conduct Gaddafi demonstrated his personal culpability to me.

I am aware that on 1/31/2001, Abdelbaset Mohmed Ali al-Megrahi was convicted by the Scottish Court that examined the evidence of 270 counts of murder for the bombing of PanAm 103. I am aware from my former position that Megrahi was involved in this act of terrorism. It was common knowledge within the Gaddafi regime.

I am also aware that Gaddafi paid money to Megrahi for carrying out his orders to commit the act of terrorism and to cover up that act. Subsequent to his arrest, and later to his release, Gaddafi provided payments to Megrahi to ensure that he did not publicly implicate Gaddafi personally in the act of terrorism.

I provide this short statement as our people are engaged in a battle for survival against the Gaddafi regime. I do so in compassion for the victims' suffering and in a desire to demonstrate how the new Libya is different to the old regime and sincerely desires democracy, social justice and wealth share for all our people. To that extent it is the new Libyan National Transitional Government's and my sincere desire to provide a more detailed statement of evidence in due course. The NTC has agreed to further liaise with the victims' representative to facilitate this within a reasonable timeframe that acknowledges the difficult situation currently on the ground in Libya.

The free people of Libya feel great compassion and sorrow towards those victims that have suffered at the hands of the Gaddafi Regime and wish to offer a hand of friendship to ease their pain.

The contents of this statement are accurate and true to the best of my knowledge and belief.

Dated 5 April 2011

Signed By Mustafa Mohammed Abdul Jalil

This statement was sent to Victoria Commeck and the lawyers acting for Victims of Terrorism in America (VTA) a few days later, on our return to London. On 14 April 2011, the VTA issued the following press release praising the statement made by Abdul Jalil confirming Gaddafi's alleged involvement in Lockerbie:

FOR IMMEDIATE RELEASE   CONTACT: Alicia Ward
April 14, 2011
  Victims of Libyan Terrorism Praise Anti-Gaddafi Leaders for Pledging to Cooperate and Expose Dictator's Culpability in Terrorism and Crimes Against Humanity
MIAMI, April 14, 2011

The Gaddafi Terror Victims Initiative praised the National Transitional Council (NTC) of Libya today for pledging to fully cooperate in assisting international victims and exposing the truth about Muammar Gaddafi's direct role in committing numerous atrocities and crimes against humanity. Crimes include the bombing of Pan Am Flight 103 in 1988 and providing plastic explosives to the Provisional Irish Republican Army (IRA) in the 1980s for acts of terrorism against civilian populations.
   The NTC has provided evidence of Gaddafi's crimes and made clear its commitment to expose the truth about his regime's many nefarious

activities. This is the first time since Gaddafi took power 42 years ago that the Libyan people have had an opportunity to speak freely about him and the crimes committed by his regime.

National Transitional Council Chairman Mustafa Mohammed Abdul Jalil's statement is the first evidence given by a Libyan implicating Gaddafi in the Lockerbie atrocity.

'This was a courageous act by NTC Chairman Abdul Jalil in shining the light of truth on this dark period in their country's history,' said Victoria Cummock, chair of the Gaddafi Terror Victims Initiative and widow of John B. Cummock, who died in the Pan Am Flight 103 bombing.

'It is our deep hope that the NTC swiftly deposes this sociopathic, mass murdering kleptocrat and ushers in a new day of cooperation, peace and reconciliation,' said Cummock. 'The evidence they have given demonstrates the positive change the NTC represents for Libya.'

Abdul Jalil, Libya's former minister of justice, confirmed in a sworn statement his prior statement to the media: 'I have personally seen official documents of the Gaddafi regime that directly implicate Gaddafi in the ordering, sanctioning and implementation of the Lockerbie terrorist incident and its subsequent cover up.' He promised to provide further evidence so the victims 'may discover the truth about how Gaddafi directly murdered their loved ones'. Abdul Jalil also testified that the only individual convicted of the Lockerbie bombing, Abdelbaset al-Megrahi, 'was involved in this act of terrorism' and received payment from Gaddafi for the Lockerbie attack and subsequent cover-up.

'This is an important first step toward healing wounds that cannot be mended so long as Gaddafi is in power and that were ripped open again in 2009 with the indefensible release of convicted mass murderer al-Megrahi by the Scottish government,' Cummock said.

'At the same time, we must express our deep sense of betrayal that the British government, with the approval of our own government, is letting former Foreign Minister Moussa Koussa off 'scot-free', allowing him to freely travel the world as he pleases despite significant evidence that he played a central role in the Lockerbie bombing plot,' Cummock said. 'As an NTC spokesman noted, Moussa Koussa "has too much blood on his hands". He negotiated the release of al-Megrahi just two years ago. It is an outrage that the current UK and US governments are continuing the policy of previous administrations to put the greed of Big Oil ahead of the need for justice among all those harmed by Libyan-sponsored terrorism. And to put him at the table in Qatar in discussions over the future of Libya is a slap in the face to the brave rebels we are supposedly assisting – it's like letting the fox decide the future of the henhouse. This cynical action stands in stark contrast to the good faith demonstrated by the NTC.'

Notably, the NTC expressed its desire to 'facilitate enquiries by the Lockerbie victims to discover the truth surrounding the Lockerbie tragedy and in particular the culpability of Gaddafi in sanctioning and conspiring in the act of terrorism against innocent people'.

'Through this generous act to the international victims of Gaddafi, made all the more remarkable for occurring in the middle of a brutal war, members of the NTC have proven that they practice what they preached in their statement committing themselves to upholding the values of democracy, social justice and international humanitarian law,' Cummock added. 'This should encourage the international community to provide the new Libya with the recognition and assistance it needs. We look forward to further discussions and cooperation with Libya's democratic forces as the truth continues to come out about the brutality and crimes of the Gaddafi regime.'

Gaddafi Terror Victims Initiative

The Gaddafi Terror Victims Initiative includes family members and survivors of those killed and injured by Gaddafi-supported acts of terrorism and crimes against humanity including those killed in the bombing of Pan Am Flight 103, the bombing of the La Belle discotheque in Germany, the IRA terrorist attacks in the United Kingdom, aboard Pan Am Flight 73, and UTA Flight 772. Statements from Mustafa Mohammed Abdul Jalil are available at www.betrayalforoil.com.

A day after this press statement was released, *The Times* newspaper ran a front page article written by its Scottish editor Magnus Linklater about the statement given by Abdul Jalil to us. It commented: 'it is the first time that anyone from Gaddafi's administration has been prepared to give evidence in public on Lockerbie, and the statement appears to confirm the verdict of the Scottish Court which convicted al-Megrahi in January 2001 [. . .] The statement opens the way for prosecutors to begin moves to bring Colonel Gaddafi before a court'. The article clearly ruffled the feathers of those campaigners who had convinced themselves of al-Megrahi's innocence and Libya's lack of involvement in the Lockerbie atrocity, including the celebrated Professor of Scots Law at the University of Edinburgh, Robert Black, who had spearheaded much of the decade-long campaign to clear al-Megrahi's name.

On his Lockerbie website he cited a blog post by Ian Bell which questioned the credibility of Abdul Jalil's statement and the BHRC's wisdom in taking it at face value. This read: 'If I follow Magnus Linklater in *The Times*, the unwitting folk from the Bar of England and Wales did not ask Libya's former justice minister to reconcile his claims with problems – six of them – encountered by the Scottish Criminal Cases Review Commission (SCCRC). Strange how that slips everyone's mind. But then, if the First Minister of Scotland hasn't wondered why Moussa Koussa is not being detained for a view on the discrepancy, and if Hague is happy for the non-suspect to keep his memories of events and files to himself, the rest of us can only guess what the SCCRC was on about.'

A fair point on one level, but Bell's blog missed the most obvious and essential one: that the brief statement from Abdul Jalil was never designed to act as a detailed rebuttal of the appeal case in support of al-Megrahi. It was an invitation to the proper prosecuting Scottish authorities to come to Benghazi to question him further on the issue. In fact, Professor Black would later face his own credibility issues when, a month later after the fall of Tripoli, the *Daily Mail* reported that secret documents found in government buildings revealed that Lord Trefgarne had attempted to charge Gaddafi nearly £1 million for Professor Black and his services in seeking the acquittal of al-Megrahi. Professor Black had previously claimed on his website that he had taken a close interest in the Lockerbie affair since 1993 because 'he was born and brought up in the town', adding that he was regarded as 'the architect of the Lockerbie trial at Camp Zeist in the Netherlands'. It appeared as if everyone connected to Libya had an interest in tapping the Gaddafi regime for something, in one way or another. As for the Scottish prosecuting authorities, they told enquiring journalists a few weeks later that they were not minded to send their lawyers over to Benghazi to question Abdul Jalil at the present time because it was 'just too dangerous'. It would take another seven months, until after the end of hostilities, before the Scottish authorities felt able to even put in a request to come to Libya to take further evidence on Lockerbie.

Announcing the Agreements

As we checked the signature of Abdul Jalil inscribed on each page, Dr Said Ali presented us with three flags of the New Libya bearing his signature – one for McCue, one for me and another for David Cameron. A little while later we showed Christopher Prentice the various agreements in the privacy of his own suite. He appeared more than a little cheered by the news, in what had otherwise been a difficult and complex day for him. He immediately called London with this message:

> I wanted to pass on some good news amongst all the second rate news you have had today. We passed on earlier to news department news about the initiative that No. 10 have been supporting to get equal compensation for the IRA victims of violence. There is going to be an announcement here shortly which I alerted news department to. I just wanted for you to tell the

Foreign Secretary and on to No 10 that it is going to be a slightly bigger announcement than expected. The National Council have today signed documents with the 2 QCs here representing the initiative on behalf of the victims. Those documents offered the first ever Libyan apology for Lockerbie; equal compensation to the American compensation for the IRA victims; full co-operation with the Lockerbie investigation; and also an MoU, which is important, for future co-operation with UK Bar Association on legal issues. So it's a full package and one other thing – the first ever apology to IRA victims on behalf of the future Libya. Now this is going to be announced here in about an hour. Its extremely good news on many fronts. I have already told news department that it is imminent. I did not know at that stage that it was going to be the full slam dunk. I'm sure the Foreign Secretary would like to know first. I have not told anyone else. But if you could tell No 10 and check that news department have got the lines ready for a warm welcome.[4]

Only time would tell whether it would be the full slam dunk. We then took a couple of photographs of us standing on the balcony with the signed statements held aloft for posterity. An hour later we took our bags to our vehicle, bade farewell to the staff at the El Fadeel Hotel for the last time, and made our way to the appointed hotel in central Benghazi where the NTC's evening press conference was to take place. Dusk descended upon Benghazi to reveal a hauntingly beautiful, luminous sky. It was time to leave for home.

9. Leaving Rebel-Held Libya

When we got to the hotel where the press conference was supposed to be held we were met with utter confusion. A notice now explained that the Council press conference was to be at another hotel, where General Younis would give a statement about the rapidly deteriorating situation at the front and the lack of assistance from NATO. Not only was Misrata said to be on the brink of falling, further news from Brega and Ajdabiya was not good. Throughout the evening dispiriting images of retreating rebels from Brega flickered across the news screens in the hotel lobbies of battle-weary Benghazi. Despite Christopher Prentice's efforts behind the scenes, the Council had felt impelled to alert the world's media to the failure by NATO Command to give adequate support to its forces. Once again the rebel city held its collective breath to see if the world would come to its rescue and avert another humanitarian catastrophe. The tension in the streets and hotel cafes was palpable. It began to feel as if Benghazi might fall.

When we got to the concrete 1980s hotel where the conference was due to take place there seemed to be a TV and satellite news team in every nook and cranny. As I stepped out into the hotel courtyard I saw Orla Guerin from BBC World News screech to a halt in a TV van that had driven straight from the front. I watched as she and her cameraman tore out of the vehicle and rushed into the hotel foyer, she bedecked in her trademark dark blue bullet-proof vest. Throughout the foyer, other news teams tested their equipment in readiness for their own interviews. You could sense the adrenalin in them all as their deadlines approached. For most journalists General Younis's statement about the situation in Ajdabiya was the big story. No one had heard a whisper about the embattled ship in the Mediterranean or about our agreements, except two British press journalists and *Newsnight*. As we descended into the basement I saw Mustafa Gheriani, the Council media spokesman, with 300 or so journalists waiting expectantly for General Younis to appear.

'Where is Hafiz Ghoga?' we asked. 'He is supposed to be making a statement on Lockerbie and IRA Semtex.' 'I don't know where he is,' came the reply from a startled Gheriani. 'You don't know where he is or you don't know about the statement?' we enquired. 'Neither,' he answered. 'What agreement?'

It was pandemonium. Gheriani had been at the press centre all day rather than at the El Fadeel Hotel where the Council was still meeting, dealing with individual journalists and giving interviews about the general situation, as I had seen him do the previous day. It was clear that strategic communications between the NTC, its members and the outside world were pretty awful. In fact, I hadn't noticed a single press attaché from the Council while it met in session at the El Fadeel. I thought of what Gheriani had told me about how there was no time to brief or be briefed by members of the Council between the long meetings they seemed to endure. A Council member would rush to a hastily arranged conference, deliver his statement, conduct a few interviews, and then disappear into the night until the next day. Special Envoy, Christopher Prentice, was right when he observed that the Council needed professional help to sort out its strategic communications. Yet there was something utterly beguiling about the nature of their makeshift press operation. It seemed to confirm the authenticity of the revolution as the people of Benghazi made it all up as they went along. These people were not stooges or placemen for the West or lackeys for a cabal of hidden Libyan strongmen, but ordinary people trying to do an extraordinary job. But as Prentice observed, in the end communication was everything in this game.

By this time Bob, our security expert, was becoming decidedly worried about the security situation. It was pitch black outside. Tensions were rising. We would have to drive through the night towards Ajdabiya. More and more people were beginning to hear about the agreements and there were still a few Gaddafi sniper cells operating in the city. It was not beyond the bounds of possibility that Gaddafi had an active cell close by. If he was willing to kill artists and citizen journalists who sought to criticise him, then why not us? Just a few weeks after we left two French lawyers were shot dead on the streets of Benghazi and a private security officer was shot in the back as he waited at a traffic light. Bob rightly wanted us out of Benghazi as soon as possible.

We pressed Gheriani to get in touch with Ghoga but he had no idea where he was or whether he would come to the press conference. All he had heard was that Ghoga had been somewhere at the front and that Younis would do the conference. It appeared more cock-up than conspiracy, but who knew the real truth? After showing Gheriani the signed agreements he suggested that we announce the agreements before General Younis made his statement on

NATO. The original idea was for the Council to issue an apology, make a statement, and then leave it for us to respond. 'Maybe we should wait to see if he turns up,' mused McCue. 'Just do it and let's get out of here,' replied Bob. He was right, of course, as we had no more time to play with. We decided to go for it.

The Press Conference

Gheriani opened the press conference in front of the world's press by explaining who we were and what we had secured. McCue then gave the following statement: 'Today, President Abdul Jalil from the Council signed some historical documents in relation to international victims of the Gaddafi regime. He has asked me to read some selected extracts to you from those documents as he couldn't be here himself to deliver them.' He then took the press through the apologies and agreements over compensation. He went on:

> If I may just say a few words as well on behalf of the victims. The Council has declared to the world that it is the antithesis of the Gaddafi Regime. That it stands for everything it declared in its national vision statement in London – that is – social justice, democracy, wealth sharing, and international normative adherence. Today it has proven this to be true in no other clearer way, in no better demonstration of its bona fides. It has shown to the world what the new Libya stands for, what it promises to be and undoubtedly what it will be. For 30 years, victims of Gaddafi sponsored IRA terrorism have sought justice and reconciliation, for 13 years [sic] the Lockerbie victims. Throughout, the Gaddafi Regime showed disdain, arrogance, and little compassion for victims. Today, the Council and the Libyan people, through the statements that have been given, indicating a clear written desire and commitment to justice and reconciliation, have shown clear compassion, respect, and justice to those victims. I will be heading back to London to provide the detail of this to the British Prime Minister and the victims. I also would just quickly like to take the opportunity to thank the Prime Minister for personally supporting this initiative along with the Foreign Office and the interim ambassador Christopher Prentice whose help on the ground has been superb in the last few days and finally to Mark Muller who will be saying a few words. Finally, on behalf of the international victims of Gaddafi, I wish to thank the Council and the Libyan people and extend our hand of friendship and support them. Long live this new Libya, thank you.

I then followed:

It gives me great pleasure to announce that the Bar Human Rights Committee of the Bar Council of England and Wales has reached a Memorandum of Understanding with the Transitional National Council in relation to the strengthening of the rule of law in Libya. This builds upon the vision statement of the Council delivered at the London Conference earlier last week and upon a series of correspondence that we entered into with the Council since the 3rd of March. The Memorandum of Understanding helps to strengthen the rule of law in seven crucial areas. The first, as Jason has alluded to, is in the provision of advice and assistance in relation to the collection and preservation of evidence in respect of human rights breaches and crimes against humanity committed in the past. And these, of course, today have included matters concerning Lockerbie and other legacy issues concerning the United Kingdom and the United States. It also includes the enhancement of the respect of international human rights standards throughout the Libyan legal and governmental sector, the provision of advice concerning constitutional and democratic reform issues, the enhancement of a fully functioning independent judiciary and local bar associations, as well as law faculties in Benghazi and elsewhere. And it also includes future advice and assistance where requested in relation to appropriate transitional justice arrangements. But let me add this. Like many of us in the UK, one month ago I watched with something approaching awe as Libyan human rights lawyers, retired judges, students, children and other sectors of civil society came together here in Benghazi to fight to build a new democratic opening in Libya. The Bar Human Rights Committee heeded the call for help because it believes the commitment to the rule of law does not start and stop in the courtroom. It starts in the hearts and minds of ordinary people in civil society and I defy anyone not to be moved by the solidarity and hope that we have experienced here in Benghazi, as ordinary people from all backgrounds seek to take control of their lives and create a better future for this country. The Bar Human Rights Committee believes there is a moral obligation, where possible, to come to the aid of those seeking to resist tyranny and reconstruct their shattered society in the name of freedom. It is part of what others sometimes refer to as a commitment to a big society. We look forward to assisting the Council and the Libyan people in building a new future based upon respect of human rights and the rule of law. Let me just end by saying this: this agreement concerning the rule of law has been reached in the teeth of war. There are young men dying but 100 kilometres from here. I believe this agreement sends out an important signal to the international community about what the new Council and New Libya is all about. We hope it is the start of a new relationship but this time one based upon mutual trust and respect between the Libyan and British people. Thank you very much.

To our surprise, the press pack burst into spontaneous applause after we had finished our remarks. After taking a few questions we collected our stuff and made for the exit. No sooner had we got off the podium than we were deluged with questions from the British press pack, including ITV, Channel 4, *Newsnight*, BBC News, *The Times* and *The Telegraph*. McCue quickly fired off a few interviews with ITN, *Newsnight* and the BBC while I talked to Martin Fletcher of *The Times*. 'Was there a deal with the British government?' asked Orla Guerin. 'No,' said McCue, 'unless you call the BHRC's offer to help strengthen the rule of law a deal.' Guerin smiled and with that we were off. As we left the building we tried to get the signed agreements copied but there were no photocopiers or scanners available. In the end we managed to get one done through an old fax machine and gave it to Martin Fletcher who we hoped might show it to others. It was now nearing 9.30 pm and we figured there was very little else we could do.

The Rise and Fall of General Younis

We left the press conference just as General Younis began to deliver his blistering attack on the failure of NATO to provide necessary military cover. Younis carried himself well. He exuded the political weight and charisma that we had seen in private. I watched as he strode confidently into the conference followed by a retinue of officials. He was in every sense the revolution's military strongman and the type of character that settled the nerves of power elites in the West, who were more used to dealing with his type than a ragtag civilian militia. There were still deep reservations within some quarters in NATO about the use of its mandate and the danger of mission creep, but Younis was having no truck with them. That night he broadcast his and the NTC's defiance to the world as he laid bare to the assembled press corps the full horror of what was befalling the Libyan people. There were very few members of the Council who could command the room as he did. He set out in stark terms the political choices facing the NATO coalition with admirable clarity. Intervene now to prevent a humanitarian catastrophe or be forced to do so later and risk the wrath of a traumatised people and nation, not to say a triumphant Gaddafi.

Yet in the end it would not be General Younis who would liberate Tripoli to the tumultuous applause of the masses. That honour would fall to a little known Islamist rebel commander called Abdelhakim Belhaj, or at least according to Al Jazeera. He had been rendered back to Tripoli under the CIA's extraordinary rendition programme a few years earlier. Belhaj was detained in Abu Salim prison and tortured by Gaddafi's interrogators for his association with the LIFG, the Islamic resistance movement that Western intelligence agencies now believed had links to Al-Qaeda. In a stark turnaround of fortunes, Belhaj would become known as the strong man who liberated Tripoli in August 2011, while General Younis would meet his demise just a few weeks before the fall of the regime, on 28 July, when he was shot dead in deeply suspicious circumstances. It was initially claimed that he was killed in crossfire with loyalist forces after he had been ordered back to Benghazi to face questioning before the Executive Committee of the Council about his failure to make military gains. Despite repeated attempts Younis was unable to take Ajdabiya. In mid-July a three-pronged assault on Brega resulted in over seventy dead and 600 wounded.[1] But later reports suggested that this was an excuse advanced to explain away Younis's execution at the hands of his own rebel guards, whose relatives had been tortured under his tenure as Minister of the Interior. Although Younis had switched sides very early on in the Revolution, and enjoyed his tribe's support in the East, as Gaddafi's Interior Minister he retained numerous enemies, particularly among those Islamist elements who had resisted the regime and been subjected to repression and torture for doing so.

Over the next month it would become increasingly clear that while Islamist elements such as the LIFG and Muslim Brotherhood heeded the NTC call for assistance in February 2011, they were disinclined to submit themselves to either the full authority of the NTC or the concept of civilian control, without further dialogue and agreement about transitional issues. Many of these Islamist elements such as the Muslim Brotherhood, LIFG and the National Front for the Salvation of Libya (NFSL) did not agree with Mahmoud Jibril's vision of a managed transition in which former senior military and security officials of the regime would be co-opted.

While they might have endorsed the NTC's aim of removing Gaddafi from power and the general political mantra of reform, and claimed not to be inspired by Al-Qaeda, it was difficult to see how such a complicated rebel fighting alliance could hold together after the regime had fallen without detailed agreements about the transitional process, post-conflict.

Certainly none of these organisations were in the vanguard of the revolution when secularists like Jibril formed the NTC and set about writing its vision statement and designing its transitional roadmap. Most if not all of these Islamist organisations had been neutered through a combination of repression and Saif al-Islam's reconciliation initiatives, which sought to reintegrate Islamist detainees back into Libyan society in exchange for political acquiescence. This happened after he made a prisoner release deal with the Doha-based cleric Ali al-Sallabi, Abdelhakim Belhaj and Sami Saadi. When the protests began, the Muslim Brotherhood presented Saif with its own reform package. It was only after the protests transformed into an uprising following Saif's infamous speech of 20 February that these Islamist leaders sought to rebuild their networks and build a wider political alliance amongst themselves. This loose alliance became known as the 17 February Coalition. Its creation was announced on Al Jazeera in early April but tensions remain between the different organisations involved in it, although virtually all of them took the view that transition could not be overseen by the NTC with Jibril as its head but only through an elected body.

This was the Islamist movement that had obsessed so many Western news editors as they tried to understand the true nature of the rebel leadership. Over the course of the next three months these Islamist elements would prove themselves adept at fighting, in contrast to their less disciplined civilian counterparts. Were General Younis's death and the rise of commanders like Belhaj ominous signs of things to come or just part of the ebb and flow of revolution? Only time would tell. Certainly General Younis constituted a threat to the growing military and political powerbase of the Islamists since he retained close contacts with the network of defected officers who supported Jibril's vision of a managed transition. Few mourned his demise when he was shot.

Yet for the moment all of these questions lay in the future, as we made our way from the press conference back to the Katiba barracks where the uprising had begun and General Younis had pledged his allegiance to the rebels, just six weeks earlier. It was here under the eerie twilight of a solitary streetlight that we rendezvoused for the last time with the Libyan driver who would take us across the desert back to Egypt. In the quiet of the night, we changed out of our dusty suits and into our jeans and head scarfs, in preparation for another bone-crushing sixteen-hour overnight drive to Cairo. After loading up with water and Libyan biscuits, and a ton of cigarettes, we silently slipped out of rebel-held Benghazi.

Terrorism and the 'Right to Resist'

It was a punishing smoke-filled drive to the Libyan border but we didn't care. We had got out of Benghazi and established what we hoped might be a fascinating dialogue with the NTC. Somewhere along the road to Ajdabiya, before turning right towards Tobruk, we met up with some clearly relieved rebels in their Toyota pickups. Jason and I took a few photographs as a memento. One rebel had come from Bournemouth, another from Manchester. We had only been in Libya for five days, yet it felt like a lifetime. During this short time the people of Benghazi and New Libya had become almost comrades. There was something elemental about these rebel fighters who would probably have been branded national security suspects by the UK authorities for their attempt to overthrow Gaddafi just a few weeks earlier. Their activities would have become the subject of intelligence briefings between Britain, the US and a succession of intelligence agencies from regimes across the Maghreb, including Gaddafi's. How would the UK authorities treat these dissident fighters now that they were on the way to seizing control of the country? Were these freedom fighters or terrorists? And if not terrorists, why not? What exactly had changed?

It was much easier for governments to adjust to the realities of revolution than for the courts, which were required to ensure that any such alteration in approach was consistent with legal principle and precedent. The full implication of what Cameron was doing in supporting the rebels was only beginning to make itself felt. Did these people have the right to take up arms and resist state oppression? His public support of regime change in Libya and Syria was in danger of driving a coach and horses through certain counter-terror paradigms, as well as the carefully constructed government legal edifice that refused to acknowledge the existence of any right to use force against an oppressive regime in defence of democracy or the right to self-determination. I left Libya that night convinced that where people were forced to take up armed struggle as a last resort against an oppressive dictator they should, at the very least, be given the ability to raise a legal defence to the charge of terrorism in UK courts. But more than anything else, I was certain to be more wary of the confines of those SIAC courtrooms in Chancery Lane, where middle-aged white men came to dubious judgments about the state of freedom and security in societies they had never lived in, and about the motives and lives of less fortunate men and women they had never met, nor were ever likely to meet.

Reporting Revolutions

Eight hours later, exhausted, dirty and parched, we finally arrived at the Salloum land port crossing just before dawn. As we drove through it we saw crumpled lumps of bodies quietly sleeping under a thousand bug-infested blankets. Jason and I pulled over to take one last photograph of this deeply desolate place. After an interminable hour of checks to our vehicle we passed into the safety of Egypt, just as the sun came up over the cliff tops of the pretty coastal town of Salloum. Within five minutes of crossing the border, McCue received news on his mobile of an article written by Chris McGreal of *The Guardian*. It read:

The revolutionary administration has denied a claim by a British lawyer representing victims of IRA attacks and the Lockerbie bombing that it has apologised for Libya's involvement and offered compensation. Following a meeting with the rebel council's leadership in Benghazi, Jason McCue, head of the Libya Victims Initiative, read a statement which he said was an 'unequivocal apology' for Libya's provision of Semtex used in IRA bombings and the blowing up of the Pan Am flight. McCue said the revolutionary council had agreed to pay compensation along the lines paid out in a deal between Muammar Gaddafi and the US government, which provided $10m for a death and $3m for a serious injury. He said there was also agreement to set up a trust for other victims. McCue said the apology and offer of compensation was in the name of the Chairman of its interim governing council, Mustafa Abdul Jalil. But Abdul Hafiz Ghoga, its deputy Chairman, said McCue's claims were 'not true'. 'We didn't apologise ourselves. We regret what happened, the catastrophic event of Lockerbie, and we will do our best to reach the truth with the families of Lockerbie. Also for the IRA. We emphasised to the British government that we will work to overcome what has happened. But there was no apology. We are not responsible,' he said. Ghoga said that the Council 'didn't negotiate anything about compensation [. . .]'[2]

And so it went on. McCue read the article with a sense of disbelief. Gheriani had seen the signed agreements before ushering us into the press conference. It was tantamount to calling him a fantasist. Why hadn't McGreal checked the story with Mustafa Abdul Jalil, or his cabinet secretary, or with Christopher Prentice, or any of the other UK journalists present who had seen copies of the signed agreement? It seemed odd not to verify the facts, given the likely distress the article would cause the victims of IRA Semtex and Lockerbie. Perhaps Ghoga had reacted spontaneously. After all, it wasn't difficult to see why an unbriefed Ghoga, coming back from the front, might have questioned the existence and authenticity of the agreements. It would stick in the throat of most rebels to be asked to apologise for the actions of a mortal enemy. Yet these legacy issues were always likely to threaten relations with the UK unless further progress was made on them. The NTC was in a perilous position, and it was in its strategic interests to draw a line under these issues so as to focus everyone's attention on its real needs.

One source had spoken of possible tensions between the ambitious Ghoga and the modest Abdul Jalil, who had always described himself as just an interim head. Had Abdul Jalil nominated Ghoga in order to bind him into the policy? It didn't come across like that but in the end it was impossible to tell. The NTC website would later describe Ghoga as being 'supportive of the Gaddafi regime almost until the very end'. Perhaps there had been an inexplicable intervention from London after Prentice had given it the heads up about the good news. What was clear was that no other news organisations ran the same story as the *The Guardian*. Martin Fletcher of *The Times* reported: 'Libya's rebel government-in-waiting offered an unprecedented and unequivocal public apology last night for Colonel Muammar Gaddafi's "despicable" acts of terrorism against the British people at Lockerbie and in Northern Ireland. The Transitional National Government pledged to facilitate an investigation of the Lockerbie bombing. It promised to pay compensation to victims of IRA bombs made with Semtex supplied by Libya, and to set up a fund for the other victims [. . .]'[3] The article went on: 'The council is still far from achieving a breakthrough and desperately wants international recognition. At a press conference in Benghazi last night, Mr McCue denied that there was any quid pro quo, but said that he believed the agreement could hasten British recognition of the council as Libya's legitimate government.' BBC *Newsnight*, ITN and BBC World all carried similar stories.

McCue now fired off a complaint to *The Guardian*. Although he didn't want to embarrass McGreal he could hardly remain silent. The difficulty was that we were still speeding back to Cairo unable to send copies of the agreements to the UK. The next day the *Guardian* correspondent conceded that: 'Mustafa Abdul Jalil had indeed signed an apology on behalf of the Libyan people for Gaddafi's provision of Semtex used in IRA bombings and for the blowing up of the Pan Am flight in 1988. It also promised compensation.' However, he now reported that the IRA and Lockerbie documents were the result of a 'misunderstanding', a 'translation mix-up', and came about because the Council had been 'pressed' by the British. It looked like Ghoga was trying to cover his earlier error. The only evidence of pressure cited came from Gheriani, who hadn't even been present at the meeting with Abdul Jalil. 'Asked if Abdul Jalil was pressured by Britain, Gheriani replied: "It depends on how you define pressure. I request something from you when you want something from me. It could be defined as pressure."' In fact, Ghoga was known for making a number of mistaken policy announcements. On 27 February he had told the world's press: '[W]e are completely against foreign intervention. The rest of Libya will be liberated by the people and Gaddafi's security forces will be eliminated by the people of Libya.' On 5 May he claimed that Canada, Denmark, Spain and the Netherlands had recognised the NTC when they hadn't. Two days later he claimed Italy had agreed to supply the rebels with weapons from funds made available from a conference in Rome when it had not.

It was becoming evident that the Council's strategic communications were as appalling as Christopher Prentice had said they were. As Mustafa Gheriani himself earlier told me: 'We are a team, but we have problems. Time is not available for us. Our executive and managers do not have the time to brief us or get briefed by us before they go out to a press meeting. They brief themselves. Sometimes they are not as available as we would like them to be. We know the media needs and is often starved of information. Yes, sometimes we have to apologise for this situation, but despite these problems we are doing a great job for the country.' More difficult to explain, however, was McGreal's claim two days later in *The Observer* that the agreement with Abdul Jalil was 'done in secret' after the 'British got him [Abdul Jalil] in a room on his own and bounced him into it'.[4] There was nothing clandestine about our visit and no British officials were present during our talks with Abdul Jalil, who was never in the room without his officials. Nor was our arrival in Benghazi a secret. Indeed, it was McGreal who had reported McCue's arrival in the city a few days earlier in his own newspaper.

Chris McGreal's personal attitude towards such apologies surfaced in an opinion piece he wrote for the Saturday *Guardian* on 8 April 2011 about the British government's ill-treatment of Mau Mau insurgents in Kenya during the 1950s:

> This week, a British human rights lawyer backed by the Foreign Office managed to strong-arm an apology out of Libya's revolutionary leadership for the actions of the man it is struggling to overthrow [. . .] This demonstration of power politics is made all the more distasteful by the contrasting attitude of the British government at the high court toward victims of the most depraved torture, gruesome killings and mass hangings by Britain during Kenya's struggle for independence. Hiding behind legal contortions, the government is refusing to apologise or pay compensation for appalling abuses done in the name of and with the knowledge of the British State [. . .] The survivors of the British camps in Kenya are asking for what the victims of the IRA and Lockerbie have now been promised from the new Libya – an apology and compensation to live out the rest of their lives with respect. But the Foreign Office believes apologies are for Libyans . . .[5]

he thundered in righteous indignation.

Few would argue with McGreal's sentiments. Yet they seemed more directed towards the application of double standards by the British government than the natural inclination of victims to seek redress and apologies from those who later sought to rule in that state's name. It was, after all, exactly what the victims of Bloody Sunday had sought from the Bloody Sunday Inquiry, as a result of which David Cameron did issue an unequivocal and historic apology. What was more interesting was McGreal's criticism of the revolution's 'self-appointed chiefs in the Council' who 'were nowhere to be seen', regarding the mounting public anger over the lack of NATO support. He quoted one frustrated official:

'They don't understand the need to communicate with the Libyan people [. . .] These lawyers and doctors in Benghazi who say they are a government, it's like kids playing dress-up for a lot of them. They don't understand the need to explain to people what it is they are doing.'⁶ The description of lawyers and doctors acting like kids was a little unfair. The NTC had been actively engaged with NATO, US, British and French officials throughout this period, but its failure to properly communicate with the public and media didn't bode well for the future in terms of public transparency and accountability. This would become a perennial problem in the New Libya.

It was fast becoming apparent that the Council was struggling not only to properly communicate but also to make its writ run across its improvised administration. One UK intelligence source told me, somewhat testily, that while the NTC had its hand on the lever it wasn't connected to anything. Many fighters on the front did not recognise its authority. On the other hand, this was a popular revolution carried out by ordinary people, many of whom were unused to strategically controlling communications or government entities. These men and women were putting their heart and soul into a better future for their country. They were caught up in a political, military and diplomatic maelstrom that would have tested the mettle of the most seasoned of politicians and diplomats. Revolutions by their very nature are messy and uncertain affairs, particularly where no organised opposition had been allowed to exist for forty odd years. Yet, if New Libya was ever to emerge with anything like a democracy, one thing was certain: the NTC had to carry the people with it and develop the requisite tools to govern them.

McGreal ended his tour of duty three weeks later with a moving portrait of the bravery of the people of Benghazi. He described how they had found courage to launch one of the 'most inspiring' revolutions he had ever witnessed. He rightly observed how middle-aged men stood against Gaddafi because they couldn't bear the thought of their children growing up devoid of hope. And how younger people had finally refused to resign themselves to a half-existence under the tutelage of the next generation of Gaddafis. He ended his portrayal by quoting a young Benghazian called Fasi: 'I really want to share in the building of this country. It's a dream to be the best country in the world. We can be that now. I think it needs democracy, and this country is rich. Democracy and oil, that's all we need.'⁷

In an earlier section of the article, McGreal described how in the early days of the uprising he was 'feted with free coffee in cafes' and 'regularly stopped on the street and thanked for coming'. Perhaps some of the free spirit of revolutionary Benghazi had entered his soul, and as a consequence he had become more than a little protective of the uprising and defensive towards the increasing number of Western interlopers and speculators who were descending upon New Libya in search of plunder, with little respect for the aspirations of its people. If that is how he perceived McCue's search for an apology, then I could forgive the scepticism. We are all immeasurably better off for having access to these types of dispatches from independently-minded foreign correspondents, whether or not they are sometimes written in passion or error. I for one salute the work of journalists like Chris McGreal, Martin Fletcher, Tim Whewell, Hala Jaber, Tim Hetherington, Chris Hondros, and the ever-courageous Marie Colvin. Without them, the reality of Libya's revolutionary spring would never have been conveyed.

A Shift in Political Consciousness

The truth is that revolutions are deeply intoxicating affairs and can both inspire and infuriate one's conscience as one becomes engrossed in the flow of events. The value of experiencing revolution first-hand was brought home to me almost immediately upon my arrival in London. As I entered my then chambers I bumped into a left-wing lawyer friend who had a particular objection to my presence in Benghazi. He had spotted me walking amongst the wreckage of the Katiba barracks on BBC *Newsnight* two days earlier. This led him to send me an e-mail in which he evinced the hope that I was not assisting NATO attacks on Gaddafi and Tripoli. It read: 'I saw you on tv a couple of days ago in Libya. I hope you are not there to gather information which can be used to justify the military attack on Libya! Kisses [. . .]' I read the e-mail as I crossed the Egyptian border and felt a ripple of anger. This lawyer knew nothing about what I was doing in Libya. The operating assumption behind his quip was that it was illegitimate to support the rebels or NATO in their attempts to stop and dislodge Gaddafi.

Yet as he accosted me in chambers it was he rather than I who became increasingly defensive as I talked about the brave people of Benghazi. When I said I was in no doubt that a bloodbath would have ensued had it not been for the no-fly zone, he declared: 'it was not about saving lives' but a broader imperialist dynamic at work. When I offered him the chance to look at my images of Benghazi, he literally put up his hand to stop me. It is interesting to note that the only e-mail concerning Libya that floated round my then chambers in the six weeks prior to my going there was one inviting members to march to 10 Downing Street in protest against the no-fly zone and the bombing of Tripoli. No one thought to march on the Libyan Embassy in protest at the mass of civilian casualties inflicted by Gaddafi on the population of Misrata. What on earth, I wondered, did they think was going on in the squares of Tunisia, Egypt and Libya? Was this not a truly extraordinary set of developments? When would these critics recognise that what was occurring in the MENA region went far beyond any conventional Left–Right analysis?

Yet to be fair to my friend, he had spent the better half of the last decade fighting to protect the civil rights of others against the more excessive aspects of the war on terror. He was part of an extraordinary network of legal activists who helped uncover the truth about extraordinary rendition and the alleged use of torture by the West's allies in places like Libya, Morocco and Algeria. Yet this very experience seemed to blinker, rather than illuminate, his attitude towards New Libya. Few lawyers where I practised had first-hand experience of how government actually formulated foreign policy. Their experience of government came principally through the courts in disputes over the disclosure of information in terror and torture related cases. The perceived failure of the authorities to adequately furnish relevant information in torture cases exacerbated their view of how government generally operated in places like the Middle East. For some colleagues it was just too difficult to accept that occasionally the UK government might act in defence of people rather than for mere profit.

In the end, what I suspect rankled with my lawyer friend was not so much my support for Cameron's intervention but my call for him to make a leap of faith. It was counter-intuitive to everything he had experienced over the last ten years. It was much easier to issue a call to faith if you had seen the effects of the intervention for yourself. I didn't blame my colleague for his apparent rage, but nor was I convinced by it. In the end, it seemed to me that what he was really grappling with was his own conscience about what should be done. To my mind, the issue was not so much whether we should have intervened militarily to save a blood bath but whether we had the stomach for what followed thereafter. If Afghanistan and Iraq had taught the West anything, it was that the difficulty lay not in winning the war but securing the peace.

I acquired two important insights as a result of my visit to Benghazi. Firstly, I realised that few calls for military intervention to avert an acute humanitarian catastrophe afford us the luxury of time to judiciously assess the merits of such an intervention, as if in a court of law. When we arrived there, Benghazi was on a knife-edge and policymakers had little scope to explore all the dynamics of intervention. It was better to gamble in favour of life and liberty than condemn people to certain death and servitude, even if the road ahead looked uncertain and difficult. After the experiences of Bosnia and Kosovo, Western statesmen, most notably Tony Blair, had pledged to ensure that never again would 'mad dog' rulers be permitted to terrorise a civilian population in Europe. What then separated the case of the Bosnian Muslim from the Benghazi Muslim other than perhaps a thinly-veiled racism that suggested Arabs were in some way not deserving of the same sort of protection?

When it came to it, Cameron heeded the call not to let another Srebrenica take place. I applauded his moral impulse and decision to call for a no-fly zone. That decision was taken so quickly, and in the face of such initial derision, that it is difficult to believe it was done for personal political gain. He acted in the moment and on instinct. Such moments come but once or twice in any premiership and often go on to define them politically and historically. These foreign policy decisions have huge consequences for which leaders must bear primary responsibility. It was a difficult judgment to make, with no obvious route map to success, but I would be interested to hear why his initial impulse in favour of intervention should be the wrong impulse to act upon. Let those who have never experienced a war zone or the terrifying spectacle of a mad dog tyrant unleashed, cast the first stone, for I certainly could not. Gaddafi was a tyrant who was unable to countenance even the simplest form of artistic criticism without resorting to the cruellest form of physical censorship, as Qais found out to his cost.

But perhaps the more important insight I discovered during those five days in April 2011 was that an irreversible paradigm shift in the political consciousness and aspirations of ordinary people in Libya and the wider MENA region had occurred. The freedom genie was out of the bottle and it was unlikely to be put back in without massive political repression. This alteration in political consciousness now required an equivalent paradigm shift in thinking in the West. An entire human community was on the march and moving closer towards us. The sheer romance of the endeavour masked a wider strategic opportunity for the West – a once in a generation chance to reset and renew its relationship with the people of the Middle East and the Maghreb.

This required both Western governments and civil society to re-evaluate their own historical approaches towards the region. Suddenly it no longer seemed possible for Western governments to prop up unpopular, corrupt regimes in the face of such widespread calls from ordinary people for political reform based on fundamental Western principles of governance. Nor was it possible for Western activists to remain locked in their gilded intellectual cages if they were serious about helping their brothers and sisters in the Arab world fight societal repression and injustice. The repercussions of the Arab Spring went way beyond the Middle East. I left chambers both exhilarated but also a little deflated by the lack of support for the rebels. What counted was not support of the military but of the civil intervention if New Libya was to have any chance of building a state based on the rule of law. Cameron and Obama had heeded the call to arms, but the real issue was whether they would heed the call to help rebuild a nation both during and after the conflict, or founder again on a heap of broken promises and rhetoric as their predecessors had done in Afghanistan and Iraq.

PART TWO: The British Intervention in Libya

10.   Towards a New MENA Policy

The day after we got back from Benghazi, McCue dropped off Mustafa Abdul Jalil's flag at the FCO for David Cameron, while I e-mailed the FCO Arab Partnership Fund about the BHRC MoU to inform it that the NTC was 'a willing partner for the purposes of any application for funds'. I then gave the BHRC co-ordinator directions to draft a broad application for submission before 27 April, in accordance with instructions I had received from officials from the Fund. I then left for a ten-day break in Zimbabwe, where I wrote up a short account about the young people I had met in Benghazi. It was somewhat surreal to record my experiences while watching herds of elephants and wild game sipping from a water hole in the depth of the Hwange National Park. Yet somehow the raw sense of physical freedom of the African plains felt fitting. I realised I had become utterly seduced by the revolutionary atmosphere I encountered in Benghazi and Cairo. The sense of democratic solidarity and hope of the Libyan people was truly astonishing. It was difficult to divine whether it was just wishful thinking or indicative of a real change spreading throughout the region. Certainly matters appeared to have taken a distinct turn for the worse for protesters in Yemen, Bahrain and Syria. Yet, remarkably, they kept protesting and demanding change. For these activists there was no going back, however dim the prospects of success appeared to be. The Arab Spring was a life-enhancing, political rollercoaster with deadly consequences for all those that lost.

An African Perspective

While in Zimbabwe I talked about this struggle with the Movement for Democratic Change (MDC) Senator David Coltart, the Minister of State for Culture, Education and Sport, as he and I and our two daughters, Charlotte and Beth, walked in the beautiful Matobo Hills just outside Bulawayo to visit the grave of Cecil Rhodes. Coltart was more than a bit interested in the struggle unfolding in Libya, since Gaddafi was no stranger to the struggle for freedom in Africa. After failing to become the Middle East's pre-eminent Arab nationalist leader in the 1970s, Gaddafi turned towards Africa and pronounced himself a great African leader. Through his financial sponsorship of the African Union and sub-Saharan African leaders, Gaddafi managed to reposition himself as a powerful regional player. Despite the humiliation of military failure in Chad, Gaddafi spread his tentacles far and wide including into southern Africa.

In Zimbabwe he had helped prop up his friend Robert Mugabe after he seized white-owned farms as a prelude to the 2002 general election. Gaddafi gave Mugabe $1 million towards his 2002 electoral campaign, as well as troops to beat MDC supporters into submission, while exhorting Muslims to rise up against white Zimbabweans. In exchange, Mugabe provided Gaddafi with 10,000 Zimbabwean passports to sidestep the international sanctions regime and supported initiatives like the one to create a United States of Africa. Gaddafi gave Mugabe further assistance in his battle with the MDC in the run-up to the 2008 election, even though, by then, Zimbabwe was in a state of total collapse. In the event, the election was won by Morgan Tsvangirai but stolen by Mugabe after he rigged just enough votes to force a second run-off. Tsvangirai finally abandoned the run-off after Zanu-PF unleashed a further wave of violence across the country in which over 200 MDC officials died. A few months later the MDC reluctantly entered into talks with Zanu-PF, sponsored by the Southern African Development Community (SADC), which resulted in the Global Political Agreement. This in turn led to the establishment of a unity government in which Morgan Tsvangirai took the premiership under the presidency of Robert Mugabe, who increasingly came to rely on the support of Gaddafi and the Chinese to prop up his embattled regime.

It was not surprising then that Coltart kept a keen eye on the conflagration in Libya, since a Gaddafi downfall meant an important nail in the coffin of Mugabe's attempt to cling to power through repressive means. Coltart had played a central part in the democratic struggle against Mugabe's excesses for the previous twenty years. He was one of the foremost human rights lawyers in Southern Africa, having previously defended many of the principal political and human rights activists in Zimbabwe. I had met him through my involvement with the Zimbabwean Defence and Aid Foundation, which I helped set up to provide defence resources to opposition and human rights figures facing unjust prosecution. It was instructive to hear him on the subject of human rights and on whether democratic reform movements should compromise their values in favour of going into coalition with dictators in order to avoid further bloodshed. In the case of the MDC it had withstood a series of murderous onslaughts during a succession of flawed elections, with little practical support from the international community. As it did so, Coltart became increasingly caught up in the interplay between law, politics, diplomacy and democratic reform. He came to believe that while it was important to advocate in favour of human rights, what was needed in Zimbabwe were men and women who were prepared to put their heads above the parapet and fight politically for democratic change and a restoration of the rule of law. He therefore stood for parliament and became first an MP and then a senator.

Yet once in office, he faced a series of difficult decisions about going into government with his nemesis, Robert Mugabe, under the power-sharing deal known as the Global Political Agreement (GPA) worked out by the SADC in 2009. As one of the principal negotiators of the GPA, Coltart was immediately subjected to criticism by former human rights colleagues, who believed the MDC had effectively sold out, particularly as an unconvinced West continued to impose a range of sanctions on the new National Unity government. By 2008 Coltart found himself between a rock and a hard place. Zimbabwe was on its knees, with outbreaks of cholera, rampant inflation, no food in the shops and little prospect of either an internal armed uprising or any external political help. Should the MDC seize the opportunity of trying to improve the lot of ordinary Zimbabweans, however incrementally, or maintain its political purity and refuse to serve in government, thus sentencing its battered supporters to four more years of repression in the political wilderness? This was a question that many opposition figures and intellectuals were asking themselves in places like Libya. In the end Coltart chose an uncertain future with a tyrant, who was just as idiosyncratic as Gaddafi.

One factor that weighed heavily with him was the failure of the international community to come to the defence of ordinary Zimbabweans. He later talked about this difficult choice at the Beyond Borders International Festival in Scotland in the summer of 2010. By then, he was desperate to get some international sanctions removed to give Mugabe enough of an incentive to stay within the terms of the GPA, which had finally begun to bear some fruit. As Minister of Education, Coltart had made a difference to the lives of Zimbabweans by restocking classrooms with millions of books for the first time in a decade. It was a small but significant indication of what the MDC could do in government to change things from within. But he needed more to keep the GPA from collapsing. Despite an initial rethink on sanctions, the new coalition government quickly reverted to the hardline position of the previous Labour administration.

As chairman of the BHRC I, along with the chairman of the Bar Council, Desmond Browne QC, visited Zimbabwe to conduct a rule of law audit in November 2009. In our report 'A Place in the Sun: Zimbabwe and the Rule of Law', we narrated that there had been no improvement whatsoever in the rule of law. The new government used the report to justify its own stance. I felt distinctly queasy about this outcome and told Henry Bellingham, the FCO Minister responsible for Southern Africa in June 2010 that in other respects the GPA was indeed worth supporting. Economically speaking things had improved under the GPA, especially after dollarisation. There was less violence in the villages and more food in the shops. Moreover, there was a slow but noticeable increase in freedom of expression, with people being at least able to access opposition newspapers.

For Coltart the impending constitutional reform process under the GPA had to be supported by the international community since it was the only game in town. Mugabe was not going to live forever. He had visited a medical clinic in Singapore eight times in 2010 and often fell asleep in cabinet. More significantly, the Zimbabwean people were peace-loving and extremely unlikely to ever take up arms. Since neither Britain nor South Africa, nor indeed the international community, had been willing to intervene, even under R2P principles, some sort of bargain had to be struck to stop the Securocrats from carrying out another bloodbath if Mugabe died. It was better to do this through politics than through the barrel of a gun, however distasteful that might be for those who had suffered under Mugabe. Coltart's arguments resonated with many who heard him speak. They evidently regarded him as a man of deep principle despite his advocacy of compromise. Even the radical lawyer, Michael Mansfield, stood up at the Beyond Borders debate to declare that he had changed his mind on the issue of sanctions and constructive engagement. It was a decision that democratic movements were often forced to face.

Many human rights advocates abhorred such compromise as it undermined the international community's commitment to uphold principles of law and justice and rewarded tyrants for not playing by the rules. Yet these advocates rarely found themselves in the political position that Coltart did. Should strict adherence to the rule of law trump the responsibility to protect civilian life and liberty in such circumstances? It was a question that many rebel movements were now asking in the MENA region as the prospect of an outright democratic victory began to recede and incumbent regimes began again to flex their muscles.

As we walked and talked in the Matobo Hills I began to understand how different the circumstances in Libya were from those in Zimbabwe. Coltart's decision to enter into the National Unity government was predicated on the assumption that no Western or African government would ever be prepared to intervene to support the struggle for peaceful democratic change in Zimbabwe. Despite the West's rhetoric in favour of non-violent democratic change, little practical help was ever given. This was ironic in the light of the previous Labour administration's avowed stance against all movements that sought to use violence in support of political change, post 9/11. However, the intervention in Libya began to change the calculus of democratic reform movements as to whether to seek compromise with dictatorship. It created a certain nervousness within regimes, such as the military junta ruling Burma, about the ability to resist all calls for democratic reform. As we finished our walk, I was beginning to realise how the British intervention in the Libya was starting to affect the calculations of other movements and regimes around the world. The stakes were even higher than I had imagined.[1]

In Search of Funding

I returned to London ten days later with renewed vigour, to meet Nick Latta from the FCO Libya desk, who was now in exile in London. Like most of the other FCO Libya desk officials, he was still ruminating over the loss of his personal belongings after Gaddafi burnt down the British Embassy in Tripoli in retaliation for the alleged death of one of his sons in a NATO missile strike. Latta advised that it would be better to submit the application in broad terms that covered the activities set out in the MoU, and then revise it with more detail as the submission progressed. The bid was eventually communicated to the FCO in the following terms:

> We hope that the draft proposal provides the basis for a successful bid, but recognise that it may be subject to revision and discussion between the FCO and the BHRC. We stand ready to assist in any way we can; Mark Muller will be available for further consultation. Please note that this is a core generic bid with a comprehensive approach concerning the rule of law in Libya, but designed flexibly for both the Arab Partnership Fund and the Human Rights & Democracy Fund to pick and choose aspects of the bid, if either programme deemed it appropriate.

As it turned out, the bid was timely. Following the London conference on Libya 29–30 March 2011, the UK became the driving force behind the establishment of the Libya Contact Group to serve as a focal point of contact with the Libyan people. It first met in Doha on 13 April 2011 to co-ordinate international policy on Libya and became a forum for discussion of humanitarian and post-conflict support.

It was within this context that in late April 2011 the UN Secretary-General appointed Ian Martin as a special advisor 'to coordinate the UN's post-conflict planning, and to engage as appropriate with multilateral and bilateral actors'. Martin attended the Contact Group and would later become head of the integrated UN Support Mission to Libya (UNSMIL) after a bitterly divided Security Council voted unanimously to establish UNSMIL on 16 September 2011. According to Martin his brief was 'to maintain a light footprint and deliver targeted assistance corresponding to Libyan wishes, respectful of national ownership while advocating UN principles.[2] This 'light footprint' approach was adopted following the UN's experience of peace-keeping in Somalia (1992–4), Kosovo (1998) and a 2002 review by Lakhdar Brahimi, who recommended its adoption in relation to the UN mission in Afghanistan.[3] From spring 2011 onwards Martin endeavoured to carry out a 'pre-assessment' process but recognised that 'with the conflict's outcome uncertain, UN engagement with Libyan actors was a sensitive issue'. As he rightly observed, 'Planning required learning the views of Libyans themselves, but which Libyans?' This question would come to haunt both the UK and UN stabilisation efforts in Libya.

However, it would take until the second meeting of the Contact Group in Rome on 5 May 2011 before any practical measures were agreed about how to approach the issue of stabilisation. The meeting established an International Stabilisation Response Team (ISRT) to build a shared international understanding of Libya's interim stabilisation needs, which again was to be led by the UK but included French and Italian technocrats to pool experience from Afghanistan and Iraq. The ISRT was due to visit Libya from 20 May to 8 June 2011 and its report was designed to identify the immediate challenges to stabilisation in NTC-controlled areas; assess the likely short- to medium-term challenges; and feed into a NTC stabilisation plan.

From its inception the ISRT was heavily influenced by Mahmoud Jibril and his circle. This circle enjoyed important international relationships and included men such as Mahmoud Shamman in Doha, Arif Ali Nayid in Abu Dhabi, Ibrahim Dabbashi in New York and Abd al-Hafiz Qudur in Italy. Together they helped shape the ISRT's perceptions of the NTC and the rebels. According to Peter Bartu, who was present in Benghazi at the time as a member of the UN's Standby Mediation Support Unit, which I later joined, this circle harboured 'an ambition to orchestrate a managed transition of power from the elder Gaddafi towards something that would realise the work they had begun under Saif-al Islam'. They had not foreseen or intended to ferment the revolution that occurred until Saif al-Islam made his fateful speech of 20 February 2011. In the run up to that speech Saif had approached certain leaders of the protests spreading across Libya on 16 February with a view to quelling them peacefully. On 17 February Hafiz Ghoga flew to Tripoli and pressed Saif to implement the political and economic reforms he had promised in the 2000s. Credible reports suggest Saif's officials drafted a speech on 18 February recommitting the regime to these reforms, but it was not to be. In the end Saif sided with his father and brothers. However, this circle still entertained the desire to effect a managed transition and mediated solution, particularly after the military stalemate of April and May 2011.

By the time the Contact Group met again in May the NTC had fleshed out its vision of a political transition in a roadmap published on 5 May 2011. Drafted by Ba'ja with input from Jibril, the roadmap was predicated on some form of negotiated ceasefire with Gaddafi, after which Gaddafi would abdicate and be replaced by a transitional or interim government drawn from the NTC, in which three technocrats, plus two senior armed and two security officials from the old regime, would serve in an effort to help avoid the chaos that engulfed Iraq in the post-conflict phase. A National Congress would then be convened to replace the NTC and appoint a committee to draft a constitution, which, if approved by the Congress, would go to a national referendum. If publicly ratified, parliamentary and presidential elections were to follow leading to the formation of a new government, all within a timeline of just nine months. It was this plan that Islamists rejected.

Despite publication of the roadmap the US expressed concern at the Contact meeting over the lack of any perceivable practical plan to stabilise Tripoli following Gaddafi's removal. According to Peter Cole, a senior analyst for International Crisis Group in Libya, these conversations led Arif Ali Nayid, head of a telecommunications firm in Libya, and a coordinating figure for a satellite node communication network between Dubai and Tripoli, to generate a two-page memo proposing a 'Tripoli Taskforce' to help liberate and then stabilise Tripoli. Nayid had been brought into the support office within the Executive Office of the NTC by Jibril on 4 April after he had made contact with the UK and US governments through Tony Blair's office. On 22 April Nayid met Abdul Jalil, who agreed to the idea of the Taskforce. Thereafter he met the ISRT where he sought to 'interpose' the Taskforce as the ISRT's Libyan interlocutor on the basis that 'the ISRT alone would not receive sufficient buy-in from Libyans'.[4]

Following publication of this plan a kind of paralysis regarding decision-making seemed to descend upon FCO stabilisation officials, who took the view that much of the rule of law streams cited in the BHRC MoU could only begin *after* the conflict had ended and an all-inclusive government had been appointed with access to unfrozen development funds. Only then would New Libya be in a position to realistically tackle issues such as the independence of the judiciary and detailed constitutional reform. They therefore asked whether we might produce a more limited proposal shorn of many of the elements of the MoU except for perhaps transitional justice. I replied that the way the application was written meant that the FCO was at liberty to slice off the element concerning transitional justice if it felt it was necessary.

As a result of these exchanges the BHRC submitted a slightly amended version to the FCO on 19 May 2011, focusing on transitional justice, constitutional reform and the protection of fundamental freedoms, with a budget of approximately £340,000, following a FCO meeting with the NTC Minister of Justice on 17 May. By then the Executive Office of the NTC had expanded to fourteen portfolios. Although I was unable to meet the Minister on that occasion, an FCO official told me that 'during a meeting this afternoon the Minister did say that he is interested in Bar Council work and is looking forward to any future work that the Bar Council will be doing in Benghazi'. However, in contrast to the view of some officials, the BHRC continued to argue that there was a discernible and pressing need to assist the NTC in all the rule of law areas from the get go, and well before any post-conflict interim government came into being.

All of this was in line with a further request for assistance made by the NTC Minister of Justice Muhammad al-Alagi to Lord Brennan (the former chairman of the Bar Council) at a meeting held at the House of Lords with Jason McCue, and the UK's exiled Ambassador to Libya, Richard Northern, on 18 May 2011. Recognising the help that independent advisors with real experience could give the NTC, al-Alagi expressed his desire for us to return to Benghazi to advise the Council on dialogue, transitional justice and constitutional reform issues as soon as possible. This was significant, as the NTC was generally wary of being seen to request, let alone accept, offers of international assistance on such sensitive matters. The request for assistance was repeated to me by al-Alagi's officials a few days later. They specifically asked that we return to Libya at the very latest by the start of July. McCue then submitted his own application for funding based upon this request. Ambassador Richard Northern politely noted the request and told McCue that he would get back to him, but he never did.

Richard Northern was a man with enormous experience of the Arab world and was part of a fast dwindling band of seasoned 'Arabist' ambassadors known as the Camel Corps. Steeped in regional language and expertise, the Camel Corps was becoming dangerously over-stretched as the Arab Spring made its impact felt on the resources of the FCO. It included men like Christopher Prentice, whom we met in Benghazi, as well as John Jenkins whom I met in Syria, and Dominic Asquith, who would both later replace Northern as ambassadors to Libya. All were Oxbridge-educated classicists who had entered the FCO in the 1970s. Prentice and Northern trained at the renowned FCO-funded language academy, the Middle East Centre for Arabic Studies (MECAS), located in the village of Shemlan high above the hills of Beirut, where students would learn 10,000 words of vocabulary in under a year. MECAS was regarded as a 'spy school' by numerous Middle East governments. It finally closed in 1978 after thirty years of service, due to the advent of the Lebanese civil war. Yet its impact on HMG's capacity to operate in the Middle East was felt for another generation, as the likes of Northern and Prentice immersed themselves in the cultural and political mores of Middle Eastern countries and their attendant elites.

By the time the Arab Spring began in 2011 there was little comparable expertise coming in through the younger ranks of diplomats, who had, in any case, switched their attention towards more lucrative postings in the UN, EU, NATO and Washington DC. As the then Defence Select Committee chair Rory Stewart MP has noted, linguistic or deep country knowledge became irrelevant for promotion after 2001 when Sir Michael Jay, then head of the FCO, deliberately reduced the weight previously given to knowledge of languages and geographical areas in favour of administrative skills. Stewart's observation about the need for the FCO to foster greater local diplomatic expertise was being borne out before our very eyes, as FCO officials with little or no experience of Libya replaced the previous country team we were dealing with, and continued to dither about whether to back the BHRC rule of law initiative. A few days after the meeting in the Lords the BHRC received this letter from the Arab Partnership Fund:

Our thanks for your proposal and my apologies that we've not been able to give you a clearer response from the Arab Partnership Fund sooner – we are in the midst of our review process – but I know you and Jason are keen for clarity.

In terms of AP, we have reviewed the bid, but as plans for Libya assistance develop it's become clear that AP will not now be involved in funding and that any Libya bids will have to be considered as part of a broader package of Libya assistance. We had got as far as assessing that the proposal was too wide-ranging for us to fund in its current form, particularly as it was too early for a number of aspects to be implemented. And we were starting to discuss with Embassy colleagues whether there might be a priority within the bid that would make sense to focus on now– hence Andrew's request to you. But it became clear this would also need to be looked at within that broader Libya package – an assessment team are now being deployed and as I understand project support is likely to be considered in the context of recommendations from that assessment.

In terms of contacts going forward, my colleague in the tri-departmental Conflict Pool (FCO/DFID/MoD), G . . . D . . . , is now coordinating potential funding along with Libya colleagues – I am copying her and Nick here, and she now has a copy of your original proposal.

I hope that provides some clarity.

With best regards,

Arab Partnership Team | MENAD

Mediating the Libyan Conflict

During this period, I went to see Jonathan Powell, the former chief of staff to Tony Blair, to discuss Libya in relation to mediation and dialogue issues. Jonathan was also a senior advisor with the Centre for Humanitarian Dialogue. In early 2011 I had helped him and Martin Griffiths set up a new mediation outfit in London called Inter Mediate. Jonathan was intent on using his experience as the UK's chief negotiator on Northern Ireland to wider effect. I therefore gave him a detailed account of my trip to Benghazi and reported on the growing need for some sort of inter-militia dialogue process. In late April I attended a meeting in the COBRA room of the Cabinet Office with Jonathan Powell, Richard Northern, Hugh Powell, head of Libya operations in the Cabinet Office, and other HMG officials working on Libya. It was a very instructive meeting vis-à-vis government thinking, as it soon became apparent just how little appetite there was on the part of officials for any initiative that sought to mediate a negotiated settlement with Gaddafi.

The government made it crystal clear that it was not prepared to fund any mediation initiative that involved Gaddafi staying in Libya or give any succour to his potential defectors about the future of the regime. It wanted to avoid sending any signal that slowed the rate of defection.

More significantly, in the view of the UK government, Libya was less tribally divided than was publicly claimed by the media. Gaddafi ran Libya with the help of around 600 influential families who, although linked to the tribal and clan system, only paid lip service to it. Many of these families lived in Tripoli despite having homes in the outlying clan areas. Turn these families and you turned the regime – or so the theory went. This analysis was borne out to some extent by the work of sociologist Mohammed Bamyeh, who examined twenty-eight of the declarations issued by tribal leaders between 23 February and 9 March 2011. He found that 'the vast majority highlighted national unity or national salvation rather than tribal interests. These declarations also demonstrate that Libya's tribes are not homogenous entities, but rather are composed of diverse members with varying social and economic backgrounds. This reality reflects the nature of Libyan society as a whole, which has a 90% urban population in which inter-marriages across tribal lines are common.'[5]

According to UK government experts then, defection was the key to success and any attempt to present potential defactors with an alternative diplomatic scenario was counter-productive to the ultimate objective of removing Gaddafi from power. All attempts at mediation were viewed through this policy prism. Officially the UK government took the view that all settlement initiatives had to 'dovetail with UN efforts to mediate the conflict' even though it knew that the UN was unlikely to ever effect such a settlement. On 10 March 2011 the UN Secretary-General Ban Ki-moon had appointed Abd al-Ilah al-Khatib, a former foreign minister of Jordan, as his special envoy to try to mediate a non-violent transition, but to little effect. I soon realised that the government's support of the UN's mandate to the exclusion of all others was based more on the UN's inability as opposed to ability to effect reconciliation. For example, on 25 February 2011 Tony Blair called Muammar Gaddafi twice in an effort to get him to abdicate and nego-tiate a solution in Libya. When asked by the Foreign Affairs Select Committee how Cameron reacted towards this initiative, the former Prime Minister replied that Mr Cameron 'was merely listening'.[6]

The position of the Cameron administration was succinctly set out in a joint opinion piece which Cameron and Sarkozy authored with Obama in the *New York Times*, which stated: 'So long as Gaddafi is in power, NATO and its coalition partners must maintain their operations so that civilians remain protected and the pressure on the regime builds. Then a genuine transition from dictatorship to an inclusive constitutional process can really begin, led by a new generation of leaders. For that transition to succeed, Colonel Gaddafi must go, and go for good.'

The sceptical disposition of the UK government and NTC certainly chimed with my own understanding of the outcome of previous efforts to mediate the conflict. While I was in Benghazi I took a call from Martin Griffiths, the former director of CHD and advisor to former Secretary-General, Kofi Annan. He informed me that Annan had been approached about possible African efforts to settle the conflict. At that time the Turks were lobbying hard to position themselves as primary mediators alongside the African Union (AU). An intelligence source in Ankara later confirmed that the Turks had opened talks with the rebels, who had sent a delegation to Ankara. I told Griffiths that from what I had seen I thought it unlikely that the Turks/AU would be acceptable to the rebel leadership, particularly given the Turks' previous scepticism over NATO's involvement in the conflict and the wisdom of supplying weapons to Misrata.

This was borne out a week or so after I left Benghazi in early April, when South African President Jacob Zuma, along with other AU officials, visited Tripoli to facilitate a cease-fire between the Council and Gaddafi to no avail. They had tried to broker a deal in which Gaddafi and his sons were to be allowed to stay in Libya, post-conflict. In so doing, they fundamentally failed to comprehend the level of sacrifice that the people of Benghazi and Misrata had made in defence of their revolution. Although a succession of other mediators made the journey to Tripoli over the next few months to try to convince Gaddafi to step down, none was successful. This even included the multi-millionaire Russian chess master and head of the World Chess Federation Kirsan Ilyumzhinov, who once played a series of games with 'Brother Leader'.

Many of these mediators failed to realise the impact of the conflict on the Libyan people's psyche. The brave people of Misrata had soldiered on for weeks under severe attack from Gaddafi's forces, who continued to encircle and bombard the embattled town. Their hatred of Gaddafi had grown stronger rather than weaker and they were determined to defeat him. The popular mood was against the idea of a negotiated transition. There were also growing demands, including some from Islamic elements, for immediate elections because of concerns about how NTC members had been initially selected. It was evident to me that the Libyan conflict was going to end with military defeat or victory for one side or the other, on the basis of which those in control on the ground would press their claim to exercise political power. The level of rebel sacrifice, together with the personality of Gaddafi, and the British government's determination to remove him at gun-point, meant this conflict was unlikely to be resolved through dialogue. Yet this policy of all-out war made it more not less necessary for the UK to develop its strategies on reconciliation, transitional justice and rule-of-law issues, especially if Tripoli fell to competing rebel factions rather than through defection, thereby creating a dangerous constitutional and security vacuum.

The Need for Rebel Dialogue

As I waited for the FCO to get back to us on funding, I continued to watch as NATO stepped up its bombing of loyalist targets. During this period, the UK made further covert efforts to weaken the resolve of Gaddafi's acolytes to try to convince certain critical players to defect. The problem was that while government experts may have been right in concluding that the tribal system was not as strong as one might have suspected in Libya, they were wrong in thinking defection was the way to effect regime change. In reality, tribes like the Warfallah and Imazighen wanted to increase power for themselves. They would go on to provide much of the manpower for the final assault on Tripoli.

Tensions were emerging between the political leaders of the NTC and the military leaders of the militias, as well as between the secular and

Islamic wings of the rebel movement, in addition to the historical regional antagonism between Tripoli, Benghazi and Fezzan, and between the fighters from Misrata and the Berber Mountains. These tensions found expression within Libya's developing civil society organisations. For example, the 17th February Martyrs Brigade in Benghazi was instrumental in creating the 17 February Coalition, while the Muslim Brotherhood was now behind the creation of the United Libyan Revolutionaries and the Youth Congregation, which were set up in a direct attempt to counter the Coalition's claim to revolutionary integrity.

During the course of April, Nayid helped the NTC expand from thirty-one members to forty, incorporating delegates from twenty-three local councils from western, central and southern Libya in an attempt to be more representative. These delegates were finally brought to Benghazi on a Qatari military plane on 12 May. But while the NTC formally recognised the existence of the tribes it did not incorporate them into its governing structures. Many of these delegates, and indeed tribes, had very different ideas to Jibril and Nayid about how Tripoli should be taken, and the transition. Nayid's sudden prominence was fast becoming an issue. So Abdul Jalil responded by curtailing the growing influence of the Tripoli Taskforce by balancing it against other forces and groups seeking to play a role in the fall of Tripoli and transition. He rejected three Tripolitanians put forward by Nayid as delegates to the NTC in favour of a list put forward by the 17 February Coalition and Sallabi, which included Abdul Aradi, a Brotherhood member who had escaped from Tripoli in April. He was selected after Sallabi and others used their international contacts to convene Islamists in a 'National Gathering' in Istanbul in late April.

Jalil's formal authorisation of Nayid's Tripoli Taskforce on 22 May sparked further tensions. While Nayid's team spent the next two weeks developing the Taskforce idea with two UK and French officers, the issue as to who should take charge between Nayid and Aradi came to a head. In an explosive meeting on 8 June, the day the ISRT completed its visit to Benghazi, Nayid argued that it would be foolish to appoint the Muslim Brotherhood or the LIFG as head because the NTC 'needed someone who had an understanding with Western allies and whose motivations were clear'. According to accounts later given to the International Crisis Group analyst Peter Cole, Aradi and the Tripoli representatives threatened to resign while Belhaj refused to bring his group under Nayid after Jibril refused to acknowledge him. The next day the Taskforce team packed up and relocated to Abu Dhabi from where Nayid placed the team under Jibril's authority as a Stabilisation Committee. Nayid had been run out of town. As a result the Qataris increasingly focused their military sponsorship towards Sallabi and Belhaj's networks, directing further shipments of arms to Sallabi's younger brother, Ismail, and away from Jibril's nework. They continued to support rebels from Misrata through a separate channel. The Qataris' change of tack was also based on their assessment of the Islamists' fighting capacities. They were intent on taking Tripoli by force without a mediated transition by using Nalat and Nafusa Mountain fighters to push towards the coast under NATO cover arranged by the Qataris. In contrast Jibril continued to plan for an internal uprising in Tripoli by training a small group of Tripolitanians to secure key installations supplemented by NATO strikes on a list of twenty-eight command centres he had been given by a defector. He now focused his attention on France, the UAE and certain Zintan commanders in a vain attempt to match the Islamists' increasingly powerful network. There was then an increasing need for some sort of dialogue process within the rebel alliance itself between these competing factions if, that is, the post-conflict period was not to descend into a violent rush for power and influence.

The prospect of inter-rebel rivalry was much more likely if Tripoli was captured by the rebel militias. Getting some agreement over future civilian control of government and political reforms, Disarmament, Demobilisation and Reintegration (DDR) and transitional justice mechanisms, both within the rebel militias and within elements of the old regime and civil society, was therefore vital. That is why the FCO had to settle its external funding policy towards non-state mediators, humanitarian and human rights organisations quickly if New Libya was to capitalise on non-state expertise in this area. The NTC had few resources of its own to deploy, given that all Libya's assets abroad were frozen. Moreover, the FCO had neither the manpower, the expertise nor the impartiality to enter into a dialogue with tribal leaders and rebel factions, especially given its previous suppression of Islamists such as the LIFG, who had dared try to overthrow the Gaddafi regime. Jonathan and I did raise the need for greater inter-militia and civil society dialogue in our meeting with UK government officials, but I detected a reluctance to involve non-state actors, other than those close to the security services, in the development of relations with the NTC.

In the absence of immediate government support, some humanitarian organisations funded their own scoping missions in Libya. Within a few weeks of my visit to Benghazi, CHD had sent out David Gorman to make contact with the NTC, with a view to running a series of dialogue initiatives with local civil society actors in rebel-held areas. I had discussed the work of CHD with Dr Said Ali while I was in Benghazi. He had previously worked for the Red Crescent and knew the interim CHD director Angelo Gnaedinger, who had served as head of policy for the Red Cross. We both felt that while there was no role for a non-state actor to mediate between Gaddafi and the rebels in light of the UN mandate, there was important work that could be done to help local communities and civil society deal with some of the effects of the violence ripping through the country as a result of the civil war. There remained an urgent need to initiate a more general dialogue between all the different stakeholders about the future needs of New Libya, particularly if there was to be buy-in in relation to any subsequent stabilisation plan adopted by the NTC and the international community. While many countries disagreed over the ways to reconstruct society in the aftermath of conflict, few, if any, formally denied the essential role that civil society should play in a peace-building and reconstruction process.

In countries that lack a fully representative democratic government, civil society is often the only vehicle through which to vocalise – on behalf of the men, women and children of all the religious or ethnic groupings – the most effective and constructive way to develop and implement a lasting peace in their society. Libyan society had the right to be consulted and engaged in any settlement that determined its future. Governments and other key stakeholders were obliged to take into consideration the views and recommendations of civil society in any peace or post-conflict negotiations. This was particularly so where, as in the case of Tunisia, Egypt and Libya, civil society had played such a crucial role in the liberation of the country from the yoke of authoritarianism and in the articulation of the revolutions' core democratic values.

CHD needed significant funding from state or international donors to pursue these processes on any meaningful scale. However, British officials continued to be more consumed with the issue of loyalist defections and how to promote a revolution from within the Libyan regime than with the political fissures developing within the rebel movement or how non-state actors might help smooth the transition from conflict to peace. By the end of May 2011 it appeared that these officials were almost exclusively focused on the military campaign to the exclusion of other important considerations concerning transition. This lack of interest would later come to haunt New Libya as it attempted to rebuild its shattered society from the ashes of the conflict. Interestingly, the FCO would take a different tack in relation to Bahrain where it would actively support dialogue efforts between the government and the opposition as well as rule of law reform.

As my attention turned to Bahrain, I remember being pulled up short some six weeks after I got back from Benghazi, while attending the launch of the Beyond Borders play *Do We Look Like Refugees?* at the Riverside Studios in London, after being shown messages from Marie Colvin, who was still holed up in Misrata. Her message described how dozens of civilians were dying every day as we enjoyed the cultural delights of London and waited to hear whether the BHRC would be given the resources it needed to help preserve and act upon the evidence of the very atrocities on which she was reporting.

Marie was a truly remarkable journalist. She had lost an eye while reporting on the conflict between the Sri Lankan government and the Tamil Tigers. Her eye-patch made her into an unforgettable character. Marie joined the *Sunday Times* twenty-five years ago after getting bored as the UPI bureau chief in Paris. From that moment on she was hooked on war reporting, covering dozens of conflicts in Afghanistan, Iraq, Somalia, Chechnya and East Timor, where she stayed behind in a UN compound to prevent the massacre of 1,500 women and children. She literally shamed the UN into not withdrawing, thereby becoming an internationally renowned figure. Colvin later admitted to one friend that staying in the compound was one of the proudest moments of her life. During this period she built a remarkable circle of friends around the world, retaining a sense of fun and generosity despite the traumatic nature of her work.

I knew her and her second husband, the Bolivian journalist Juan Carlos Gumucio. Carlos, like Marie, was a larger-than-life character who partied and worked hard, but ended up shooting himself in the heart ten years ago. Even though they had split up by then, she was devastated. As I read her e-mail messages to her friends I was immediately transported back to Freedom Square. The next day I called the FCO for an update on the BHRC bid, but to little avail. They were still deliberating over how to fund external civil society organisations, following the Department for International Development (DFID) Secretary of State, Andrew Mitchell's decision to send the first-ever International Stabilisation Response Team (ISRT) to Benghazi. It would report back to the International Contact Group sometime in June.

Towards a New Middle East Policy

While FCO officials dealing with Libya deliberated on what strategy to adopt, their political masters in Whitehall were busy framing an altogether more dynamic and radical shift of policy towards the MENA region. The contrast between the two approaches was startling. It soon became clear that Cameron's decision to intervene in Libya was not just based on moral and humanitarian grounds but was part of a wider geo-political response to the Arab Spring. A fresh strategic vision of the West's role in the Middle East was being mapped out. The emergence of a new governing reality in the Middle East started on 2 May 2011 with the news of the death of Osama Bin Laden. While not exactly heralding the end of the 'war on terror', it certainly hinted at its demise and replacement with a broader-based, more positive approach. In a statement made to the House of Commons on 3 May

2011, David Cameron had this to say on Bin Laden's effect on the developments in Middle East:

> Mr Speaker, bin Laden and Gaddafi were said to have hated each other. But there was a common thread running between them. They both feared the idea that democracy and civil rights could take hold in the Arab World. While we should continue to degrade, dismantle and defeat the terrorist networks a big part of the long-term answer is the success of democracy in the Middle East and the conclusion of the Arab-Israeli peace process. For twenty years, bin Laden claimed that the future of the Muslim world would be his. But what Libya has shown – as Egypt and Tunisia before it – is that people are rejecting everything that bin Laden stood for. Instead of replacing dictatorship with his extremist totalitarianism, they are choosing democracy. Ten years on from the terrible tragedy of 9/11, with the end of bin Laden and the democratic awakening across the Arab world, we must seize this unique opportunity to deliver a decisive break with the forces of Al-Qaeda and its poisonous ideology which has caused so much suffering for so many years.

One day later, at the Lord Mayor's banquet at Mansion House in London, the Foreign Secretary William Hague delivered an even more emphatic speech on the importance of the Arab Spring uprisings. Hague declared 2011 to be 'a momentous year' where the 'confluence of events' occurring in the Middle East were so 'extraordinarily significant' that they were bound to 'change the course of history'. 'The eruption of democracy movements across the Middle East and North Africa is, even in its early stages, the most important development of the early twenty-first century, with potential long term consequences greater than either 9/11 or the global financial crisis in 2008,' he declared. According to Hague there were three lessons to be learnt: 'The first is that the forces that led to the Arab Spring will sweep more widely across the globe. Demands for open government, action against corruption and greater political participation will spread by themselves over time – not because Western nations are advocating them, but because they are the natural aspirations of all people everywhere.' Here, Hague encapsulated in a sentence the sheer democratic sweep and potential of the Arab Spring that David Coltart and I had talked about in Zimbabwe.

Hague's second lesson was that 'Governments that set their face against reform altogether – as Libya had done and Syria sadly was beginning to do – were doomed to failure. Simply refusing to address legitimate grievances or attempting to stamp them out will fail. The idea of freedom cannot be confined behind bars, however strong the lock.' This statement had huge strategic import as it implied that the West's obligations towards those protesting in favour of democratic reform might extend beyond merely providing humanitarian protection to backing regime change. The third lesson he identified concerned economics. He claimed that:

> while the people of Egypt and Tunisia made a monumental effort to bring change in their countries, the economic challenges they now face will be at least as great. There is a potentially explosive tension between people's expectations of immediate economic benefits from their revolutions and the need for these new governments to take difficult measures to open their economies and offer more opportunity to their citizens. We have to do our utmost to help the Arab world make a success of more open political systems and economies, and it is massively in our own interest to do so.

He ended his address by declaring that if the Arab Spring did lead to more open and democratic societies it would be the 'greatest advance for human rights and freedom since the end of the Cold War'. If it did not, however, he predicted that we could see a collapse back into more authoritarian regimes, conflict and increased terrorism in North Africa, on the very doorstep of Europe. The scenarios and decisions facing the West could not have been more starkly set out. These policy pronouncements would become the yardstick by which Cameron's coalition government and the FCO would, and should, be judged, particularly in relation to the stabilisation of the region.

A Seismic Shift in Policy?

This change in strategic vision by Western leaders was crystallised when Barack Obama gave a speech on 19 May 2011, in which he tried to redefine America's relationship with the Arab world. Obama had been previously criticised for his failure to give a sufficient lead in the wake of the Arab Spring. This speech was billed as the US's historic response to it and built on an earlier speech he had made in Cairo in 2009 at the start of his tenure, which had been well-received. In that earlier speech he had called for a new beginning in relations between the US and the Muslim world, in words that to some extent prefigured the aspirations of the Arab Spring. Obama now declared that the United States and the West intended to pour billions of dollars into the Middle East in support of Egypt, Tunisia and other countries embracing democracy, on a scale of aid similar to that given to former communist countries after the fall of the Berlin Wall in 1989.

He told a packed audience that the US must commit itself unequivocally to nurture and support the Arab Spring and back human rights for all in the region who were willing to make the transition from repression to democracy. 'Failure to speak to the broader aspirations of ordinary people will only feed suspicion that has festered for years that the United States pursues our own interests at their expense [. . .] A failure to change our approach threatens a deepening spiral of division between the United States and the Muslim communities.' That was why the US had to open a new 'chapter' in US diplomacy, which placed Washington on the side of popular uprisings not only in Egypt, Tunisia and Libya, but also in Syria and Bahrain – a long-time ally of America. 'We have insisted publicly and privately that mass arrests and brute force are at odds with the universal rights of Bahrain's citizens, and will not make legitimate calls for reform to go away,' Obama said.

Yet crucially, Obama failed to make a single reference to Saudi Arabia. For seasoned commentators like Robert Fisk of *The Independent*, Obama's speech was pure rhetoric. 'It was the same old story,' he wrote, opining that such declarations were unlikely to stop America 'giving unconditional craven support to Israel' or lead to the end of the siege of Gaza, talks with Hamas, or restrictions on the further colonisation of Arab land. While the more democratic-reform-minded wing of the State Department might have won out against those more concerned to defend the US's vital oil interest in the internal policy debate about how to respond to the Arab Spring, Fisk believed that business with the dictators of the Arab world would continue just as before, albeit in a different form.[7]

After all, Obama's initial response to the protests in Cairo's Tahrir Square had been to send veteran diplomat Frank Wisner to Egypt. Wisner had been stationed in Cairo between 1986 and 1991 and had been instrumental in getting Egypt to support the US in the first Gulf War of 1991. He was a very close friend of Mubarak and urged him to step down, but not until September. Wisner later told a security conference in Munich, shortly after his Cairo trip: 'You need to get a national consensus around the pre-conditions of the next step forward, and the President must stay in office in order to steer those changes through.' But while Obama might initially have hedged his bets in relation to Egypt, these new declarations did point to a new and radical political dispensation.

The direction of policy was quickly reiterated in a joint article by Obama and Cameron, published in *The Times* just after Obama's speech on 19 May.[8] They now publicly proclaimed democracy or some variant of representative government as the only viable long-term model of political development for the Middle East region. For decades, ordinary people had spoken of the need for radical reform only to be met by a wall of silence, until, that is, Tarek Bouazizi set himself ablaze. Now that the people had spoken with their blood, it ill behoved any US or UK leader to turn their back on those who gave up their lives for democratic freedom. Having imposed a 'war on terror' upon an entire region, in which Western values were trumpeted as the only alternative to Islamic extremism, there was very little option other than to embrace what was occurring on the streets of Cairo, Benghazi and even Manama. Obama and Cameron may only have heeded the call for democratic change after their client regimes failed to control the situation, but heed the call they eventually did. In their article they both recognised that the political landscape had changed forever and that some form of democratic reform, even in places like Bahrain, was probably inevitable if long-term stability was to be achieved. These speeches and articles provided a clear policy framework by which civil society could hold the UK government to account.

Such new public policy pronouncements contrasted with the early reaction of other policymakers such as Tony Blair, who had argued for 'managed change' by the Mubarak regime. This recommendation was quickly blown out of the political water by the protesters in Tahrir Square, never to be repeated by Cameron, Sarkozy or Obama. The idea that an autocratic ruler who had stifled all reform for the better part of thirty years could engineer a meaningful process of democratic reform was extremely doubtful. For many radical commentators the protests in Tahrir Square constituted high noon for both these Arab rulers and the Western statesmen who had courted them so assiduously, both in and out of government. A new democratic spirit and narrative was emerging in which old elites held little authority.

Although this manifested itself most potently in the Middle East during the Arab Spring, it was also evident in the West. Throughout the summer of 2011 groups of ordinary people – young and old, rich and poor, black and white – began to eschew official political and parliamentary processes to occupy a series of public spaces all over the Western world, in protest against the general lack of democracy, transparency, and economic and social fairness that underpinned capitalism in the world. For many radicals the Occupy movement pointed to a new dawn in global civic political consciousness, as ordinary people realised the awesome power of civil society when it was unshackled from the traditional political and diplomatic system.

Obama seemed to understand this shift in consciousness. That is why, a week after Blair issued his call for 'managed change' in Egypt, Obama moved from supporting to jettisoning Mubarak, a staunch US ally of some twenty-four years' standing, within the space of just twenty-four hours. Despite the somewhat overblown rhetoric of his 19 May speech, Obama's words did indicate a new strategic vision for the region. Henry Kissinger probably got it about right when he said that the US and UK had decided to move as much as possible in favour of human rights and values without courting strategic suicide by creating absolute chaos in places like Saudi Arabia. Only time would tell whether or not these policy pronouncements would usher in a new era of sustainable change in the Middle East. Yet, with the people of the region clamouring for reform, there seemed little point in not welcoming them. The policy changes made the role of civil society even more critical to the stabilisation and future political development of the region, nowhere more so than on the streets of Manama in Bahrain, where the tension between reform and repression continued to deepen with each passing day.

11. Bahrain

On the same day as Obama delivered his speech in Cairo, David Cameron met the Crown Prince of Bahrain at No. 10 Downing Street. The next day *The Independent* printed the following on its front page: 'As Obama tells the Middle East to embrace democracy [. . .] Cameron embraces tyranny.'[1] Yet this was by no means the whole story. A Downing Street spokesperson confirmed that the Prime Minister had 'stressed the importance of the government moving to a policy of reform rather than repression'. It was the Crown Prince who had sought to negotiate a reform package with the Shia opposition in early March 2011, before Saudi forces moved into the country to put an end to negotiations that threatened to galvanise their own Shia minority in favour of reform. The position was therefore much more complex than *The Independent* made out. There were both modernists and traditionalists within the ruling Bahraini family and government. Moreover, following widespread condemnation of the authorities' violent reaction to the protests and the killings of civilians, prominent members of the US administration such as Samantha Power were now committed to reform in Bahrain.

Yet Power had her work cut out. Further gruesome reports of human rights abuses perpetrated during the protests in Manama in March of 2011 continued to surface. By May the Bahrain authorities were preventing certain international human rights organisations from entering the country. Through my previous work I had established fairly good relations with Bahraini government departments with a legal focus, as well as with all the principal opposition political parties and societies. The BHRC enjoyed a standing that pre-dated the Arab Spring, as it was seen as more of a legal institution than an outright human rights advocacy NGO. I therefore decided to try to help promote dialogue between the parties. The sixty-four-thousand-dollar question was whether the government in Bahrain was willing or able to enter into the type of all-inclusive dialogue that William Hague now demanded? This was no easy question for the FCO to answer, let alone a civil society organisation like the BHRC, particularly when political events moved at such breath-taking speed. Different answers would lead to radically different policy approaches. Yet answer the question we had to – and in real time.

What seemed clear to me was that if the international human rights community wanted to stop further human rights abuses and help promote change in Bahrain it had to understand both the culture and political dynamics that underpinned the conflict there, as well as the personalities that dominated this small, but strategically important, island. It was within this context that in May 2011 I met with a number of leading members of the Shura Council and the Lower House of Parliament at the Bahraini Embassy in London. I had been asked to listen to their explanation of events in Bahrain and to see whether they had any ready solutions to the human rights crisis. They had been sent to Europe by the Bahraini government to try to counter some of the appalling press Bahrain was getting. The Embassy lined up a number of human rights organisations for them to talk to, including Amnesty International, HRW and the BHRC. The delegation included Ali Saleh al-Saleh who was appointed head of the Shura Council in 2010 and would become the Minister for Human Rights in 2012. As I stood in line to be received by the delegation I realised there was little point in repeating the identical concerns of the other more powerful human rights bodies. I therefore decided to concentrate on exploring whether there was any prospect for meaningful dialogue between the parties.

I had already talked extensively to a number of mediators about Bahrain, and had canvassed Jonathan Powell about what role Inter Mediate might play, given its links to Tony Blair and, through him, to the Crown Prince. I had been told by a source that the Crown Prince had recently met President Obama and his officials and had been told that the King had to 'open up a human rights file to deal with the abuses allegedly perpetrated by the state'. Pressure was growing upon Bahrain from all sides to engage in some form of dialogue that might heal the growing rift between the Sunni and Shia communities. It rapidly became obvious, however, that the Crown Prince still felt severely burnt by his earlier attempt at reconciliation and had little political capital to play with. Although it was said he did not necessarily believe the opposition Al-Wefaq was in the pay of the Iranians, he now had to concentrate on rebuilding relations with Saudi Arabia, his uncle the Prime Minister, and the ordinary Sunni community in Bahrain, who felt he had given too much away in the March dialogue process.

Sunni outrage at Shia conduct had quickly manifested itself during the protests, with the development of new movements such as the Sunni-dominated National Unity Gathering (NUG), which formed itself into a movement within ten days of the start of the protests, with the covert support of the government. It thereafter brought large sections of the Sunni constituency onto the streets of Manama to send a clear message of defiance to the Shia community and the likes of the Crown Prince. Rumours circulated that this was just part of another government-inspired propaganda coup, but it soon became apparent that a semi-independent new political force had been born, whether the government had intended this or not. Led by the Sunni opposition figure Sheikh Abdullatif al-Mahmood, the NUG continued to make its presence felt long enough after the crackdown to ensure that the Crown Prince knew that the moment for compromising with the Shia had passed.

None of these developments ruled out the possibility of creating a discrete, deniable, back channel, provided of course that confidentiality could be guaranteed. Throughout May of 2011 both Jonathan Powell and I met with various Al-Wefaq representatives in London to see whether such an arrangement was either of interest or possible. For its part, Al-Wefaq confirmed it was willing to enter talks in what it called 'a spirit of reconciliation' despite previously winning 64 per cent of the popular vote and holding eighteen out of the forty elected seats in parliament. One former MP stated that Al-Wefaq was now willing to agree to the seven guiding principles put forward earlier by the Crown Prince, even if they were no longer formally on the table following the imposition of martial law. He also accepted there was an urgent need to discuss the growing incidence of sectarianism and inequality. Thus on 30 May, two days before the end of the state of emergency, the prominent Shia cleric Sheikh Ali Salman communicated to the royal court that he was committed to the establishment of an elected civil rather than Islamic state, that retained the Al-Khalifa family at its head.

In response to the original seven-point plan put forward by the Crown Prince, Al-Wefaq had stated that any dialogue process could not occur without all the parties first accepting that the eventual goal would be that of an elected government. The former Al-Wefaq MP now added that no process could start without some reform to the five governates' electoral system before new elections were held on the 24 September, otherwise Al-Wefaq would boycott them. Powell counselled against imposing any conditions for talks, referring to how parties in Northern Ireland entered talks without pre-conditions. Both of us pushed the former MP on whether a transitional phase of reform might leave the Prime Minister with his position and powers intact. 'There is flexibility,' he replied.

We now encouraged him to widen the agenda to include security and economic issues as well as constitutional issues. For his part the former Al-Wefaq MP told me that the visiting Shura members I met at the Bahraini Embassy in May 2011 had no power whatsoever. 'They will say they support dialogue but they have no authority. Two weeks ago they said we didn't need one [dialogue]. Now after the King intimated he might set one up they say we do.' This was somewhat unfair. Although the vast majority of the delegation was immutably tied to the regime, there were one or two independent thinkers and others who were more than a little disturbed by the increasing sectarianism. In the event, the delegation and I talked for over two hours about the situation in Bahrain and the prospects of dialogue, the differences between mediation and dialogue, and how to construct a confidential, deniable back channel. They promised to report back to Manama but gave little away.

In the meantime I informed them that I was minded to visit Bahrain in the next two weeks with Tim Phillips, a former advisor to US President Clinton with a history of helping to resolve conflict, who was committed to helping Bahrain see its way through its political impasse by supporting efforts to strengthen the moderate centre ground. Phillips was principally known for setting up Beyond Conflict (formerly known as Project on Justice in Times of Transition) and the Club of Madrid, an organisation comprising more than seventy-five former heads of state and prime ministers. As a visiting lecturer at Tufts University, he taught courses on the critical role of leadership in conflict transformation and had published on transitional justice, conflict resolution and national reconciliation. He also served on the board of directors of numerous international organisations and cultural and educational institutions.

None of them sought to dissuade me from coming and many produced business cards stating how willing they were to meet us in Bahrain so that we might better understand the situation there. It would be instructive to see how many would make good their promises. The plan was to go with Phillips along with Roelf Meyer (former South African Defence Secretary to President F. W. de Klerk), who negotiated the release of Nelson Mandela, and Mohammed Bhabha, a senior African National Congress (ANC) negotiator and former Constitutional Affairs Minister, who had been Roelf's opposite number in the South African reconciliation process, with a view to sharing their experiences about peace building and reconciliation with both the Bahraini government and opposition alike.

Beyond Conflict was another small innovative organisation that I admired, which was engaged in tackling complex challenges concerning societal transformation. Established in 1992 it was based in Boston and affiliated with Tufts and Columbia universities. It emerged as a consequence of an experimental meeting held in Salzburg, Austria, in March 1992, the purpose of which was to figure out whether the new leaders of post-communist Europe could learn from the experience of leaders in other countries who had successfully guided their own nations through the painful legacies of the past to move from dictatorship to democracy. Phillips recalled that early meeting well: 'Many insisted that their nation's history and challenges were unique and that there was nothing to be learned from the experience of other countries. But gradually, over the course of several days of discussions and informal conversations over beer and fine food, they began to see parallels and lessons in the experiences of Argentina, Chile, Spain, Uruguay and other countries. The East Europeans returned to their own countries with new perspectives and constructive approaches.' As a consequence, Václav Havel, Czechoslovakia's first democratically elected President after the Velvet Revolution, urged Phillips to continue using this pioneering methodology. Within a few years, the project was deeply engaged in Northern Ireland and the Balkans. It was Phillips who took Roelf Meyer and Cyril Ramaphosa to Northern Ireland to share the South African experience to great acclaim, just as Gerry Adams and John Hume would later do elsewhere.

Tim's move into Bahrain was of obvious interest to me. I too had been involved in peace processes where I had witnessed the transformative effect of former adversaries and deadly foes beginning to talk to each other in the right environment. I had seen how it was possible for armed group and government representatives to change their personal behaviour and outlook towards a conflict as talks deepened. In one such mediation, within a few months, hardened enemies who could hardly look each other in the eye began to refer to each other as 'friend' and enquire politely about each other's respective personal situations. Such courtesies didn't necessarily stop the killing but their personal journey did represent a small and significant step towards creating the conditions for an overall peace that would eventually led to a lasting cease-fire. Both Phillips and I believed some of these experiences were transferable. Thus, although no two conflicts were alike, it was important to understand the underlying mechanisms of human behaviour that drive individuals and groups away from repression and violent conflict towards negotiation and peace.

Considerable human, political and financial resources have been devoted to resolving conflict over the past century, yet war and repression remain with us. Even where peace has been declared, achieving a durable peace through democracy has proven difficult, be it in Israel and Palestine, Bosnia Herzegovina, Sri Lanka or Colombia. For that, what is needed is to identify the fundamental changes in perceptions and actions that lead to genuine change. While it is true that every country has its own unique national history and experience, how people respond to terrifying, humiliating and dehumanising experiences of life under dictatorship and civil war is fundamentally the same around the world. Phillips understood intuitively that people in such situations struggle as individuals with the burdens of violence, fear and repression on a deeply personal and psychological level. He had seen how it was possible for them to move beyond their experiences through learning about the experiences of others, thus speeding up the process of internal and societal change. And so it was that I agreed to go with Tim to Manama in June of 2011.

Manama, June 2011

As it turned out the Shura Council's trip to the UK and Brussels failed to quell any of the growing international criticism of Bahrain. Matters were so fraught that, by the time we flew into Manama, Tim and I had no idea whether we would get through passport control. Almost immediately I was pulled aside by a Bahraini official and questioned about the purpose of my trip. I told them it was legal business and not tourism. Other NGOs were later banned for having given false information at the border. After an hour or so I was eventually let through to join the rest of the group. For the next few days we met with representatives of Bahraini civil society and opposition movements. They confirmed the haunting stories that had appeared in the world's press. Of particular concern were the doctors and lawyers who remained in detention, ostensibly for performing their professional duties.

Nabeel Rajab, the celebrated human rights activist and director of the Bahrain Human Rights Centre, talked passionately about the need for the government to adhere to the rule of law both as a matter of principle and in an effort to stem the growing tide of sectarianism: 'The conflict in Bahrain is not about a Sunni/Shia divide but the distribution of wealth and power. It is about social and political reform and an end to human rights violations.' Rajab would later be arrested and tried for his efforts to highlight alleged human rights abuses, which the authorities regarded as seditious. Yet ours was not primarily a human rights mission. We needed to talk to members of the government, the Sunni community, the opposition and resident diplomats to get their perspective, with a view to assessing whether a dialogue about reform was in fact possible.

This difference in perspective between the human rights advocate and the humanitarian reconciler was graphically brought home to me while dining with an influential liberal Bahraini Sunni friend in Manama two and a half months after the protests were suppressed. She took me to task for the BHRC's criticism of the conduct of the Bahraini government concerning the brutal arrest and maltreatment of Shia doctors and lawyers. I knew nothing of the real circumstances in Bahrain, she remonstrated. Otherwise I would know that Iran was trying to meddle in its internal affairs. I would know that the Shias' allegiance was to their clerics and not to king and country. I would know that many of the Shia protesters were intent on bringing down the regime, and not interested in adopting the piecemeal reforms offered by the Crown Prince. I would know that many of the young protesters deliberately goaded and attacked the police in the villages to provoke a response – a response that their leaders could then exploit internationally in order to influence people like me. And I would know that these doctors were not as innocent as the world imagined, but were instead part of a movement that was intent on destroying Bahrain's way of life.

To be clear, this outburst came from a sensitive woman who over the last decade had given generously to both Shia and Sunni communities in a spirit of cultural reconciliation, through her sponsorship of artists and the arts. Yet her anger was so powerful that she had seemingly dismissed accounts of mistreatment. She felt the Shia response to the Arab Spring had assaulted everything she held dear about Bahrain. When she finished I asked her whether that would be her opening statement in any national dialogue if the King had asked her to preside over such a process. As I repeated my question she looked at me as if a juggernaut had just hit her. 'What!' she screamed. I repeated the question. This time she fell into silence as her intellect finally took over from her rage. 'No,' she quietly replied.

I told her that I fully sympathised with her dilemma. For me it all depends upon what angle you come at it from. People see it differently according to whether they are Shia or Sunni, a subject or a ruler, a mother or a father, a victim or an abuser, a human rights defender or a security official tasked with keeping order. But your perspective changes altogether when you are charged with establishing reconciliation between all these groups through national dialogue. Suddenly you have to accommodate all sorts of different perspectives. The task becomes not so much how to hold criminal elements or government agencies to account, but how to bring conflicted parties together in an effort to bring the violence and instability to an end. This inevitably raises the spectre of compromise.

Diplomatic Blues

We encountered similar views to Nabeel Rajab's from a senior but outgoing British diplomat about the prospects of a successful dialogue. He remarked upon the optimism of our team, commenting that he in contrast was 'very depressed' about the situation. According to him, the people running the country during the state of emergency were arch-conservatives. 'Someone told me that during the state of emergency they set up a National Security Council consisting of five men including the Royal Court Minister and the Chief of Staff, as well as the head of the National Security Office. The Prime Minister was not on the committee but it expressed his view. I find it difficult to see a way forward as there is almost no moderate constituency in government. The King was marginalised although there is some evidence he is coming back into play. But it's a case of hardline from ultra-hardline.' He went on:

> They believe the crisis finished on 18 March after they regained security. They kettled the protests into the Shia villages as they did in the 1990s, and now believed it had worked. However, there is a distinction between security and stability. Stability is where you can take soldiers off the street. The first thing is to persuade them that things will have to change. I made a speech a few days ago in which I described the lifting of the state of emergency and the opening of a national dialogue as good steps in what was a long road. I'm not sure that anyone on the government side – leaving aside the Crown Prince who has no power – is in fact willing to go down this road. It's all rather cosmetic.

The diplomat, who clearly loved Bahrain and its people, admitted to us that he had become a busted flush after he had visited Al-Wefaq and assisted the Crown Prince's dialogue, to the consternation of the hardliners in the Prime Minister's office and the Ministry of the Interior. 'I told Al-Wefaq they must support the dialogue after the Crown Prince made concessions. But it was difficult to know how much the street led them or they led the street. The Khalifas can't see why the UK does not stand by them through thick and thin.' I later heard how the King of Bahrain had personally commiserated with him about his diplomatic demise, calling him a 'brother', while being unable to rehabilitate him in the eyes of others. 'Is there anything that could change this picture?' asked Roelf. 'Where can you work in the hierarchy to support moderates?' 'I can't see anywhere,' he replied despondently. The diplomat also confirmed that even liberal Sunnis in the artistic and business community were beginning to turn against their Shia brothers in this polarised climate. 'Two weeks ago I had a conversation with a member of the business community who was head of an Islamic bank. I always marked him down as a liberal. No beard and with liberal social attitudes. I said to him he must be interested in stability. He said the opposition must apologise first. Certain businessmen and bankers who three years ago were forward looking are now very vindictive towards the Shia.'

Similar sentiments were echoed by Sager Shaheen, the deputy chair of the Chamber of Commerce, who told us about his own experiences of the protests:

> The 14th of February was a shock. When it first started in Pearl Roundabout it was peaceful. They were demanding the right to more

housing and jobs. Between the 14th and the 17th of February they were allowed to stay. Then it got out of control, escalated and became unsafe, as there were no police on the street. I believe in the right to freedom of expression but not the right to hurt others or block roads. People were afraid there was going to be a sectarian conflict. I live in a Shia district. They were waiting with steel rods. Standing at a checkpoint. Eighteen- to twenty-year-olds. They began to decide whether you could go in or not. My wife was very scared. So the security forces intervened and all of this happened. Many Shias were against what happened but were told they couldn't say anything. They remained quiet as they would have been seen as traitors, but 70 per cent–80 per cent of the Shias are with the Al-Khalifas.

Shaheen went on to blame the problem on religion: 'There are extremists in both sects but it is the religious leaders who are creating division. Shias from one year old spend every day in the mosque, so by the time many are ten years old they hate the regime. Iran plays a big role through its TV channels. They took over parts of Lebanon and then Iraq and they now want to do it here. Al-Wefaq almost achieved an agreement with the Crown Prince after the Roundabout was cleared. Ali Salman told me he went back to check with his chief cleric but the cleric said no.' As far as Shaheen was concerned it was far better if the business community handled the dialogue. 'We all learned new things – including the need to develop the constitution and integrate people together – it wasn't to be.'

A similar message came from the US Embassy. 'We are hearing rhetoric from Sunnis that 'we are the real victims' and that 'the people sentenced to death must die', explained one analyst. Bahraini and Saudi hardliners were furious with President Obama for his general failure to stand by Mubarak. It was telling that the Bahrain cabinet formally referred to Obama's 19 May speech in their meetings. They were surprised, as they didn't expect him to link Bahrain to the other places that had experienced uprisings. 'You can't underestimate the toxic media environment,' confided the analyst. It was within this context that the US-based National Democracy Institute was banned from entering the country for trying to assist the opposition Shia parties with building internal capacity. According to the analyst, this was an unfair reading of America's intent:

The problem is they don't get out. They just travel to the Gulf, which is an echo chamber. The Prime Minister talked about a schism in society for the first time the other month. He met with one hundred prominent Shia families but then told them that his feelings had been hurt by their conduct. Another problem is that Bahrain has not evolved as a society. The middle and upper classes don't want to get involved in politics. The King tends not get involved in detail and there are no 'process people' close to him to advise him how to build a viable dialogue.

Al-Wefaq and the Shia Opposition

Despite the pessimistic message we encountered, we resolved to press on to discover whether there was any basis for dialogue by calling in all possible favours to get meetings with both sides. On 16 June we met with the leadership of the Sunni National Unity Gathering through Faisal Fulud, the Secretary General of the Bahrain Human Rights Watch Society (BHRWS), a government-sponsored NGO. Faisal was originally an activist in the student and trade union movements. Jailed twice in the 1990s, he came in from the cold and joined the establishment after the new King introduced his 2001 reforms. After being appointed to the Shura Council he set up the BHRWS in 2004 on the basis that 'it did not mix politics and human rights unlike other NGOs such as the Bahrain Human Rights Centre'. The BHRWS comprised eleven members of all denominations, including the Bahraini Ambassador in the US, and was allegedly dedicated to the protection of democracy, free and fair elections, and freedom of expression. In reality it seemed extremely close to the government.

Faisal echoed many of Sager Shaheen's criticisms of Al-Wefaq:

The Crown Prince told the opposition that he would sort out the problem through a national dialogue. Al-Haq refused. Hassan Mushaima declared that the opposition wanted a republic. Iran fomented the conflict. The Hezbollah leader in Lebanon made a number of statements that scared the GCC. The Crown Prince tried his best. We met with him twice. The opposition said they didn't want the Prime Minister in government. At the same time government hardliners were working against the Crown Prince. The Crown Prince called us and said he only had hours before Saudi Arabia would invade. He went to Ali Salman and told him he had seven principles. I said please let's go before tomorrow but Al-Wefaq refused, saying 'We are the government now!'

Whether this account was strictly accurate was debatable. While Al-Wefaq had undoubtedly prevaricated over the Crown Prince's offer, it did not reject it outright. The former Al-Wefaq MP later told me that Sheikh Ali Salman had offered to go and see the King after proposing a power-sharing arrangement with Abdullatif Mahmood of the NUG, in which he offered the Sunnis an effective veto in parliament, but Mahmood prevaricated and then refused.

By the time Faisal had managed to hook us up with the NUG, the King had already announced the establishment of a one-month-long national dialogue to start at the beginning of July and end before Ramadan in August of 2011. He now appointed the Speaker of the Parliament as chair with the responsibility to report back to him on possible reforms. The Speaker was generally known to be a pliant regime man who inspired little confidence. It soon became apparent that the King had consulted neither Al-Wefaq nor any of the other political societies about the nature and form of the purported dialogue. Matters were not helped after the regime allocated to Al-Wefaq just two of out twenty places around the table, notwithstanding its huge share of the popular vote. It was difficult to place much faith in such a process given its limited scope, design and inclusivity. Whether the lack of consultation was a deliberate ploy or the result of ignorance about how best to frame such a process was difficult to divine. On the face of it, it looked more designed to reduce the level of international pressure on Bahrain than to engender any long-term consensus over political reform.

Even Faisal was sceptical about its likely success: 'I feel that if the national dialogue fails then there will be no trust left. The hardliners want everything under their control and are afraid they will lose power. Nobody knows at the moment which groups will be invited. There are rumours they are construct-ing a media centre and that over sixty political and civil society parties will be invited. But if Al-Wefaq don't come then the national dialogue will fail.' Faisal went on to explain how so many political and civil societies came into being after the Shia opposition boycotted the first parliamentary elections of 2001 on the basis that the National Charter failed to embody the full rights referred to in the referendum. The government, in effect, encouraged and paid for the creation of a number of Sunni-based societies in an effort to give Sunni groups greater representation in parliament. 'You cannot put 300 people in a room and expect to get consensus,' observed Meyer. 'You need to work with smaller parties away from the television cameras. Above all you need to create an environment in which one can first of all listen to one another.'

From the outset it was clear that the 2011 national dialogue neither enjoyed the support and confidence of the main two political opposition parties nor the people on the street. The attempt to dilute Al-Wefaq's presence in the talks placed it in a particularly difficult situation. The need to placate its own constituency, which was becoming increasingly agitated at the lack of progress, was obvious to all and sundry. One prominent resident Shia politi-cian explained Al-Wefaq's dilemma:

The royal family places the dialogue between the people when it should be between the people and the government. Our problem is with the government and the fact that the Prime Minister will not cede any authority. We have a problem with the King and his uncle so why should we go and negotiate with other groups? They should recognise that Al-Wefaq has the support of 65 per cent of the population. Yet we are going to get just two votes in the dialogue. They are deliberately trying to open a national dialogue on everything but if Parliament couldn't solve it in forty years how can we solve it in one month? They are trying to dilute the problem. The King and Crown Prince talk of 'consensus' but how can we achieve this? Two days ago they started to sack those suspended from municipal education. How does this assist the dialogue? They want to tell the international community that they tried dialogue and that Al-Wefaq was too sectarian. It's untrue. We have said we welcome dialogue in principle but we need to discuss its structure. We met Michael Posner and told him we have not taken a decision yet to boycott or participate in the dialogue but we feel it is going to be a failure. If we pull out they will blame us.

We spoke to Sheikh Ali Salman, the leader of Al-Wefaq. He was forced into exile in 1992 after he called for a restoration of the 1973 constitution. Following the adoption of the National Charter he created Al-Wefaq to contest the 2006 elections, after he and other opposition figures split from Al-Haq. He repeated many of the concerns about the proposed dialogue: 'Many things are unclear about the dialogue. We don't feel the government want a real political solution that deals with the people's demands. They talk about dialogue because the international community says a security driven policy is not enough. If they were serious the Crown Prince should lead it and concentrate on political reform.' Yet by the time we talked this through with Sheikh Ali Salman, the concerns of Al-Wefaq had already been communicated to the Crown Prince through intermediaries. But he was taking no chances. Having been seriously burnt in the last dialogue he made it clear that he would not become embroiled. Like many of us, his officials probably thought the process was bound to fail given its uncompromising unilateral design.

That is why we underscored with both opposition groups how useful secret back channels could be in creating trust where consensus about dialogue was lacking. Talks about talks helped prepare negotiations for talks about substance. In one conflict I was involved in, there were four years of talks about talks before the parties met to discuss the actual dynamics of the conflict. As Meyer commented: 'Process is equally important to content. You can't expect to get a successful outcome if there hasn't been a successful process.' For five years before the first official talks began in South Africa, high-level officials from both sides met regularly with Nelson Mandela in his prison cell to discuss the process and build trust and confidence with one another. Both sides would later draw upon this repository of trust when they encountered hurdles and breakdown in negotiations. This was particularly the case between Meyer and the ANC's chief negotiator, Cyril Ramaphosa; their personal chemistry was extremely good after each man built upon a careful understanding of the other. Yet as Roelf himself observed, such chemistry would have been largely irrelevant had there not been some sort of paradigm shift in thinking on the part of the Afrikaners.

A leader from the Democratic Progress Tribune, a secular democratic society committed to political reform that often worked with Al-Wefaq over human rights issues, confirmed that no such paradigm shift had yet occurred. He explained:

> The government is trying to say the threat is from Iran but it is not true. Yet our political struggle started in the 1920s. There has been a political and economic problem ever since 98 per cent of the population approved the National Charter ten years ago but then didn't faithfully implement it. Between 2002 and 2006 I was an MP and noticed that the government was never serious about further reform. It feels that what happened ten years ago is enough. The difficulties in Bahrain are due to the royal family keeping too much power. There is no underlying conflict between Shias and Sunnis. We were the first to accept the dialogue offer from the Crown Prince. He sent us a letter on 1 March 2011. We replied on 3 March. He said the government would change within two months but then the hardliners intervened. Bahrain needs the help of the international community. The people feel left alone. Your role can definitely help.

As for the events in February 2011, the leader was adamant that:

> The protests in Pearl Roundabout were completely peaceful. It was the government that tried to make them violent. Hassan Mushaima, who was not part of the legitimate opposition said from London that this protest will be peaceful until somebody dies by the government in jail or outside. The next day on 16 February two people died. One died outside my home. The other died outside the hospital. It was deliberate. It is true that some kicked police vehicles but it was the security forces that instigated the violence. From 16 February we pleaded with the government to stop the killing. The King said it must stop. At that time there were over 1,000 Sunnis at the Roundabout. Then on 26 February Hassan [. . .] arrived from London. We told him Bahrain didn't just belong to us and we had to negotiate but Hassan went to the Roundabout and said we want a republic.

Abdullatif al-Mahmood, who had been threatened with exile, then proposed to create a militia 'to defend our people and the Sunni'. It was the beginning of the end.

Meyer talked to the Sheikh about how important it was in any process to take ownership of the problem, including of the design of the dialogue process and thus its eventual outcome. The King's failure to consult about either process or substance meant there was little 'buy in' from any groups other than the regime's placemen. Yet this did not mean Al-Wefaq should refuse to participate in the dialogue. Roelf and I both felt it was imperative that Al-Wefaq did not withdraw from the process. At the very least it should use the opportunity to register its objections about the procedure and structure of the proposed talks, if only to help frame any future process. 'This is the time for the opposition to come together,' advised Roelf, continuing:

> As the US politician, A. Stevenson, once said, 'Sometimes you need to stand upon the hilltop and see the big picture.' This is a crucial moment for Bahrain. An inclusive approach requires leadership, as it is a 'step by step' process. One month is a ludicrous time frame but the first step is to work at the design of the process. Over the next two weeks perhaps you and others should sit down to agree a statement of intent that governs the whole purpose of the dialogue. It must be strategic in intent as this is a chess game. It should be a document that seeks common ground rather than one that satisfies all the parties. It should be one that puts you on the hilltop about the future of Bahrain. At the very least you can use this process to prepare for real negotiations.

Mohammed agreed. 'You need to think about what kind of internal decision-making structure you should adopt for the dialogue. Appoint a chief negotiator. Select a face for the media. Think about the structure of the negotiating table and your relationship to other parties. Respond to the invitation to participate in the dialogue with a submission of your own.'

The prominent Shia politician listened intently then said: 'But the fundamental issue is the lack of participation of the royal family in the dialogue.' 'Dialogue is not a monologue. The more you engage the more it will strengthen you,' chipped in Phillips diplomatically. 'Either you find a problem for every solution or a solution for every problem,' replied Roelf somewhat more forcefully.

188 STORM IN THE DESERT

The NUG and South Africa

It was within this context that we finally met Abdullatif al-Mahmood and other members of the National Unity Gathering. They had initially set aside one hour for us, but in the end we talked for seven. Abdullatif was a charismatic opposition leader who had spent some time in jail during the 1990s for his criticism of the regime. He explained how the NUG came into being on 19 February 2012, as a reaction to the protests at Pearl Roundabout. It organised a number of mass Sunni rallies after the government released twenty-three opposition detainees previously charged with political offences. At the start of the meeting the leadership were polite, formal but demonstrably suspicious, while Abdullatif plainly felt that South Africa was a world away from Bahrain. Yet he retained a modicum of curiosity and was probably tasked by the government to find out just exactly what we were up to. Roelf began by telling the NUG that he had witnessed numerous conflicts over the last fifteen years where outside intervention had prevented people from taking ownership of their own situation. As a result, these conflicts were not resolved. 'The international community can exert all the pressure it likes on a country, but if its people have not recognised the need for change, then no lasting progress will be made. It's up to the people to do it themselves,' he declared.

I watched as the leadership of the NUG slowly began to take an interest. Roelf described both his own story and that of South Africa. He reminded everyone how few had expected apartheid to end peacefully. Even fewer expected that the system of white supremacy, which had been so rigorously enforced by the National Party between 1948 and 1994, would be dismantled by a privileged member of Afrikaner society, particularly one who would probably have become President had apartheid not been dismantled. Yet this was Roelf Meyer's story, and his personal transformation mirrored that of his country. It was a journey from an entrenched notion of racial superiority to one that realised the need to strive for equality for all. As he spoke about how his shift in thinking occurred, the NUG's interest visibly increased. It had taken fourteen years for this change to occur, he explained, but when it did it enabled both sides to build a communication process in which they could properly talk to each other. 'In the end the process worked because we built it together. It was very inclusive. Not only were the two major parties engaged, other smaller parties of all affiliations were accommodated and made to feel welcome. That helped us reach a settlement that was approved by everybody.' This was clearly relevant to Bahrain and the current attitude of the NUG towards the national dialogue.

Meyer explained how he had grown up in a privileged world not unlike the one enjoyed by many Sunni leaders in Bahrain. It was a life of advantages and opportunities of which his black compatriots could only dream. Yet, as a young lawyer, grappling with a personal sense of fairness and justice, he was soon confronted by a system that did not allow blacks even the most basic of constitutional rights. The denial of personal dignity was enshrined in the very system of law Meyer now professed to practise. Thousands could not get citizenship or access to official papers, jobs and housing. Meyer told Abdullatif how he found himself on a personal journey of discovery as the conflict in South Africa ratcheted up. He recalled the time he spoke with a former farmhand to find out why he had joined the ANC. The young man recounted how he had ridden in the back of a white farmer's pickup truck when he was a child, along with the farmer's dog. When it began to rain, the farmer brought the dog into the cab so it could stay dry and left the boy in the open for hours to get drenched in the downpour. This simple but profound act of humiliation directed towards such a small defenceless human being stung Meyer's moral sensibilities. It was an act he could no longer explain away or justify. Through such acts he began to understand how his fellow black South Africans felt alienated and radicalised. Repeated exposure to such acts of dehumanisation and inequality gradually ate away at his convictions and belief in the sustainability of the regime.

Then a few years later, while serving as Vice Minister of Police during a national state of emergency, Meyer was tasked by President P. W. Botha to learn why blacks were rioting. He spent eighteen months visiting black townships to gain an understanding about the unrest and what might be done to stop it. Few whites, let alone government officials, ever ventured into the townships to witness first-hand just how harsh the reality of black life in South Africa was. He now began to understand that while he remained an elected representative to Parliament, he in no way represented the people of South Africa. His flock was only a tiny white minority whose advantages and privileges he could no longer morally support. More importantly, Meyer could see the need for not only a pragmatic but a paradigm shift in thinking within the National Party, which in his view needed not only to embrace drastic social and political change, but to deal with the ANC's militant wing and its leader, Nelson Mandela.

Meyer told Abdullatif how long it took for this to register at the emotional and political level. At first, he said, the National Party tried to negotiate a piecemeal deal with the ANC, designed to retain as much power for the white minority as possible. Meyer then told his assembled audience how:

> The 1992 political breakdown forced us as a government to go back to the drawing board and say to ourselves, 'What Now? What is it that we want from a future constitution in South Africa?' It was then that the paradigm shift occurred. It finally dawned on the National Party government that this notion of reserved rights, of group rights, of minority protection in the

South African environment, was not going to work. We had to intervene to make it one of equality for all. I'm absolutely convinced that if we hadn't made that paradigm shift peace would not have been sustainable. One might comment it was damn long before I saw the light but there it was. All in all, it took at least fourteen years for me to complete this personal transformation and leave the paradigm of white supremacy behind. Suddenly I was able to speak to the other side. I was within this new paradigm in which I realised that South Africa's future could only be based on equality for all in a democratic environment. Not only had I come to understand the need for this change, I had embraced it.

It was even more compelling to listen to Meyer's story with Mohammed Bhabha in the room. After Roelf had told his story Bhabha recounted his experiences from an ANC perspective. They had been archenemies and yet here they were swapping notes about how they finally came to negotiate with each other. It had taken a long time for the National Party leadership to recognise the need for change. In the end change came about as the result of four factors: economic sanctions and other punitive measures enacted by the international community; the growing effectiveness of the ANC, which essentially made part of the country ungovernable and led to years of state of emergency; the internal recognition by white South Africans that 'change had to come, because the country was bleeding itself to bits'; and the growing realisation that the existing course would inevitably lead to full-scale war. But the possibility of non-violent change was only possible in South Africa because the National Party had in the ANC a potential partner with which to negotiate peace and a new constitutional framework for the country. Bhabha now described how the ANC brought its own radical constituency in from the diplomatic and political cold. It was something that Al-Wefaq and the NUG would also have to do if there were to be any chance of resolving the conflict in Bahrain. Some of these stories resonated with the NUG, who themselves had to deal with a heavily polarised and increasingly radicalised Sunni constituency who were not at all convinced about the utility of the King's proposed national dialogue.

It is difficult to believe in the transformative effect of this type of dialogue process until you witness it in action. As Roelf and Brahba talked about their experiences in South Africa you could see the mists of incomprehension lift from the faces of some members of the NUG. Although they were far from convinced that Bahrain was comparable to South Africa, they did understand that some of the questions that had been bedevilling them were ones that both Roelf and Bhabha had had to confront. Within an hour or so, the NUG leaders were not only listening intently to Meyer and Bhabha but, more importantly, asking detailed questions on all aspects of the South African process. When and how did each side decide to negotiate? Why did each side enter talks without pre-conditions? How did they choose which confidence-building measures to sequence first? How did they manage to park difficult issues such as past human rights abuses? And so on. It was within this context that we invited them to come to South Africa to find out the answers to these questions for themselves. Suddenly one hour turned into seven and lunch turned into dinner.

Over the next few hours we learned that the NUG had remarkably similar constitutional goals to Al-Wefaq, despite their antipathy towards the Shia opposition and its religion. Although the NUG was subject to government control, its leadership evinced a barely disguised ambition to deepen its power and influence through constitutional reform. Like Al-Wefaq, it too had an interest in a national dialogue leading to greater parliamentary representation and powers, even if it had no desire to see the power of the Shia opposition increase. It was fascinating to see how the conversation opened up once a certain level of trust was established. 'The Shia opposition did not consider us a legitimate body. It was a shock for them when they saw our numbers. There are good and bad people in their movement but we know there are some people on their side who will help resolve this problem. We have many points that we agree upon and we can improve our relations. We can raise our heads to them in the interests of Bahrain,' explained one NUG member. Suddenly we were exploring various different constitutional models of parliamentary representation. It was difficult to pinpoint the exact moment when the alchemy of tentative trust between different men, women and cultures occurs, but occur it did, and in that moment we knew we were in with a chance to help strengthen the centre ground.

Exclusion as a Driver of Conflict

I now talked about my experiences with the Kurds in Turkey, who, like the Shia, had been lobbying for equal rights and greater political participation for the better part of four generations. Throughout its ninety-year history the Turkish Republic had been racked by conflict, rebellion and military coups, primarily as a result of its unrepresentative and discriminatory structures. While these structures were sustainable during the Cold War and the so-called 'war on terror' years, they were unlikely to survive the Arab Spring now that the democratic genie had been let out of the bottle. Given all that had transpired, it was extremely unlikely that the Kurds or the Shia opposition would meekly accept a return to the status quo for any length of time. The point of our discussions was not to prescribe to Bahrainis or Turks how they should ultimately solve their political problems, but to help them identify what the issues were and how other countries had dealt with similar issues and conflicts, from both a political and a psychological perspective.

In the case of Turkey, the ethnic and cultural conflict had led to a pernicious armed struggle that consistently threatened to tear the country apart. The PKK derived its power, whether it admitted this to itself or not, less from its Marxist-orientated ideological platform than from the general discrimination and indignity meted out to the Kurds. What most Kurds wanted was what ordinary people wanted – human dignity, cultural freedom, and a chance to live a happy, prosperous life with the same opportunities as other citizens. This was also true of most Shias in Bahrain. How that was to be achieved was a matter for national dialogue, but it was clear that many of the issues that fuelled the political conflict in Bahrain related to years of political, social and economic discrimination.

On one view this discrimination could be tackled without massive constitutional reform, provided of course the political will was there. There was everything to play for. It was possible to conceive of how the Al-Khalifas could embark upon a round of economic and social reform while retaining power and marginalising those on the extremes. Yet it was equally clear that the conflict was likely to continue and intensify, as it had done in Turkey, unless some of the basic demands of the Shia population regarding discrimination and dignity were addressed and accepted by all. Meyer ventured to Abdullatif that Bahrain was somewhat like South Africa in the 1980s. The only way to keep a grip on the mounting opposition was to lock up and torture even more dissidents. 'The only way out is dialogue,' urged Meyer, 'a dialogue that is not window dressing. It is not enough to lift the state of emergency.'

Much of this analysis was difficult for the NUG to swallow in one short gulp. It was one thing to listen to other people's experiences; quite another to accept the existence of certain parallels. The NUG believed Shia political leaders were controlled by outside religious and political forces. As a result, the NUG were deeply sceptical about joining any national dialogue where Al-Wefaq predominated or was officially recognised as the principal negotiating party. The issue of discrimination was just a smokescreen behind which lay a Shia grab for political power. Yet the prospect of a month-long national dialogue starting in July 2011 was plainly a tantalising prospect for them: 'We believe everybody should respect each other but as I said the Shia opposition do not consider us as a legitimate body. It was a shock to them. They never thought we could get the numbers we did. They want to portray us as just a plaything of the regime but there are three of us – the regime, the Shia and us. We believe the dialogue should be for all of us and that there should be no conditions. We hope the other side does not impose conditions to block the dialogue whether before or after it begins. We know there are some people on their side who will help resolve the problem.' For our part we were convinced that Al-Wefaq was a party with which the NUG could do business.

Our initial talks with Al-Wefaq in Manama had convinced us that there was a moderate centre ground around which most political societies could coalesce. While some radical groups such as Al-Haq looked to certain outside powers for inspiration, there was little evidence that Al-Wefaq was the plaything of either Tehran or Baghdad, although it communicated with them. Abdullatif now disclosed to us that the NUG had discreetly met with representatives of Al-Wefaq on at least three previous occasions. We urged the NUG to establish a confidential back channel with Al-Wefaq in order to test out the other's position on the proposed national dialogue, and the range of issues that was likely to arise within it. Only time would tell whether these words would have any effect on the conduct of the opposition parties. We had made significant progress with both the Sunni and Shia opposition but those at the very centre of power in government and within the royal court continued to elude us. While we had met with some of the Prime Minister's advisors who promised to connect us up with their political masters on the next occasion (including a curious little birdwatching Brit called Howard King, who had no doubt been tasked with keeping a tab on us during our stay in Manama), we had not yet secured their trust or confidence.

In the end we had to remind ourselves that dialogue initiatives were marathons rather than sprints, and that we had to *earn* the trust of all the relevant parties. How could we ask others to look beyond their interests and suffering if we were not ourselves willing to bleed a little? In any case, it was a common feature of groups caught up in conflict to develop a very insular view of their own reality. They often believed that no one had suffered the way they had. As a result, they were extremely reluctant to listen to, or respect, the view of outsiders. Each of the groups we met in Bahrain felt in their own way that they were the victims. This made it more difficult to talk about a shared future or engage in talks about a meaningful dialogue. Such feelings of victimhood often stymied each side's attempt to engage with the enemy or pursue reconciliation, at least until their suffering was acknowledged.

I remember talking about this phenomenon at a breakfast meeting in Manama with a former deputy governor of the World Bank, who was there on business. He was an Iraqi Christian with an encyclopaedic understanding of the economic and political realities of the region. He gave us an intimate portrait of the regime and its psychological and policy fixations. Even he was slightly dumbstruck at our initiative, given the manifest paranoia that he had encountered in the country. 'You know what you guys remind me of ?' he said. 'No,' replied Phillips. 'Storm chasers,' he replied. 'You're like those guys who chase tornadoes in the southern states of America. You literally seek out the eye of the storm in an attempt to understand it. I wish you well and hope you can find at least some shelter on the way but I somehow doubt it.'

The Manama Dialogue

As was widely predicted, the one-month-long national dialogue of August 2011 neither halted the descent into sectarianism nor achieved any consensus about the nature of long-term political reform in Bahrain. While its announcement did buy the regime time to regroup over the summer, few were convinced by the dialogue chairman's orchestrated and piecemeal recommendations given to the King. They failed to tackle either the underlying political conflict or any of the burning human rights issues thrown up by the protests. It appeared to some observers as if the royal court was living in a cosseted and closed world, in which it believed the King's dispensation could resolve entrenched problems within just a matter of weeks. The dialogue's lack of inclusivity meant it was bound to fail. As Roelf Meyer had warned, none of the parties had ownership of the procedural or substantive agenda. Before we left Bahrain in June 2011 we just about managed to convince Al-Wefaq to enter into the dialogue process, if only to lodge their criticisms about its nature and structure. However, it was no surprise when two weeks later we were informed they had walked out of the talks.

More surprising was Al-Wefaq's decision, a month later, to boycott elections to the lower parliamentary house. The boycott constituted a serious strategic mistake by Al-Wefaq, as it deprived itself of an elected long-term platform from which to trumpet its cause both domestically and internationally. Although the electoral parliamentary districts were designed to deprive it of an overall majority, the legitimacy that came with being elected still gave it a unique status as the principal elected opposition party in parliament and the country. Moreover, even though it had acquired only eighteen out of the forty seats available last time round, no one who understood Bahraini politics was under any misapprehension about who enjoyed a democratic majority within the overall electorate. By boycotting the elections Al-Wefaq gave its political opponents the chance to enhance their political legitimacy. It also undermined its own ability to garner wider external support. It would have been more advantageous for Al-Wefaq to enter a new, if compromised, parliament with a popular mandate to reform it, than to put all its eggs in one basket in a single symbolic act of rejection that was bound to be forgotten within a few weeks.

Not unlike the failure to respond timeously to the Crown Prince's offer of reform in March of 2011, the decision to boycott elections was taken on a purely tactical level. It was adopted in order to assuage an angry Shia constituency fed up with the government's failure to acknowledge its equitable demands. Al-Wefaq leaders knew they had to control the street if they wanted to control the politics of opposition. The prominent Shia politician I talked to in Manama explained to me in a private meeting in London on 2 September:

> The government is trying to make this a sectarian issue. As soon as the youths get out onto the streets there is a huge security response with tear gas. There is no state protection for ordinary Shias. We are trying to control the youths and are succeeding but the reformers in the royal family are doing nothing. The arrests are continuous. We clearly see a power struggle in the ruling family. The King in his last speech put things in a softer way. He expressed the desire for the 3,000 people whose jobs and scholarships were revoked to return, and issued a decree to this effect, but nothing was acted upon. There was supposed to be a transfer of jurisdiction from military to civilian tribunals. He is not really in control. The youth want something to happen and we need to send a signal.

In reality, however, the boycott did nothing to increase pressure on the government, which quickly used the manoeuvre to discredit the opposition both at home and abroad. It would have been more problematic for the government if Al-Wefaq had contested the elections and then refused to take up its seats in parliament until a viable dialogue was up and running. Instead, Al-Wefaq gave the hardliners in the government an open goal, as it desperately sought to explain to a bemused international community the tortured reasoning behind its tactical decision-making.

More significantly, the decision to boycott betrayed a fundamental lack of understanding about what any future proposed dialogue was about. As William Hague himself acknowledged, any 'meaningful dialogue' was bound to look at electoral reform at some time or another. It became clear to Tim and me that Al-Wefaq were in desperate need of assistance in strategic thinking if, that is, it was serious about achieving long-term reform through non-violent means. The government quickly pounced on Al-Wefaq's failure to engage with it. The resultant government media onslaught merely fuelled the increasing polarisation between the two religious communities. What happened in Ramadan 2011 told its own story. In previous years, Shia and Sunni families would routinely visit each other in their homes. The season afforded Bahrainis an important opportunity to discuss pressing issues and overcome personal slights and sectarian conflicts in a calm and friendly atmosphere. But not this time. There was a discernible lack of fraternisation in the summer of 2011, as a blatantly biased media ratcheted up sectarian divisions with yet more inflammatory stories of how the Shia were controlled by clerics from Tehran. 'All of this segregation is deliberate,' complained the prominent Shia politician. 'Even moderate Sunnis now have fears. It is difficult to reach out to anyone in the Sunni community. The government are trying to make this a sectarian issue and this freezes politics.'

The use of the media by the Bahraini government to discredit the Shia was counter-productive. Despite the obvious historical tensions between the Shia and Sunni communities, members of both still regarded themselves as Bahrainis first, and an inclusive national identity was an important basis from which to build a new political dispensation, albeit within the context of an Al-Khalifa constitutional monarchy. By ostracising the Shia as alien Iranian sympathisers, the government reduced the space for compromise and reconciliation. Whether this was a deliberate policy or just a knee-jerk response by Sunni hardliners remained unclear. It too was another tactical decision taken for short-term gain, which flew in the face of the government's own stated strategic objective of controlling and ameliorating the level of Shia protest on the streets.

As Syria has learned to its tragic cost, it is far easier to tear apart a mosaic of co-existing confessional identities, built up over thousands of years, than to reconstruct it – a task which requires decades of inter-communal hard work. If the war in the Former Yugoslavia in the 1990s had taught the international community anything, it was that local attempts to polarise sectarian differences for short-term tactical political gain had strategically explosive effects on the search for a non-violent solution to political conflict. Thus, as summer gave way to autumn, it became clearer that *all* parties in Bahrain were indeed in need of some form of assistance if the centre ground was to be strengthened, whether they recognised or accepted it or not.

The BICI Commission

After Al-Wefaq boycotted the elections all eyes turned towards the Bahrain Independent Commission of Inquiry (BICI), which had been quietly beavering away over the summer to unearth the truth about the crackdown of March 2011. On 29 June 2011, while we were in Bahrain, the King – under extreme pressure from the international community, particularly the US – announced by Royal Order No. 28 the establishment of a commission to investigate the events of February and March, to determine whether violations of international human rights law and norms had occurred. Importantly, the Commission was given powers to make appropriate recommendations concerning any breaches found by it to have occurred. A deadline was set for late October 2011. The international community's desire for dialogue and accountability for human rights abuses was not cosmetic, as its pressure led directly to the creation of the BICI by the King. Had he refused to appoint one, he would have had some sort of UN commission of inquiry with a route back to the Security Council forced upon him.

Samantha Power had played a critical role in pressurising the King into appointing a team of distinguished international experts to carry out the independent inquiry. The Commission was to be chaired by Professor Cherif Bassiouni, a leading authority on international criminal, human rights and humanitarian law. The commissioners included Professor Sir Nigel Rodley, the former UN Special Rapporteur on Torture; Judge Philippe Kirsch QC, the first president of the International Criminal Court; Dr Mahnoush Arsanjani, a distinguished international lawyer from Iran, who served in the legal offices of the UN for over thirty-two years; and Dr Badria Al-Awadhi, a renowned expert in international and sharia law from Kuwait, who was also the director of the Arab Regional Centre for Environmental Law.

The first independent, credible, international commission began its work in the region and sent shockwaves through certain Arab capitals. For some commentators it was indicative of US determination to make good some of the promises made by President Obama in his speech of 19 May 2011. For others, the appointment of the Commission was just another example of a face-saving device dreamt up by the West in an attempt to delay real reform. Certainly many of the regime's opponents believed the government would never introduce any substantive reforms that actually prohibited the incidence of torture or ensured a fair justice system. They pointed to how throughout the autumn of 2011 the trials of protesters and oppositionists continued unabated, including those of lawyers and medics, as did restrictions on the media and dismissals of Shia employees and students. The debate about the significance of the BICI rumbled on until late autumn when the government finally announced it would present its recommendations to the King in public on 23 November.

It was obvious from the outset that this was to be a highly orchestrated public ceremony, designed to convince a sceptical world that Bahrain was on the mend. All of the principal human rights NGOs, including the BHRC, received gold-leaf-adorned invitations requesting our presence in Bahrain to witness the official handover. I was aware through confidential sources that there had been some tensions between Chairman Bassiouni and other members of the Commission about the extent to which it should name and shame individual perpetrators and ministers for their complicity in the perpetration of human rights abuses. Certainly the late Nigel Rodley fought admirably to ensure as much accountability as possible. Many suspected, however, that the wily Bassiouni would produce something just short of a whitewash, though some maintained that he would deliver, since both his own credibility and that of his colleagues were on the line. In reality few knew what the BICI would ultimately find or recommend.

The Commission eventually presented its findings to the King in Arabic and English on 23 November 2011. The report ran to 612 pages in Arabic and contained a detailed narrative of events and analysis of the copious evidence gathered by the Commission, as well as recommendations to the government. Paragraph 1,234 of the report detailed some of the indignities visited upon Shia Bahraini citizens, including: rape; the threat of rape; sexual molestation; punching; beating with rubber hoses, electrical cables, whips, metal bars and wooden boards; the application of electrical pillows; the exposure to large differences in temperature; sleep deprivation; blindfolding; handcuffing; forced standing; verbal abuse; and the making of religious insults, to name but a few. All of the above were contrary to Article 19 of the Bahraini constitution and the United Nations Convention against Torture, the International Covenant on Civil and Political Rights and the Arab Charter of Human Rights. In an appendix to the report the BICI had reproduced the summaries of sixty cases it investigated and found proven.

In the event the report fell short of opposition expectations concerning culpability, but went much further in its factual findings than those who had predicted a whitewash had anticipated. Although it failed to attribute criminal culpability to any individual police officers or ministers in charge at the time, the BICI did issue a set of searing factual findings concerning the use of violence and torture by state authorities. The report did not pull its punches about the 'systematic use' of torture or the failure to investigate it, setting out in graphic detail the nature of the treatment. More significantly it identified 171 recommendations for the King to enact. These focused on training and reform of the security forces, as well as changes to the judicial and military court system. The proposed reforms were designed to reduce the incidence of torture, strengthen the independence of the judiciary and increase the prospect of internal investigation and state accountability for abuses. What the report did not do was deal with any of the long-term political grievances that underpinned the protests, other than to recommend a series of social and economic measures to remedy discrimination in employment, healthcare and the public sector.

To my mind the BICI report was anything but a whitewash. While it did not explicitly address the issue of democratic reform, it was never specifically asked to do so. Although I could understand the disappointment of Al-Wefaq leaders who believed that this was the international community's chance to push for real state accountability and political reform of the system, it was always unlikely that a set of international lawyers would unilaterally elect to enter into such shark-infested waters without a specific mandate. Despite the public relations fanfare that accompanied the delivery of the report – a fanfare that, if anything, detracted from the power of its findings – this was a watershed moment in state accountability in the Middle East. The King had indicated he would accept the BICI recommendations without reservation and take all necessary measures to improve the human rights situation through the creation of a BICI follow-up committee.

It was true that the self-congratulatory nature of the report's presentation rightly fuelled NGO suspicions that this was yet another PR exercise to buy time. Nevertheless, the acceptance of the BICI was a progressive and open-ended move, for which the King should have received more international praise, as it set an agenda for institutional reform across government. One need only cast one's mind back to the long fight to establish the Bloody Sunday and Hillsborough inquiries in the UK to realise that all states, even Western ones, are generally reluctant to order open-ended inquiries with full investigative powers into state misconduct, let alone give such powers to a collection of independently-minded outsiders.

The King's announcement of the BICI follow-up committee undoubtedly set the agenda in Bahrain for the next few months, and relieved some of the international pressure on the government as the anniversary of the uprising and 14 March crackdown approached. It also gave the government a credible foundation on which to build a new political narrative of wider political reform if it was so minded. The BICI did not explicitly provide an over-arching political narrative to its recommendations and proposed reforms. But without such a narrative there was great danger that the street would view the BICI reform measures as technical, cosmetic and of little relevance to their daily lives. To make any difference within the Shia community the BICI follow-up measures had to be seen as part of a wider commitment to political reform and reconciliation on the macro level.

Whether the government understood this fact or even recognised the existence of the opportunity was hard to discern. Certainly the Prime Minister and his cohorts remained deeply sceptical about the whole BICI exercise. That is probably why ministers and advisors known to be on the doveish wing of the government did not publicly advocate going further than just calling for the implementation of the BICI recommendations. We would have to see if the BICI report and its follow-up committee would actually precipitate the development of a wider narrative of political reform, but as 2011 drew to a close the omens did not look promising. Most ordinary Sunnis in Bahrain felt the King had conceded quite enough to the international community and Shia constituency already.

Notwithstanding this bleak mood, Beyond Conflict continued over the next three years to work with both Shia and Sunni leaders in an effort to dampen the prospect of violence. Both sides were taken to South Africa, Northern Ireland and Scotland to learn how conflicts could be resolved peacefully and how gradual radical constitutional change was possible through the parliamentary process. Young emerging leaders in the government were taken by Tim Phillips and me to Boston for adaptive leadership courses at Harvard while other civil society leaders were selected for the Rule of Law MENA Fellowship Programme run by the John Smith Memorial Trust, sponsored by the FCO. More to the point, the FCO, under the leadership of Ambassador Iain Lindsay, who quickly mended fences with the royal family after his appointment in 2011, put in place a detailed programme of rule-of-law assistance, designed to try to stop the incidence of torture and enhance principles of good governance across a range of ministries. This was precisely the type of detailed assistance the NTC should have been offered. Throughout this period there were a number of dialogue initiatives, some more cosmetic than others. In the summer of 2013 Al-Wefaq came tantalisingly close to forming a national unity government. Matters took a turn for the worse after Al-Wefaq once again elected not to stand for parliament in late 2014, which precipitated a rapid decline in relations. Arrests followed in 2015, as the hawks in the Bahraini administration took advantage of growing conflict between Shias and Sunnis, Iran and Saudi Arabia, in places like Syria and Yemen.

I remain convinced that a reasonable constitutional settlement is attainable in Bahrain, and that the people of Bahrain see themselves as Bahrainis first rather than Shia or Sunni. It could even act as a template for how reconciliation between different confessional communities in the wider region could be achieved if given the right international support and encouragement. It is beyond the confines of this book to properly and fairly evaluate the impact of all this work, but it is clear that without this type of prolonged engagement by the FCO and other non-state actors, like Beyond Conflict, the John Smith Memorial Trust and Beyond Borders, with political, cultural and civil society leaders, there was every chance that matters could have turned more violent, potentially even ending in the type of political and social chaos that would finally engulf New Libya.

Libyan refugees at the border, trying to reach Egypt on 2 April 2011

The Katiba barracks on the outskirts of Benghazi after it was stormed by rebel forces in February 2011

An iconic Libyan rebel Toyota on the approach to Benghazi, sporting the rebel flag and a machine gun

The courthouse of Benghazi, where protests against the Gaddafi regime began on 17 February 2011

A wall of Freedom Square, visited by the author on 3 April 2011, where those who died in the battle for Benghazi were remembered

A placard held by a female protester in Freedom Square, Benghazi, on 4 April 2011

Jason McCue and the author in Freedom Square on 4 April 2011

Young boys helping to clean the streets of Benghazi in April 2011. Many children, including the Boy Scouts and the Girl Guides, were responsible for the delivery of public services during the early part of the revolution

Citizens of New Libya sign petitions in Freedom Square, Benghazi, April 2011, asking for NATO's help in the battle for Misrata

Placards held aloft by revolutionaries in Freedom Square, Benghazi, 4 April 2011. An arresting sign in the centre reads 'We are not AlQaida. We want freedom'.

Above. A striking work of graffiti art, which the author came across on 3 April 2011, painted by the Banksy of Benghazi, Qais Ahmad Hilal, who was shot dead by a sniper cell sent into Benghazi by Gaddafi

Right. Qais Ahmad Hilal, a graffiti artist who was shot dead by a sniper in an attempt to stem the flow of satirical art that appeared across Benghazi. Qais's murder in fact urged other young artists to take to the streets and create art in his name

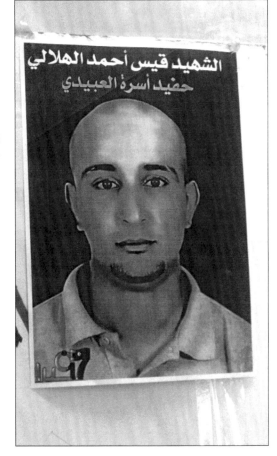

الشهيد قيس أحمد الهلالي
حفيد أسرة العبيدي

The author with young men and women at the Benghazi courthouse, where young artists came together to make art in support of the rebels after protests erupted in February 2011

Two artists at the Benghazi courthouse showing the author their anti-Gaddafi artwork on 4 April 2011

Above. Jason McCue giving interviews to UK press and media at El Fadeel Hotel in Benghazi with the author on the morning of 3 April 2011

Right. Iman Bugaighis, TNC spokeswoman and sister of Salwa al-Dighaili, member of the National Transitional Council, who was assassinated in 2014. Bugaighis was one of 13 original members of the February 17 Revolution Committee which ran the city from the courthouse; she went from professor of dentistry at the Garyounis University to revolutionary spokeswoman in little more than two weeks.

Jason McCue and the author announcing the Agreements reached with the NTC to the world's press on the evening of 5 April 2011

Jason McCue and the author holding the signed Agreements with the UK Special Envoy to Libya, Christopher Prentice, at the El Fadeel Hotel in Benghazi on 5 April 2011

Above. Jason McCue and the author meeting rebel fighters on their return from Ajdabiya as they made their way towards the Egyptian border during the night of 5 April 2011

Right. Exhausted, at 4.30am on 6 April 2011, Jason McCue and the author waiting to cross the Libyan–Egyptian border

Friday afternoon opposition rally in Sitra, Bahrain, in the summer of 2011

Roelf Meyer, Tim Phillips, Mohammed Bhabha and the author talking with the NUA leadership in Manama in the summer of 2011

The author with Callum Macrae of Channel 4 news and colleagues from the BHRC and KHRP taking a rest while documenting human rights abuses in a burnt-out Kurdish village in south-east Turkey in early 1994

The author with Sydney Kentridge QC and Tim Otty before opening the case of *Ocalan* v. *Turkey* before the Grand Chamber of the European Courts of Human Rights sitting in Strasbourg on 9 July 2004

Delfina Entracanales, of the Delfina Foundation, looking at the work of young artists with the author in the old town of Damascus in 2007

Delfina Entracanales and the author at the home of Boutros Boutros-Ghali, the former UN Secretary General, in Cairo in 2009

Beyond Borders team and Lord Steel with representatives of the Omani Lower and Upper Parliament at Traquair House in the Scottish Borders in March 2013

The last session at Beyond Borders Thought Festival on Islam and the West with Malian Director of the Festival in the Desert, Manny Ansar; former US Ambassador for the Clinton Administration, Cynthia Schneider; writer and barrister Sadakat Kadri; historian William Dalyrmple; and the author

With Bill Clinton and thirty other former presidents and prime ministers at the Club du Madrid 2012 Conference in Little Rock, Arakansas, where the author was Master of Ceremonies

The author looking on at 11 Downing Street as Prime Minister David Cameron meets Fellows of the John Smith Memorial Trust in June 2011

Roelf Meyer, Tim Phillips and the author enjoying themselves after a speech at the 2012 Edinburgh Festival

Sir Kieran Prendergast, former head of the United Nations Department of Political Affairs and Chair of the Beyond Borders Patrons, in conversation with First Minister Nicola Sturgeon, Martin Griffiths, Executive Director of the European Institute of Peace, and the author, talking about Scotland and peacemaking at Traquair House during the 2015 Beyond Borders International Festival

The author in talks with US Secretary of State John Kerry and UN Special Envoy to Syria, Staffan de Mistura, in Vienna in May 2016, in his capacity as a senior mediation advisor to the UN Department of Political Affairs and the Office of the Special Envoy to Syria

12.   Stabilising Libya

This then was the diplomatic and policy landscape in mid-June 2011, as a small group of bespoke humanitarian and dialogue organisations waited to see how the ISRT report to the International Contact Group on stabilisation in Libya might utilise their expertise. Some suspected that the publication of the report had provided the UK government with a convenient cover by which to delay making funding decisions concerning non-state assistance. Others were more sympathetic to the situation with which the FCO had to deal. The lack of information about conditions on the ground in a fast-moving political and military situation made it extraordinarily difficult for any government institution to evaluate bids. As Rory Stewart and Gerald Knaus observe in their book *Can Intervention Work?* (2011), 'International policy-makers have a muddled and half-understood picture of the country before intervention, perhaps an equally muddled and half-understood picture of their own society in the West, and some generally doubtful guesses about how to get from one to the other.'[1]

Yet the task was not as difficult as it appeared when one considered the relatively small sums involved. As McCue rightly reminded one earnest FCO official, each NATO missile that landed in Libya cost the coalition about £1 million. The BHRC were asking for a fraction of that sum to assist on transitional justice and constitutional issues. Stephen R. Grand, director of the Project on US Relations with the Islamic World, wryly observed: 'Often small amounts of money targeted at the right individual or organisation can be far more effective than large, expensive top-down programs. In a moment of tremendous change, assistance needs to be delivered swiftly and nimbly, which is not something governments always do well. This task may be better performed in many instances by private foundations and civil society groups.'[2]

In fact, it would take David Cameron to nudge the FCO on BHRC involvement, after McCue wrote to him directly to elicit his help. In a letter dated 8 June 2011 Cameron informed McCue that he had asked the FCO to open discussions with a view to harnessing the Bar Council's expertise to help strengthen the rule of law in Libya, within the context of the government's wider post-conflict strategy, which was still being worked out.

10 DOWNING STREET
LONDON SW1A 2AA

THE PRIME MINISTER

8 June 2011

Dear Jason

Thank you for your letter of 18 May, and for keeping me updated on your contacts with the National Transitional Council. They deserve credit for taking an early stand on legacy issues, and I am sure that the approach of building long-term contacts as the situation develops is the right one.

Building up the capacity and credibility of the Council as the legitimate interlocutors for the Libyan people remains central to our Libya policy. The engagement of partners such as the Bar Council is welcome, and I have asked the FCO to contact Mark Muller so that the proposals can be considered urgently as part of the wider strategy being developed by the new international Stabilisation Response Assessment Team. The nature of this process, and the need for us to leverage wider sources of international funding than the UK alone can supply, means that we do not yet have the agreement and funding for your team's immediate deployment to Benghazi. But the FCO will come back to you as soon as possible to discuss how your idea could sit within the approach that is being developed.

Mr Jason McCue

But in late June 2011 we discovered that the officials dealing with the BHRC application weren't even aware of the Prime Minister's letter or intervention on our behalf. On 23 June I wrote to the FCO requesting an 'update to be given regarding possible funding re aspects of the original Bar Council BHRC bid which is no longer being considered under the AP'. The only reply I received from the FCO, despite sending the request to a number of officials, was as follows: 'Hi Mark, I've now moved on from Libya issues. Grateful therefore if you could remove me from your distribution list. All the best.' Four days later we received this further response:

Thank you for your bid to the Arab Partnership Fund. Apologies for only responding to you now.

After wide discussion in the FCO and Whitehall it has been decided that the Arab Partnership Programme will not accept bids for Libya at present.

All support for any stabilisation/reconstruction work in Libya is now under the authority of the Libya sub-Board of the Conflict Prevention Pool. This board will now consider your proposal and contact you in due course.

Whitehall, it appeared, was still struggling to deal with issues involving a multitude of countries as a result of the Arab Spring. The bureaucratic fog was only mitigated by the failure of the Libyan rebels to bring down the regime, thereby giving all concerned much needed breathing space. Yet it did seem strange that while the Prime Minister acted with admirable speed in redefining the policy landscape, and the military could conduct its campaign with conspicuous efficiency and with few civilian casualties, Whitehall found it virtually impossible to decide how to urgently assist the NTC on transitional justice and reconciliation issues that were bound to affect the course of any stabilisation effort sooner rather than later.

It was probably disconcerting for officials to have to deal with the BHRC and victim associations led by characters like McCue so early on in a conflict, particularly given the FCO's own initial shaky efforts to establish relations with the NTC. And then there were the skeletons in its cupboard concerning Britain's relationship with the Gaddafi regime and its alleged involvement in the CIA rendition programme. Perhaps they thought it might not be such a good idea to let human rights lawyers lead on transitional justice issues even though they had secured an agreement with the NTC, particularly given Jibril's ambition to effect a managed transition with the help of former members of the regime. In the event, it would take a full month, four weeks after the Prime Minister first wrote to McCue, before the FCO came back with a response to the BHRC bid. By then, the officials who, in April 2011, had advised the BHRC to put its bid in a broad way had been replaced by other officials who now wanted it drafted in a different way. Apparently there was now a new fund involving other ministries such as DFID, which – wait for it – could only make a final decision once the ISRT report had been considered by an inter-departmental committee meeting in mid-July.

We received this response on 8 July 2011:

Mark Muller, QC
Chair, Bar Human Rights Committee of England and Wales

Dear Mr Muller

I understand that you are concerned that you are still waiting for a response on the Bar Human Rights Committee rule of law proposal for Libya which you submitted to the Foreign Office for consideration. I did speak briefly to your colleague Jason McCue about 10 days ago, when he asked about progress on the proposal, to explain that consideration would be given to the proposal after the International Stabilisation Response Team had undertaken their mission, made their recommendations and HMG had decided how we intended to respond to those recommendations.

I thought it might be helpful if I set out the procedures and structures within HMG regarding how we are handling support for Libya in order to explain the reasons for what must seem to you an unnecessary and bureaucratic delay. These have changed several times over the last few weeks owing to the fluidity of the situation in Libya.

As you are aware, your proposal was initially considered by both HRDF [Human Rights Democracy Fund] and the Arab Partnership. Subsequently, Ministers decided that all funding for Libya, both support for the NTC as well as post-conflict stabilisation work, should be channelled through a single source. On formation of a separate Libya Conflict Pool your proposal was referred for consideration by the Libya Sub Board. This Fund has limited monies as yet allocated to it and the principal use of the Fund to date has been to sustain the Transitional National Council for urgent immediate priorities.

Funding for stabilisation work, which includes rule of law, has not actually been considered as yet although some major advance planning has been undertaken. An International Stabilisation Response Team was despatched to Libya, NATO has set up a Stabilisation Planning Team and the UN Department for Political Affairs, who are in the lead on post-conflict work, are developing a post crisis plan in support of the NTC for when a political settlement has been reached. These are the only initiatives which have received funding from the Libya Conflict Pool to date.

I understand that the recommendations of the International Stabilisation Response Team will be discussed at the International Contact Group on 15 July, following which, the UK will draw up its own programme of response. Inside HMG, a specialist stabilisation team has also been set up to plan the UK's response. Your proposal has been forwarded to them, to our team in Benghazi and to the Ministry of Justice's International team for comment.

My colleague from the Arab Partnership, wrote on the 20 June to Joanne at the Bar Council to explain that you would receive a response after the Libya Conflict Pool Board meeting, the date of which had not then been set. It will now take place on 12 July.

The Board of the Libya Conflict Pool will have its first full meeting since its establishment next Tuesday. The Bar Human Rights Committee proposal will be considered at that meeting along with other proposals, in the context of recommendations from the various international plans. I would re-iterate that the UN is in the lead on post-conflict reconstruction and stabilisation and the UK's primary focus will be to support its work.

I hope this explanation clarifies the situation for you and explains the reasons for delay. I will write to you immediately after the Board meeting to let you know the position.

The contents of the letter raised a number of concerns. Firstly, it proceeded on the basis that the BHRC application was a post-conflict stabilisation bid, when it was nothing of the sort. Rather, it was a bid for funds for immediate rule of law work to be undertaken during the conflict. Secondly, it did not come out of thin air. It came from a MoU signed with the NTC, which the rebel Minister of Justice endorsed in his later visit to London on 17 May 2011. Thirdly, the strengthening of the rule of law, transitional justice issues, the preservation of evidence concerning crimes against humanity, and wider constitutional dialogue were immediate priorities for the NTC. That is why they signed the MoU in the first place. It was deeply disappointing to realise that by the time the Libyan conflict entered its summer fighting phase, a full three months after we had returned from Benghazi, all external bids for funding to the FCO concerning transitional justice and immediate dialogue issues were still on hold pending 'official consideration' of the ISRT report. This, despite one MI6 source publicly describing the report as a 'Noddy guide' to stabilisation that wasn't worth the wait.

The ISRT Report

When the seventy-page stabilisation report was eventually published towards the end of June it gave little explicit guidance about what type of projects should be supported by the international community. While it did include abstract statements in favour of civil society dialogue, and the involvement of the non-state sector in post-conflict reconstruction, it contained few concrete recommendations concerning implementation. Instead, it was littered with policy wonk phraseology for which most English speaking Libyans needed expert translation. As noted in *The Times*, the report concluded – wrongly as it turned out – that there was a low probability of both a successful advance on Tripoli by rebel forces and of Gaddafi being hit by NATO forces in a missile strike. Instead, it expected the regime to crumble from within through a popular uprising or coup. The plan was therefore highly reliant on the defection of parts of the existing Gaddafi security apparatus to the rebels, and Jibril's vision of a mediated transition. It had wholly failed to take account of the emerging divisions between the 'securalists' and the increasingly powerful 'Islamist' networks or the views of other rebel militia in places like Misrata or indeed civil society. As Ian Martin observed, much depended on which Libyans one talked with. The ISRT seemingly confined its exchanges to the NTC in Benghazi and Jibril's network in UAE.

According to *The Times*, the report included a proposal for a 10,000–15,000-strong 'Tripoli Taskforce' of guards, resourced and supported by the United Arab Emirates (UAE) whose purpose was to take over the Libyan capital, secure key sites and arrest high-level Gaddafi supporters. The document disclosed detailed planning for key security, telecommunications, power and transport infrastructure to be secured in the immediate aftermath of the collapse of the regime. It also foresaw an internationally backed one-month programme for the emergency supply of $550 million of gas and petrol to western Libya that would begin immediately after the fall of the regime, as well as a UN-supported programme to deliver immediate humanitarian aid by land, sea and air, with support from key Muslim-majority countries such as the UAE, Qatar and Turkey.

What it did not do was plan in any detail for the possibility of different power centres emerging within New Libya, post-conflict, or draw upon the full power of civil society both within Libya and abroad to help reconstruct and reconcile the country. This, despite a plethora of UN declarations that emphasised the crucial role that civil society and women should play in post-conflict reconstruction and reconciliation processes. It was obvious to most independent observers that to achieve any sort of long-term reconciliation in Libya, the NTC had to involve the Libyan people in the rebuilding of its shattered society. It also had to reintegrate rebel factions into an agreed cohesive political framework to have any chance of success. Anyone who had experienced stabilisation efforts in Iraq and Afghanistan knew that government could not achieve such transformation by its efforts alone. Yet the report failed to properly address these issues, preferring instead to predicate its response on an internal uprising in Tripoli that would, conveniently enough, have required a monopoly of power to be given to state and international bodies over which Western states had most control. It failed to materialise. In the event there were no widespread defections to make the regime collapse from within. Instead, Tripoli was captured by a ragtag bunch of rebel militias who thereafter refused to give up areas of control to the regular Libyan army. In fact, the regime continued to fight on well after it had lost Tripoli, thus allowing rebel militias to consolidate their positions in the absence of any agreed post-conflict division of the spoils.

The Lessons of Iraq and Afghanistan

To my mind senior officials in 10 Downing Street should have asked themselves just how successful previous state-based stabilisation efforts had been in rebuilding societies elsewhere, before they decided to put their faith in another one. The deployment of government 'stabilisation units' reached its zenith in Afghanistan. A cursory glance at Sherard Cowper-Coles's observations in *Cables from Kabul: The Inside Story of the West's Afghanistan Campaign* (2012), which detailed his time as the UK Ambassador and Special Envoy to Afghanistan and Pakistan, told you all you needed to know about the reality of these initiatives. The failure to politically engage with real opposition elements in Afghanistan meant much of the hard work done by stabilisation officers in the field was of no relevance whatsoever. The only local Afghan communities that worked with these units, in places like Helmand Province, were the ones in their pay. Unsurprisingly, they told their paymasters what they wanted to hear. This situation was not best assisted by the short six-month battlefield and one-year diplomatic rotations, which meant troops and officials were often shipped out just when they began to understand the terrain. Cowper-Coles's experiences of stabilisation efforts in Afghanistan should have served as a warning to those government advisors who remain attracted to the idea of co-ordinating reconstruction in Libya through government-based institutions and larger development agencies, without the involvement of opposition and smaller civil society elements.

In fact, Cowper-Coles's experiences mirrored my own with the BHRC. In November 2008 the BHRC won the Attorney General's Pro Bono Award for its FCO-funded work in strengthening the rule of law in Afghanistan. But to what end? The real story behind the award was much more depressing. In 2006 the BHRC had been actively engaged on the ground in Afghanistan building law libraries, working with women's shelters, lawyers, law officers, the Afghan Human Rights Commission and local NGOs from across the country. This was possible because the BHRC had been allowed to operate freely and interact on its own initiative with local players and real communities. Yet within two years of the British takeover of Helmand, the BHRC was locked down in the British Embassy in Kabul. From that point on it was only able to give what felt like stage-managed seminars with carefully selected actors in the secure confines of a UNDPA building, under the watchful eyes of our close protection units. New security protocols and the need to co-ordinate everything through stabilisation units snuffed out all independent initiative to work with ordinary Afghans in any meaningful way. The new legal 'duty of care' imposed burdens on the embassy to ensure civilian staff and contractors took no risks. Many of my later visits to the country were spent within embassy or international compounds or having dinner with Rory Stewart at his remarkable Turquoise Foundation. Ironically the Turquoise Foundation remained one of the few shining examples of what could be achieved when the power of civil society was harnessed both domestically and internationally.

After ten years of hugely expensive intervention, it seemed to me that all the West had managed to do in Afghanistan was to create a hermetically sealed bubble in a heavily protected area of Kabul, in which Western government officials and representatives from international NGOs and development organisations spent most of their time meeting with each other and Afghan ministries to 'co-ordinate' increasingly ineffectual policies on the ground. Rory Stewart, who spent the better part of six years in Kabul, later commented on 'the extreme isolation of international lives, their surreal optimism, and their abstract jargon'. Civilians employed by Western governments were generally locked within the guarded embassy compounds, which kept them brutally segregated from local life while 'development officials were absorbed in [. . .] writing 'strategic plans' and 'feasibility studies', submitting reports, and ensuring the proper processing of 'contracts, invoices, and receipts'.[3] It is telling that Cowper-Coles only publicly revealed the true extent of the mess in Afghanistan after he had left the Foreign Service. In truth, it was probably impossible for even a high-ranking official such as him to come clean while in office. The truth was that no individual was in a position to turn around the juggernaut of Western self-delusion that was stabilisation in Afghanistan and Iraq. Had they tried to do so, I have no doubt they would have been on the first helicopter out of Kabul, for the alternative was to rip up the entire policy framework and start afresh.

It would take President Obama to finally call time on the fiction of state-building that was going on in Afghanistan and, indeed, Iraq, but by then its lessons were clear. The official historian of the US military, Lieutenant Colonel Isaiah Wilson, wrote of the Iraq war that 'there was no Phase IV plan' to occupy and stabilise Iraq once the regime collapsed. When the Coalition Provisional Authority did try to put Iraq back on its feet it disbanded the military and imposed de-Baathification in relation to all government administrators, including teachers and technical experts of all kinds, to disastrous effect. The closure of state-owned businesses and the introduction of free market practices led to a rapid contraction of the economy. This in turn led to the creation of widespread grievances that resulted in renewed resistance. Within a few months of the war ending the Coalition Provisional Authority faced a full-scale insurgency. When asked about the resulting chaos, looting and executions, Donald Rumsfeld, the Secretary of State for Defense, simply shrugged his shoulders and responded by saying, 'Stuff happens.'

It was clear from conversations I had with NTC officials in London in May and June of 2011 that they had no desire to repeat the Iraqi experience by letting 'stuff' happen in Libya. That is precisely why they agreed to a plan in which police officials, administrators and experts vital to maintenance of basic services were to be kept on after the fall of the regime and a MoU would help strengthen the rule of law *before* the conflict ended. If Afghanistan and Iraq had taught us anything, it was that to stabilise a country properly you needed not only to start planning from the outset of any intervention but you also had to ensure that the private sector and local civil communities were included in the development and subsequent implementation of any stabilisation plan. The 'buy-in' of local non-governmental players was particularly essential in efforts to rebuild respect for the rule of law, for it was not government but the people who ultimately built, dispensed and voluntarily became subject to the rule of law.

The Mercy Corps Report

This insight tallied with the conclusions of a report written by the US-based humanitarian organisation Mercy Corps which, together with the Governance Network, sent out a small team to eastern Libya to carry out an assessment of the immediate governance issues facing Libya in early July of 2011. It also hoped to identify areas where international assistance would be of use in Libya and to examine the potential barriers to success of internationally supported interventions. Unlike the ISRT, the Mercy Corps team travelled to Benghazi, Derna, Bayda and Tobruk to conduct interviews with over forty NTC members, government officials and civil society leaders. Crucially, it also held meetings with youth, the media and academics. An overarching theme of the assessment was the strong sense of ownership that civil society had in the transition, which required the establishment of an all-inclusive process. According to this report, civil society had expanded massively since February 2011, 'reflecting the significant hope and determination of a population in the process of liberating themselves and eager to help lead what is next for the country'.

Before the uprising, Libya had only twenty-two registered civil society organisations (CSOs) and it was impossible for them to function independently. As of 24 July 2011 that number had risen to 250 in Benghazi alone. However, problems remained concerning entrenched corruption, over-centralised decision-making, a lack of transparency and inexperienced leadership, engendered by a regime that had stifled all governance systems both inside and outside of the public sector. Indeed, the assessment reported that Libya ranked last or second to last in the region in four of Kaufman and Mastruzzi's five Worldwide Governance Indicators (WGI), despite a better ranking on the United Nation's Human Development Index (HDI) due to its free access to health care and education.

As Dr Lamia Abusedra of the NTC's Executive Office of Cultural Relations and Civil Society (EOCCS) admitted: 'Goodwill is running the country now, but soon we have to build real institutions with real participation by the people.' Thus, in the view of the Mercy Corps it was absolutely essential to: determine meaningful dialogue between citizens and government about the future of the Libyan state; negotiate afresh the relationships between the new government, nascent civil society and the private sector; determine how to reform ministries and reintegrate old regime technocrats; and capitalise on 'new-found national identity to further develop an emerging sense of citizens' responsibility'.

But even in July 2011 there were already worrying signs that effective civil society engagement with the NTC was just not happening. The assessment reported how many in civil society felt left out of decision-making processes that related to the future of the country, citing the drafting of the transitional constitution as an example. The NTC leadership had formed a committee of academics to do the work 'without realising the need or at least making the effort to include a wider population in the process'. Thus, the NTC intended to present a draft constitution to Libyan citizens with 'apparently little provision for inclusion, discussion or debate'. This attitude replicated the psychology of the old regime and its refusal to consult anyone who did not count politically, which deeply concerned active civil society groups who had 'high expectations' about reform and 'things being done differently' in the new Libya.

The Mercy Corps' observations about the lack of NTC communication and engagement with Libyan society were beginning to gather resonance. As Stephen R. Grand has noted:

> The success of democratisation efforts in the Middle East over the long term will depend in good measure on the existence of public demand for reform and democracy. Well-designed constitutions are important [. . .] but they will be rendered meaningless if the public is not willing to stand behind them to ensure they function as intended. Transitions to democracy are more likely to remain on track and be successful with the help of an empowered and engaged citizenry, capable of reminding politicians that there will be a price to pay should they deviate from the new rules of the game. All else remaining equal, one can expect countries with citizens who are more educated, more exposed to the outside world, and more highly networked together to fare better than those whose citizens are not.[4]

The Mercy Corps report concluded that civil society was 'at risk of becoming alienated if the current approach was not altered'. When this was raised with Dr Atia Lagwal, executive officer of EOCCS, he replied that it was 'too political' to talk about right now. Instead, he repeated the oft-quoted refrain of NTC leaders that, unlike Egypt, Libya had sufficient money to ensure that Libyans did not become impatient with the pace of change. 'We will figure it out and once Gaddafi is gone there will be no problems,' he opined. One might have added 'Inshallah'.

If the primary objective of the ISRT report was to put forward viable and practical recommendations about how to actually construct a stable, inclusive and democratic Libya, post-Gaddafi, then it failed in its task. It read like a beginners' guide to state-building, in which the platitudes and abstractions about civil society were designed to avoid rather than engage with the difficult issues that threatened the West's relations with the NTC. This failure to make civil society a partner in the development of New Libya's constitutional and political future as the conflict was ongoing would come to haunt efforts to build a viable post-conflict future for the country for years to come.

In the event, the only private organisations funded by HMG in the early part of the Libyan uprising were the large development agencies, apart from small companies that specialised in the field of strategic communications or security, who enjoyed distinctly comfortable relations, not to say connections, with the British security establishment. The FCO and DFID were altogether more comfortable dealing with development agencies such as Oxfam, Save the Children and CARE in these types of conflict situations. They understood the humanitarian purpose of these agencies, which did not trespass on policy areas historically the preserve of states. So while the UK government had certainly adapted over the last quarter of a century to the increasing role that non-state development agencies played in the field of post-conflict or natural disaster reconstruction, it continued to struggle with the emergence of smaller, more esoteric, players in the field of conflict resolution and transitional justice, which often cut across complicated state interests.

In previous conflicts like Afghanistan and Iraq, rule of law actors like the BHRC had only appeared on the scene after and not at the start of military operations, and only after stabilisation policy was settled. Yet the BHRC's early involvement in the Libyan conflict was not an isolated incident. It was indicative of a new type of private diplomacy emerging in international relations in the twenty-first century, in which NGOs and groups representing victims of terrorism were simply no longer willing to leave negotiations on crucial legacy, human rights, transitional justice and conflict resolution issues exclusively to state institutions. The failure of the ISRT to fully harness the private sector did not, however, stop the development of other non-state dialogue initiatives. After being rebuffed by the UK government, CHD managed to secure funding from the German government and Norway to start its dialogue with local representatives of Libyan civil society about future democratic reform and reconciliation.

With the help of Hana el-Gallal, the former NTC spokesperson on education who resigned her post in May 2011 because of the NTC's lack of dialogue with Libyan civil society, CHD went on to bring together local political, tribal and civil society representatives from Libya's rebel polity, in a series of remarkable conferences and reconciliation meetings. The first one was held in Benghazi, where 100 people from the opposition were invited to discuss the issues that Libya would need to address in the future. Similar meetings occurred in Tripoli and Misrata in September 2011, but by then much of the discontent and alienation we had sensed building had set in. CHD would follow up these meetings after the fall of Gaddafi with a series of public dialogues and discussions, in late 2011/early 2012, regarding the drafting of electoral and constitutional laws. But by then serious public distrust about the transparency of decision-making concerning the NTC had embedded itself, following its non-consultation with others about reforms. The failure to identify and support these types of initiatives at an early stage revealed a demonstrable and growing need for a new independent international rapid response fund, which small non-state mediators and humanitarian institutions could draw upon to begin urgent innovative initiatives in emergency conflict situations. If the international community was to take advantage of such expertise, then these actors had to be able to access emergency funds without having to artificially fit themselves within the specific aims and objectives of the funding priorities of governments and international institutions, which often took months to process applications in any case.

To my mind the approach taken by CHD to stabilisation was critical as it tried to support the development of a pluralistic political arena in Libya, by generating grass-roots consensus and ownership over post-conflict reform, through encouraging significant 'buy-in' from wider society. Rebuilding government legitimacy, national infrastructure and institutions all required recognition of the principles of good governance in order to prevent new outbreaks of violence and civil despair. An essential element of good governance was an empowered and informed civil society. Successful reconstruction efforts elsewhere demonstrated that civil society had a crucial role to play in ensuring government upheld its commitment to the rule of law at both the local and national level. Civil society did this through cultural expression and criticism, media monitoring and lobbying activities, and delivering civil education at the grass-roots level. This was precisely what I saw the fledgling elements of Libyan civil society do in Benghazi in early April 2011.

The Rejection of the BHRC Bid

On 13 July 2011 the BHRC finally received a response from the FCO rejecting its bid, moments before a meeting arranged to consider its implementation. The Libya sub-board had rejected the bid as 'premature'; too wide-ranging and comprehensive; and only capable of being implemented in eastern Libya. It observed that courts could not be expected to function on day one of peace. I wrote back in the following terms:

> Thank you for your e-mail the contents of which are duly noted. As you know the original bid was submitted immediately after our visit to Benghazi in April to the Arab Partnership Fund under pressure of time and not to the Pool Fund of which we learnt about only relatively recently. We share

many, if not all, of the observations made by the relevant Government Departments about the original bid save for one and that is that it might have been worthwhile for such observations to have been communicated a little earlier so we might have responded to them or refined our bid. We have not pursued our dialogue with the NTC as we were waiting for the FCO response. We remain firmly of the view that civil society in the UK has an important role to play in strengthening the rule of law in Libya both *before* and *after* the NTC assumes a position of power with or without the support of HMG. However, we very much hope there may be an opportunity to contribute and work with the FCO and UN in the future when matters are a little clearer.

For his part, McCue was a little less diplomatic, writing a blistering letter pointing out that:

the proposal was drafted in broad terms after detailed discussions with the FCO. It was drafted that way to meet the tight April deadline re the Arab Partnership Fund and because the BHRC was specially told that the bid could be refined later as matters became clearer. Mr Muller was later asked to refine the bid and to just concentrate on transitional justice issues. He was then told to hold off after all Libyan bids were removed from the Arab Partnership Fund. He has been waiting for the FCO to revert back to him on the substance of the bid ever since. Your comments concerning the broad nature of the bid takes no account of this history or what the BHRC was in fact proposing to concentrate on. When we met with Justice Minister al-Alagi in London, he made clear that he had been asked by the Chairman Abdul Jalil and the NTC to raise the matter of our Programme and push it forwards. In front of Richard Northern, we had no option but to apologise for the delay and explain to the Minister that we were waiting still on FCO funding. The Minister asked then whether we could be ready to deploy British lawyers in Benghazi before the end of July.

As to substance, McCue stated: 'There is simply no common sense reason for HMG not to embrace and fund this Programme immediately.' FCO sent out the 'wrong signal' by indicating that 'HMG does not want private civil society engagement' in transitional justice issues in which 'it cannot engage itself'. As to the assertion that the bid was premature, he claimed it was 'completely responsive to the current situation in Libya and the very immediate needs of the people'. Such conflict resolution rule-of-law work needed to be 'commenced in the midst of conflict' not just after it. The idea that you needed to stabilise the situation 'before much of the activity can be carried out' made no sense 'as the higher echelons of the judiciary have had no independence for thirty years'. Judges, he railed, 'need to be trained now, outside the conflict zone, so that they can be reactivated immediately when conditions allow'. Lastly McCue pointed out that he had been in constant contact with the Lawyers' Trade Union and that Minister al-Alagi had expressed his desire to set up a working group. He ended by claiming the way the FCO dealt with the proposal fell 'far short of what is expected of it and what we all know it is capable of'.

For Jason the rejection of the bid was a cruel blow. He was someone who had campaigned against Gaddafi's excesses for over twenty years and had made the long arduous trip to Benghazi in an effort to reset relations with what he thought was the moral support of the British Prime Minister. But it was time to move on and I told him so. What should not be allowed to pass, however, is the assertion by certain former government ministers before the Foreign Affairs Select Committee in 2016 that the government did 'all it could' to help create the conditions for a successful stabilisation of Libya both during and after the conflict.

13. Endgame in Libya

As the conflict slid into mid-July 2011 it began to look to some as if a stalemate might be developing in Libya. During this period the NATO coalition experienced a flurry of nerves after rumours spread that the French were having second thoughts about the intervention, and were thinking about cutting a deal with Gaddafi. Yet we knew through other reports that things were moving slowly, almost imperceptibly, in favour of the rebels. The British government had increased its stabilisation unit from six to over forty, while the French had installed an even bigger presence in Benghazi. Moreover, both countries finally got over their legal concerns and, in July 2011, recognised the diplomatic credentials of the NTC as the legitimate government of Libya, thereby allowing it to begin the process by which it could access locked and frozen funds. By the end of July, French nerves had settled and most of NATO was fully on board and reconciled to its mission, especially after Turkey and the African Union, led by President Zuma, finally failed in efforts to secure a negotiated settlement.

But perhaps the most important reason for the end of the military stalemate was the arrival of foreign ground advisors. They not only coordinated the delivery of arms and trained rebels but also helped break the siege of Misrata as well as secure the approach into Tripoli from the Nafusa Mountains. Up until June 2011, NATO deployed few reconnaissance missions to Tripoli or the Nafusa Mountains as it regarded Brega, and then Misrata, as the more important priority. According to Frederic Wehrey, a senior associate in the Middle East Programme at Carnegie Endowment for International Peace, 'this limited the number of strikes that could be carried out, since NATO's rules of engagement required that the target be verified via sight . . . The scarcity of NATO airpower effectively stalled the Nafusa offensive once the mountain towns of Zintan, Yefren, Nalut and Kikla had risen up. Without airpower these towns were unable to move out of their foothills and into the plains north of Nafusa.'

The arrival of foreign advisors in June changed all of that by improving the flow of information to enable precise airstrikes to take place. British advisors were particularly effective in calling in and coordinating strikes in Misrata, while Qatari and Emirati advisors played a similar role in the Nafusa Mountains by enhancing communication, training and weapons shipments. However, there was much competition between the Qataris and Emiratis due to the tension between Jibril and Belhaj, which in turn led the British and the French to set up their own operations room in Zintan after the Qataris began to eclipse the role of the Emiratis.

NATO commanders also utilised a network of former military and air-force officers who had set up operating rooms in Benghazi, Misrata and Zintan. These officers enjoyed longstanding relationships with their Western counterparts through security co-operation and training. While these defectors had little control over the makeshift battalions that characterised the early effort of the revolution – battalions full of civilian volunteers with no military experience – they did provide valuable information to NATO planners. For example, an operations room was set up in Dubai in March 2011 by Mahmoud Jibril with the assistance of MI6. By mid-July NATO had other operations rooms to draw upon apart from the one set up in Benghazi by a former colonel from the Libyan Special Forces commanded by Yuonis, who quickly became sidelined as the division between secularists and Islamists camps intensified. This included a room in Zuwaitina, which the Qataris helped set up, linked to the Islamists. All of these rooms fed information to NATO if not to each other.

More to the point British efforts to depose Gaddafi were no longer limited to guiding in air strikes. On the ground – and on the quiet – special-forces soldiers were blending in with rebel fighters. Arguments about how far the UK should go, given the legal constraints, were finally resolved in a series of meetings of the National Security Council at Downing Street, under the chairmanship of Prime Minister David Cameron. At the outset of the NATO air campaign there had been real divisions about men 'directing air strikes' from the ground. However, the erroneous bombing of NTC columns by NATO aircraft in early April provided those who wanted to give more direct assistance with the argument they needed. From then on British and French officers were permitted to co-ordinate more closely with the NTC and rebels in Misrata, ostensibly for the purposes of 'deconfliction' or preventing such accidental clashes from happening again. Meanwhile, the Chief of Staff General Richards began to liaise with his counterparts in Qatar, who by June had agreed with the UK and France to provide material back-up as well as training to the NTC. But while France and Qatar were ready to provide weapons directly, the UK was not. This made little practical difference, however, since the SAS was operating closely with Qatari special forces, which had reportedly delivered items such as Milan anti-tank missiles to rebel personnel.

As to the contribution of British forces, General Richards, speaking later at a public event, commented that though the NTC forces 'were the land element [. . .] integrating the Qataris', Emiratis' and Jordanians' troops into the operation was key'. He failed to mention the presence of more than twenty other British operators on the ground. The truth was that by mid-August the SAS had strayed beyond its training facility, with single men or pairs accompanying NTC commanders back to their units after training. They dressed as Libyans and blended in with the units they mentored. There were concerned that they might be spotted but this did not happen. 'We have become a lot better at blending in. Our people were able to stay close to the NTC commanders without being compromised,' one insider later told the BBC's defence correspondent, Mark Urban. This dovetailed with the admission made by the Chief of the Qatar Defence Staff in October of 2011 that 'hundreds' of his troops had been on the ground in Libya, although sources close to Urban suggested that the number committed on the ground by all nations probably did not exceed a couple of hundred.

By the end of July 2011 a twenty-four-strong British Special Forces team from D Squadron of 22 Regiment had been put in place, including members of the Special Reconnaissance Regiment who were expert in covert intelligence gathering. Their job was to train and mentor NTC units in Libya. These forces linked up with members of the Commandement des Opérations Spéciales (COS), the elite parachute regiment of the French army, at Zuwaytinah, the command headquarters for the eastern front, ninety miles south-west of Benghazi. From there, officers were sent to the west of the country via Tunisia to train rebel volunteers in the western mountains, in places like Zintan. Libyan exiles from Manchester, Birmingham, London and Dublin, many of whom had never seen their homeland before the conflict, also received training in the western mountains, from French, American and Qatari special forces.

The Emergence of Two Plans for the Liberation of Tripoli

The problem was, however, that by late July there were two rival plans to liberate Tripoli trading on the international market. On 4–5 July Mahmoud Jibril met with his supporters in Abu Dhabi and set out his strategy for liberation, which once again rested in part on an internal uprising supported by a network of security service defectors in the capital. He now divided the NTC Stabilisation Committee into two parts with Hisham Bu Hajar from the 17 February Coalition leading a Liberation and Securing Committee and Nayid a reformed Stabilisation Committee designed to secure and maintain key installations and services. Jibril had developed a close relationship with some Zintani commanders and persuaded both the UAE and France to supply them with weapons and train them, respectively. The Liberation and Securing Committee set up an operations centre in Djerba in Tunisia from where it identified a list of at least twenty-eight targets for NATO to strike before its Tripoli network struck. In early August Jibril relocated his team to Zintan next to the French and UAE operations room. It was here in the Nafusa Mountains that Jibril and Nayid trained a small group of rebels from Tripoli, which they called the 'Tripoli Guard', with the help of their Western and Gulf allies. The purpose of the Guard was to secure key facilities which, according to Peter Cole, a senior analyst from the International Crisis Group, numbered around 430 by early August. However, the concept of a Tripoli Military Council of defected regime officials was resisted by Tripoli's NTC representatives, who wanted to see the Tripoli militias in Nafusa take the lead.

The Qatari-backed plan, on the other hand, centred around Ali al-Sallabi, Abdul Aradi, Abdelhakim Belhaj and Islamist rebels in Tripoli, who were intent on not compromising with former elements of the regime. By August they had succeeded in diverting Qatar's loyalties away from Jibril after presenting a plan to the chief of staff of the Qatari Armed Forces and the Emir in June. As a consequence, from June onwards Qatari weapons shipments in Nafusa were routed through Belhaj, who had developed relations with Nalut, where his forces were based. While some of these supplies went to Nalut more went to the 17 February Battalion in Tripoli led by a LIFG commander, and to the Islamist Tripoli Revolutionaries' Battalions, who had been trained by the Qataris. The Qatari-backed plan sought to give these fighters, including Misratan and other rebels from certain parts of Nafusa, the means by which to surround Tripoli and close off access routes to allow battalions from and in Tripoli to take the capital by force.

Qatar also used the recaptured airport in Misrata to fly in weapons not just to Misratan rebels but also to the Islamist 17 February Coalition in Tripoli. These weapons were taken into Tripoli by three ships acquired by Misratan rebels, who would offload the contents into dinghies to take ashore. The 17 February Coalition began to look towards Misrata and the Tripolitanian armed groups in the Nafusa Mountains after visiting Jibril's team Djerba in July. They quickly became disillusioned with his team's lack of military planning. It was clear Jibril had little appetite for taking the city by force whatever his associations were with their colleague Bu Hajar. Accordingly, over the course of August, the 17 February Coalition in Tripoli organised the framework for a 'popular uprising' by dividing the city into areas in which small volunteer units were required to secure and then take control of their streets and neighbourhoods.

While each of these plans relied on NATO airstrikes and did not envisage Misratan or Zintani militias entering, securing or occupying Tripoli, the method of liberation chosen by each camp could not have been more different. This situation cried out for further inter-militia dialogue and co-operation on the military and political level. Yet while there was some military liaison between the two sets of groups during July and August via the Qataris, neither side shared details of their plan with each other. Nor was there much liaison by the ISRT with these camps even though the stabilisation fissures were there for all to see following the death of General Younis on 28 July 2011.

Over the previous month a massive argument had erupted between these camps after a detailed draft framework to implement the NTC's 5 May Roadmap entitled 'Constituent Covenant for the Transition Period' was endorsed by the NTC Executive on 21 June. Under Article 30 the NTC was permitted to continue as the interim administration until elections and the constitutional-making process were complete. This was met by a storm of protest in Benghazi from Islamist, secular and civil society elements alike. The Covenant also relied on a wholly unrealistic transitional timeframe, put forward to quell objections to the perpetuation of the NTC's rule. This led to a raft of new transition plans being put forward by numerous groups, including Islamist ones. Ali al-Sallabi presented a 206-clause draft constitution, while the Muslim Brotherhood and the other Islamists groups continued to maintain that an elected body had to preside over transition. It is unclear whether the ISRT attempted to engage with any of these alternative plans.

In the event the Islamist elements won the day. On 3 August 2011 the NTC finally published its Constitutional Declaration, which stipulated that the NTC should dissolve after elections to a new National Congress within 240 days of the formal end of the war. The Congress would then choose a Prime Minister, endorse any cabinet selected and appoint a committee to draft a Constitution within ninety days, which would then be put to referendum. The Islamist victory occurred in part due to their growing prominence on both the military and political front. But it was also due to luck and lack of planning. When the vote was taken on 3 August many of the key players in the NTC were away, including Ba'ja, who was in Washington. According to Peter Bartu, the Muslim Brotherhood and others had taken advantage of the drama and tension of the moment (Younis's murder) to push through a fundamentally different sequence to what was envisaged:

The NTC apparently had no internal bylaws for managing absentee voting at the time. On 10 August, when Ghoga and the chief of the NTC legal committee, Salwa al-Dighaili, introduced the Constitutional Declaration in a Benghazi press conference, they were almost mobbed by an angry audience that included original members of the 17 February Coalition who felt the whole process had been conducted furtively and without genuine consultation. From their perspective, the Constitutional Declaration showed how the Islamist (or Muslim Brotherhood) and secular (or pro-Jibril) factions of the NTC had already started to position themselves for political power after the fall of Tripoli. In this respect, the 17 February Coalition saw both camps as being as bad as each other, with each supporting a transitional sequence which they thought would benefit them politically.[1]

It was within this febrile atmosphere that on 8 August Abdul Jalil dismissed the entire Executive Office ostensibly for its alleged role in the Younis affair. In reality Jalil had become increasingly sceptical and cautious about Jibril. Unlike Jibril, Jalil was required to pay heed to all revolutionary forces and justify the NTC's actions to an increasingly intemperate and exasperated public. In the end Jalil kept Jibril on as head of the Executive but instructed him to put forward a new board for approval.

Throughout this period Jibril's Stabilisation Committee continued to work with both the UN and international community, including with the ISRT, without involving other revolutionary forces on the ground. Not that this was of too much concern to the FCO, which issued the following statement in reaction to the dismissal of the Executive:

We understand that a new committee will be appointed in the very near future and that this will continue to be representative and inclusive. The move has not affected the NTC's ability to govern, nor hampered its ability to continue fighting for greater freedom.

The Capture of Tripoli

This then was the military, political and stabilisation environment when on 17 August Nafusa fighters finally swept down to surround the capital with the help of seventy Qatari special forces, thereby tipping the military balance in favour of the Qatari-backed plan. Their action precipitated a hastily organised meeting between the two camps to unite the different Tripoli battalions under a 'Tripoli Brigade'. However, Belhaj refused to accept Bu Hajar, who had organised the military wing of the Islamist 17 February Coalition and was on good terms with Jibril, as its leader. On 18 August Belhaj finally consented to Bu Hajar having general responsibility on the basis that he could lead a Tripoli Military Council to 'secure' Tripoli after the regime's demise. In reality the Tripoli Brigade was a façade behind which lay deeply unresolved military and political fissures between Western-backed rebels and Islamists, who retained widely different visions of what victory and any transition looked like. Yet, somehow, despite all the infighting and chaos, NATO planners and commanders through careful diplomacy managed to stay above the fray and as a consequence the stage was now set for the takeover of Tripoli.

Looking back, it is abundantly clear that the capture of Tripoli could not have occurred without NATO's special forces and RAF Sentinel aeroplanes, which mapped the location of Gaddafi's troops using radar imagery that could track the smallest vehicle from 100 miles away. They in turn were assisted by two RC-135 Rivet Joint US spy planes based at Souda Bay in Crete, which monitored mobile and satellite telephones as well as standard military radio frequencies. Throughout August, NATO drones beamed real-time images of loyalist positions on the ground to the rebels, while special forces, acting as forward air controllers, called in yet more jet fighters to bomb and attack Gaddafi's tanks and command posts. These attacks were supplemented by further NATO attacks on ammunition stores and communications facilities, whose locations were identified by rebel units who had been given satellite phones supplied by the British and French. There could be little doubt now that the NATO mission had transformed itself from a humanitarian mission into one hell-bent on removing Gaddafi, a fact not lost on either the Russians or the Chinese.

Mahmoud Jibril would later confirm that the assault on Tripoli had in fact been delayed three times. It was supposed to take place on 14 July and was then pushed back until 17 August, before NATO delayed matters again for another three days. On 18 August, the RAF took out a vessel packed with loyalist forces which had been sent to defend the regime's last functioning oil refinery at Zawiya, thirty miles from Tripoli. Within a short time, the refinery fell and Gaddafi was left with no fuel supplies. The next day rebels launched Operation Mermaid Dawn to take the capital. An RAF Tornado GR4 aircraft was called in to attack the Baroni Centre, a key communications base in Tripoli, while nine Paveway bombs were dropped onto another critical military command centre.

On 20 August Jibril broadcast a speech on Libya TV from a channel based in Qatar, which was the sign for the underground resistance movement inside Tripoli to rise up against the regime. According to *The Sunday Times*, resistance leaders had for months been smuggling weapons into the capital, while other residents mapped out where Gaddafi's snipers were holed up, sometimes bringing them food and water, pretending to be Gaddafi loyalists. These residents now set about taking out these snipers' positions, with some using only meat cleavers. But whereas NATO was originally supposed to hit eighty-seven targets, these targets subsequently got whittled down to twenty-seven. Mahmoud Jibril would later tell the newspaper *Asharq Al-Awsat* that NATO's reticence allowed Gaddafi to escape, claiming that although states sometimes say one thing their intelligence communities do another. Nor was it coincidence that during this period two cargo planes from South Africa allegedly picked up cash and gold just before the assault on Tripoli began.

Hundreds of firefights now erupted across Tripoli's neighbourhoods. Gaddafi's security brigades quickly lost confidence. In June Saif al-Islam had created a volunteer reserve force called the People's Resistance Forces (PFR) in which civilians were armed and ordered to man checkpoints in their communities. These civilians were badly trained and lacked martial spirit. When the 17 February Coalition's neighbourhood units attacked, many of the volunteers just deserted their posts. By the morning of 21 August most PFR volunteers had fled while regime security brigades had retreated to Bab al-Aziziya or towards Bani Walid.

None of this was intended to happen. The Zintani fighters had agreed with NATO planners and Jibril to come down as far as the coastal road at Zawiya. But it turned out that many of the Tripolitanian rebels allied to them in the Nafusa Mountains were not ready to move on 20 August. With 17 February Coalition units calling frantically for help, one part of the newly constituted Tripoli Brigade started to fight its way into the capital from outside Zawiya on the west. On Sunday 21 August 2011 the Brigade tore out of Zawiya in a convoy of pickup trucks and mini-vans along the coastal highway, past the burnt-out remains of vehicles from previous battles. Until, that is, they were met by a hail of mortars from Gaddafi's artillery units stationed on higher land, as they approached the heavily fortified headquarters of the elite Khamis Brigade, which protected the western approaches to Tripoli. Suddenly two NATO bombs were dropped on the barracks, resulting in hundreds of Libyan soldiers abandoning their positions and leaving their munitions behind.

Belhaj now drove up the southern route into Tripoli to where the Zintani fighters were camped. He was immediately told they were also not in a logistical position to move although they could clear the airport road. In the event they went on to occupy the airport, which they would continue to do for over a year. The spoils of war proved to be just too attractive. Meanwhile, 500 Misratan rebels, who had arrived by boat on 19 and 20 August, now attacked from the east and also poured into the city. They went straight for Gaddafi's palace, where a vicious firefight ensued, with sniper, RPG, mortar and machine-gun fire being exchanged by both sides. Men fought each other street by street, alleyway by alleyway, for control of the compound. As night fell on Sunday, more and more rebels streamed into Tripoli, where ecstatic crowds greeted them as heroes, while tracer rounds lit up the night sky. They were now joined by fighters from the Nafusa Mountains.

TV screens were quickly filled with images of Tripoli residents tearing down images of Gaddafi in an orgy of jubilation. Despite rebel claims that Tripoli had been liberated, Gaddafi forces still controlled pockets of the city, such as the palace and government buildings. It was during this period that Saif al-Islam showed up at the Rixos Hotel to brief Western journalists for the very last time. By Monday night it was effectively all over. Saif eventually fled the capital just before rebels, who had encircled the Bab al-Aziziya compound, began their final assault. After taking out the remaining snipers in a crescendo of machine-gun fire, rebel fighters from Misrata smashed through the perimeter wall with the aid of a tractor to breach the palace defences.

One *Sunday Times* journalist later described the scene as he and the rebel commander he accompanied stared in elated disbelief at the scenes unfolding around them: 'Black smoke billowed from Gaddafi's bedouin tents in the distance. The rebels ran through the smoke towards his residence, storming the building as mortars, RPGs and heavy machinegun fire continued to boom and snap past them. Inside the building there was, of course, no sign of Gaddafi, but Mehdi and 15 of his men sat down on sofas inside one of the rooms and wiped the sweat from their brows. "I can't talk now," said Mehdi, reloading the magazine of his assault rifle. "You don't know how I feel. Now Libya is free. Everything will be right again. Thank you France, Qatar, Obama, Cameron," he added, with tears filling his eyes.'

As the rebels poured over Gaddafi's compound, an Al Jazeera cameraman drove with Belhaj to the front of the compound where Gaddafi's infamous statue of a clenched fist crushing a US fighter plane was situated. Here Belhaj presented himself to the world as the leader of the Tripoli Military Council that had just liberated the country. Misratan and Zintani militias were furious. Belhaj was a leader who commanded fewer than two hundred men, yet he, rather than Jibril or any other rebel leader, would adorn the front of the world's newspapers the next day to pronounce the end of Gaddafi's forty-two years of reign.

This was particularly galling for the Zintani Brigades, whose contribution towards the war effort exacted a heavy toll on the town of Zintan, just as the war had done in Misrata. Zintan was left with more than 800 disabled men out of a population of 40,000. This fact alone should have impressed upon the ISRT the urgent need for some form of reconciliation process to be put in place in Libya, if further violence and retribution was to be avoided and the country knitted back together again. Yet nothing was done, even though by mid-August it was highly unlikely that the policy of procuring regime change through defection was likely to win through.

Over the next couple of days, hundreds of rebels scoured Gaddafi's compound to see how the great dictator lived. Gauche images of rebels standing with two-fingered salutes next to Gaddafi's white baby grand pianos and his daughter's gold mermaid sofa flashed around the world. In that moment I thought of Qais and what he would have made of these ludicrous scenes. As Marina Hyde of *The Guardian* noted at the time: 'It's hard not to be swept along in the exhilaration of the great dictator becoming a joke. Ridicule is powerful, which is why the likes of Gaddafi threaten everything to suppress it, and in the free exchange of irreverence is the seed of Libyan democracy.'[2]

More worryingly, and contrary to the expectation and planning of the ISRT, rebel brigades from Tripoli, Misrata, Zintan and the Berber mountains now took up strategic positions across the city. Overnight these militias became one of the most important political constituencies with which the NTC and the wider world had to deal. They were very different from the young people I had met in Benghazi back in April. As *Time Magazine* commented: 'The Berber guerrillas of the Nafusa Mountains didn't pause to set up Facebook pages as they swept into the plains south and west of Tripoli.'[3]

Throughout this period, the ISRT continued to consult only with those it felt most comfortable with, despite the changing dynamic on the ground. The lack of engagement by the ISRT with either Islamist elements or civil society over constitutional, security and rule-of-law issues that were likely to dominate any transition was inexplicable. This was unfortunate as the optimum time to try to forge a wider consensus about transition across Libyan society was before not after the liberation of Tripoli, while the West and its Gulf allies enjoyed real leverage with all relevant groups. The UK only formally recognised the NTC on 27 July 2011 after an agreement was hammered out at a Contact Group meeting on 15 July to help the NTC deal with its liquidity problem and negotiate with the UN Sanctions Committee to access millions of dinars frozen by sanctions on humanitarian grounds. This was needed to pay salaries and acquire crucial supplies such as refined fuel products. The liquidity crisis had been kept at bay after the Contact Group pledged $250 million for humanitarian assistance at its 5 May meeting. These funds were siphoned through a Temporary Financial Mechanism (TFM) that bypassed sanctions and was of the type McCue and I had talked about in April 2011 with Christopher Prentice in Benghazi. At the fourth Contact Group meeting in Istanbul held on 15 July, thirty-two countries, as well as the UN, EU, NATO, the Arab League, the OIC and other BRIC countries, finally recognised the NTC as the 'legitimate governing authority in Libya'. Its resolution read as follows

Henceforth and until an interim authority is in place, participants agreed to deal with the National Transitional Council (NTC) as the legitimate governing authority in Libya. The Group welcomed the role of the NTC in leading the transition process in Libya and expressed support for its efforts to broaden its popular base to embrace all Libyan people. The Group urged all relevant parties to explore ways and means of paving the way for the formation of an interim government to ensure a smooth and peaceful transition of power with the widest popular support possible . . .

The participants reaffirmed that the Contact Group remains the appropriate platform for the international community to be a focal point of contact with the Libyan people, to coordinate international policy and to be a forum for discussion of humanitarian and post-conflict support.

It also made clear that any 'transition process' should 'be inclusive, Libyan-owned and representative, including the potential participation of select members of the previous bureaucracy as stipulated in the NTC Roadmap; the opposition; and other elements of Libyan society'. Finally, it reaffirmed the role of the UN as the leading international entity post-conflict but was silent on how these matters should be progressed during the conflict phase. This was no doubt because it had created the ISRT precisely for this purpose.

Following the UK's recognition of the NTC on 27 July, De La Rue, a UK-based company, released over two billion dinars to the NTC, which eased the immediate liquidity crisis and paved the way for the transition after the fall of Tripoli. It was a perfect moment for the UK or the ISRT to intervene to pressure Libyan stakeholders to come together to sort out a more meaningful agreement over the nature, sequencing and pace of transition. At the very least the ISRT should have demanded a place for civil society so that its voice could be heard given that its buy-in would be essential if Libya was to move from conflict to any form of societal peace in the long term. That it did not seek to do so constituted a major failure of policy and planning.

Supporting the Culture of Democracy in Libya

With the BHRC bid to the FCO rejected, I began to think about the informal groups of young artists, musicians, journalists and writers that I had met in Benghazi, who were unlikely to fall within any of the recognised political or civil society groups identified by the ISRT or under the CHD initiative. To my mind these people were crucial to the long-term nurturing of democracy and freedom in Libya and the understanding of this in the West. The revolution would be lost if these young people, who had been so instrumental to its early popularity and survival, were not recognised or catered for in New Libya's future. Like many of the others I had met in the MENA region through the Delfina Foundation, they looked beyond the shores of Libya towards the West for support and solidarity. They constituted an unorthodox but critical component in any strategy to strengthen the rule of law and proper governance. As Islamist elements increased their prominence within the rebel movement through their fighting prowess, it was vital that the free cultural spirit of Benghazi did not dissipate or become crushed by more powerful conservative forces.

The more I talked with people from the cultural sector the more I felt the need to acknowledge the work of the young of Benghazi and their struggle for freedom and democratic change. I had opened up a dialogue with Nick Latta of the FCO about a potential exhibition concerning Benghazi revolutionary graffiti. Nick had been stationed at the UK embassy at the time of the uprising and had to be airlifted out of Tripoli to Malta at the start of the conflict, in traumatic circumstances. He was extremely supportive of the idea and talked of an exhibition being showcased at the Brighton Festival under its Human Rights Programme being curated by Burmese opposition leader, Aung San Suu Kyi. But within a month he found himself being moved from the Libya desk. This was not an unfamiliar occurrence within the FCO. I therefore turned to the private sector, which is more entrepreneurial when it comes to the business of taking fast decisions to support important cultural projects.

As executive director of Beyond Borders, a Scottish-based initiative dedicated to the promotion of small nation dialogue and cultural exchange, particularly in relation to countries emerging from conflict, I decided to try to convey to a wider public audience some of the struggle that these young people from Benghazi were engaged in. The Edinburgh Festival, held during each August, seemed an appropriate forum. It was a small gesture of support, but an important one for the type of work in which these people were engaged.

Beyond Borders uses cultural exchange to help overcome misunderstanding between different peoples, cultures and nations. Founded in 2010, it enjoys the support of a variety of senior Scottish statesmen and women, including Baroness Smith, Lord Campbell, Lord Browne, Lord McConnell and Angus Robertson. It sought to extend what the Delfina Foundation did in the visual artist field to seven other cultural media including literature, performing arts, visual arts, heritage, film, law and the spoken word, by using Scotland's unique cultural and political heritage as a platform for dialogue and exchange. In 2010 it launched a series of artistic, literary, film and dialogue festivals during the Edinburgh Festival including its Beyond

Borders International Festival of Literature and Thought at Traquair House in the Scottish Borders, where each August numerous thinkers, writers, film makers and civil society leaders from the Middle East and elsewhere gather to exchange ideas, share experiences and discuss some of the most pressing issues of our time.

This festival has been instrumental in developing new ways of getting across old concerns about inequality and human rights abuses to wider audiences. For example, the Palestinian author and activist Raja Shehadeh used the festival to talk eloquently about the plight of Palestine. He managed to move audiences with simple tales from his book *Palestinian Walks: Notes on a Vanishing Landscape* (2008) that told the story of Israel's occupation of the West Bank through his personal family history. Raja managed to reach and touch more people through his literature, talks, films, podcasts and use of new media, then he had ever done as a human rights advocate, notwithstanding his ground-breaking legal work as the founding member and director of the Palestinian human rights organisation, Al-Haq. Al-Haq's work in defence of ordinary Palestinians had become legendary among the civil rights community, but was still largely unknown to the wider Western public. The writer's pen and TED-type podcast were fast becoming more potent than the advocate's nib as a force for change in the twenty-first century.

The increasing importance of these types of exchanges was not lost on policy formers like Stephen R. Grand, the director of the Project on US Relations with the Islamic World at the Brookings Institution. In considering how America should support transitions to democracy in the Middle East, he rightly observed in a Brookings pamphlet that: 'large scale grants and contract programmes that have sought to impose a parochial, American vision on another society, for example, have done much harm and little good. The practice of dispatching waves of high-priced American consultants with little familiarity with the local context has not worked'. Instead, he argued, the United States should consider 'the importance of attitudinal aspects to democracy' and recognise how American technologies, music, film, universities and example of democracy all played some part in the dramatic cultural and attitudinal changes that have taken place in the Middle East. According to Grand, all these mediums could be used to help accelerate these changes. He advocated greater Internet access and freedom, to allow Arab and Western youth to connect via social and virtual mediums, as well as the development of exchange programmes 'to get as many Arab youth and professionals out to other parts of the world so that they can experience other cultures and observe first-hand how citizens mediate relations with political authority in other settings'. He called for the provision of financial support for 'civil initiatives that bring like-minded citizens together for common purposes'.[4]

This is why Beyond Borders commissioned the exhibition on Libyan Graffiti Art and curated a series of debates on the Arab Spring involving participants from the region and the West as part of its wider summer programme of events across Scotland. The exhibition was designed to run alongside a short film about the young people I had met in Benghazi. Some of the graffiti images that subsequently appeared in the exhibition feature in this book. They are dedicated to all those Libyan artists and journalists that risked or lost their lives during the Arab Spring. Participants at the festival included the fearless and passionate journalist Marie Colvin, who had visited Libya on many occasions and knew Gaddafi personally, as well as singers and activists who had taken part in some of the protests. It seemed to me that this was the very least we could do as the military endgame began to play itself out across the cities and deserts of Libya under a baking summer sun, and the long-suffering people of Libya once more held their breath to discover whether they would be finally delivered into a new democratic world of personal and societal promise.

Beyond Borders and Marie Colvin

In fact, I was hosting a dinner at the Beyond Borders International Festival at Traquair House the weekend Tripoli fell. Sitting round the table was a host of intellectuals with an interest in the Arab world, such as Dr Izzeldin Abuelaish; journalists such as Marie Colvin and the BBC's Alan Little; and former diplomats like Sir Kieran Prendergast and Jonathan Powell, many of whom had come to debate the Arab Spring. On hearing the news, Marie Colvin instantly left the table to organise her departure to Tripoli the next morning for *The Sunday Times*. She was desperate to get to Libya and suddenly looked like a cat caught in a cage, unable to pounce on her prey. Marie was never happier than when dashing towards her next big story, and this was a big one. She wanted to find Gaddafi, whom she had interviewed on a number of occasions over the course of her career.

She had developed a remarkable relationship with the idiosyncratic dictator after their first meeting in 1986, when President Reagan bombed his compound in Tripoli. At 3 am she was summoned from her hotel room. 'In walked Gaddafi,' she told me, 'dressed in a red silk collarless shirt, white silk pyjama trousers and lizard-skin slip-ons. Over it all he wore a gold cap. He turned, locked the door, put the key in his pocket and said, "I am Gaddafi." I remember saying to myself, "No Kidding." ' On a subsequent occasion Gaddafi confided in her that he had fallen for Madeleine Albright, the US Secretary of State. Another journalist told her of her own hilarious encounter with Gaddafi in the late 1980s when he demanded to know Marie's whereabouts. 'When will she return to Libya? I miss her,' he declared, having selected a white dress and green shoes for her to wear. It wasn't difficult to see why Marie wanted to interview Gaddafi before he was either killed or captured.

As I tried to secure her a seat on the first flight out of Edinburgh we tuned in to CNN and BBC World News to watch amazing images of the Libyan people dancing and rejoicing in Tripoli's Green Square and in the streets of Benghazi. Other images showed rebel fighters holding up luxurious personal possessions of Gaddafi and his family from their compound, Bab al-Aziziya, as they continuously fired their Kalashnikovs into the air. One man held aloft a jewel-encrusted Samurai sword. Another sat on a leopard-skin throne inlaid with mother of pearl. Other rebels shot up and tried to fell the famous statue of a giant gold fist clutching an American fighter plane. In the villas rebels found huge swimming pools and whirlpools surrounded by plasma TV screens and high tech gadgets, all set against garish décor, and a catastrophe of gold leaf furniture, statues and ornaments. Gaddafi had been but one week away from celebrating his forty-second year in power, in what was now dubbed Martyrs' Square. What I would have given to go back to Libya with Colvin to witness the end of the forty-two-year nightmare.

As I rejoined my dinner guests, the conversation turned to what might happen next in Libya. The expected protracted battle for Tripoli never materialised. We now learnt that rebel forces under Commander Belhaj had entered the city from the east with little resistance, after he brokered a deal with a loyalist Gaddafi commander. Everyone was worried about civil order and whether the country would descend into anarchy, like Iraq, especially given the speed of the final liberation. This sense of foreboding was partly fuelled by the civil disorder that had rocked the UK the previous week. A series of unprecedented riots had taken place in London, Birmingham and Manchester, in which incensed youths had gone on the rampage, looting and burning sections of their own communities. I remember reflecting upon just how impressive the young people in Cairo and Benghazi were compared to their counterparts in London and Manchester. They could also have turned years of economic frustration and envy into similar wanton street violence, yet there was little or no looting during the early days of the uprising. Nothing remotely comparable to what occurred in London happened in Benghazi and Tripoli after the downfall of the regime, despite a similar dearth of state authority on the streets. Instead, Mahmoud Jibril urged rebels not to loot or engage in reprisals to 'sully the final page of the revolution' as 'the eyes of the world are upon us'.

22–23 August 2011 was historic not simply for Libya but for the whole of the Arab region and the West's relationship to it. The regime's demise in Tripoli brought immediate and unbridled joy to the majority of Libyans for the first time in forty-two years, but it also sent shockwaves through a number of Arab capitals. It was difficult to see how opposition elements could elsewhere have emboldened their struggle for freedom had Gaddafi beaten the NATO-backed rebel uprising in Libya. But I will always associate 22 August 2011 with Marie Colvin, for it was the last time I would ever see her. I recall her sitting with my friend Dr Izzeldin Abuelaish, the Palestinian surgeon whom I had interviewed the previous day at the festival, and who had lost three daughters in the Israeli bombing of Gaza in January of 2009. Quite remarkably, Marie had met him at an Israeli checkpoint some three months earlier, as he tried to get his wife, who was battling leukaemia, to the Israeli hospital where he worked. This then was a poignant reunion in which we discussed the futility of conflict and the capacity of human beings to forgive atrocities. Little did Izzeldin and I know that this would be the last time we would see Marie alive, or that the last story she would file would be about a bombardment similar in effect to that experienced by Izzeldin's daughters. Marie eventually left Traquair in the small hours of the next morning after she had, typically for her, managed to hitch a ride to London on board a cargo plane. Unfortunately, she never got to interview Gaddafi again.

On the day she left Traquair Marie was due to attend a Beyond Borders rule of law lecture given by Mordecai Malunga on Zimbabwe – there was no country or people she was not interested in. Thereafter, she was supposed to join Mordecai in a further debate about the Responsibility to Protect, a subject she was passionate about. By this time the Russians and Chinese were expressing deep concerns about how the NATO mandate had been implemented in Libya. At the debate Sir Kieran Prendergast, ever the cautious diplomat, warned of how the intervention in Libya might have put back the cause of humanitarian intervention through mission creep and the failure to deal with dissenting concerns of more sceptical members of the Security Council. I for one would have liked to have heard Marie's response to Kieran's worries, but it was not to be. I have little doubt about what she might have said, given her twenty-five years of experience on the front line.

Marie Colvin and Homs

Marie died in a bombardment of the Baba Amr district in Homs, Syria, on 22 February 2012, six months to the day after she left Traquair. She went there clandestinely, intent on braving the dangers in order to bear witness to the suffering of ordinary people caught up in a conflict not of their making. By February 2012 the Syrian government was involved in a bitter struggle with armed opposition elements. Marie was determined to get in to report what was happening on the ground. After being refused a visa by the authorities she flew to Beirut and illicitly crossed into Syria from the Lebanese border. In an e-mail dated 10 February to her friend Sara Hashash she wrote: 'The overall picture I have been told about is that Homs is ringed by the army and tanks, and the army is stopping anyone from entering and leaving. I may have found a way in.' As she waited for her fixer to get her across the border she dined for the last time with her close friend Lindsey Hilsum, the international editor of Channel Four whom I had met in Benghazi in March of 2011.

Lindsey warned her friend that it was too dangerous to cross the border. 'It's what we do,' was Colvin's emphatic reply. A few days later, on a cold, dark night, Colvin and *Sunday Times* photographer Paul Conroy slipped into Syria and made their way to Homs. 'There is a lot of shelling and snipers during the day,' she reported. The only form of viable communication out of Homs was through Skype via a satellite feed at a makeshift media centre rigged up in Baba Amr, where activists uploaded images to the Internet. Colvin's Thuraya Satphone was too easily intercepted by government forces. That is why Colvin would find herself returning to the same building time and again. Paul Conroy, the photographer who accompanied Colvin into Syria, later told me his story:

> I'd been in before, a few weeks earlier, and the situation was critical. I got the call again, 'Paul, go to Syria today. You know, get out there. Meet Marie in Beirut.' So I went and we met up. We made contact with smugglers. A bit of money passed hands and very clandestinely we crept through minefields and past army posts. By then Homs had been under bombardment for about fourteen days. Assad military forces were trying to crush the revolution, the heart of the revolution. There were people broadcasting live images of the attacks. It was kinda strange. You'd see this complete devastation going on and you'd think, well that's where I'm trying to get to. It was a strange feeling but we got in with the Free Syrian Army. We had to crawl through a three-kilometre storm sewer drain under the freeway into the city. There was no oxygen in there. They were taking weapons and bringing bodies out, all in this tiny little tunnel that we had to go through. It was hell because of the lack of oxygen and your muscles cramped. It was like coming out into Armageddon when we emerged. You knew you were in Homs as you could see the white flashes all around.

Colvin and Conroy made their way to an improvised media centre in Baba Amr. The next morning Colvin counted forty-five shells landing in just seven minutes, admitting in an e-mail to her friend Lucy Fisher that 'I did have a few moments when I thought, what am I doing.' Yet she ended the e-mail and answered her own doubts with characteristic clarity of purpose – 'Story incredibly important though. Mx.' That night she smuggled herself out of Homs to send back an account of the latest fighting and bombardment. A few days later she was back in the epicentre of Baba Amr, which now resembled something out of Hell. Shell upon shell landed upon the district as water and electricity supplies gradually ran out. Paul later recounted the trip in and out of Homs:

> We came out for a few days but then we went back again. We didn't tell our editors. We just sneaked back in. The situation, even over a few days, had deteriorated. The first day back we could not leave the building. We counted thirty to forty shells per minute around the building we were in. I've done a few wars, but this was the most ferocious bombardment I'd ever experienced. Both Marie and I said, 'I've never seen anything like this.' The next day, we woke up and the shelling intensified again. We more or less knew we weren't gonna get out. We thought, right we've got a problem. We're in the middle of the story – 28,000 civilians trapped in this neighbourhood – and we're not gonna get a story out by Sunday. We knew something was about to happen and we didn't think we'd get out alive to be honest, so we made the decision with the media guys, the activists who were transmitting and getting stuff out, to do live broadcasts with CNN, BBC and Channel 4, because there may be no tomorrow. So we did the transmissions and thankfully they went out.

The next day Conroy and Colvin managed to make their way to a field clinic. In an e-mail sent to Sean Ryan, foreign editor of the *Sunday Times* Colvin wrote: 'It is sickening that the Syrian regime is allowed to keep doing this. There was a shocking scene at the apartment clinic today. A baby boy lay on a head scarf, naked, his little tummy heaving as he tried to breathe. The doctor said, "We can do nothing for him." He had been hit by shrapnel in his left side. They had to just let him die as his mother wept.' Over the next few days, Colvin told the world about what in her view was happening in Baba Amr through satellite interviews with the BBC, *Channel Four News* and CNN. Most of all she railed about how the outside world was failing to act.

By now her companion, Paul Conroy, was worried that Marie's profile and broadcasting were seriously endangering their lives. But Marie wanted to stay one more day to file another story. Government forces now knew that foreign journalists were operating in Baba Amr and had the capabilities to locate satellite transmissions. In an e-mail to Ryan published in the *Sunday Times* after her death, Conroy wrote: 'As I am sure you are aware Marie can be tricky to convince once she has the bit between her teeth.' The next day, in the early hours of 22 February 2012, the shelling of Baba Amr began again, but this time the area of the media centre was targeted. As the first explosion hit the building Marie ran to the hall where she had left her shoes. It was a fatal mistake. The next rocket landed in front of the building, killing her and the French photographer Remi Ochlik instantly. Conroy and another journalist, Edith Bouvier, were hit by shrapnel in the room next to the hallway, each sustaining serious injuries to their legs.

Paul later described to me the moment when the bombs hit the building:

> We decided to try and visit a field clinic. I heard two rockets land about a hundred metres either side of the building. Thirty seconds later another two rockets hit and at that point, as an ex-artilleryman, I realised they were bracketing and walking [. . .] walking the shells and they had a drone flying above. As I began to understand what was happening the first rocket came into the building and the room that Marie and I had been sleeping in. My reaction was to say, 'My camera's in there.' So I ran back in, saw my bag in the rubble, grabbed it, and I ran down the corridor back to the main room, that had no windows in, and into the street. Another shell took out the corridor that I'd just run down. By then the house was black and thick in dust from the explosions of the shells. It was chaos. There were people injured. And then another shell hit above us and so part of the ceiling collapsed. And I thought at that point it was over. I thought, three shells, you know, had done their damage. So I bent down to pick up the camera I'd dropped and just about took a shot when there was an almighty explosion. This was the biggest of all. I was still standing but felt something hit my leg, like a piece of rubble or something. I put my hand down but it just slipped and came out the other side of my leg. I stood there with my hand through my leg and thought that's not good. Rather bizarrely, for the first ten seconds, I just thought of hospital food – rubbery potatoes and cold custard. Then I snapped back into reality, located the main artery and checked that it and the bone were intact and tied my Keffiyeh scarf round the leg to tourniquet it. And then I thought, got to find Marie. I thought she had got out of the building because someone had been screaming 'GET OUT! GET OUT!' So I took a few steps and my leg just buckled and I fell over. In fact I fell next to Marie, who was obviously dead. I double-checked that she was dead. Remi Ochlik was also dead. But in the time it had taken me to get there and fumble about, the drone above had spotted me moving in the rubble

so they opened fire again and started shelling the street. I was pinned down in the rubble while the next attack went on as the guys from the media centre tried to come out and drag me in. There was so much shrapnel flying about that if they'd come out they'd have just been ripped to pieces. It was only because I was so low in the rubble that I survived. The shrapnel was whizzing past my face. So I just lay there. I saw an Ethernet cable, grabbed it, and tied it round my leg as tight as I could. After about fifteen minutes the shelling stopped and they just dragged me inside. Up until that point I hadn't felt any pain. My body had flooded itself with endorphins.

The media activists managed to get Paul out of the area and to a makeshift clinic, leaving the dead bodies of Colvin and Ochlik to an uncertain fate:

After about fifteen minutes we heard a car screech up. It was the Free Syrian Army. They yanked us out of the building and threw us into a car and took us, ironically, to the field hospital that we'd been trying to get to. I knew the doctors. We'd been there before to film and shoot. The Doctor looked up and said: 'Paul, what are you doing here?' I said: 'I've got a hole in my leg.' He laughed and said: 'Oh, so you do. But you know we've got no anaesthetics and I'm gonna have to operate on you now. Here's some Paracetamol.' 'Nice one,' I replied. I had this great big lump of hamburger meat hanging out my leg. He just got a pair of scissors and I said, 'Can I smoke?' He said: 'You can do anything you want to.' So I literally sat up having a fag while he cut this muscle out. As soon as I put out a cigarette the nurse lit another and put it in my mouth. And then he says: 'Now we've got to clean it.' I thought, great. It couldn't have been as bad as cutting the muscle out. He got a bottle of iodine and a tooth-brush. Poured the bottle of iodine in and just scrubbed it with the toothbrush. All the time this was happening the hospital was being shelled and the building was being hit. Every time I thought it was clean, another shell would hit and the dust would fall into the wound and he'd have to do it again. And then he got a staple gun and sealed both sides of the wound. Normally they'd leave one side open but we had to escape. He bandaged it up and put us in a house about fifty metres away from the hospital, which was also targeted.

Conroy and the other journalists faced days of further agony as diplomats tried, unsuccessfully, to get the government and opposition to agree to a cease-fire to let the injured out. In the end they made their escape on the back of motorbikes ridden by activists through the sewers of Homs. At least a dozen opposition activists died in the escape as security forces fired a rain of bullets into the sewers. Conway later explained how it happened:

> We ended up staying for five days in this building. The regime knew which building we were in, so for five days we just sat in the pitch black. We put mattresses up against the window. They sent in the Syrian Red Cross to get us out after some cease-fire was negotiated. But the head of the mission said to me: 'Look, don't get in the ambulance, they're going to execute you when you get out. Throw your bodies on the road and make it look like the Free Syrian Army attacked us and that we were killed by the rebels.' So we let the ambulances go and didn't get in them. Then just when we thought it couldn't get any worse a guy comes in and says: 'Paul, bit of bad luck [. . .] bad news.' I said: 'There can't be any more bad news.' He said: 'The tunnel's been blown up.' Our only other option by which to escape had just been blown up after a shell had hit the tunnel and blocked it. Suddenly there was no escape and we just had to sit it out. The city was surrounded, completely. It felt like a medieval siege.

He went on:

> Eventually, after five days, they came in and they said, 'We've fixed the tunnel. We've dug out the dirt. Get in the trucks.' So they put a pair of trousers on me and dragged me out and they threw me in a truck in a last ditch attempt to get us out. We then just drove through bombardment. They began to target us as we had the lights on. There were mortars, shells, machine-guns, sniper fire. It was a crazy four-mile drive to the tunnel. When we got there they tied me on a rope, dropped me down the hole, where they had converted a motorbike to run in the tunnel. I had to get on it and lay flat with the driver. They put a kid behind me that had all the flesh blown off his legs and we just drove through the storm drain until we reached the blockage. I thought they'd cleared it, but it was actually just a hole. They said, 'Get in there and crawl through.' I had no choice. I got halfway down and got stuck as a big piece of reinforced concrete steel went through my leg and into the wound. It was like barbed wire hooked into me. In the end the only way I could get free was to wrench it off, as I couldn't go backwards. So I pulled my leg off this metal hook and ripped it open even more. I finally got through the tunnel. With the help of a couple of rebels I crawled a couple of hundred metres across a field. There were snipers everywhere. Two rebels then grabbed and supported me as we walked for four miles across walls, ditches and farmland. Eventually they got me to a vet who

cleaned and washed and then stitched me up again. I think it was another two or three days before we crossed the front line on motorbikes and in cars and finally got into Lebanon. Once in Lebanon we had to dodge Hezbollah, who were patrolling the area. They were looking for people coming out of Syria. By hook or by crook, we finally made it to Beirut, where I was greeted with a bottle of Scotch and forty valium. I just sat up all night with a guy from the *Sunday Times* who had been co-ordinating attempts to get us out. In the end we were left to do it ourselves. He eventually put me on a little jet that News International lined up. There was a really hot nurse and a doctor on board. He said: 'You've got two options. You can either have ibuprofen and paracetamol or whisky and morphine.' I just replied: 'Fill me up, Doc.' And with that I went home.

It would take a year or so before Paul's remarkable escape was fully told. Most journalists concentrated their attention on the demise of Marie and her last dispatch to the *Sunday Times*. It was a graphic account of a widows' basement, where 300 people were huddled together, having lost their loved ones after two weeks of relentless bombing. 'The widows' basement,' she wrote:

reflects the ordeal of 28,000 men, women and children clinging to existence in Baba Amr, a district surrounded on all sides by Syrian forces. The army is launching Katyusha rockets, mortar shells and tank rounds at random. Snipers on the rooftops shoot any civilian who comes into their sights [. . .] Almost every building is pockmarked after tank rounds punched through concrete walls [. . .] The building I was in lost its upper floors. On some streets whole buildings have collapsed – all there is to see are shredded clothes, broken pots and the shattered furniture of families destroyed [. . .] There are no telephones and the electricity has been cut off. Few homes have diesel for the tin stoves they rely on for heat in the coldest winter that anyone can remember [. . .] On the lips of everyone was the question 'Why have we been abandoned by the world?'[5]

It was the type of question that the residents of Benghazi might have asked had not the international community got its act together to pass the R2P resolution against Gaddafi's Libya in the Security Council a year earlier.

In 2001 Marie Colvin said this of her motivation in covering wars:

Simply: there's no way to cover war properly without risk. Covering war means going into places torn by chaos, destruction, death and pain, and trying to bear witness to that. I care about the experience of those most directly affected by war, those asked to fight and those who are just trying to survive. Going to these places, finding out what is happening, is the only way to get at the truth. Despite all the videos you see on television, what's on the ground has remained remarkably the same for the past hundred years. Craters. Burnt houses. Women weeping for sons and daughters. Suffering. In my profession, there is no chance of unemployment. The real difficulty is having enough faith in humanity that someone will care.

Marie was a war correspondent rather than a foreign correspondent. She described the utter futility and horrors of war rather than the origins and factors behind the war in Syria, which were multifaceted in nature and involved a range of regional players and shadowy forces that ultimately helped stoke and fuel the conflict. Certainly it is way beyond the confines of this book to explain how and why the conflict in Syria developed in the way it did, save to say that it was not comparable to the situation that prevailed in Libya. What is clear, however, is that it is doubtful whether the Security Council would have come together to appoint Kofi Annan as the UN and Arab League's first Peace Envoy to Syria in February 2012 were it not for the reportage and bravery of journalists like Marie Colvin and Paul Conroy.

Marie was a remarkable journalist and human being, whose reporting and inspirational personality touched thousands. She left an indelible mark on people. After she died, I was struck by how many people were affected by her loss. I had never bargained for the outpouring of sentiment that hit the Beyond Borders website from people who had heard her speak, or the reaction of ordinary people in Innerleithen and Traquair who had met her – from the taxi driver who drove her to the festival, to the waitress who served her tea, to the site manager who miked her up. All had a story to tell of Marie and her kindness. She had kept in touch with many of them, writing to them and calling them, and telling them about her desire to sail, or see this or that film. She was an inveterate texter and Twitter user. There wasn't a dry eye in the house at the 2012 Beyond Borders International Festival of Thought and Literature when Paul Conroy recounted their last few hours huddled together in a bombed-out basement on a winter's day in Homs in February 2012.

Final reflections from the 2011
Beyond Borders International Festival

Two days after the R2P debate in Edinburgh, as the celebrations in Tripoli continued unabated, I attended the premiere of my short film about the young people I encountered in Benghazi in April 2011. It ran alongside another film about the aftermath of the 1989 Romanian revolution, produced by the Scottish film maker Rupert Wolfe Murray some twenty-one years earlier, in a session entitled '21 Years of Revolution'. The two films provided the backdrop to a fascinating Q and A discussion about how the ideals that drive revolutions often become contorted by groups jockeying for power in the immediate post-revolutionary period. It was remarkable to watch similar scenes of people rejoicing and then demonstrating in defence of 'their revolution' twenty-one years earlier in Bucharest.

In the case of Romania, the revolution was quickly hijacked by the mili- tary, acting in cahoots with former high-ranking members of the regime and security forces. Within the space of two months the revolution was all but over. Although Ceausescu and his wife were summarily executed after a trial lasting no more than a couple of hours, the original aspirations that had fuelled the hopes of so many ordinary Romanians about a new Romania turned to dust as the *ancien regime* metamorphosed into new political parties bent on retaking power. Wolfe Murray's film captured this swirling period of intense political activity, from the recriminations on the street to the backroom deals and the stage-managed political press conferences of the new political parties. Was this also to be the fate of the Libyan revolution? Would the aspirations of the people of Benghazi for a state based on the rule of law be similarly dashed? Would they have to wait for another twenty years before real progress was made? There were already signs in Egypt that remnants of the Mubarak regime were regrouping under new guises. In 1989 the Western world heralded the revolutions of the Cold War as inaugurating a new era of freedom. Yet in places like Romania it took another twenty years before it began to emerge from its corrupt and authoritarian past, and then only after massive internal investment by the EU as part of its long-term objective in securing European integration. Time would tell how long it would take for Libya to move forward, but it was bound to take much longer without a similar degree of investment and long-term commitment from the West.

I finished the Beyond Borders season the next day with a final debate on the Arab Spring, with BBC journalist Alan Little, Egyptian film maker Omar Hamilton and a NATO official, at the Scottish Parliament's Festival of Politics organised by the Carnegie Foundation. All the panellists reiterated the need for New Libya to get its act together on transitional justice and rule-of-law issues if a vengeful bloodbath was to be avoided. With each passing day casualties were mounting on both sides, but these issues failed to move up the diplomatic agenda. As Berber, Islamist and Misrata fighters continued to seize yet more territory in Tripoli, it became harder to see how the NTC could flex its muscles across the country particularly on justice and reconciliation issues.

14. Whither the Revolution?

While the people of Tripoli rejoiced to the sounds of celebratory rebel gunfire, anxieties quickly surfaced in a number of Western ministries about the failure of the NTC to fill the emerging political vacuum emerging in the city. Abdul Jalil had decided to remain in Benghazi for the time being as he did not want to convey to the people of Benghazi that there was just one centre of power in Libya. Elsewhere Mahmoud Jibril was criticised for failing to stamp his authority on the liberation and appearing too hesitant about coming to Tripoli from Doha.

The speed of the liberation had taken everyone by surprise. Anger was mounting on the streets as running water and petrol began to run low in the capital, while numerous civilians began the desperate search in hospitals, mortuaries, military bases and prisons for loved ones who had been detained by Gaddafi's forces during the six-month civil war. Rumours spread of underground bunkers where thousands of prisoners had been abandoned to a slow, gruesome death. The sense of impending grief was palpable. It was obvious that the NTC had to act faster if it was not to lose control of both the political situation and the loyalty of ordinary residents of Tripoli.

There were already worrying signs that the triumphant militias from Misrata and Zintan were disinclined to hand power over to their political counterparts. Misratan and Zintani commanders were losing control of their fighters as they started to loot the capital. Militias and volunteer units as well as criminal opportunists were now occupying not just security establishments and depots across the capital but also private villas. In an attempt to fill the power vacuum Tarhouni and al-Alagi flew to the capital via Zintan to announce the liberation of Tripoli, to the evident irritation of Belhaj. Belhaj now called on the British government to issue an apology to him, after documents surfaced concerning its alleged involvement in his rendition back to Tripoli a few years earlier.

Two competing stabilisation organisations quickly emerged on the scene. The First was Jibril's Stabilisation Committee, which had been liaising with the UN and the international community over the previous months. It met Contact Group members in Dubai between 21 and 25 August. The second was the Tripoli Local Council set up by the 17 February Coalition in August. It brought together a network of Tripolitanian professions and engineers under a civil contingency committee which had been stockpiling medicine, food and communication systems in anticipation of the liberation. Its engineers now played a crucial role in preserving water supplies from the source of the Great Manmade River Gaddafi built 600 km south of Tripoli. However, while it was prepared to reach out towards the International Committee of the Red Cross it was not prepared to do so for Jibril's Stabilisation Committee, which it viewed as lacking legitimacy as a result of being led by non-Tripolitanians. Thus the same schism that scarred the conflict phase repeated itself in the post-conflict phase.

At first glance then there was little evidence that the much-vaunted ISRT stabilisation plan was being implemented. Yet by the second week of September 2011 the NTC and its allies had succeeded in restoring electricity and water supplies to the capital. Petrol stations began to open, albeit with long queues, while fresh fruit, vegetables and meat appeared once again in the shops. Other reports claimed that barricades, rubbish and graffiti were being removed from the streets as the first flights for six months began to land at Tripoli Airport. Jibril's Stabilisation Committee's planning appeared to be working to a degree, but huge problems remained. Notwithstanding, Libya had clear advantages over countries like Iraq. It had enormous oil wealth and a small population of 6.6 million with little religious or sectarian division. It also enjoyed a higher literacy rate than either of its neighbours, and a wide range of professional expertise existed within its diaspora who, as the former UK Envoy Christopher Prentice rightly observed back in April, seemed willing to return to help put the country back on its feet. Moreover, Gaddafi's frozen assets, totalling an estimated $100 billion, could be used to jumpstart an economy ravaged by six months of civil war. These resources were probably enough to keep the loose coalition of rebel forces together, at least for the medium term, as the spoils of war were divided on the street and in the political chamber.

Yet in reality Jibril's Stabilisation Committee could only act as an emergency relief provider unless it obtained wider political support for its activities. This was unlikely to be forthcoming given the frictions with Belhaj and other militias. Belhaj was still nominally head of the Tripoli Military Council but had his own problems with Zintan for having supplied competing towns in Nafusa with weaponry. In an effort to bolster the Council's standing, Ali al-Sallabi now embarked on shuttle diplomacy between various commanders from Tripoli, Zintan and Misrata to rebuild bridges. He was regarded with much greater respect and as a consequence was able to formally announce to the world the establishment of the Tripoli Military Council on 25 August. The Misratans now accepted Belhaj as head and Bu Hajar as deputy, along with ten heads of local area military councils, but the Zintani rebels did not.

In an effort to counter these developments, Jibril's colleague Tarhouni announced the creation of a Supreme Security Council Committee (SSC) on 7 September, which included Zintan representatives as well as Bu Hajar. It nominally had oversight of all fighting groups in Tripoli but to little effect as new groups continued to emerge in Tripoli to take advantage of the spoils of the chaos. The resultant tensions between the two camps led Abdul Jalil to finally fly to Tripoli on 11 September to bring some semblance of order and unity. He immediately chaired a series of meeting with commanders from all sides, which led him a week later to transfer control of the Supreme Security Council away from the Executive Office's to three NTC members in a deliberate clipping of Jibril's wings.

These NTC members now began to register fighters by promising to pay their salaries, resulting in an immediate diminution of Belhaj's stature and influence. However, the move created a highly politicised and unstable parallel security structure and economy. Zintani and Misratan rebels had suddenly been given every incentive to remain in Tripoli. Commanders now began to position themselves for jobs in the Security Council and ministries as attention turned to the creation of a new interim administration. This did not include Belhaj, as his badly judged speech before Gaddafi's iconic statue had effectively put paid to his political ambitions. He would later contest a seat but lose in the elections of 7 July 2012. The transfer of power away from the Executive Committee also marked the end of Jibril's dream of a managed transition in which he would head an interim administration. A few days later he announced he would resign as head of the NTC's Executive Office as soon as the fighting was over. But in contrast to Belhaj, Jibril would later emerge from the elections with the largest number of seats of all party leaders.

All eyes now turned towards the United Nations and what it would do. On 7 September 2011 UN Secretary-General Ban Ki-moon proposed to the Security Council that the UN formally establish a comprehensive Support Mission in Libya (UNSMIL) under the leadership of Ian Martin. On 16 September, the Security Council unanimously agreed. It empowered UNSMIL 'to support' and 'assist' Libyan national efforts to restore security and state authority. Ian Martin elected to focus his energies on three areas – elections, security and the rule of law. He later described the UN's approach in the following terms:

To combine the objectives of speed of response and national ownership, the secretary-general proposed a phased approach, deploying a team for three months for immediate support . . .

We offered support to the NTC's Executive Committee and Stabilisation Team, but despite their efforts encountered an initial vacuum of governance. It gradually became clear that Jibril and other key members of the NTC Executive Committee would not be part of the interim government, which the NTC's Constitutional Declaration said would be formed within thirty days of the announcement of liberation.

Accordingly, the deployment of UN staff was deliberately gradual. The key consideration was Libyan counterparts' readiness to engage in different fields, which developed slowly. As there was no government for the UN to consult with in undertaking full mission planning during the initial three-month mandate, the Security Council on 2 December agreed to a three-month extension. Meanwhile, growing international concern regarding the flow of arms and ammunition out of Libya led the Council to explicitly mandate UNSMIL to assist Libya efforts to address the threats of proliferation.[1]

The baton was passing from NATO to the UN but it had little to work with. It would be interesting to see how the UK and France intended to support the NTC and the UN mission on a bilateral level given their stated committed to the democratic development of Libya.

Luckily for the Council, the liberation of Libya was not yet complete, as there were still important battles for the militias to fight. Gaddafi and his sons remained at large, while forces and tribes loyal to him continued to offer vigorous pockets of resistance in his hometown of Sirte and in the desert town of Bani Walid. These military diversions were a godsend to the NTC. It would take a few weeks for the rebel militias to mop up this resistance, thus giving the NTC more time to move its operations. This kept the tensions between militia leadership and the NTC at bay, at least for the time being. Even then, huge problems remained. Most of the foreign workers that had serviced Tripoli had left in the wake of the fighting. The long-neglected infrastructure was even more damaged as a consequence of war, apart from those big gilded projects supported by Gaddafi that were poorly executed and maintained in any event. Production of oil was down by 60 per cent. The huge public sector was warped by corruption, while the tiny private sector lacked regulation or any semblance of the rule of law likely to attract investors back any time soon. The country remained badly in need of foreign expertise, from the ports to the oil industry, to the sanitation system and on to the creation of new telecom, banking and governance structures.

The UK should have provided such expertise from the outset. And the ISRT should have helped the NTC to thrash out some basic agreements with the militias in advance of the assault on Tripoli, particularly about how the remnants of the regime were to be treated in defeat. If Iraq had taught the international community anything, it was that there had to be a cogent strategy in place to deal with post-conflict justice issues in the run-up to any military dénouement, if the political authorities were to have any chance of keeping and exercising power on the streets. Yet despite the huge NATO effort to remove Gaddafi there appeared to be no effective plan about how the NTC proposed to disarm, demobilise and reintegrate into civil society those militias, now that they had taken Tripoli.

The NTC also had to deal with a tribal culture that involved more than 140 clans, many with deep-seated enmities, and also the ancient ethnic and linguistic fault line between the Berber minority and the Arab population. Gaddafi had co-opted these disparate elements through patronage, bribery and repression. Just how the NTC would manage to move from a form of government based upon the illusive system of 'people's' committees to an all-inclusive elected, transparent and constitutional form of government, without alienating crucial tribal or ethnic elements was a big question. The need for support and advice in the post-conflict period seemed as acute as ever. All of this cried out at the very least for a process of consultation involving the tribes and civil society. Initiatives like the ones promoted by CHD remained crucial to New Libya's ability to confront and overcome some of the most deep-seated suspicions and enmities that lay just below the surface of Libyan society. Laying the foundations for lasting peace and security in any country emerging from internal conflict is a complex process involving many opposing factions. It was therefore essential that reconciliation and reconstruction programmes involved all parties at an early point and took an integrated approach to the political, civil, economic, social and cultural context of the specific conflict. The prospect of recovery and peace-building in places like Libya, and other countries affected by the Arab Spring, rested in part on the ability of the international community to harness the power of civil society, and the ISRT should have promoted this policy.

As we have seen, the experience of places like South Africa and Northern Ireland demonstrates how civil society can act as a vital catalyst for social, political and economic change. It has a key role to play in broadening popular understanding and advocating measures to bring an end to ongoing violence and human suffering. Moreover, civil society organisations have the moral legitimacy to act as custodians of peace and to help oversee government accountability. This was particularly the case in Arab countries such as Libya, where the capacity to deliver essential services to citizens had become weak due to poor governance and a 'democratic deficit'.

The NTC and Libya's rebel factions needed to recognise that the exclusion of a range of civil society and clan groups from the formal peace and reform process threatened the sustainability and durability of any future constitutional settlement agreed by New Libya's political powers. Formal stabilisation and peace processes needed to be complemented by other initiatives that reached out to wider constituencies, so that they too became stakeholders in any overall post-conflict settlement. Yet the British government's decision to merely back the UN mission, rather than get its hands dirty by intervening directly to support the NTC's fledgling civil administration and civil society, seemed more an act of hope than conviction. All of this raised questions about what exactly the UK intervention in Libya was designed to achieve, if not a democratic transformation.

A New Doctrine of Democratic Intervention?

What is clear is that victory in Libya represented a major boost for the NATO alliance, at least in terms of the success of its military intervention. After ten years of being bogged down in places like Afghanistan and Kosovo, NATO leaders finally had something to celebrate. In the Libya campaign its warplanes had flown roughly 26,000 sorties, including more than 9,600 strike missions. It destroyed about 5,900 military targets, including Libya's air defences and more than 1,000 tanks, vehicles and guns, as well as Gaddafi's command and control networks. The air strikes broke the back of Gaddafi's forces and paved the way for the rebel onslaught on Tripoli in August 2011. In doing so, NATO restored some of its faltering confidence, although it was sharply criticised by Russia, China, South Africa and other nations for overstepping the terms of UN Security Council Resolution 1973.

The debate about the true nature of Britain, France and then NATO's intervention had intensified over the summer of 2011. By late August it was obvious to everybody that NATO's intervention was directed not just toward humanitarian protection but efforts to create a new democratic dispensation for Libya through regime change. What did this mean for the R2P doctrine? Just before his death in 2011, Václav Havel, the former Czech President and dissident, described 'Responsibility to Protect' as the most significant development in the defence of human rights since they were codified in the Universal Declaration of Human Rights after the Second World War, though one which had proved to be a 'frustratingly elusive promise' despite its adoption at the 2005 World Summit. He wrote movingly about the development of the doctrine:

> It is a journey that began in the gas chambers of the Holocaust and moved through the killing fields in Cambodia to the machetes and rapes in Rwanda and into a stadium in Srebrenica. Time and again, the world has watched and waited as human beings planned and implemented genocides, war crimes, ethnic cleansings, and crimes against humanity, enveloping states and destroying lives. In Rwanda and Bosnia, the world even watched as UN peacekeepers sat impotent, as innocents were slaughtered. The enormity of the international community's failure to respond to government sponsored mass murders resulted in a rethink of traditional notions of state sovereignty and the development of the R2P doctrine.[2]

For Havel, R2P was much more than an 'aspirational' doctrine. It was 'a clear and unequivocal public commitment' by world leaders 'to prevent mass atrocities'. For him, the 'most important question' was how R2P was to be implemented. Havel wrote these words just after the intervention in Libya began, which he believed was more likely attributed to 'a host of political factors than merely to R2P'. Unfortunately, he died before being able to assess its full impact in Libya. It is clear, however, that he remained deeply hopeful about the future utility of the doctrine: 'Although there will surely be stumbles as the doctrine is implemented, R2P remains the international community's greatest hope for being able to one day truthfully claim, "Never Again!"'

Was the R2P promise redeemed or hijacked for other political purposes in Libya? The answer to this question had profound consequences for the protection of other civilian populations. Sir Kieran Prendergast cast doubt upon the intervention in Libya. He regarded the level of support offered to the Libyan rebels by the UK under R2P principles as not only impermissible but dangerous to the future diplomatic world order. The illegitimate extension of R2P to regime change in Libya would stop effective action being taken elsewhere, such as in Syria, due to the way in which the Security Council vote had been manipulated. Certainly Russia and China had become increasingly sceptical about the West's motivations.

For some it marked the beginning of the end for a concept that had only just begun to take hold. The military intervention in Libya raised fundamental questions about when, how and in what circumstances the international community should be allowed to intervene in the domestic affairs of a state that perpetrated gross human rights abuses to suppress democratic reform. What action did UN Resolution 1973 exactly authorise? Was it limited to the provision of military assistance to stop an imminent humanitarian catastrophe, as the Russians contended? Or did it implicitly authorise military action in support of regime change if that action prevented further catastrophes from occurring in the future?

For David Cameron the position was clear. The intervention constituted a supreme example of how the international community could and should act in concert, under legitimate UN authority, to protect civilian populations from brutal regimes intent on crushing democratic reform. This was consistent with the sentiments expressed by Barack Obama and David Cameron in their joint article in *The Times* published five days after Obama's speech on 19 May 2011, which states:

> What we are seeing is there is a groundswell of people demanding the basic rights, freedoms and dignities that we take for granted. We all share in their success or failure. Progress in the region will be uneven and it is not our place to dictate the pace and scope of this change. But we stand with those who want to bring light into dark, support those who seek freedom in place of repression, aid those laying the building blocks of democracy. We do so because democracy and respect for universal rights is a good for the people of the region, and also the antidote to the instability and extremism that threatens our security. And we will not stand by as their aspirations get crushed in a hail of bombs, bullets and mortar fire. We are reluctant to use force but when our interests and values come together *we know that we have a responsibility to act.* That is why we mobilised the international community to protect the Libyan people from Colonel Gaddafi's regime [. . .] And continue to support the legitimate and credible Transitional National Council and its efforts to prepare for all inclusive, democratic transition. Together we show the world that the principles of justice and freedom will be upheld.[3]

Cameron put the position of his administration beyond doubt in a speech to the 66th General Assembly of the United Nations in September 2011, where he urged the UN to put its money where its mouth was and henceforth take 'action' rather than voice platitudes in defence of democracy and freedom. His opening salvo to the UN came in his first sentence. 'Libya and the Arab Spring shows the UN needs a *new way of working* not just united in condemnation, but united in action,' he declared.

> Last week I was in Tripoli and Benghazi. I saw the hunger of a people eager to get on with reclaiming their country, writing themselves a new chapter of freedom and democracy. This has been the most dramatic episode of what has been called the Arab Spring. My argument today is that Libya and

the Arab Spring shows the UN needs a new way of working. Because the Arab Spring *is a massive opportunity to spread peace, prosperity, democracy and vitally security but only if we really seize it.*

According to Cameron this included a responsibility to help bring about democratic government.

You can sign every human rights declaration in the world but if you stand by and watch people being slaughtered in their own country, when you could act, then what are those signatures really worth? The UN has to show that we can be not just united in condemnation, but *united in action*, acting in a way that lives up to the UN's founding principles and meets the needs of people everywhere [. . .] Just as after 1989 we helped those who tore down the Berlin Wall to build robust democracies and market economies. Just as in 1994 we welcomed South Africa back into the Commonwealth of Nations when it chose the path of reconciliation and democracy instead of racial conflict. So now in 2011 as people in North Africa and the Middle East stand up and give voice to their hopes for more open and democratic societies, we have an opportunity and I would say *a responsibility* to help them.

Stirring words, but what did this mean in terms of action post-conflict?

Cameron's speech to the UN effectively hinted at a new doctrine of intervention which went beyond the R2P humanitarian precepts that underpinned the two UN resolutions passed on Libya. He went on:

Here at the UN, we have *a responsibility* to stand up against regimes that persecute their people. We need to see reform in Yemen. And above all, on Syria, it is time for the Members of the Security Council to *act*. We must now adopt a credible resolution threatening tough sanctions. Of course we should always act with care when it comes to the internal affairs of a sovereign state. But we cannot allow this to be an excuse for indifference in the face of a regime that week after week arrests, intimidates, tortures and kills people who are peacefully trying to make their voices heard.

Cameron's speech was entirely in keeping with his earlier statement on the subject, published on 14 April 2011 in the *New York Times*, when he set out the position of the UK government towards intervention in terms of democratic regime change. It also dovetailed with the Presidential Study Directive on Mass Atrocities (PSD-10) issued by the Obama administration during the Libyan conflict, which authorised an escalating series of actions against a country failing to protect its citizens. It defined the prevention of mass atrocities as both 'a core national security interest and a core moral responsibility of the United States'.

According to the eminent academic Adam Roberts, president of the British Academy and Emeritus Professor of International Relations at Oxford University, Cameron's speech was akin to Tony Blair's 1997 Chicago foreign policy speech on liberal intervention before NATO's military campaign in Kosovo. It seemingly prepared the ground for a new doctrine of democratic intervention. In a talk given at the Kennedy School of Government at Harvard University in October 2011 reflecting on his arguments in *Civil Resistance & Power Politics: The Experience of Non-Violent Action from Gandhi to the Present* (2009), Professor Roberts described the UK's involvement in Libya as an 'almost unabashed intervention in a civil war', where R2P was used to authorise international support for democratic reform against the Gaddafi regime. For Roberts it was impossible to disconnect civilian protests and resistance in Libya from the struggle for political power. Civil resistance was not, and had never been, a phenomenon unconnected to other forms of power, whether economic, social or military.

There was no better illustration of the relation between civil resistance and political power than the recent case of Libya. Unlike Somalia, the international community had in the NTC a political entity it could support; and do so against a regime that did not enjoy the strategic backing of Russia, China and Iran, in contrast to the regime in Syria. Gaddafi invoked relatively little regional support and was isolated politically through an internal idiosyncratic system that lacked any coherent ideological framework. Moreover, Libya did not have any of the religious or ethnic fissures that plagued Bosnia or Iraq, or allow neighbouring powers to act as spoilers. As a consequence, the international community was able to eschew the studiously detached disposition it had adopted in Bosnia fifteen years earlier. The lack of an alternative power base within an ethnic community or the military meant support for democratic reform was an altogether viable proposition in Libya. More significantly, Libya benefited from enormous oil reserves and a small and well-educated population from which to build a new democratic settlement. In these circumstances Cameron believed there was a duty on the international community both to intervene on humanitarian grounds, but also to aid the development of democracy where possible. It was not difficult to see how the international protection of the civilian population under R2P principles quickly transformed itself into a latent and then explicit struggle for democratic change in the case of Libya.

Cameron's General Assembly speech combined the principles of R2P with the evolving right to democracy, and applied it to circumstances where none of the inhibiting political factors that stopped international action taking place in countries such as Syria or Bahrain were present. In doing so, the speech built upon some of the UN, international and regional instruments and declarations in support of democratic government cited earlier. Although there was no established legal right to democratic governance in international law, the international community had emphasised the centrality of democratic rights time and again in a whole host of UN resolutions. These developments, together with the Arab Spring, meant that it was no longer open for the West to back weak and illegitimate authoritarian governments out of a preference for short-term stability, without recourse to the principle of democracy.

Cameron's doctrine of democratic intervention seemingly arose where a critical mass of civilians came together to protest in favour of democratic change against an authoritarian regime with no legitimate support – and were threatened with widespread reprisals within the meaning of R2P; in circumstances where regime change through democratic reform was likely to prevent further abuses from occurring in the future; and where the case for intervention was not opposed by the Security Council so as to render democratic regime change impractical. In short, Cameron seemed to be advocating that where these conditions were met, the international community was not just under an obligation to physically protect a defenceless population but also one to help it achieve democratic change. Where R2P principles were satisfied and such reform seemed possible, therefore, it was his view that the international community had a duty to intervene using whatever diplomatic, military or political means necessary.

But if Cameron's administration was committed to removing Gaddafi's regime in principle, in practice it was less gung-ho about wading in by itself to help rebuild the country or deal with legacy issues that still haunted UK–Libya relations, instead preferring to support the UN in its efforts. I took a call from an FCO official in Tripoli on the subject in mid-September. In the end he declared that henceforth all requests for non-state support for the rule of law and transitional justice sector had to be channelled through the EU and UN, whose institutions had taken lead roles in helping the NTC to rebuild New Libya. I was immediately reminded of Afghanistan and everything David Marshall, the UN official, had observed about the UN's capacity to deliver rule of law programmes in conflict areas in a book entitled *The International Rule of Law Movement: A Crisis of Legitimacy and the Way Forward* (2014). It detailed just how ineffectual UN efforts had been to strengthen the rule of law in fragile states or those experiencing traumatic political transition. Letting the UN and the EU take the lead on rule of law and transitional justice issues constituted an abdication of responsibility on the part of the UK government. What was needed was not more UN consultants with MAs in conflict transformation, but independent legal practitioners who actually practised in the rule of law sector and knew how to build institutions on the ground, and who could give bespoke advice to Libyan ministers without fear or favour. One initiative obviously did not exclude the other. Quite why HMG was not willing to assist the NTC on a bilateral basis in relation to these issues remained a total mystery to me.

Rendition

Interestingly it was during this period that the issue of the previous Labour administration's attitude and conduct towards the Gaddafi regime reared its head again after documents were found in Moussa Koussa's office that seemingly hinted at its involvement in rendition and the possible facilitation of torture of rebel commander Abdelhakim Belhaj and other LIFG targets. Mr Belhaj originally fled Libya as a dissident in the 1990s, and ended up in China with his wife Fatima Bouchar, where he made no secret of being a leader of the LIFG. The documents revealed that Koussa was informed as early as November 2003 that MI6 was seeking the assistance of their counterpart in China to deal with 'the Islamic extremist target in China'. Belhaj was finally detained in Malaysia in March 2004 after he tried to obtain asylum through the British High Commission. He had left China and attempted to travel to the UK on a false Iraqi passport. On hearing the news, MI6 tipped off the CIA about his whereabouts. Belhaj and his wife were informed that they would be allowed to board a BA flight to London via Bangkok, despite having no EU passports or UK visas. This was contrary to the stringent immigration regulations that applied post 9/11. When Belhaj and his wife touched down in Bangkok to change planes they were immediately taken into 'custody', and transported to a cell close to Don Muang International Airport. Belhaj's detention occurred just days after SIAC freed 'M', after it criticised the Home Office for its 'consistent exaggeration' of the links between the LIFG and Al-Qaeda.[4]

The existence of a CIA secret detention facility in Thailand, whose location was hitherto unknown, is not without relevance. Tied and gagged, Belhaj and Bouchar were forced by US officials to fly to Libya. They arrived just days before Tony Blair shook hands with Gaddafi, in what became known as the 'Deal in the Desert'. Back in London, Shell announced a £110m gas exploration deal. For his part, Tony Blair triumphantly proclaimed that Libya had recognised 'a common cause, with us, in the fight against Al-Qaeda extremism and terrorism', seemingly oblivious of SIAC's judgment. Belhaj's thirty-year-old wife Fatima Bouchar was four months pregnant at the time, and gave a graphic and heartrending account to the *Guardian* newspaper of her rendition from Bangkok to Tripoli. According to Bouchar, upon arrival in Bangkok she was quickly dragged away from her husband and shackled to a cell wall for five days, without food or being able to move. 'They knew I was pregnant. It was obvious,' she reported.[5] The Americans forced her to lie on a stretcher and began wrapping tape around her feet. They moved upwards along her legs, tightly binding her stomach, arms and chest to the stretcher so that she was unable to move. They then wound the tape around her head and eyes, placing a hood and ear muffs on her, but not before she saw three Americans dressed in black with balaclavas, two men and a woman.

After that she was bundled into an aircraft unaware of where she was going. For the next seventeen hours she claimed she was unable to move any part of her body apart from her right eye, which remained taped open throughout the flight. 'It was agony,' she recalled. On arrival she was driven to Tajoura prison in Tripoli, where she spent the next four months being interrogated five hours a day. She had no idea whether her husband was alive or dead. 'I really thought I was going to have my baby there. The time around the birth of a first child should be among the happiest in a couple's lives, but it is very difficult for me to look back at that time because I wanted to die rather than be going through what I did,' she recalled in horror. She was eventually released just before the birth of her son, when word of the couple's capture reached the outside world. When Tony Blair said that the rules of the game had changed after 9/11, he wasn't being rhetorical.

Belhaj was similarly blindfolded, hooded and then hung from hooks in his cell wall by American agents, in poses reminiscent of the abuses that occurred in Abu Ghraib prison in Iraq, which the Bush administration claimed had been perpetrated by renegade military personnel acting on a whim. He was also subjected to loud music consistent with the type of enhanced interrogation techniques approved by the Bush White House. After being flown to Tripoli, Belhaj was taken to the infamous Abu Salim prison, where he suffered six continuous years of abuse at the hands of Gaddafi's henchmen. During this period, he was allegedly interrogated by MI6, including by a female agent. He was also injected with truth drugs and suspended by his wrists in his cell, as his interrogators beat him and demanded to know the whereabouts of Osama bin Laden.

He was told that his treatment would improve if he linked LIFG members active in Britain to Al-Qaeda and told the British the same. Unbeknown to Belhaj, just three days after his abduction another leading LIFG member, Abu Mundhir al-Saadi, was likewise rendered back to Tripoli after being forced into a plane in Hong Kong, in a joint

British–Libyan operation. He too was subjected to torture and questioned in a similar manner before being released six years later. His wife and four children, including a six-year-old girl, were forced back to Libya and endured two months of detention at Tajoura. For Gareth Peirce, the solicitor acting for 'M', the UK's 'complicity in these renditions' and 'synchronisation with the obtaining of perceived missing intelligence for domestic proceedings' was utterly 'sickening' as well as damning of both enterprises equally.

A *Daily Mail* journalist later claimed that Whitehall sources confirmed that a cabinet minister must almost certainly have had to approve MI6 agents turning Belhaj over to Gaddafi, although the Foreign Secretary at the time, Jack Straw, denied any knowledge of the rendition. For its part, the Foreign Office repeated its oft-quoted mantra on the subject of torture, after Belhaj instructed Leigh Day to bring an action against the government following its steadfast refusal to issue an apology. 'The government,' opined an FCO spokesperson, 'stands firmly against torture and cruel, inhuman and degrading treatment or punishment. We do not condone it, nor do we ask others to do it on our behalf.' It was unclear whether the spokesperson was speaking for the past as well as the present. Sapna Malik, the couple's lawyer, was probably closer to the truth when she said: 'The barbaric treatment which our clients describe, both at the hands of the Americans and the Libyans, is beyond comprehension and yet it appears that the UK was responsible for setting off this torturous chain of events.' Anthony Layden's emphatic statements underlining the UK's zero tolerance of torture before SIAC in the Sihali case flooded my mind.

Was Chris McGreal of *The Guardian* therefore right when he complained about British government double standards and its double-dealing on legacy issues? After all, what could be clearer then the cringe-making note from Mark Allen, head of counter-terrorism at MI6, to Moussa Koussa, dated 18 March 2004, found in Koussa's office after the fall of Tripoli. In the note Allen, who later took a lucrative job with BP working on Libyan oil contracts, described how a rendition target's safe arrival in the hands of Gaddafi's security forces was 'the least we could do for you and Libya to demonstrate the remarkable relationship we have built over recent years'. Such remarks chimed with Prime Minister Gordon Brown's 2008 reply to Jason McCue that Libya was now an important partner in the fight against terrorism. Allen also made it clear that it was British intelligence that had effected the target's safe arrival and that as a result he expected the fruits of his interrogation to be passed on to him first rather than to the Americans. The note read as follows:

London
SE1
18 March 2004

FOR THE URGENT PERSONAL ATTENTION OF MUSA KUSA
DEPARTMENT OF INTERNATIONAL RELATIONS AND COLLABORATION

Following message for Musa in Tripoli from Mark in London. I am so grateful to you for your help in sorting this visit to the Leader by our Prime Minister. The diplomats had failed to get organised. What you did made a great impression at No 10. They are grateful too.

....

No 10 however are keen that the Prime Minister meet the Leader in his tent. I don't know why the English are fascinated by tents. The plain fact that the journalists would love it.

....

Most importantly I congratulate you on the safe arrival of Abu 'Abd Allah Sadiq. This was the least we could do for you and for Libya to demonstrate the remarkable relationship we have built over recent years. I am so glad. I was grateful to you for helping the officer we sent out last week. Abu 'Abd Allah's information on the situation in this country is of urgent importance to us.

Amusingly, we got a request from the Americans to channel requests for information from Abu 'Abd Allah through the Americans. I have no intention of doing any such thing. The intelligence about Abu 'Abd Allah was British.

I know I did not pay for the air cargo. But I feel I have the right to deal with you direct on this and am very grateful to you for the help you are giving us.

M.

The disclosure of these communications was acutely embarrassing for the government, not to mention BP, for whom Allen now worked. It also sent shock waves through a series of companies which did illicit business with the Gaddafis, particularly after Peter Bouckaert and his Human Rights Watch team uncovered further intelligence documents in Tripoli, which allegedly exposed deals between them and companies from Britain, France, Belgium, South Africa and Spain, concerning the sale of a comprehensive surveillance system to the Gaddafi government and covering landlines, mobile phones, the Internet, satellite communications and microwave communications. Within days, numerous private security companies were deployed by a number of Western companies to seize embarrassing or incriminating material left behind by their staff in Tripoli.

15.   The Fall of the House of Gaddafi

One major test for any New Libyan commitment to the rule of law would be how the interim government dealt with the likes of Gaddafi and his sons once they were captured. Its reaction would say a lot about New Libya's stated commitment to the rule of law and desire to reconcile the country. It is not known what advice the UK government gave, if any, on this point. However, as the NTC focused on forming an interim administration in Tripoli to govern the country until the election of a constituent assembly, rebel militias continued to search for Gaddafi and his sons the length and breadth of Libya. It would take another six weeks before Gaddafi was located and captured. In fact, Gaddafi and his son Mutassim secretly fled Tripoli on 21 August, after he elected to hide in his hometown of Sirte. They travelled there in a small convoy via the loyalist bastions of Tarhuna and Bani Walid, despite being counselled against doing so by the leader of Gaddafi's feared People's Guard, Mansour Dhao Ibrahim. The decision to stay in Sirte was made by Mutassim. He reasoned that this was the last place NATO would look for his father. But this decision meant that the escape route south into the vast Libyan desert was less accessible than it would have been had Gaddafi remained in Bani Walid.

Sirte was a deeply loyalist town that had been rewarded handsomely for its support of the regime. When Gaddafi was born in 1942 it was just a desolate coastal village; by 2011 it was full of whitewashed houses and streets with new shop fronts and gleaming cars. It stood in marked contrast to the dusty, dirty streets which littered Libya's other towns. Gaddafi later populated Sirte with thousands of black Africans, proclaiming it to be an 'Arab space and African space'. He even once proposed it as the capital of a Pan-African union after holding an African Union summit there. By choosing to go back to Sirte, Gaddafi effectively prolonged the war, as fiercely loyal African cadres fought desperately to ensure the survival of the last vestiges of the regime, and to save their own lives. Witnesses to the ensuing battle in Sirte during September 2011 alleged that many of these

African loyalists used families as human shields and kidnapped daughters to prevent others from leaving. Other reports claimed that soldiers who refused to continue fighting for the regime were summarily executed. Sirte continued to hold out, despite repeated suicidal onslaughts by rebel brigades from Misrata, until NATO launched a ferocious bombing assault on 8 October, when according to one *Sunday Times* report: 'the ground did not stop shaking all night'.

The next morning the rebels pushed forwards into the south and east of the city expecting the usual fierce resistance, but this time none was forthcoming. For the next few days the Misratan rebels bombarded the other parts of the town with everything at their disposal, bringing their tanks and heavy guns in 'and blazing away at every building standing between their own positions and the sea'. Through their own homemade form of 'shock and awe' the rebels finally breached the psychological ramparts of defiance. From that moment on more and more loyalist fighters surrendered or just faded away, as the sheer futility of their resistance became obvious. Bit by bit, Gaddafi's hometown was blown apart all around them.

As rebel forces encircled the last vestiges of opposition in Sirte, Gaddafi rapidly became cut off from the outside world. His only means of communication was a phone that he used to make statements to a Syrian television station in Damascus and taunt the rebels. Over the next few days, rebel forces continued to fire rocket after rocket into areas not under its control, on one occasion wounding three of Gaddafi's guards in the house in which he was staying. According to one graphic account in *The New York Times*, Muammar Gaddafi spent his last days hovering between defiance and delusion, surviving on rice and pasta that his guards scrounged from the empty civilian houses he moved between every few days.[1] As the weeks passed he began to ask with incredulity why there was no electricity or water. Then on 19 October, some six weeks or so after he fled Tripoli, Gaddafi and his son found themselves cornered in District Two of Sirte, after rebel forces finally stormed their way into the city centre. It was then that Gaddafi decided to flee.

Revolutionary Injustice and the Execution of Gaddafi

At about 8 am the next morning, after a fatal delay of some five hours, a huge convoy of over fifty cars with heavy armaments left Sirte, with Gaddafi placed in the middle in a Toyota Land Cruiser. Jibril Abu Sharaf was one of the surviving defenders who got in a civilian car and joined the end of the convoy. 'We tried to escape along the coast road. But we came under heavy fire so we tried another way.' Within half an hour NATO jets, including RAF Tornados, had spotted them. An American Predator drone piloted from a control site in Las Vegas fired the first missile and destroyed eleven vehicles, burning many of the occupants alive. A French Mirage jet quickly followed suit. Jibril recalled: 'Then the only thing I saw was dead bodies all around, dust and debris. It went dark.' The rest of the convoy split up, with Gaddafi's core group of about twenty vehicles turning south-west at high speed on the main highway. This convoy was then attacked by a Mirage 2000D fighter plane from a base at Souda Bay in Crete, which dropped a 250kg, laser-guided GBU bomb on the convoy, while a Mirage F1CR monitored the situation.

At the time NATO was unaware of Gaddafi's whereabouts. British military sources had previously told *The Sunday Times* that the colonel was believed to have fled to a third country after the fall of Tripoli in August. Other Western diplomats thought he was on the run in the vast desert of southern Libya, bribing locals to give him refuge. Fierce armed resistance in Bani Walid strengthened suspicions that he was hiding there. Sirte, by contrast, seemed too obvious a place to hide. Little did the Mirage NATO pilot know that his bomb had just got lucky. Shrapnel from one of the missiles hit the Toyota in which Gaddafi was travelling. The impact released the airbags. Gaddafi, his Minister of Defence Abu-Bakr Yunis Jabr, Dhao and four volunteer soldiers were forced to decamp from the vehicle. They staggered through a line of trees towards a local farm, bruised, bloodied and battered. From there they made the fatal mistake of hiding in a drainage pipe as missiles continued to rain down on them. Dhao, who had been struck by shrapnel, rapidly lost consciousness. It was deeply ironic that in the end Gaddafi found himself alone, defenceless and cowering like a rat in a sewer. He had used similar words to describe those dissenters he vowed to crush who had had the temerity to challenge his rule in Benghazi some six months earlier.

I was in Boston at Harvard Law School when news of his capture flashed across screens. It was astonishing to watch how quickly his authoritarian regime fell apart once the security forces were defeated in the capital. Watching images of Gaddafi's capture reminded me of Saddam Hussein, who was also found in a rat hole near his hometown of Tikrit, where he was hiding out after the capital, Baghdad, fell. Saddam would later be hanged after standing trial for his crimes, but his humiliation was nothing compared to the fate that was to now befall Gaddafi.

Within a few minutes of NATO hitting Gaddafi's convoy, rebel fighters were scouring the bombsite area in search of survivors. Ahmad al-Ghazal, a twenty-one-year-old kitchen shop manager and his rebel team drove right by the culvert without noticing Gaddafi. Suddenly, someone started firing. Ghazal and his men immediately leapt from their pickup and returned fire with their Kalashnikovs. The firefight was fierce but decisive.

Suddenly one of the enemy fighters dressed in civilian clothes screamed, 'My leg is broken, I can't help, Sayeedi,' a term which means 'respected one'. Within seconds Gaddafi appeared, half in and half out of the tunnel. Ghazal threw away his Kalashnikov and jumped on him. Gaddafi did not fire a shot, despite having a number of weapons on his person, including a fully loaded gold pistol inscribed with 'Muammar Gaddafi' on one side and an engraving of his green flag on the other. It featured an Arabic strap line declaring: 'The sun never sets on the revolution.' As Gaddafi was dragged bloodied but alive out of the drainage pipe the sun began to set on his revolution with deadly speed. He now found himself surrounded by jubilant rebels, who immediately began to taunt him and slap his face. Some were nearly hysterical, shouting 'Ya kalb!' ('You dog'), while others shouted, 'Keep him alive! Keep him alive,' as half a dozen rebels held his arms on either side of him.

Some proceeded to put their prize aloft a yellow Toyota pickup, but Gaddafi slid forward off the bonnet. Mobile phone footage showed him in a blood-soaked shirt leaning up against the vehicle, restrained by fighters, as other rebels continued to taunt him and fire their weapons in the air in celebration. I remember watching intently as Gaddafi touched his bloody brow and then looked at his hands, confused and disorientated, unable to compute the blood pouring from his head. A rebel fighter held up a black boot to the phone and shouted, 'Muammar's boot! His boot! Victory! This is victory!' In a later account, Gaddafi was reported to have asked one of the rebels what he had ever done to him. Another clip from a different phone showed Gaddafi lying on the ground with three men around him holding him down. Shouts of 'Keep him alive!' could be heard before a man gave out a high-pitched hysterical scream. Gaddafi then went out of view as gunshots rang out. Within seconds he appeared to be dead, as rebel fighters rolled his body over on the pavement. By this time, he was semi-naked with a pool of blood around his head and his arms raised above his head. The rebels then paraded his body through the town on a vehicle surrounded by crowds chanting: 'The blood of the martyrs will not go in vain!'

A young fighter from Benghazi, called Sanad Sadek al-Ouraybi, was later hailed as the rebel who had fired the fatal shot into Gaddafi's head, as he lay pinned to the ground. Gaddafi was whisked to hospital in an ambulance with bullet wounds in his head and chest. The rebels later claimed that Gaddafi died in the ambulance after being shot in crossfire, but ambulance driver Ali Jaghdoun disputed this, telling Reuters that Gaddafi was dead when he picked him up and drove him to Misrata. 'I didn't try to revive him because he was already dead,' he said.[2] Other mobile footage indicated that not only had Gaddafi been shot in cold blood, but that he had also been tortured with a knife up his rectum, by an adrenalin-fuelled rebel intent on revenge and revolutionary glory. Commander Shaibani, head of the Ghiran rebel fighters in Sirte, finally conceded to *The Sunday Times* that: 'Everyone was firing. Our young men were hysterical. I don't know who killed him, but I am not sorry.' Another rebel commander confessed anonymously to Reuters: 'We wanted to keep him alive, but the young guys – things went out of control.' Shaibani was later captured and tortured by loyalists in the town of Bani Walid.

The manner of Gaddafi's passing was both truly shocking and corrosive for the revolution. It was a deeply uncomfortable moment for all of us who had bought into the revolution's stated commitment to the rule of law. But perhaps we should have been less shocked than we were. As the BBC's Alan Little later commented, it was 'inevitable' that Gaddafi would be killed in such circumstances. What did we expect after forty-two years of dictatorship and a vicious and bloody civil war in which many rebels had lost numerous relatives and comrades? Gaddafi was captured not by the NTC but by rebel fighters from Misrata – a town that endured unimaginable suffering at the hands of his forces. His spontaneous execution was a supreme act of revenge, but it also brought instant closure for all those who had suffered at his hands. In reality, similar acts of brutality were being perpetrated every day during the war. It was somewhat unrealistic to expect many of these fighters to comply with the NTC's insistence that Gaddafi be detained and tried for crimes against humanity before the International Criminal Court, in some far-off land with all the attendant uncertainty that involved. Although some of the fighters present at his capture tried to do just that, we in the West should not be so surprised by such acts of revolutionary justice or injustice, just as, perhaps, we should not be so convinced about the merits of victor's justice delivered in an alien courtroom in The Hague a thousand miles away from the people of Libya.

It is instructive to note that not many international lawyers who toured the TV studios to talk about the rule of law in the aftermath of Gaddafi's execution spoke about the bodies of fifty-three loyalist fighters who were found in Sirte with their hands bound behind their backs and a single bullet wound to each of their heads. In many ways their cold-hearted execution was far more disturbing for its deliberate orchestration. Yet this story failed to engage the attention of the world's media as much as the tabloid images of Gaddafi's last moments. It was Gaddafi's Shakespearean demise that truly captured the imagination of the West. For the first time, Western news channels broadcasted largely unedited grainy mobile phone footage of a terrified Gaddafi being tortured and put to death, which had earlier sped, unedited, around the world on the Internet. Ordinarily, such graphic images of acts of barbarism would be censored by media outlets, since they would be judged to be beyond the pale. But this was somehow different. It was a dénouement that had to be witnessed because of its symbolic and narrative effect. Gaddafi's death, more than any other event in the Libyan revolution, brought a certain closure to the conflict. It also brought home to Western audiences the unvarnished truth about its brutal nature. Yet if we are honest we all knew that the filtered news we were being fed was hardly reflective of the conflict, and that such acts of inhumanity were far more commonplace in war than we in the West ever cared to admit.

While Westerners expressed their horror at Gaddafi's execution, others in Libya, whose relatives had suffered a similar fate at his instigation, took a completely different view. For many Libyan people, traumatised by the conflict, Gaddafi's killing not only constituted the ultimate act of closure, it also lessened the desire for vengeance within society against other less elevated members of the former regime. It was a truly cathartic moment for society as a whole, particularly for those traditional communities where tribal honour required blood to be paid with blood. Of course it would have been better for the rule of law if Gaddafi had been treated more humanely and detained to face justice in a court of law. But the spectre of a long, drawn-out trial, whether in Libya or The Hague, was equally problematic for a country that desperately wanted to move on, not to mention for those senior politicians in the West who had courted Gaddafi too assiduously. In the end Gaddafi's physical demise was convenient for all concerned. Con Coughlin of *The Telegraph* probably got it right when he commented: 'No one in London or Paris is making any serious demands that the perpetrators be called to account. All that really matters is that Gaddafi's regime is history and that the task of rebuilding Libya can now begin in earnest.'[3]

But questions did have to be asked about the apparent lack of any forward planning on the part of the NTC about how to deal with Gaddafi's capture by rebel forces not subject to its direct command. It didn't even appear to have a strategy about what to do with his body in the event of him being killed. In the event, the bodies of Gaddafi and his son Mutassim were placed in a meat locker in Misrata, ostensibly for the purpose of carrying out an autopsy after the NTC in Benghazi ordered an investigation into whether they had been deliberately killed in custody. What followed was an even more macabre spectacle as thousands of people queued for a half a mile to catch a once in a lifetime glimpse of the battered corpse of the fallen dictator and his son. One report talked of two little girls, dressed in their finest dresses, holding their father's hand, skipping as they left. Others talked of men smiling as they knelt down by Gaddafi's head in the bright light, making the V for victory sign, as if they had just bagged a big game animal in the wild. 'I drove from Tripoli to see him,' said Ahmad al-Nuda. 'I wanted to make sure it was Gaddafi. The man who has made our life hell for 42 years. It is him. Thank you God.' In many ways these sacrilegious images were even more damaging to the NTC than the initial assault on Gaddafi, which at least had the mitigating feature of being spontaneous. This humiliating ritual was both deliberate and contrived, and had the effect of inducing a measure of sympathy for a man and his family who had shown little or no mercy to his own victims.

No one was surprised that the militia in Misrata were disinclined to institute a protracted enquiry into Gaddafi's killing, which it continued to maintain was the result of crossfire. All the post mortem examination revealed was that he had died of gunshot injuries. After five days of increasing international disquiet about the public displaying of his body, Gaddafi was secretly driven to an anonymous grave in the Saharan desert, where he was interred by a small group of Misrata rebels. They were sworn to secrecy about the location, in an effort to stop his final resting place becoming a martyr's site for loyalist supporters. As the international community once again called for an investigation into the treatment of Gaddafi and his son, the irrepressible Abdul Hafiz Ghoga, now the vice-chairman of the NTC, gave a press conference in which he said that whoever killed the former dictator would be 'judged and given a fair trial'. In response to the UK Defence Secretary Philip Hammond's comment that Gaddafi's death had 'stained' the reputation of Libya's fledgling interim government, Ghoga hit back immediately: 'With regards to Gaddafi, we do not wait for anybody to tell us. We had already launched an investigation. We have issued a code of ethics in handling prisoners of war. I am sure that was an individual act not any revolutionaries or the national army.' Time would tell whether Ghoga's overblown intervention would come to anything.

An End to Hostilities

The death of Gaddafi heralded the end of hostilities on the battlefield. Three days after his capture and execution on 23 October 2011, the NTC declared the country liberated and formally launched the roadmap for New Libya. Many observers pointed to the NTC's continued inability to rein in the power of Islamist elements and the revolutionary militias such as those in Misrata who had displayed Gaddafi's body in breach of Islamic practice. By the end of hostilities Libya was still left with hundreds of armed groups in a multitude of different cities and towns with no overall chain of command. Some of these groups had fought for the revolution from the outset and gained control of their own territory. Others saw little fighting and only joined the battles in Tripoli, Bani Walid and Sirt later on in an opportunistic bid to take advantage of the security vacuum emerging in their localities. Many of these groups now controlled vital installations. Few pledged allegiances to either the NTC or its democratic reforms. The executive branches of the NTC's simply did not possess the capacity to implement its democratic vision. Nor did they enjoy a monopoly of coercive power to enforce their writ across the country.

As Dirk Vandewalle, field office director for the Carter Centre in Tripoli, later noted in his perceptive essay 'Libya's Uncertain Revolution', 'Tripoli's new rulers were faced with new revolutionary battalions whose power they could not control, cities and towns largely running their own affairs and a longstanding desire for greater autonomy in Cyrenaica that harkened back to Libya's original 1951 constitution.'[4] Most of these divisions and historical tensions were known when the ISRT wrote its report in June and dealt with the NTC throughout August and September. They were certainly apparent in late July in the run up to the NTC's Constitutional Declaration of 3 August 2011 when Abdul Jalil tried to placate Islamist complaints about Jibril's centralising roadmap of 5 May 2011. The ISRT's lack of cultural and political expertise about conditions on the ground had come home to roost. It would be interesting to see whether and how the UK government intended to support the NTC going forward given David Cameron's admonishment to the UN to 'act' rather than 'talk' in support of democratic reform.

Under the terms of the Constitutional Declaration adopted in August 2011, the NTC had agreed to hand over power to an elected assembly within eight months. The NTC was now required to pass electoral legislation and establish an electoral commission within ninety days of the declaration, leading to the election of a 200-member General National Congress within 240 days. A constitution would then be drawn up with a twenty-month countdown to a general election. The UN's Electoral Assistance Division (EAD) and UNSMIL advisors quickly set about assisting the NTC in this process through the creation of a High National Election Commission. However, the focus on electing an assembly rather than dealing with the practical problems that faced the country, such as the security and rule-of-law situation, was later conceded by one senior UN official to be a major mistake.

For his part Mustafa Abdul Jalil now declared three days of celebration in a speech to tens of thousands of Libyans, in which he called for national reconciliation and the upholding of the rule of 'Islamic law' which, he intimated, would be the 'basic source' of legislation in the country. He told the cheering crowd:

This revolution was looked after by God to achieve victory. I call on every-one for forgiveness, tolerance and reconciliation. We must get rid of hatred and envy from our souls. This is a necessary matter for the success of the revolution and the success of the future Libya. I call on all Libyans to resort to the rule of law and nothing but the law and not to take rights by the use of force [. . .] We are seeking organised national security and a national army that will protect the borders and the nation.

The Islamist tone to the speech was unmistakable. A week later, after Gaddafi's burial in the desert Mahmoud Jibril stood down as promised. He was replaced by Abdel Rahim al-Keib, a little-known professor of electrical engineering from Tripoli, who was elected in the first round of a public vote of the members of the NTC, after garnering twenty-six out of fifty-one votes. Council members were asked to choose from five candidates after the with-drawal of five others, including NTC vice-chairman Abdul Hafiz Ghoga. Mustafa Abdul Jalil hailed the vote as proof of the Libyans' ability 'to build their future'. Abdul Jalil also declared the intention to uphold all interna-tional agreements and treaties, a fact not lost on McCue. This was important to the restoration of business and financial confidence as well as to the rule of law more generally. I remember watching many of the Council members I met take their place on Libya's national podium, as the Council declared the country free.

The Capture of Saif al-Islam

With Gaddafi gone, attention now turned to Saif al-Islam. He was one of just a handful of national figures left from the Gaddafi era who remained at large, and he was capable of rallying loyalist forces. More to the point, he – more than anyone else alive – knew where the real bodies were buried, both literally and figuratively. It was as if New Libya could not sleep until he and his wagging finger were captured and put out of commission. It would take another six weeks before rebel forces finally located and captured Saif al-Is-lam as he tried to smuggle himself out of the country to Niger. He was detained at about 1.30 am on 18 November, thirty miles west of the oil town of Obari in southern Libya. Initial reports claimed a unit of fifteen fighters from the Zintan Brigade, travelling in three vehicles, intercepted two cars carrying him and three companions, following a tip-off from intelligence sources about an unknown VIP in the area. Later reports claimed Saif was captured and sold by local tribesmen. Whoever the occupants of the three vehicles were, they immediately fired in the air to halt the two cars.

Suddenly a man emerged in traditional desert robes with a Tuareg scarf pulled across his face. He introduced himself as 'Abdelsalam', meaning 'servant of peace'. The bearded man claimed to be a local camel keeper. Saif, it transpired, had grown a bushy beard in a bid to disguise his features after he fled Tripoli, but to little effect. His facial features were infamous across Libya and the retention of his trademark rimless glasses probably didn't help his cover. Saif was detained without a fight, after he made a last-ditch effort to evade capture by leaping from his Jeep to cover his face with sand. The so-called Lion of Tripoli, who had vouched to fight to the bitter end, failed to utilise the dollars he had with him to make a final bid to escape. Instead he shivered in absolute terror. As one of Saif's captors, Ahmad Ammar, a professor of marine biology, later noted: 'At the beginning he was very scared. He thought we would kill him.' But luckily for Saif there was to be no orgy of retribution as in the case of his father; this time the rebels had learnt their lesson.

Within hours Saif al-Islam was put on a Soviet-built cargo plane and flown from Obari to the rebel stronghold of Zintan. Huge crowds surrounded the plane in Zintan as the plane taxied in from the runway. Men fired in celebration at his detention, while others climbed onto the fuselage and tried to prise open a door to demand his death. 'I'm staying here,' said Saif recoiling in terror. 'They'll empty their guns into me the second I go out there.' His demeanour was in stark contrast to the arrogant, aggressive posture he had adopted in his widely reviled television appearances some six months earlier.

Saif's aides later confirmed to interrogators in Zintan that he had left Tripoli on 21 August to hide in the besieged city of Bani Walid, after making a defiant appearance at the Rixos Hotel in Tripoli, where he used to routinely brief international journalists during the war. He finally fled from Bani Walid on 19 October into the Southern desert the day before his father was captured and killed in Sirte. It was then that his convoy was caught in a NATO strike, allegedly injuring his fingers. Yet this account conflicted with more disturbing reports that medical officials in Zintan who examined the injuries concluded that his amputated fingers were not consistent with an air strike, hinting at darker acts of retribution on the part of the Zintan Brigade. This was no doubt in retaliation for Saif's arrogant finger-wagging forty-minute 'rivers of blood' speech delivered on Libyan television at the outset of the uprising. In fact, it would take a further three hours before the baying crowd around his plane finally dispersed to allow a clearly relieved Saif to be driven to a private house on the edge of town.

As news spread of his detention, the sound of celebratory gunfire and car horns rang out across the towns and cities of New Libya. Once again a multitude of people rushed onto the streets waving rebel banners and revolutionary flags. Stung by international criticism of Saif's father's earlier execution, the local Zintani commander Bashir Thaelba immediately declared that Saif would be held in custody in Zintan until the formation of a stable Libyan government that would decide when and where he would be tried. For its part, the International Criminal Court issued a statement noting that Libya was under a legal obligation to co-operate with its international arrest warrant issued against Saif al-Islam for crimes against humanity: 'If they decide they want to try the suspect in Libya instead of before the International Criminal Court, there's a necessary process.' Saif had already tried to contact the ICC while on the run in the Libyan desert, in a desperate attempt to secure safe passage out of the country. ICC Chief Prosecutor Luis Moreno Ocampo now announced that he would fly to Tripoli to hold talks with the NTC about where Saif al-Islam should be tried. Although he recognised that national governments had first right to try their citizens for war crimes, he needed to make sure Saif al-Islam would be given a fair hearing.

In reality, his much-trailed trip to Tripoli was of little import, as the die had already been cast. Despite Ocampo's somewhat flamboyant efforts to steal the Libyans' thunder, this was always likely to be a Libyan-directed affair. Within a day of his capture, Libyan interim Minister of Justice, Muhammad al-Alagi, confirmed that Saif al-Islam would be put on trial in Libya for criminal offences that carried the death penalty. 'He has instigated others to kill, misused public funds, threatened and instigated and even taken part in recruiting and bringing in mercenaries.' It was unclear what fair trial assurances Ocampo had secured during his two-day talks with the NTC. All al-Alagi told Al Jazeera was that 'we Libyans do not oppose the presence of international monitors'.

For his part, David Cameron issued a statement that the Libyan authorities had given an assurance that the trial would be conducted in accordance with international standards of justice. Information minister, Mahmoud Shamman, seemed to encapsulate the mood when he observed that this was 'the final chapter in the Libyan drama': the curtain, it seemed, would come down in their own land. Thus was the stage set for the biggest trial in Libya's history, a trial not simply judging Saif's alleged involvement in crimes against humanity, but also New Libya's stated commitment to the rule of law. It was within this febrile context that NATO Secretary-General, Anders Rasmussen, finally announced that all operations would cease as of 31 October 2011. Saif's capture effectively brought combat operations to an end and ushered in the start of the post-conflict reconstruction phase, to borrow from the lexicon of the stabilisation unit of Her Majesty's Government.

Continuing Human Rights Abuses

The joyous scenes that greeted Saif's capture proved to be short-lived. While they certainly brought a close to the civil war, much uncertainty and tension remained over what the future held for the country, now that the Gaddafis were vanquished. Although many Libyans respected how Mustafa Abdul Jalil tried to maintain unity within the NTC during the uprising, it became clear just how riven with rivalry it had become in the post-conflict period, as officials jockeyed for power. Mahmoud Jibril's announcement that he would resign as interim Prime Minister once Libya was liberated followed months of tension with Mustafa Abdul Jalil, and there was public criticism of Jibril for spending large parts of the summer out of the country. 'I put forward my resignation because I have no influence. We make decisions that are then put in the trash bin,' he declared ominously. The creation of a new transitional government headed by Abdel Rahim al-Keib on 22 November 2011 did little to relieve the pressure. While al-Keib confirmed that elections would be held in the summer of 2012, he further declared that any newly elected body would not elect a government but bring together a national convention to draft a new constitution, define the political framework and appoint the next transitional government. Yet throughout this period, his administration remained largely incapable of delivering the most basic services. Into this vacuum stepped the militias and radical religious groups. They were already settling scores and meting out their own rough justice on the streets of Libya in the absence of a functioning justice and security system.

Few were surprised when, one week after Saif al-Islam was captured, the UN Secretary General Ban Ki-moon released a report to the Security Council confirming that thousands of people, including women and children, were being illegally detained by militias in private jails beyond the control of the NTC, and were being systematically abused. The report alleged that, while thousands of Gaddafi's political prisoners had been released, over 7,000 new enemies of the state had also been detained. Many were black Africans without papers, such as those that Jason McCue and I had encountered when crossing into Libya at the Egyptian border in April 2011. These Africans were accused of helping the former regime and singled out for particular racist mistreatment.

Elsewhere, Patrick Cockburn of *The Independent* reported that people in Gaddafi's hometown of Sirte were facing a 'continuing reign of terror'.[5] For his part Ban Ki-moon expressed the hope that the NTC would make good its intention to follow a democratic path and introduce a functioning legal system sooner rather than later. Quite how the Secretary General thought this might be achieved, in the absence of a worked-out justice plan or DDR agreement to politically integrate militia leaders into a country now awash with weapons, was left unexplained. By the time he expressed this hope the UN was already two months into a three-month support mission to assist Libya's political transition, with little noticeable effect. This was because most of UNSMIL's resources were directed towards planning for the elections and while the UN quickly deployed police advisors in its initial team in September 2011 they encountered much confusion on the Libyan side caused by poor control and coordination within the Interior Ministry. Ian Martin was not wrong when he observed that the international community needed to offer a strategic and coordinated approach, and not merely isolated training packages.[6]

With little structured international support in place and the Libyan armed forces and police severely depleted, Al-Keib was forced yet again to turn to the very elements that were creating the chaos after being surrounded by fighters at his office intent on getting a share of the $100 billion that had just been released under UN Security Council Resolution 2016 on 5 December. On 18 December he personally vouched that anyone who registered with the Supreme Security Council (SCC) would be paid, thus bringing yet more thousands onto the government payroll in a vain attempt to assert control over armed groups operating in Tripoli. In practice the government and the central headquarters of the SSC exercised very limited authority over local SSC branches. In the event over 200,000 signed up to a Warriors Affairs Commission, particularly after the new government announced that 75,000 revolutionaries would also be integrated by the Ministries of Interior, Defence and Labour into the police, armed forces and workforce. The consequences of the lack of forward planning concerning security and the rule of law was now there for all to see. It led directly to the haphazard creation of an entrenched parallel parasitic security force and economy. By this time Cameron appeared to have washed his hands of the matter and moved on to other issues elsewhere.

Further allegations of human rights abuses soon emerged concerning rebel 'cleansing' of loyalist areas in Tawergha and Sirte. Matters became so fraught that by 23 January 2012 Mustafa Abdul Jalil was obliged to warn the public of the prospects of years of 'internecine strife'. Two weeks later, an Amnesty International report confirmed the militias remained 'out of control'[7] and were committing gross human rights abuses, including torture, rape and murder. Much of the bloodletting took place in the southern desert town of Ghademes where Tuareg tribesmen were forced out because of their support for the former regime. Many crossed the border into Mali to join the National Movement for the Liberation of Azawad, which went to war against the Malian government in January 2012. The inability of the NTC to make its writ run across Libya was having serious repercussions both in and outside the country, as a welter of criminal and tribal elements adjusted their calculations to take advantage of the situation. This was nowhere better illustrated than in the south of the country, where thousands of weapons were regularly smuggled out of Libya into the hands of Al-Qaeda in Islamic Maghreb (AQIM) by semi-nomadic Tuareg tribes operating across the porous borders of the Sahara desert that straddled Mali, Algeria, Niger and Chad.

As I read these human rights reports, echoes of the BHRC's earlier Memorandum of Understanding rippled through my mind. The most pressing issue facing the NTC in the immediate post-conflict period, then, was not so much political reform as the restoration of some semblance of the rule of law. Human Rights Watch's 2012 World Report rightly observed that the NTC and Western donors needed to make it an 'urgent priority to build a functioning justice system [. . .] that protects human rights'.[8] As Ian Martin later observed:

> the lack of action by the government was highly disappointing. It was international and local pressure, as members of local councils became concerned for their communities' reputation, and some non-governmental organisations began monitoring detention and speaking out, which led to some mitigation of treatment and a handful of releases. All these challenges required a functioning judicial system, not just as a matter of principle, but as a very practical necessity for resolving conflicts, which persisted or flared up in different parts of the country, creating conditions for new human rights violations.[9]

These challenges became even more acute after Abdullah al-Senussi, the former head of Gaddafi's internal security, was stopped on a flight from Casablanca to Nouakchott by Mauritanian officials in mid-March 2012, and then extradited back to Libya on charges carrying the death penalty.

It was alleged that nearly $200 million was paid over to secure his capture. His subsequent detention in Libya set up a further jurisdictional tension and conflict between the domestic authorities and the ICC. Matters were not best assisted when a few months later the Zintan militia decided to detain three ICC officials and a defence lawyer acting for Saif al-Islam, allegedly for unlawfully colluding to pass on secret information from 'dangerous allies' of Saif. The uprising that had put the rule of law at the centre of its focus was in serious danger of turning in on itself. It was particularly interesting to note that the new Libyan government felt able to instruct a scion of the UK liberal legal establishment to represent it at the ICC to assist in its submission that New Libya was now a state subject to the rule of law, one that had capacity to both try and sentence individuals in accordance with international norms and standards of criminal justice.

16.   Ambassador Stevens

Despite the deteriorating security and rule of law situation, steps were taken during this period towards the establishment of a democratic electoral system. Early 2012 witnessed the formation of new political parties consistent with a move towards multi-party democracy as set out in the NTC's draft constitution. On 24 December 2011, the Libyan chapter of the Muslim Brotherhood created the Justice and Development Party. This was followed by over forty political organisations, NGOs and independents electing Mahmoud Jibril to lead their national alliance in the July elections on 13 March 2012. Ali Tarhouni, the former Finance Minister, quickly followed with the establishment of his own political entity. Yet little consensus existed about the character of any future political system. Huge tensions remained between the militias and the NTC, the Islamic and secular parties, and Tripoli and eastern Libya where certain elements were clamouring for a federal structure.

In an attempt to head off growing calls for secession, al-Keib declared the NTC would henceforth pursue a policy of decentralisation. The move defused tensions and just about kept elections on track. On 17 May 2012 Libya held elections for local governing councils in Benghazi, Misrata and Zintan. Quite remarkably, the one in Benghazi resulted in the election of Najat al-Kikhia, a female university professor, as mayor. More significantly, electoral monitors declared the elections free and fair, thereby providing Libyans with a rare glimpse of a better future. This mood carried forward into the national elections of 7 July 2012, despite a delay in holding them. In the event, 62 per cent of voters elected more than 3,000 candidates in a peaceful and fair contest in which over 80 per cent of those eligible to vote were registered in the months preceding the election. For many Libyans, the summer elections of 2012 were both an emotional and a deeply cathartic moment, that demonstrated Libyans could work together to create a better future. To the surprise of an increasingly sceptical outside world, Mahmoud Jibril's secular centrist party took thirty-nine seats against the Muslim

Brotherhood's seventeen. An alliance of non-Islamist candidates had won 80 per cent of the vote in Tripoli and 60 per cent of the vote in Benghazi. They even secured a majority in Derna, the city most associated with Islamic fundamentalism. Despite all Libya's other problems, a new political dawn seemed to be on the horizon. Ian Martin was right to claim that 'the UN's greatest contribution in the first year was to the credibility of the election, which was not only a matter of confidence in the technical assistance of the UN's electoral support team, but also of UNSMIL's constant interaction with key Libyan political actors and civil society'.[1]

Another encouraging development that accompanied the creation of the multi-party system was the growth of freedom of speech and civil society. The years 2011–12 saw the publication of dozens of new, private magazines such as *Miyadeen*, *al-Libi* and *Arus al-Bahr* as well as new radio stations. The period also witnessed the emergence of hundreds of little NGOs and community organisations. Although these organisations were weak and under-funded, their existence reinforced New Libya's commitment to respect freedom of expression and increase the participation of women in the nation's social and political affairs. It was satisfying to see CHD's capacity-building programmes beginning to transfer to Libyan society the tools by which it could make its voice heard. Furthermore, while parts of Tripoli remained in the grip of militias it was claimed that over 50,000 ex-militiamen had been integrated into the fledgling Libyan army, with salaries being paid. Further acute economic problems continued as a result of a lack of liquidity, but Libyan banks were beginning to reopen with the help of foreign banks which were buying back into the financial system. The problem was not so much Libya's macro-economic future, but the continuing institutional fragility of the NTC and the total lack of a governmental infrastructure. Although the Libyan oil industry had managed to emerge from the conflict largely undamaged, little else did. What Libya needed above all else was a functioning bureaucracy that could help the NTC set priorities, structure and process investment properly, and then allocate and implement budgets. Yet such institutions took years to build, notwithstanding the provision of some technical assistance from neighbouring Arab states and Western allies.

The Rise of the Islamists

Other factors militated against this process, however, most notably the existence of a number of shadowy domestic and international spoilers, all of whom had an interest in diminishing the NTC's power and influence within New Libya. These spoilers, together with their local actors, made the NTC's job of reconstruction even harder, despite backing the NTC during the early days of the revolution. Qatar and Saudi Arabia were now known to be supporting different Islamist groups by providing them with arms and finance. So, too, was Turkey. Few in the NTC trusted the Russians, the Chinese or the Algerians not to meddle in the affairs of New Libya. It was an open secret that Algeria continued to provide succour and sanctuary to a number of Gaddafi loyalists. And then there were the criminal elements let loose during the revolution, including Mafioso elements in places like Tobruk and Benghazi, which, along with corrupt units in the militias and police force, were quick to take advantage of the chaos. But perhaps the greatest threat to the authority of the NTC came from the porous borders of the south where emboldened Islamic fundamentalists connected to Al-Qaeda were seeking to overthrow the government in Mali.

There were signs that radical Islamists were intent on upping the political ante, particularly in places like Derna and Benghazi. Early 2012 witnessed a series of violent attacks on pro-Western targets that would culminate in the audacious assault on the US Consulate in Benghazi on 11 September 2012. On 4 March 2012 Mohamed al-Hassi, the head of security in Derna, was gunned down on a street in broad daylight. This was followed by the assassination of Abdel Hakin al-Hasadi, a former LIFG cadre member, who denounced Al-Qaeda after joining the uprising. On 10 April 2012 a bomb was hurled in front of a UN convoy containing the UN Special Representative, Ian Martin. On 6 June 2012 an improvised device was placed outside the US Consulate in retaliation for the assassination of Libyan-born Al-Qaeda leader Abu Layth al-Libi, a fact that would assume much greater importance after Ambassador Stevens's assassination.

Four days later, on 10 June, the UK Ambassador's convoy suffered an attack by a rocket-propelled grenade. The Libyan authorities later identified the culprits as members of the Jamarat Islamiya al-Moutashedida. On 18 June Salafists attacked the Tunisian Consulate in Benghazi for an artist's disrespectful depiction of the Prophet. As a result, the British decided to leave the city, and were followed by the International Committee of the Red Cross, who suspended operations on 5 August after a series of strikes on its offices in Benghazi and Misrata. Thus, despite the apparent success of secularist elements in the national elections of July 2012, sceptics were not muckraking when they pointed to the increasing threat of Al-Qaeda within the region in general and towards US interests in Libya in particular.

This was the political landscape in the summer of 2012 with which Western diplomats like the US Ambassador, Chris Stevens, had to deal. Yet for Stevens all of this came with the territory. It came as little surprise when President Obama chose to appoint him as America's first Ambassador to the country following Gaddafi's fall from power. Nor was there much surprise when Stevens resolved to continue to nurture the personal relationships he had forged during the revolution in Benghazi. He chose to stay in Benghazi, rather than operating from the isolated and protected environs of the US Embassy in Tripoli where he would have had to rely upon second-hand reports collated by Internet-based analysts. Unlike a lot of other more cautious traditional diplomats Stevens preferred to get his information first-hand from the street. He believed in getting his hands dirty by drinking coffee with the men who inhabited the ministries, cafés and checkpoints, and actually controlled New Libya in all its guises. He therefore eschewed the practice of more traditional diplomats who chose to deconstruct political events within smaller, diplomatic and better-protected circles. Stevens's passion for the streets would ultimately lead to his demise, but whether it would lead to the demise of this form of diplomacy was something else.

In a *Vanity Fair* exposé of the circumstances surrounding Stevens's assassination on 11 September 2012, Fred Burton and Samuel M. Katz described the atmosphere in Benghazi just before his death in the following terms:

> In the northeastern city of Benghazi, Libya's second-largest city, men in blazers and dark glasses wandered about the narrow streets of the Medina, the old quarter, with briefcases full of cash and Browning Hi-Power 9-mm. semi-automatics – the classic killing tool of the European spy. Rent-a-guns, militiamen with AK-47s and no qualms about killing, stood outside the cafés and restaurants where men with cash and those with missiles exchanged business terms. It was a le Carré urban landscape where loyalties changed sides with every sunset; there were murders, betrayals, and triple-crossing profits to be made in the post-revolution. The police were only as honest as their next bribe. Most governments were eager to abandon the danger and intrigue of Benghazi. By September 2012 much of the international community had pulled chocks and left. Following the kidnapping in Benghazi of seven members of its Red Crescent relief agency, even Iran, one of the leading state sponsors of global terror, had escaped the city.[2]

Theirs was a chilling description of a city in chaos and conflict, in which men in Saudi robes and with Yemeni-looking features carried RPGs and PKM machine guns, and looked for yet more weapons to buy to send to their brothers fighting in Syria. Ambassador Stevens was all too aware of the deteriorating security situation. On 15 August, the temporary staff at the US Special Mission in Benghazi held an emergency meeting. They expressed concern that the Diplomatic Security agents would be unable to defend the Mission if it came under sustained attack, given the limited manpower and weapons at their disposal. Stevens agreed that security was at best tenuous. Ordinarily the safety of the Mission would have been the responsibility of Libyan intelligence and police forces, but that was not possible in New Libya. The State Department therefore had little choice but to rely for protection on the 17 February Militia, who were financed by the Gulf States. They were augmented by local security guards contracted to a Wales-based security firm named Blue Mountain, which had won a $387,000 contract to provide unarmed guards at the Special Mission Compound. These guards were paid roughly $4.15 an hour for their services. Despite this precarious security situation, Stevens continued to believe that he should remain in the city. It was after all where tens of thousands of good men and women turned out for the revolution in support of democracy and a return to the rule of law. They went on living in Benghazi and depended more than ever on the efforts of the US and UK to help the NTC take on those who had come to hijack the revolution. Thus, despite the bleak security situation described by Burton and Katz, Stevens continued to work from the US Special Mission in Benghazi that he used during the revolution.

The Execution of Chris Stevens

On 11 September 2012 Ambassador Stevens found himself at the US Mission along with five Diplomatic Security agents who were detailed to protect him. Burton and Katz would later describe them as inexperienced, yet willing to do what they were told and to work the worst shifts: 'The men in Benghazi were a mixed bag of over-achievers: former street cops, US Marines, a US Army Iraq-war veteran, and academics. All had under ten years on the job; some had less than five years.' After an evening meeting with the Turkish Ambassador at the compound, Chris Stevens decided to turn in for the night. It was about 9.30 pm. A few minutes later the attack began. The unarmed guards at the perimeter fled, as did elements of the 17 February Militia. The security agents were left to fend for themselves against dozens of armed jihadists. Within minutes the jihadists had surrounded the villa and begun to shoot it up. Inside Stevens and two agents desperately sought sanctuary in the strong room. The jihadists then set fire to the villa, after failing to find their prey. As smoke engulfed the building the agents decided to make a run for it. Crawling on their bellies the three men left the strong room to try to exit through a window. But when the agents got to the window the Ambassador was not behind them. Despite repeated attempts to find Stevens the agents were forced to retreat. A fire-fight ensued until finally help arrived from the local CIA facility who managed to extract those who were still alive.

An hour or so later the CIA facility also came under fire. In total three US officials died in the attacks apart from Chris Stevens. In the ensuing chaos it was difficult for those in the State Department in Foggy Bottom in Washington to know whether this was a spontaneous or carefully orchestrated attack. Not only was information sparse about the scale of the attack, other factors pointed to a spontaneous incident. The attack on 11 September had been preceded by large protests in Egypt in front of the US Embassy in Garden City, Cairo. This occurred after Arab television networks picked up a story on 8 September about a fourteen-minute video posted on YouTube on 1 July 2012 entitled 'Innocence of Muslims', by an Egyptian-born Coptic American. The BBC described the film as depicting Islam as a 'religion of violence and hate and its Prophet Mohammed as a foolish and power-hungry man'. The following day, US embassies across the MENA region became the subject of frenzied protest. Many therefore believed the attack on the US compound in Benghazi to be part of a series of violent protests spiralling out across the region. News of the attack spread like wildfire in Benghazi, producing rejoicing and shame in equal measures.

Once the attack had subsided and the jihadists had moved on to the nearby CIA facility, an assortment of onlookers and looters descended on the US Benghazi Mission. Within seconds eerie images of the compound were posted on the Internet, including footage of the lifeless body of the US Ambassador. Stevens's body was subsequently rescued by some men dressed in Western clothes, who thereafter commandeered a car to take it to a nearby hospital. Ironically Chris Stevens had intended to visit this hospital the very next day. He had been due to meet Dr Thomas F. Burke, the chief of Massachusetts General Division of Global Health and Human Rights, who along with Boston's Massachusetts General Hospital, had partnered up with the Benghazi Medical Centre (BMC) in an act of international solidarity. Stevens wanted to pay homage to that solidarity and spoke to Dr Burke at 8.30 pm on 11 September, an hour or so before the fatal attack on the compound. At 9.40 pm Dr Burke was on the phone to a security agent at the compound when he heard the words, 'We've got a fucking problem.' According to Burton and Katz's account, at 2.15 am a phalanx of young men burst through the emergency room of the BMC carrying Stevens's body. Dr Abu Zeid tried desperately for ninety minutes to resuscitate him, but to no avail. In the early hours of 12 September Chris Stevens was finally pronounced dead, due to smoke inhalation. He was fifty-two years old. It was said that some of the doctors cried over his crumpled body. They knew all too well that another morsel of hope for a state based on the rule of law had disappeared overnight. Across town, in the villa of the US Mission in Benghazi, someone had scrawled along the bathroom wall: 'I am Chris from the dead.' If ever there was a tale of two cities that night, it was here in Benghazi.

The bodies of Ambassador Stevens and the three other US officials were flown back to a hangar in Washington a few days later, where President Obama addressed grieving relatives and colleagues of Chris Stevens: 'Chris Stevens was everything America could want in an ambassador, as the whole country has come to see – how he first went to the region as a young man in the Peace Corps, how during the revolution, he arrived in Libya on that cargo ship, how he believed in Libya and its people and how they loved him back. And there, in Benghazi he laid down his life for his friends – Libyan and American – and for us all. Today Chris is home.' Obama then gave this message to 'people in every corner of the world', that 'America is a friend, and that we care not just about our own country, not just about our own interests, but about theirs, that even as voices of suspicion and mistrust seek to divide countries and cultures from one another, the United States of America will never retreat from the world. We will never stop working for the dignity and freedom that every person deserves, whatever their creed, whatever their faith.' For her part, Secretary of State Clinton observed, 'There will be more difficult days ahead but it is important that we don't lose sight of the fundamental fact that America must keep leading the world.'

These words were important. On 21 September 2012 tens of thousands of Benghazians took to the streets to demand more control of the militias. The new government led by President Mohammed al-Magariaf responded by trying to appoint its own officers to work alongside the three biggest brigades in the country's eastern region, in an effort to rein them in and restore some semblance of the rule of law. Since Gaddafi's death, these brigades had acted as the government's main military and police force in the region. But few were convinced that their ultimate loyalty lay with the institutions of state. Notwithstanding the stirring words of the US President and Hillary Clinton, Stevens's tragic death invoked a renewed sense of crisis about the direction that New Libya, and the Arab Spring more generally, were taking. As Burton and Katz later observed: 'Ambassador Stevens, because he looked at the Arab Spring through that eternally American ailment of passionate optimism, had been Libya's most ambitious advocate in Washington DC and elsewhere in the world. His murder was a fatal sign, perhaps, that Libya was destined to suffer through many more years of hell.'[3] It became obvious that the assassination of Stevens would have immediate ramifications for the 2012 US election between President Obama and Mitt Romney, and for American policy towards the MENA region more generally.

The Republican candidate used Stevens's death to call into question the administration's entire policy towards New Libya and the MENA region. The President and the State Department, Romney said, had put American interests and officials in harm's way, by failing to back its traditional allies in favour of heeding spurious promises of democratic reform by largely unknown rebel groups, many of who were affiliated to Al-Qaeda. Obama rejected the criticism, accusing Romney and the Republicans of the worst sort of opportunism. Despite the election mudslinging, worrying questions remained as to what exactly had happened in Benghazi on 11 September 2012, and what it signified for US policy towards the region.

The Republicans now alleged that the Obama administration had deliberately mischaracterised the assault on the US Mission as a spontaneous event. They pointed to statements made by the US Ambassador to the UN, Susan Rice, to the press, which claimed that the attack formed part of a set of wider demonstrations that had occurred in Cairo that same afternoon, in protest against Western depictions of the Prophet Mohammed. This, they claimed, was a smokescreen used by the State Department to hide wider security failings on the part of Hillary Clinton, including not properly securing the protection of diplomatic officials or heeding warnings relating to the growing threat of Islamic fundamentalism in New Libya. Hillary Clinton rejected any such conspiracy, reaffirming both the integrity of her officials and US policy towards the region.

Clinton was followed by President Obama, who on 25 September delivered an impassioned address to the United Nations General Assembly in defence of his policy. He started this address with a tribute to Chris Stevens: 'I would like to begin today by telling you about an American named Chris Stevens.' Obama talked of Stevens's love of the region and its people, and of how he used to walk the streets of the cities where he worked 'tasting the local food, meeting as many people as he could, speaking Arabic and listening with a broad smile'. Obama then went on to reassert America's enduring belief in the universal value of freedom of speech, challenging MENA democracies to ensure that right even in the face of violence:

> We do so because in a diverse society, efforts to restrict speech can become a tool to silence critics, or oppress minorities. We do so because given the power of faith in our lives, and the passion that religious differences can inflame, the strongest weapon against hateful speech is not repression, it is more speech – the voices of tolerance that rally against bigotry and blasphemy, and lift up the values of understanding and mutual respect.

He added that Americans 'have fought and died around the globe to protect the right of all people to express their view'. Obama returned to the Envoy in his closing remarks: 'I promise you this: long after these killers are brought to justice, Chris Stevens's legacy will live on in the lives he touched.'

Stevens's Legacy

President Obama won the presidential election of 2012, but the debate about whether it was wise for the US and the UK to intervene in the MENA region to back democratic reform continued, despite Obama's stirring vow to protect Stevens's legacy. Obama's farewell ode to Chris Stevens certainly resonated with me. His life had touched mine, but then I shared his view of the world, and of the need for Western diplomacy to engage with the MENA region long-term, and in a democratic and culturally sensitive fashion. Like Stevens, I too was moved by how ordinary people in Benghazi rose up to take on an all-powerful tyrant against the odds. The sheer romance of the early part of the Libyan uprising infected my soul. I remained convinced NATO's initial intervention in Libya was both justified and instrumental in averting a humanitarian catastrophe. Nor was I too alarmed when that intervention mutated into a campaign to remove Gaddafi from power in order to effect democratic change. This was necessary to ensure R2P succeeded in Libya on a long-term basis, although I decried the failure to properly explore whether a negotiated exit for Gaddafi could have been effected in May of 2011. I suspected the UK government's refusal to countenance such an outcome was not simply based upon its disinclination to send mixed messages to the regime at time of military conflict, but was also because of the political dangers of having Gaddafi loose and free to talk in Caracas or Havana. Gaddafi knew where the bodies were buried, just as Moussa Koussa and Saif al-Islam did. But unlike Moussa Koussa, Gaddafi would have had little reason not to spill the beans.

The UK's murky political, security and economic relationship with the Gaddafi regime cast a long shadow over its conduct in Libya, whatever the new Conservative and Liberal Democrat coalition government maintained. Its emerging role in rendition and possible complicity in torture; its failure to detain or investigate Moussa Koussa for murder and crimes against humanity; and its disinclination to heed the invitation of Mustafa Abdul Jalil to investigate Lockerbie all hinted at darker pre-occupations. Despite David Cameron's warm words of support for the BHRC, the FCO were reluctant to let Jason McCue and me become too closely involved with the NTC on legacy issues, particularly in respect of Lockerbie, IRA Semtex or the murder of WPC Fletcher. There is some evidence relating to this. After the fall of Gaddafi, *The Telegraph* managed to get hold of a confidential e-mail sent by Sidney Blumenthal, a former aide to US President Bill Clinton, to Hillary Clinton. It hinted that the British government may well have been playing both sides of the conflict and seeking to preserve its relationship with key members of the Gaddafi regime.

It referred to information gleaned on 8 April 2011, just a couple of days after McCue and I got back from Benghazi, and read as follows:

On the morning of April 8 [2011], an individual with direct access to the Leadership of the Libyan National Council [NTC] stated in strictest confidence that members of the Military Committee of the LNC are concerned that, despite the involvement of NATO against the forces of Muammar Qaddafi, the government of Great Britain is using its intelligence services in an effort to dictate the actions of both the LNC and the Qaddafi regime. These individuals add that they have been informed by contacts in France and Italy that, while they have been engaged in discussions with the LNC regarding possible assistance, British diplomats and intelligence officers have maintained contact with members of the Qaddafi government, In [sic] an effort to protect the British position in the event the rebellion settles into a stalemate. These LNC officials believe that the defection of Libyan Minister of Foreign Affairs, Moussa Koussa, to the United Kingdom was part of this effort. By the same token they say that British Intelligence officers are in discussion with associates of Saif al-Islam Qaddafi, regarding future relation between the two countries if he takes power from his father and implements reforms.[4]

To my mind, none of this should have prevented the UK government from developing its own response to the wider issues identified by the BHRC, whatever its pre-occupation about the past might have been. The greatest failure of the UK government's intervention in Libya was not its decision to pursue regime change, but its inability to ensure a viable civilian transition before the conflict ended. Instead of learning the lessons of Afghanistan and Iraq, it blithely continued to place faith in government-led stabilisation units, which had manifestly failed to stabilise either country, let alone inculcate a respect for the rule of law. The people who paid the price of this blunder were not only those Libyan citizens who supported the establishment of a secular state, but innocent civilians in neighbouring countries whose societies were awash with weapons, as lawlessness spread across the region.

The refusal of the UK government to allocate any real funding to this issue or promote an inter-militia dialogue was frankly inexcusable, particularly given the NTC's direct call for assistance, as articulated in the BHRC's Memorandum of Understanding. Anyone involved in Libya could not have missed seeing the emerging power of the militias in Benghazi, Zintan and Misrata vis-à-vis the NTC, as Chris McGreal's articles in the *Guardian* newspaper made abundantly clear. The capacity of organisations like CHD to engage with these problems should have been properly explored. While it was true that the UK government was unused to private organisations involving themselves in such issues before a military conflict was over, this should not have stopped the FCO from recognising the emergence of a new reality. The BHRC had demonstrated that it could be trusted to work with the FCO in difficult places such as Afghanistan and Palestine. Moreover, there was a world of difference between non-state actors giving neutral advice to the NTC and state diplomats, whose allegiances restricted their ability to build requisite trust, credibility and impartiality between the key players.

The problem I suspect lay not so much in the past record of these non-state organisations but within Whitehall, where few officials were willing to recommend innovative approaches if this might mean reducing HMG's direct influence over the NTC while a NATO campaign was going on. We detected a general reluctance to fully recognise the growing capacity of the non-state sector to help resolve these types of issues. As noted earlier, the FCO and DFID preferred to work either with major humanitarian agencies that avoided sensitive political issues, or bespoke private communication and strategy companies that enjoyed close relations with its security services. There was then a natural inclination within government to monopolise relations with rebel groups such as the NTC, and where possible to restrict the access, influence and power of private entities to affect matters during military operations. In hindsight the FCO's non-engagement with the BHRC regarding its application for funding probably reflected this anxiety. On the one hand it shared the BHRC's commitment to the rule of law. On the other, it might have been sceptical of its ability to toe the line when it came to difficult legacy issues. Thus, despite David Cameron's written instructions to co-operate with the Bar Council, the FCO funding application got passed on and somehow lost in the system.

All this made the publication of the international stabilisation plan for Libya in June 2011 more, not less, important. Yet a cursory glance at that plan told you all you needed to know about the ability of governments to effect societal change by themselves. Once again the UK foreign policy establishment elected to stay within its own comfort zone when it came to the business of planning for transition. Stabilisation experts, with little experience of Libya, simply lifted approaches and terminology that had been used elsewhere and only paid lip service to the role of civil society. Matters were also not best helped by the FCO's continual rotation of personnel. It would often take months for new officials to get on top of events before they felt any confidence about recommending innovative steps. In the space of just a couple of months following the imposition of the no-fly zone the entire Libya team was replaced. The new team that came on board seemingly adopted the somewhat naïve position of Ghoga, namely that everything would come good in Libya because of the NTC's stated commitment to the rule of law and the country's undoubted financial resources. Such a stance chimed with the immediate objective of ensuring military victory first and officials safeguarding their career trajectory. Thus Rory Stewart's pertinent observations about the need for a team of country experts committed to that country proved correct. All of this made for a deeply flawed policy-making process that affected the lives of millions of people.

The UK Foreign Affairs Select Committee

It was then with more than a little interest that I noted the opening of the Foreign Affairs Select Committee inquiry into the UK's involvement in the Libyan intervention, following the general election in 2015. Quite rightly, the new parliament wanted to learn lessons and asked the FCO and other ministries for an account of efforts to help stabilise the country. The FCO told the Committee that 'the guiding principles of the UK's response planning on stabilisation were that it should be Libyan-owned and co-ordinated by the UN', but was utterly silent about stabilisation policy before the conflict ended.[5] The FCO felt able to capture the government's contribution towards the transition effort in just a few short paragraphs. The summary fashion of its response is worth repeating in its entirety:

> Following the London Conference on Libya on 29 March 2011, the UK was a driving force behind the establishment of the Libya Contact Group. The Group first met in Doha on the 13 April 2011. It served as a focal point of contact with the Libyan people, coordinated international policy on Libya and was a forum for discussion of humanitarian and post-conflict support. The Group's work was further reinforced by mobilising the FCO's global network to influence partners and ensure effective implementation of UNSCR 1973.

> The Second Contact Group on Libya in Rome on 5 May 2011 established an International Stabilisation Response Team (ISRT) to build a shared international understanding of Libya's interim stabilisation needs. The ISRT was led by the UK and visited Libya from 20 May to 8 June 2011. The ISRT's report, produced at the end of June 2011, identified the immediate challenges to stabilisation in NTC-controlled areas; assessed the likely short- to medium-term challenges; and fed into an NTC Stabilisation Plan.

> HMG's cross-Whitehall Stabilisation Unit (SU) was closely involved in policy development throughout the planning and implementation of the

intervention and post-conflict response to Libya. In particular, the SU led on the UK contribution to the ISRT. The SU contribution is detailed further in **Annex C.**

Annex C: Initial Phase and the SRT
The SU was closely involved in policy development and initial analysis from the very beginning of the Libya crisis, bringing vital know how to early scenario planning discussions and engaging UK based Libya experts. Additional non-government staff were brought in to support the core SU Libya team, and several SU staff members were deployed to support the FCO-led missions in Malta, Cairo and then finally in Benghazi.

The SU's most substantive contribution during this initial phase was through its generation and deployment of the first Stabilisation Response Team (SRT) in May 2011, following NSC(L) agreement. The SRT deployed within 14 days, and included UK and international staff. The SRT provided an initial analysis of the situation in NTC controlled areas, outlining the immediate challenges and medium term political, security and economic challenges the new Libyan authorities faced. The SRT put forward a number of broad areas for priority action, including support to civil society, the security forces and the need for the NTC to ensure sustained, legitimate leadership. A subsequent SU 'lessons' analysis of the SRT deployment identified various issues, including whether adequately clear objectives for the SRT were agreed and whether clear command and control arrangements were in place. The review also highlighted the sensitivities of the SRT's handling of the final report with the Libyan interim authorities and whether the tight timelines for deployment allowed for an adequate consideration of value for money.

The UK Special Envoy to the Libyan Political Transition
In the autumn of 2013, the FCO undertook a review of its policy towards Libya to assess whether support provided was having the desired effect on progress towards peace and security. As a result of that review, in April 2014 the Prime Minister appointed Jonathan Powell to reinvigorate political negotiations and resolve competing visions between Libyan groups on the future of Libya. Jonathan Powell began work in May 2014, developing relationships with military and political figures on both sides of the divide. He has worked throughout 2014 and 2015 in support of the UN-led process. In September 2014, the UN appointed Bernadino Léon as Special Representative of the Secretary-General (SRSG) to lead a political process to end the escalating violence. At the request of SRSG Léon, Jonathan Powell is currently working on the UN's security track, promoting dialogue

between militia leaders and supporting ceasefires on the ground. He travelled repeatedly to Libya in 2014, focusing his efforts on Benghazi and Tripoli. In 2015, the security situation has made it more difficult for him to travel to Libya. Instead he has held meetings with Libyan contacts in the region and Europe and has continued to focus on promoting engagement in Tripoli and Benghazi. He works closely with other international envoys and the UK Ambassador.

On reading this FCO account I felt a chill down my spine. I, of course, wholly supported the appointment of Jonathan Powell, but even that was more than a little ironic. Far from engaging in a proper lessons-learned exercise, the submission sought to hold to the line rather than actively analyse the real impact of the International Stabilisation Unit and plan. Andrew Mitchell, the DFID minister who oversaw the Stabilisation Unit, was on record for trumpeting its contribution. Recalling those crucial days back in April/May 2011, he said: 'I came straight out of the cabinet and ensured I was fully briefed on what we thought are the lessons of Iraq. I then put together a cross-departmental team from the MoD, FCO and the cabinet office to work on stabilisation. It culminated with the deployment to Benghazi of a stabilisation response team – William [Hague] and I saw them when we were down in Benghazi.' As to that trip, he told *The Guardian* in October 2011: 'The NTC are much better than anyone thought they would be. The thing I noticed was how quickly, when they had driven out the Gaddafi forces, they stabilised Misrata, which was in a bad way. I saw it for myself in Benghazi – there was traffic control. Although the rubbish wasn't being collected, the fact was the police were evident and they were able to provide order.' Perhaps someone should have told Mitchell that it had been the Boy Scouts who had been controlling the traffic for most of the revolution. Mitchell's quick visit to Benghazi was just that – quick – and so was his judgment, despite his having been fully briefed on what the lessons on Iraq were.

One short trip to Benghazi by his team did not make for a sustainable stabilisation policy. Other ministers, with a little more experience of the MENA region, took a more realistic tack. The former international development minister Alan Duncan, who served directly under Mitchell, felt impelled to scribble 'fanciful rot' over Mitchell's much-vaunted plan when it was placed before him. It was, he ventured, 'an unrealistic desktop exercise', 'very theoretical'[5] and took no account of the tribal forces that would be unleashed if Gaddafi's government fell. Instead it relied upon the 'whopping assumption that anything that follows Gaddafi will be better. It did not foresee the real historic and tribal tensions that would be unleashed and act as a source for conflict and not unity.' Duncan was right in his

analysis, but it was not so much a matter of not foreseeing such an even-
tuality as dismissing it out of hand. Whether Duncan was aware or not,
both Jonathan Powell and I had raised this very issue with government
officials back in April 2011. Our analysis was not accepted or given any
weight. Countering Mitchell's earlier view, former Defence Secretary Liam
Fox admitted to *The Guardian* newspaper that in October 2011 he was
made 'acutely aware' by Mustafa Abdul Jalil, the chairman of the NTC,
of how disunited the militias had become. Patrick Wintour, the *Guardian*'s
political editor, was moved to observe that 'his remarks reflect a growing
acceptance within Whitehall that Britain's intervention in Libya misjudged
the political forces in the country'.[7]

So what of William Hague's evidence to the Committee? He believed the
Arab Spring to be the most important event of the twenty-first century, even
outstripping 9/11. He rightly told the Committee that the decision to intervene militarily was the correct one: 'their stated intention, from Gaddafi
himself, was to go house to house, room to room, exacting their revenge on
the people of Benghazi [. . .] It would be a brave assumption, given the
history of Gaddafi, the situation and the disposition of forces, that his
army would drive into Benghazi and they would all behave like pussycats.
A lot of people were going to die.'[8] But he now conceded that Libya had
been left in a 'terrible state'. 'In Libya we had plenty of plans but no power
to implement them,' he told the Committee. 'One of the lessons of this is
not that there was a lack of planning, but that transition takes a lot longer.'
Transition had been too quick, and rapid elections meant senior, experienced figures in the NTC 'disappeared' too quickly. Passing the buck onto
the United Nations, whose mission started in Libya in September 2011, he
stated its assistance was 'not prescriptive enough in identifying the priorities for a Libyan Government' and not 'forceful' enough in implementing
plans for crucial areas such as policing. He could have been talking about
his own department.

However, Hague correctly observed that 'the decision by Libyan leaders to
involve militias in trying to stabilise the security of the state, rather than
progressively exclude militias from one city and then another city, which
would have been an alternative model, meant that the state's security in order
to mobilise its resources was never there'.[9] According to Sir Dominic Asquith,
the number of revolutionaries mushroomed from between 20,000 and 25,000
who fought in the revolution to 140,000 in the aftermath of the revolution.[10]
Ian Martin later acknowledged that the international community's 'greatest
failure was the lack of progress in the security sector'.[11] Notwithstanding that
admission, I believe it was unfair to lay the entire blame upon the United
Nations. As Martin notes: 'the failure to secure Gaddafi's extraordinary
stockpiles of arms and ammunition, or to more urgently address Libya's

border security, severely exacerbated the crisis in Mali, and posed wider regional threats. These went far beyond UNSMIL's limited mandate and capacity, and should have received a higher and earlier level of attention and commitment by the intervening states.'[12] Much more planning could and should have been done earlier by those who intervened militarily, including thinking through how to deal with security and the militias. As Hague himself concluded, 'a coalition of the willing working on Libyan stabilisation and reconstruction might have been more effective than a UN-led process'.[13] The real question was why this was never considered by the UK given the 'light-foot approach' adopted by the UN.

But was the failure of the British government to assist Libya in its transition due to the UK's lack of implementing power, as William Hague intimated to the Select Committee? From where I stood the answer was no. The government had been informed in early April 2011 of the need to help the NTC bolster the rule of law *before* Gaddafi fell. This was some six months before the UN even appeared on the scene. The NTC Justice Minister had pleaded with the exiled British Ambassador for more assistance when he met him with Jason McCue and Dan Brennan in the House of Lords in May 2011. When the Libya sub-Board of the Conflict Prevention Pool did consider the BHRC bid in June it took the view it was 'premature' to concentrate on rule of law issues. There was, then, no lack of power to implement plans. Instead, there was a lack of resolve to get involved at all.[14] All of this chimes with the evidence of Liam Fox, the former Defence Secretary, who admitted to the Select Committee that Britain knew that weapons were being transported in convoys out of the collapsing Libyan state into Niger in the aftermath of the fall of Gaddafi, but was unable to stop it as 'an unavoidable consequence of the lack of troops'. The decision not to bolster the transition in Libya with UK troops was not due to a heartfelt belief in the capacity of the UN to deliver on policing, including of Libya's borders. It was due to an unspoken but operating assumption not to deploy regular troops on the ground in support of a civilian transition. As David Richards, Chief of the Defence Staff, later conceded to the Select Committee, the outcome was 'a strategic failure', where the diplomats 'somehow hoped that it would work out on the night when self-evidently it did not'. He added: '[I]f you don't do it properly or you don't have the resources, do not do it at all. If you want to win wars, mass matters, you need troops on the ground.'[15]

Richards also admitted that British military intelligence had little knowl-edge of anti-Gaddafi forces in Libya, and that the decision to base the campaign and subsequent plan for stabilisation on the assumption that there were no tribal forces inside Libya was a diplomatic and policy failure. According to Professor Joffé 'people had not really bothered to monitor closely what was happening'.[16] US intelligence officials reportedly described the intervention as 'an intelligence light decision'.[17] Iraq should have taught policymakers the perils of basing an entire intervention on limited intelligence. Yet the FCO was put on notice as early as April 2011 that if New Libya was to avoid the political vacuum that occurred in Iraq it had to develop a strategy to deal with the different irregular militia stakeholders, be they tribal in nature or otherwise. As we have seen, this did not happen because HMG's own assessment was that Tripoli would fall through internal defection. Again the failure to develop a Plan B was not due to a lack of implementing power but a failure of policymaking and leadership.

This analysis chimes with the claims of the Deputy Prime Minister of Libya's new unity government. In a direct repudiation of William Hague's claims, Ahmad Maiteeg told the *Observer* in January 2016 that Britain and France had failed to provide the necessary help after Gaddafi's removal from power even though their initial intervention was right:

> There was a lot of misunderstanding. People were thinking that Libya had stable and strong institutions, but this was not the case. It was a one-man show for 42 years. Once this man had gone away we did not get the right help from our friends and allies from the West and Britain. What we need now is our friends and allies to help us build the institutions to start to build the country in the right way. They did the right thing at that time [in 2011] to help the Libyans but this help did not continue for a period of time.[18]

In the same interview Maiteeg also gave cause for hope to families of victims of IRA Semtex about their compensation claim:

> The right thing is that our justice minister will form a committee and take care of this matter. We have to study the case by our committee and see how far we go [. . .] Of course, our relationship with Britain is very important to us and Britain stands by Libya at many delicate times. The minimum we can do is look at this case and study it well, and we will do the right things for our country and our friends in Britain.

Jonathan Powell was also questioned by the Committee about his role as the UK Special Envoy from 2013 onwards, and he did observe that 'if you look back at the earlier period before I was involved, there is certainly a question about how far national Governments should have been involved relative to the UN'. Like me he thought the intervention 'was the right thing to do'. He went on:

> I think it would have been very difficult to have turned down that opportunity when Benghazi was under attack. When I started going to Libya two

years ago, Libyans would say to me, 'Thank you very much, indeed, Britain, for supporting us in the revolution, but why did you go away and desert us after the revolution and leave us by ourselves?' I think that is an unfair criticism, because the people on the ground at the time were trying to help the Government. It was more Jibril and people in the Government who were telling them to go away.

I do think there were people maybe drawing the wrong lesson from Iraq. They thought we don't want any more Bremers [Paul Bremer was the US official put in charge of Iraq under the coalition's occupation] telling them what to do on the ground. Actually, again, you were dealing with a country with no institutions, no tradition at all of how to do this Government. We should have been more proactive. I note that President Obama, interviewed last year in *The New York Times*, said: 'We [. . .] underestimated the need to come in full force,' and that there should have been a 'much more aggressive effort to rebuild societies'. He said he thought that was his biggest mistake in foreign policy and I think there is something to that.
Q492 Chair: But doesn't that fly in the face of what the Prime Minister recently said? He intimated pretty strongly that he thought it was the fault of the Libyans at the end of the day. He is on record as saying that we gave them their chance but they blew it.

Jonathan Powell: He is certainly right to say that the Libyans have to be responsible for their own fate. We can't take over their fate for them, but I do think we should have done more. I agree with President Obama that we should have been more willing, and ignored them when they told us to go away and leave them alone. We should have actually tried to help them with the institutions in a more proactive way.[19]

Commenting on the situation in Libya, in a speech given during the 2015 general election Ed Miliband, the former Labour leader, was a little more emphatic in his criticism of David Cameron. He alleged that David Cameron had been wrong 'to assume that Libya was a country whose institutions could be left to evolve and transform on their own'. In his view, the tragedy could have been anticipated and should have been avoided. 'Britain could have played its part in ensuring the international community stood by the people of Libya in practice rather than standing behind the unfounded hopes of potential progress only in principle,' he said. Miliband's speech was met by a storm of protest, as it implied Cameron might be responsible for migrant deaths. But on the more general point it contained more than an element of truth to it from where I stood.

Conclusion

In conclusion, it seems the failure to provide the NTC with necessary transition assistance both during and after the military campaign contributed directly to the political and security vacuum that enveloped the country, post-Gaddafi. This in turn helped fuel inter-militia rivalry, a resurgence of terrorist activity across Libya's porous and unmanned borders, as well as the eventual rise of Islamic State and other jihadist groups in Libya. By leaving it all to the UN, and concentrating on early elections, the UK helped denude the NTC of power. The failure of the international stabilisation plan to properly address inter-militia rivalry, disarmament and demobilisation, or transitional justice arrangements regarding those detained after the conflict, was inexcusable. The critical period to work on the division of responsibilities between the NTC and the militias, and treatment and prosecution of loyalists and the Gaddafi family, was not after but before the fall of Tripoli. The cost of paying non-state actors to assist in these matters, who had already established relations with the rebels, was minimal when compared to the expense of continuous civic instability.

As the Foreign Affairs Select Committee reported, the UK spent some £320 million on bombing Libya and approximately £25 million on reconstruction programmes, most of which went to the UN.[20] HMG's conflict advisors should have recognised what David Marshall's work at Harvard demonstrated, namely that the UN and international community's record of promoting the rule of law in conflict situations left a lot to be desired. It is therefore wrong to blame all the ills that subsequently befell Libya in 2012 on NATO's military intervention, or the subsequent action and inaction of the Libyan people. The failure to build a viable state was not so much due to military intervention but the West's failure to intervene on a civilian level. R2P, as conceived by Cameron and Obama, was never just about military intervention and immediate humanitarian protection. It also required a civilian intervention committed to building a viable peace that kept both Libya and neighbouring populations safe from further violence. If the West was politically wary about using troops or governmental institutions to carry out this task, then it should have enlisted the help of the private sector or not intervened at all.

President Obama got it about right when he described post-intervention Libya as a 'shit show'. Expressing his disappointment in the UK and France for not exercising leadership on stabilisation and reconstruction he told *The Atlantic Magazine* in 2016, 'I had more faith in the Europeans, given Libya's proximity, being invested in the follow-up,' adding that the then Prime Minister David Cameron stopped paying attention and became 'distracted by a range of things'. The Foreign Affairs Select Committee found it difficult to disagree with Obama's emphatic conclusion. It found that the UK along with France led the military intervention and 'had a particular responsibility to support Libyan economic and political reconstruction'.[21]

As I ruminated on what had transpired in Benghazi since I left in April 2011, the words of a Tripoli-based blogger quoted in *The Guardian* newspaper on 1 March 2011 finally came back to haunt me:

> This is a priceless opportunity that has fallen into your laps. It's a chance for you to improve your image in the eyes of Arabs and Muslims. Don't mess it up. All of your previous programmes to bring the east and west closer have failed, and some of them have made things even worse. Don't start something you cannot finish, don't turn a people's pure revolution into some curse that will befall everyone.[22]

It was difficult to decipher whether the UK government's intervention in Libya was indicative of a real and sustained commitment towards democratic change and reform, or of a desire to simply remove a dictator it had come to dislike and could no longer do business with. But if it was the latter it could expect to continue to earn the wrath of a new generation of civil society activists across the MENA region. In its report the UK Foreign Affairs Select Committee stated that it had heard 'from all but one of the key British protagonists involved in the decision to intervene in Libya in 2011'. It invited the then Prime Minister, David Cameron MP, to provide oral evidence to the inquiry in March 2016, but he declined, citing 'the pressure on his diary'. If he had done so he might have been able to assess his government's performance in relation to its intervention, by recalling his own statement given at the start of the conflict:

> To those who say it is nothing to do with us, I would simply respond: Do we want a situation where a failed pariah state festers on Europe's southern border, potentially threatening our security, pushing people across the Mediterranean and creating a more dangerous and uncertain world for Britain and for all our allies as well as for the people of Libya? My answer is clear: This is not in Britain's interests. And that is why Britain will remain at the forefront of Europe in leading the response to this crisis.

PART THREE: The Aftermath

17. Reflections for the Future

Human Dignity

So what lessons should policymakers learn from the UK's intervention in Libya and the Arab Spring more generally? Let me put forward some observations that they might reflect upon as the situation mutates. The first concerns human dignity and the right to be treated equally and with respect. UK policymakers would do well to recognise that the demand for human dignity animated much of the protest in 2011, and that such a demand is unlikely to go away any time soon. The multitudes that took to the streets were young, and their desire to hold government to account and see long-term political reform remains undiminished. If the UK is to regain credibility with the people in the region it needs to demonstrate its commitment to the concept of human dignity in both word and deed, something it very much failed to do during the 'war on terror' years. This entails recognising that the Arab Spring, with its demand for an end to corrupt, unrepresentative and unresponsive government, has – at the very least – put paid to the cosy, post-colonial arrangement that tacitly existed between the West and a series of democratically weak regimes. The UK can ill afford to ignore the democratic aspirations of the people in the MENA region, as sustainable government and security ultimately rest upon the consent of the people.

The former British Foreign Secretary William Hague, in his Mansion House Speech of 4 May 2011, rightly recognised the transformative power of the Arab Spring and the need for the West to develop a new relationship towards the MENA region based upon democratic principles. Today, we need to remind ourselves that what most ordinary people in the Middle East want is not more religion or ideology or security, but the same things as people in the West: peace, jobs, healthcare, education and transparent, responsive, representative government. These wants cannot be silenced, repressed or dismissed on any long-term basis. President Obama was therefore right to offer the region a new type of Marshall Plan in his Cairo Speech of 19 May 2011. But offering is one thing and delivering is another. President Donald Trump will need to redeem this promise if the region is to avoid sliding back into protest, instability and political chaos.

The real problem with a security-focused analysis of the situation is that it does not address the ordinary needs of the MENA people. Long-term political stability will only be achieved if there is a new social contract between governments and the governed based upon core, enduring political principles. In his Cairo speech, Obama wisely recognised the idea of human dignity as universal. He understood that it forms the philosophical basis to human beings' entitlement, irrespective of status and wealth, to claim a set of inalienable human rights. As the philosopher Kant once observed in *The Metaphysics of Morals*, a person 'is not to be valued merely as a means to the ends of others or even his own ends, but as an end in himself, that is, he possesses a dignity (an absolute inner worth) by which he exacts respect for himself from all other rational beings in the world'. The protests felt iconic because they confirmed, if confirmation was needed, that human dignity is a paramount value in any human society, and that there is no such thing as Arab exceptionalism, either then or now.

Such observations are foundational to much libertarian thinking. The concept of human dignity has been recognised by the international community as a guiding principle in the affairs of man. In 1986 the United Nations General Assembly resolved that all new human rights instruments should 'derive from the inherent dignity and worth of the human being'. In 1993 over 170 governments came together at the Second World Conference on Human Rights in Vienna, and chose human dignity as the value that generated human rights. It is why the Rome Statute of the International Criminal Court of 1998 borrowed the phrase 'outrages upon personal dignity' from Common Article 3 of the Geneva Convention, to make it the basis of its mandate. It is also why numerous regional human rights mechanisms and constitutional courts across the globe recognised in their jurisprudence the paramount place dignity occupies in the pantheon of human rights. As the former UN Secretary General Boutros Boutros-Ghali observed: 'just like democratisation within States, democratisation at the international level is based on and aims to promote the dignity and worth of the individual being and the fundamental equality of persons and all peoples'. The Quran states: 'whoever kills a fellow being unjustly [. . .] has murdered all of humanity'. The UK government needs to respond to the call for greater dignity by incorporating it into its overseas development and dialogue strategies, by giving more focus to the individual and society and less to government and the state.

Britain's Own Human Rights Stain

Sceptics should also reflect upon the success of current counter-terror approaches in identifying and stopping the tide of Islamic fundamentalism in the region. In reality these have done little to stabilise the situation. At the very least the security pacts between the UK and regimes such as those in Libya and Algeria need to be rethought and replaced by more durable and principled agreements, if the UK is to have any hope of establishing an enduring concordat between it and people of the MENA region. Policymakers must accept that excesses were perpetrated and then make some admission about the UK's role during the last decade in facilitating some of the darker arts practised by certain regimes.

It was high-handed of the former UK Defence Secretary, Philip Hammond, to admonish the NTC for its failure to investigate Gaddafi's execution and other human rights abuses, given his own government's failure to publicly confront the UK's murky past with Libya. It took years for the coalition government to even order an inquiry into allegations of UK complicity regarding torture through rendition. This only came after dogged attempts to bring the government to account through a series of cases and parliamentary protests undertaken by Liberty, Reprieve and Amnesty International, as well as media investigations by newspapers such as *The Guardian* and *The Independent*. David Cameron's failure to issue an apology to Belhaj or accept the force of his complaints was not rescued by his subsequent reference of the case to the Gibson Inquiry into torture and rendition. By that time the Inquiry had already stalled under the weight of other criminal and civil investigations and proceedings, and lost credibility in the eyes of the British human rights community. Liberty's withdrawal from the Gibson Inquiry, following publication of its terms of reference and secret operating procedures, told its own story.

It was unsurprising when Belhaj and Saadi launched civil proceedings against MI5, MI6, the Foreign Office and Sir Mark Allen for complicity in their illegal rendition and torture. Yet one intelligence source told me that Mark Allen felt he was being hung out to dry by his political masters. Interestingly, the *Daily Mail* reported in April 2012 that well-placed sources had confirmed that the operations were 'ministerially authorised government policy'. I was told that a high-level source implied that authorisation might have been given orally. Despite repeated requests from *The Guardian* to Jack Straw to indicate if he or any other minister authorised the operations, no answer has ever been forthcoming. A writ against Straw has now been issued. Figures released under the Freedom of Information Act reveal the extraordinary lengths to which the government is going to prevent the civil case against it, former Home Secretary Jack Straw and Sir Mark Allen coming to court: by 10 September 2015 the government had spent £355,000 on internal legal advice and £259,000 on external advice, as it sought to have the case dropped. Of this, £27,000 was spent on advice relating to Straw and £110,000 on advice relating to Allen.

But the most telling aspect of the story was the revelation that the target may have been rendered back to Tripoli via Diego Garcia, a British Overseas Dependent Territory, where a US military facility was located. This, despite assurances given by Jack Straw, the former Foreign Secretary, to both parliament and the Bar Human Rights Committee in writing that it was not used as a base for rendition. According to the *Guardian* correspondent Ian Cobain, '[B]y piecing together air traffic control logs and matching them with a document found in the Tripoli cache, it is possible to trace the route taken by the aircraft that rendered Bouchar and Belhaj from Bangkok to Tripoli in March 2004.'[6]

The aircraft used was allegedly a Boeing 737 with tail number N313P, operated by a North Carolina company called Aero Contractors, which had been widely reported to be a CIA front. According to the records of the European air traffic management agency, Eurocontrol, and the Federal Aviation Administration in the US, N313P took off from Dulles airport in Washington DC at 2.51 am on 7 March 2004, and landed at Misrata in Libya shortly after noon local time. When N313P departed from Misrata, it flew beyond Eurocontrol's area of responsibility and disappeared, temporarily, from its records. But a flight plan prepared by the CIA the previous day, and faxed to Libya, was found among the secret cache of letters and faxes recovered from Koussa's office after the fall of Tripoli. For Cobain, this showed 'that after the date when Bouchar and Belhaj were forced on board in Bangkok, the aircraft was then due to fly to Tripoli via Diego Garcia, where it would refuel during the early hours of 9 March'. This all dovetailed with the contents of other CIA papers found in Tripoli, including a fax from 2003 detailing the British arrest of LIFG head, 'Emir Abu Mundhir', in Hong Kong, for passport violations. 'We are also aware that your service had been co-operating with the British to effect Abu Munthir's [sic] removal to Tripoli [. . .] and that you had an aircraft available for this purpose in the Maldives.'

If true, this had implications for both the previous Labour government and the new coalition government's stated commitment to combating torture and respecting the rule of law. On a number of occasions both Tony Blair and Jack Straw stated in parliament that there was 'no evidence' to support the contention that Diego Garcia played a part in the global rendition programme. These statements reflected the Bar Human Rights Committee's own enquiries at the time. Back in March 2004, the BHRC wrote to Jack Straw in express terms to enquire whether Diego Garcia was being used as a detention facility or stop-off point for rendition, including in relation to any US vessel moored off its shores. We received express written assurances from the Foreign Secretary that it was not being used for these purposes. After a deluge of new evidence began to emerge concerning the operation of the CIA's rendition programme, David Miliband, Gordon Brown's Foreign Secretary, felt compelled by 2008 to apologise to the House of Commons for the inaccurate information previously given by the government on this point. He reported that, upon further investigation, two rendition flights had in fact been allowed to refuel at Diego Garcia in 2002. However, he said nothing of Belhaj's flight in 2004.

But the issue relating to the use of Diego Garcia was plainly troubling the Blair administration even back in 2004. After the BHRC had received assurances from Jack Straw, its then chairman Peter Carter QC and I, acting in my capacity as vice-chair, had a meeting with the then Attorney General, Peter Goldsmith, on the subject of Iraq in which the issue of Diego Garcia was tangentially raised. The meeting took place in a small room off the lobby of the Houses of Parliament in March 2004, and had been ostensibly arranged to discuss ILAC, an international legal organisation concerned with the reconstruction of the judicial system in Iraq. We wanted to see if there was a role for the BHRC. At one point during the course of our discussions the Attorney General asked his officials to leave the room. I cannot now recall at what point in the discussions that occurred. What I do recall, however, is that after they left he orally repeated the written assurances that we had received from Jack Straw in relation to Diego Garcia. Both Peter and I were struck at the time by this unprompted intervention, made outwith the hearing of his own officials. We had not asked him about the matter, for there was no further evidence before us to challenge the good faith of the assurances that we had been already given. Looking back, it is clear that the Labour government was extremely sensitive even back then to any allegation concerning Diego Garcia. This further intervention appeared unnecessary if, as David Miliband later suggested to parliament, the two rendition refuelling flights that had occurred were only discovered by officials in 2008 and were not part of any deliberate attempt to conceal rendition flights from parliament.

Faced with the prospect of a slew of civil claims for damages and redress from former rendition detainees, the coalition government brought forward yet more proposals to extend the application of SIAC-style secrecy hearings to any civil trial or process in which a minister concludes that evidence or foreign intelligence material is too sensitive to be aired in public. It remains a deeply troubling response to a set of disturbing allegations, particularly given successive governments' publicly stated policy of a zero tolerance of torture and public misfeasance.

All of this stands in marked contrast to the early apology issued by the NTC for the human rights abuses committed by the previous Gaddafi regime. The NTC offered the UK the chance to build a new political dispensation with New Libya through a compensation agreement. It was a concordat that was based upon the mutual acceptance of the rule of law, democracy and trans-parent governance, free from the corruption and misdeeds of the past. Did parts of Cameron's administration refuse to recognise this concordat due to queasiness over its own legacy issues? Who knows, but whatever the real truth it ill-behoved Philip Hammond to lecture the NTC about its commitment to human rights, democracy and the rule of law, given the UK government's fail-ure to support it or look at its own record with any degree of transparency.

Writing from an American perspective, Ethan Chorin, the former official at the US Liaison Office in Tripoli between 2004 and 2006, talks of the 'venal interests of individuals and organisations' in the post-rapprochement Gaddafi period, in which the 'sheer speed and size of the revolving doors between government, lobbyists, individual politicians, oil companies, arms dealers and their counterparts' was 'truly astounding'. He reserves his greatest crit-icism for his own government but it could apply to others:

> While the US preached 'good governance' under the administration of George W. Bush, it was simultaneously an egregious violator of these same principles, selling arms to Libya, and worse, literally delivering individuals to Gaddafi's front door with all but the weakest caveats against torture – without really knowing much about these people or their motives. The fact that so many weapons were sold with zeal by the West to Gaddafi in the lead-up to the revolution, and that the US, the UK, and other countries actually participated in a programme to deliver some of Gaddafi's enemies to him on a plate for torture, should by rights be cause for far greater outrage by the American public than has hitherto been the case.[1]

IRA Semtex Victims

The UK government should also recognise that the issue of human dignity does not just relate to those who have been abused in the region. It includes IRA Semtex and other victims who continue to suffer as a consequence of Gaddafi's actions and the UK government's own inaction on this festering legacy issue. Many felt the coalition government was under an obligation to bring closure to these legacy issues as quickly as possible while the NTC felt still in debt to those who had helped it liberate Libya. That is certainly what many victims believed after David Cameron report-edly gave a private commitment to the victims to make the settlement a priority in September 2011.

As a result, *The Sunday Times* felt able to report that 'the deal, revealed on the exaronews.com website, will see families of IRA victims killed by Libyan Semtex receive $10m (£6.3m) each, while those who were injured will get about $3m (£1.9m). A total of 156 victims or families of victims will receive the payouts'.[2] 'There is light at last for our international victims after the darkness of the Gaddafi era,' McCue told *The Sunday Times* after suggesting that formal liberation had triggered the MoU agreement. McCue would later travel to Libya to start the dialogue on how to implement the legacy agreements, after a new interim government was selected and sworn in, in early December 2011. The commitment allegedly given by Cameron was consistent with certain exchanges in parliament on this subject. On 9 September 2011, Northern Irish MP Nigel Dodds asked the then Prime Minister: 'Can I seek an assurance from the Prime Minister that he continues to back the case for justice, and that he will do what he can to secure compensation from the new regime?' The Prime Minister's reply was: 'I certainly will do that and it is a vital issue. There is no doubt that the Libyan provision of Semtex to the IRA was immensely damaging over many years, and it possibly still is today. We need to be clear that this will be an important bilateral issue between Britain and the new Libyan authorities. Clearly we have to let this government get their feet under the desk, but this is very high up my list of items.'

But it was not to be. Despite further promising noises from Cameron following the appointment of the new Libyan Prime Minister in autumn of 2011 little progress was made. In September McCue's Northern Ireland–Libya Reconciliation Unit pass was revoked. On 11 September 2012 he was informed that the Unit that had previously been dedicated to securing compensation for the UK victims had moved to working with Libya to promote 'broad and lasting reconciliation' between the two countries. Foreign Office Minister Alistair Burt and Northern Ireland Office (NIO) Minister Hugo Swire had written to the Libyan government setting out how the UK and Libya could work together to promote 'broad and lasting reconciliation' between Libya and the UK communities directly affected by Gaddafi's support of terrorism, through a 'range of activities' that would benefit all communities. The FCO and NIO had identified a potential reconciliation package including: sharing UK knowledge and experience of reconciliation and post-conflict issues; 'commercial activities'; establishing links between Libyan and UK institutions and communities; gestures of reconciliation (it was suggested that the Libyan Prime Minister could place a wreath at WPC Fletcher's memorial during his next visit). What there was not was any mention of a humanitarian compensation package for IRA or other victims of Libya's intervention in the conflict in Northern Ireland.

When the UK victims later asked what this meant for their compensation claims, the FCO explained that they would have to explore this directly with the Libyan government themselves, through their own private campaign, though the FCO could continue to provide 'facilitation support'. The FCO's role would henceforth be limited to helping set up meetings with the Libyan Embassy in London, offering updates on the situation in Libya, and providing advice on any approaches to the Libyan authorities. On 15 November 2011 the Prime Minister finally wrote to McCue in reply to a letter of his dated 2 September. He told McCue that he had asked the FCO 'to prepare detailed plans for a comprehensive structured bilateral dialogue with the new Libyan Government with a view to establishing a sustainable and effective partnership with Libya'. According to Cameron, 'this will provide a forum to address all outstanding legacy issues resulting from the Qadhafi period and the many victims affected by his actions'. But he added this important rider: 'Our objective is a comprehensive resolution of these legacy issues. For this reason, I do not think it would be right or productive to pressure the NTC to settle just one element now.' In fact, the agreements signed in Benghazi also referred to the provision of a humanitarian compensation fund for other victims of the Northern Ireland conflict.

On 19 February 2013 McCue and partners were further informed that following a meeting between the NIO and the Libyan Foreign Minister in December 2012, the UK would draft a set of proposals which would set out five key areas: political gestures; trade and investment; developing community links; policing in post-conflict communities; and scholarships. Cameron's commitment to do all he could for the victims was slipping down the list of priorities. Further bad news came on 4 August 2013 when new information came to light about the circumstances surrounding how President Bush came to sign an Executive Order which effectively torpedoed the British victims' claim in the US courts. *The Telegraph* reported that Tony Blair made a secret trip to the White House to broker a deal on behalf of Gaddafi that deprived British victims of Libyan terrorism of millions of pounds in compensation. Quoting a 'senior source', it alleged that Mr Blair acted 'as a go-between in negotiations between Gaddafi and President George Bush over payments to terror victims'. It quoted the senior source as saying: 'You will find that Mr Blair called on Mr Bush in Washington in February 2008. I do know there was a meeting between Mr Blair and Mr Bush subsequent to one of Mr Blair's visits to Libya.'[3]

At the time Libya was being sued through the US courts for terror atrocities. Billions of dollars of Gaddafi's assets were at risk of being frozen as a result of a new law Congress passed called the National Defense Authorisation Act 2008. This allowed victims of state-sponsored terrorism to collect court-awarded damages by either seizing the terror state's assets or taking money from companies doing business with them. Gaddafi had taken fright and was concerned it would jeopardise oil and gas contracts with US companies and so allegedly enlisted the help of Mr Blair. As noted earlier, the deal struck led to US victims receiving over $1.6 billion out of a compensation fund, but in exchange for all court cases being dropped under an act of Congress. In a letter dated 27 February 2008, written after his visits to Tripoli and then Washington, but discovered only after Gaddafi's downfall, Mr Blair wrote: 'Dear Muammar [. . .] I also raised some of our conversation with President Bush and would be very happy to let you know how those talks went, with best wishes, yours ever Tony.'

The Telegraph source now made it clear that those talks may have included discussions about compensation. Up until then, Blair had always insisted he had 'nothing whatsoever to do with any compensation legislation signed by President Bush' and he continues to maintain this position. The senior source's allegations dovetailed with other events. According to WikiLeaks, on 12 March 2008 the US Embassy in Tripoli sent a classified message which read as follows:

> 1. (C) Summary: Leader Muammar al-Qadhafi, National Oil Corporation Chairman Shukri Ghanem and Deputy Foreign Minister Siala stressed to American interlocutors in recent meetings that the GOL [government of Libya] views the recent confluence of the UTA [aircraft] bombing case judgment against Libya and a new US law intended to assist victims of terrorism as serious threats that could jeopardize further development of US-Libya bilateral ties and prompt Libya to expel US oil and gas companies and reduce oil production. End summary.[4]

All of this was consistent with a *New York Times* report that in March 2008 Libya's Ambassador to the US, Ali S. Aujali, signed a $2.4 million contract with the prominent Washington lobbying firm, the Livingston Group.[5] Together with the Livingston Group, Aujali had a series of meetings with Congressional leaders to secure a waiver from the law. Separately, David Goldwyn, head of Goldwyn International Strategies LLC, 'an oil industry group' and the Libyan Government approached the White House, the State Department, the Energy Department and the Pentagon: 'A battalion of top oil industry executives – from companies including ConocoPhillips, Hess, Occidental and Marathon Oil' were reported to 'have been making the rounds on Capitol Hill'. The report claimed 'ExxonMobil, Chevron and Dow Chemical also supported the effort', which resulted in four of President Bush's cabinet members – Robert M. Gates, the Defense Secretary, Condoleezza Rice (who would subsequently be instrumental in brokering the Libya Claims Resolution Act [LCRA]), the Secretary of State, Samuel W. Bodman, the

Energy Secretary, and Carlos M. Gutierrez, the Commerce Secretary – writing a letter to Congress urging it to agree to Libya's requested exception. The letter said that the law was putting American oil companies at a disadvantage in competing for access to Libya's 40 billion barrels of proven oil reserves.

Another e-mail obtained by *The Sunday Telegraph* after the fall of Gaddafi had been written to Mr Blair's office in June 2008 by the then British Ambassador to Libya, Sir Vincent Fean, to clarify the timeline. It advised:

> TB should explain what he said to President Bush (and what Banner said to Welch) to keep his promise to intervene after the President allowed US courts to attach Libyan assets. He could express satisfaction at the progress made in talks between the US and Libya to reach a Govt to Govt solution to all the legal/compensation issues outstanding from the 1980s. It would be good to get these issues resolved, and move on. The right framework is being created. HMG is not involved in the talks, although some British citizens might be affected by them.[6]

This was a reference to Lockerbie, plus some Northern Irish litigants going to US courts seeking compensation from Libya for IRA terrorist attacks funded/fuelled by Libya. As we now know, on 30 July 2008 USDOS (US Department of State) submitted to Congress the draft Libya Claims Resolution Act 2008 (LCRA). In August Bush signed the LCRA into law. On 14 August the US and Libya signed the US/Libya Claims Settlement Agreement. The e-mail not only fixed Blair with knowledge of this matter, it specifically contemplated the plight of IRA Semtex and UK Lockerbie victims seeking compensation through the US courts. Quite why Mr Blair failed to make any representations on behalf of the victims, given that he was informed of their direct interests, remains somewhat of a mystery. He would later tell a parliamentary committee that he never tried to get the Americans to exclude the claims of IRA victims: 'I did not raise this issue with President Bush. The email from former Ambassador Vincent Fean to my office evidences no such thing, it was simply a reflection of government policy at the time. I was in favour of the USA having good relations with Libya for the same reason as I favoured the UK having such relations: it assisted in the fight against terrorism. [. . .] the attempt to implicate me in deliberately trying to stop IRA victims receiving compensation is utterly without foundation and wrong.' That such representations were made by the new government of Gordon Brown was, however, made clear by the FCO in a statement dated 6 October 2008 and issued by Kim Howells on behalf of the then Foreign Secretary David Miliband. He stated that:

> during the course of negotiations between the US and Libya, the Government made representations to the US Administration that the

families of Lockerbie victims and existing UK claimants, with claims before US courts against Libya for its past sponsorship of Irish Republican Army (IRA) terrorist acts (the McDonald case), should be included as recipients of any compensation package. In the event, it proved not possible to include the McDonald case claimants in the recipients of compensation under the US/Libya Agreement.

It was within this context that the new Prime Minister Gordon Brown yielded to McCue and created the FCO Northern Ireland–Libya Reconciliation Unit, after Northern Irish parliamentarians pressed the Labour government about why the victims were not properly protected. But in hindsight it appears clear that all governments of whatever hue were reluctant to tackle this legacy issue. Thus, despite the words of encouragement written by David Cameron to McCue that propelled him to take the hazardous trip to Benghazi in March 2011, it now appears that his administration was never committed to pursuing compensation for IRA Semtex victims with any degree of vigour. The position of the coalition government was put beyond doubt by Baroness Warsi in response to yet another parliamentary question on 22 January 2014:

> The Government is not involved in any negotiations with the Libyan government on securing compensation payments for the British victims of Qadhafi sponsored Irish Republican Army (IRA) terrorism. The Government considers individual compensation claims that are being pursued to be a private matter and best pursued directly with the Libyan government. However, the Foreign and Commonwealth Office does provide facilitation support to a number of private compensation campaign groups, where it has been requested.

Finally, on 3 March 2015 the tireless Nigel Dodds asked the then Foreign Secretary Philip Hammond yet another question: 'Following engagement with ourselves, the Prime Minister appointed the National Security Advisor to engage with the Libyan authorities on reconciliation and finding ways forward for compensation for victims of IRA terrorism that was sponsored by the Gaddafi regime. Will the Foreign Secretary update the House on what progress the National Security Advisor has made in that work?' Mr Hammond replied:

> I regret to have to tell the Right Hon. Gentleman that the reality on the ground in Libya is that there is no authority to engage with. I am afraid that at the moment I can report no progress on those measures. The urgent need now is to see a Government of national unity created and for the

Libyan people to deal collectively with the threat to their society that is posed by the establishment of ISIL cells. Once we have such an authority in place, we will of course re-engage with that agenda.

Cameron's coalition government was now seeking to hide behind the very chaos it had helped engender through its own inaction. The victims and McCue's campaign were back to square one.

Some form of respite for McCue and the victims finally came on 2 May 2017 with the publication of the House of Commons Northern Ireland Affairs Committee Fourth Report of Session 2016–17 into HM Government support for UK victims of IRA attacks that used Gaddafi-supplied Semtex and weapons. This report was rushed out after Prime Minister Theresa May called a general election. It concluded that successive governments had badly let down the victims and their legal representatives. It paid 'warm tribute to the quiet dignity and determination of those individuals and organisations who have campaigned tirelessly over the years to rectify this injustice'. It also encouraged the next government to adopt a fresh approach 'to secure the compensation these people deserve'. More significantly, it noted that

Whilst there was initial optimism that the Coalition Government would take a different approach on the issue of compensation after the fall of Gaddafi, that Government's rhetoric did not translate into any tangible progress. This was, yet again, a missed opportunity. The fact that lawyers acting on behalf the UK victims were able to have the then Chairman of the National Transitional Council of Libya sign a statement in support of providing compensation early in 2011, suggests to us that, if the Coalition Government itself had taken up this issue at that time, it would have had a good chance of reaching an agreement.

The report further disclosed 'the FCO itself admitted to us in its oral evidence that it could not see any legal reason why the UK Government could not espouse a claim by its citizens – it was simply a longstanding Government practice not to do so'. It concluded that:

with sufficient determination, the UK Government should be able to reach an agreement. But, as one of our witnesses said: 'it requires somebody to bang on their door, not with a wet sponge, but [with a] bang'.[7]

The UK Human Rights Community and the MENA Region

But if the Arab Spring raised some uncomfortable questions for the UK government it also raised others for the UK's civil rights community. A number of Arab colleagues argue that sections of this community had become far too obsessed with litigating the war on terror in courts back in the UK, rather than helping others confront wider societal injustice in the region. This was perhaps why the Arab Spring came as a shock, as by then their perspectives had become singularly framed by the war on terror paradigm. Few anticipated that after ten years of unremitting conflict, carnage and legal intrigue, the people of the MENA region would take to the streets to validate and claim Western principles of governance for themselves.

I salute the extraordinary effort of long-time activists like Clive Stafford Smith and Gareth Peirce, who worked tirelessly to expose the injustice of Guantanamo Bay, but perhaps too much attention was given by other lawyers to war on terror cases in the UK, to the relative exclusion of other human rights issues in the region. As Stafford Smith himself confided to me at one BHRC seminar in 2011, very rarely, if at all, was any detainee released through a court order. The graphic pictures from Abu Ghraib and Guantanamo may have presented the civil rights community with difficult issues about how to combat state impunity, but they did not challenge it ethically other than to defend the universal nature of the prohibition against torture. The BHRC might have filed a successful amicus brief in Hamdan v Rumsfeld before the US Supreme Court to reaffirm the right to habeas corpus, even for Guantanamo detainees, but we should not kid ourselves about the innovative nature of the submissions made. In the end it merely contained a basic restatement of all that we have fought for since the time of Magna Carta.

In the end it was not these test cases that put paid to Bush's counter-terror paradigm, but the emergence of an urgent public political discourse over the utility of the 'war on terror', including its inability to prevent soldier deaths or resolve conflicts in Afghanistan, Iraq and the wider Middle East. Indeed, a study of the effect of litigation against extraordinary rendition and use of torture techniques by the CIA and UK by Professor Suzanne Egan, a prominent member of the Irish Human Rights Commission (who tried to investigate CIA flights flown through Shannon Airport in Ireland), concluded that not much headway had been made through the US and European courts in halting these practices.

For Egan, it was the power of information rather than law that had helped bring an end to these practices. The sustained public campaign and debate engendered by journalist enquiry, and the lobbying of civil rights organisations, such as Reprieve, Liberty and Amnesty International, were far more effective in getting detainees released than the gilded speeches of advocates in any court of law. Professor Philippe Sands QC probably reached more people through his compelling account of the Bush administration's assault on the precepts of international law in his book *Lawless World: Making and Breaking Global Rules* than through any court advocacy.

More to the point, as the defence solicitor Gareth Peirce has observed, it was not neo-con politicians but ordinary lawyers in our civil and court service who built the legal edifice of the war on terror, with its system of secretive tribunals, special advocates and black holes of injustice.

Perhaps we lawyers should have given ourselves fewer human rights prizes about litigating the war on terror and been a little harder on ourselves when considering our record in helping other campaigners to combat some of the wider economic and social human rights abuses that were occurring in the MENA region. For throughout this period the sheer injustice of life for ordinary people there went largely unnoticed. Until, that is, those people took to the streets in 2011. My Arab colleagues were therefore probably right when they observed that if you were not an alleged terrorist or victim of terrorism, then you and your community didn't get very much of a look in.

It is interesting to note that some of the leading lawyers who sought to prosecute UK soldiers for alleged crimes in conflict zones rarely set foot in the region to take evidence while the conflict was going on. I recall when, in 2005, as vice-chair of the BHRC, I offered one of Liberty's award-winning solicitors the chance to actually travel to southern Iraq to take detailed evidence from his Iraqi clients about torture claims allegedly inflicted by British troops. He was offered the assistance of Arabic speaking lawyers and translators, whose expenses the BHRC would pay. 'I'm not going to southern Iraq,' he replied incredulously. He looked at me as if I were mad. It appeared his primary concern was to obtain a legal aid certificate to kick-start a human rights case in the UK, capable of triggering an inquest or torture enquiry into the conduct of British troops in Iraq. He had obtained just enough evidence via newspaper journalists and local interpreters to issue a writ in the UK domestic courts to raise the issue of whether Article 1 jurisdiction of the European Convention of Human Rights covered British forces operating in Iraq.

There was little doubt that such cases needed to be tested, if based on credible evidence, and perhaps he should be applauded for his tenacity in litigating such alleged abuses, but it was equally troubling to note his reticence to visit the very society he sought to litigate about. This particular solicitor went on to ask another charity I was involved in for repayment of £4,000 he had personally paid to bring the father of his dead client to the UK for a press conference. I felt distinctly queasy about his whole approach, including how he offered to sack one prominent QC in favour of me, provided I let his team lead on a European Court of Human Rights case called *Issa v. Turkey* that I had been litigating for the past six years, for the Kurdish Human Rights Project (KHRP). This concerned whether ECHR jurisdiction extended to northern Iraq to cover the alleged torture and slaughter of seven Kurdish shepherds by Turkish forces, who had entered Iraq and detained them as result of their onslaught on PKK guerrillas. The legal parallels with his case were obvious, but while our KHRP team walked for three days over the mountains from Iran in order to gather testimony from local villagers, he merely dispatched his interpreter to Iraq to get legal aid forms signed. His overtures were rejected by the charity. He was later criticised for ambu-lance-chasing in contradistinction to legal campaigners like Gareth Peirce, who resolutely kept an eye on injustice both at home and abroad, in all its facets. No one could accuse Gareth or any of the other solicitors at Birnberg Peirce of enriching themselves on the back of those they represented.

The Need to Engage with Indigenous Communities – an Example from Turkey

With the benefit of hindsight what the civil rights community and UK govern-ment should have been doing during the war on terror years was to build relationships with civil society communities in the Middle East who were fighting injustice beyond that of the war on terror. My experiences suggest we need to return to a more comprehensive civil society approach that focuses on improving actual conditions in the region. As chairman of the KHRP between 1994 and 2009, I witnessed how the fortunes of Kurds were partially, but nonetheless significantly, transformed in both Turkey and Iraq, over twenty years. This was after a number of human rights lawyers in Europe teamed up with activists from the region in the 1990s and early 2000s to confront injustice in all its forms. This was achieved through the creation of new regionally focused NGOs, and the deployment of innovative legal and public awareness strategies.

The KHRP was dedicated to the protection and promotion of fundamen-tal freedoms across the Kurdish regions of the Near East and not just in Turkey. The suppression of Kurdish identity, culture and existence was prev-alent among all states in the region, but most acute in Turkey and Iraq. It was originally set up by my friend and colleague Kerim Yildiz but thereafter devel-oped by us together in association with a number of legal colleagues and chambers including the Chambers of Mark Muller at 10–11 Gray's Inn Square. When I first met Kerim in early 1993 the KHRP had just a small room off Oxford Street in London, complete with a dodgy Amstrad computer, a picture of a burning Kurdish village up on the wall, and a secretary who came in two afternoons a week for free when she felt like it. By 2010 it had devel-oped into a well-respected international organisation with a full-time staff of dozens of people and a legal team of over sixty lawyers. Its fellows and interns came to work at the KHRP from all around the world. Although it may not have looked very impressive back in 1993 from this small acorn grew a mighty tree. Kerim had stumbled across an elemental idea while studying for an MA in Human Rights at Essex University. The idea was to systematically use the right of individual petition to the European Court of Human Rights (ECHR), which Turkey had recently signed, to help bring a measure of redress to the people of south-east Turkey, whose rights were being violated by the Turkish authorities in the wake of its conflict with the PKK. The idea was a dream for any young would-be human rights lawyer like myself.

Much of this legal work was achieved within the context of a bitter counter-insurgency struggle involving the Turkish Government and the PKK. For thirty-five years the PKK had fought against the Turkish state allegedly in support of greater Kurdish cultural and political rights in a war that had killed over 40,000 people. The PKK began its armed struggle in 1982, although the party itself was formed in 1978 after its leader, Abdullah Ocalan, left Ankara as a student in 1976 to return to the Kurdish areas of south-east Turkey to recruit militant revolutionary cadres committed to the establishment of a separate state for Kurds. Ever since the creation of the Turkish Republic in 1923 Kurdish identity had been suppressed as a territorial threat to the indivisible unity of the nation state. Kemal Atatürk, the father of the nation, had carved out a homeland for Turks from the embers of the Ottoman empire in the teeth of opposition from the Great Powers in a war of liberation that followed the First World War. He was determined that the new secular modern state of Turkey would not be torn apart by either religion or unruly minorities supported by foreign powers, as the previous empire had been. The result was that all manifestations of Kurdish political and cultural identity were banned. Kurds were henceforth to be regarded as 'Mountain Turks'. To enforce this fiction Kurdish language and culture were prohibited from being taught in schools or used in public life. Over the next seventy years, numerous popular uprisings by the Kurds were brutally suppressed by the Turkish military. The Sheik Said revolt of 1926 led to 248 Kurdish leaders being beheaded and put on pikes outside the gates of Diyarbakir in a scene reminiscent of the film *Spartacus*. The Dersim Uprising of 1938 led to whole communities being uprooted and displaced to the west of Turkey. The ritual humiliation of Kurds in public life continued unabated for the next four decades, until the PKK emerged to take the fight to the Turks, particularly after the 1980 military coup, when it set up bases in northern Iraq and Syria along the border of Turkey. Within a few short years, the PKK had taken out all competing left-wing opposition forces in the region with a brutal efficiency that put fear into the heart of most Anatolian conscripts. The Turkish military hit back through its special forces by trying to 'drain the swamp' through the deployment of classic counter-terror tactics learnt in the Vietnam War. The resultant conflict led to a vicious dirty war in the south-east during the 1990s in which over three million Kurdish villagers were forcibly displaced from 3,000 villages. Hundreds of intellectuals, journalists, lawyers and politicians were detained, killed or tortured in an iron-fist effort to quell dissent.

It was within this conflict-ridden context that Kerim Yildiz and I developed the KHRP. With the help of my chambers, the Bar Human Rights Committee, and some legal academics from Essex University, the KHRP embarked upon a series of human rights test cases against Turkey. Together we brought over 400 successful cases to the European Court of Human Rights, establishing test cases in relation to most of the principal articles under the Convention. This resulted in compensation being paid for village destruction and displacement, security courts being reformed, detention times being shortened, Kurdish language restrictions being lifted, and the death penalty being abolished, as well as new norms being established in relation to fair trials, freedom of expression, association and movement.

Over the course of the next fifteen years the KHRP routinely came to the aid of numerous Kurdish and Turkish intellectuals, journalists, human rights defenders, artists and ordinary villagers whose rights had been violated. Importantly it obtained compensation for Kurdish villagers whose homes had been destroyed in all three countries, and without the need to exhaust domestic remedies. It established that rape was torture in international law. It helped develop the jurisprudence of the ECHR on investigative measures that were required to be taken by states in death-in-custody and disappearance cases. It also extended the jurisdiction of the Convention to cover the acts of state agents of member states who detained people overseas or breached human rights in effectively controlled territory outwith national boundaries, through cases such as *Ocalan* and *Issa*. Through these cases the KHRP challenged the conduct metered out towards Kurds by the Turkish, Armenian and Azerbaijan governments.

Yet none of this could have been achieved were it not for indigenous human rights defenders on the ground, who in turn desperately needed to be given both moral support and a measure of protection from state attack. In early 1992 the Turkish government and security apparatus adopted a scorched-earth policy towards its conflict with the PKK. It was intent on smashing all forms of resistance in relation to the Kurdish issue. Suddenly, human rights organisations, Bar associations, journalists and democratic politicians all found themselves coming under legal, extra-legal and physical attack. These indigenous organisations were crucial not only to the success of the KHRP's evidence collection programme, but also to the future existence of civic society in the Kurdish areas of Turkey. Without these fledgling institutions, ordinary Kurdish villagers and peasants were cut loose with little or no protection or avenues of redress against the brutal iron fist policies of the security forces. This was a recipe for disaster for both ordinary Kurds and Turks alike. State repression almost inevitably resulted in further polarisation between the warring parties, forcing those caught in the middle to choose between one side and another. The response of the West and Europe was therefore crucial. Yet, while its governments remained largely silent, European civil society heeded the call.

Over the next few years the KHRP, UK Parliamentary Human Rights Group, and other well-known human rights advocacy groups such as Article 19, Human Rights Watch and Amnesty International, conducted fact-finding missions to the region to investigate allegations of torture, extra-judicial killings and the interference with the right to freedom of association and expression. They also conducted sustained trial observations of politicians, lawyers, human rights activists, writers, politicians, who all found themselves in one way or another the subject of continued prosecution for merely speaking out against these abuses. These trial observations helped hold the judicial authorities to account and challenged the immunity of those who had perpetrated human right violations. As a result, the KHRP advised most of Turkey's key opposition leaders, both Kurdish and Turkish, including those in the AKP Party who were themselves being persecuted by the Kemalist state for their espousal of moderate Islam, such as the future president of the Turkish Republic. The Kurdish issue only began to ameliorate after the AKP took power in 2001 and began a campaign to join the European Union, which resulted in some significant reforms to Turkey's Kemalist ideology and nationalist legal structure. Notwithstanding these reforms, however, the discrimination against the Kurds in Turkey festered on, partly fuelled by Turkey's concerns about its neighbours' efforts to destabilise its power and influence in the region.

However, through its integrated litigation programme, training seminars, sustained trial observations and public awareness programmes, the KHRP helped break the pervasive culture of military and state impunity against Kurds in the Near East. It also transformed the international community's understanding of the Kurds, in what was on any view a complex region. The publication of a series of ground-breaking reports concerning freedom of expression and association, especially in relation to minority cultural identity and rights, helped educate the wider public about the plight of Kurds not just in Turkey but also in Iraq, Iran, Syria and the Former Soviet Union. The KHRP then was always more than a litigation clearing-house. It represented a beacon of light to an unrecognised people hitherto shrouded in official darkness and silence from Baghdad to Ankara. Over time, host governments in the region were forced, both legally and politically, to extend unrecognised rights to a hitherto oppressed ethnic community. More recently, the KHRP was at the forefront in efforts to assist states in the region voluntarily to comply with their human rights, European Union and international obligations. As such it made a significant contribution to reform in Turkey and its compliance with the EU accession process. Elsewhere, it increased environmental consciousness by running innovative and popular campaigns, such as the Ilisu Dam Campaign, which brought together human rights activists with environmentalists, such as the inspirational Nicholas Hildyard of the Corner House, as well as comedians, like Mark Thomas, from the broadcast sector, to save a 2,000-year-old UNESCO ear-marked village along the banks of the Tigris in south-east Turkey.

Yet despite the KHRP's hugely successful record of litigation and hard-hitting influential public awareness campaigns, by the end of the first decade of the twenty-first century it was in danger of becoming irrelevant. By 2010 Turkey and northern Iraq had changed considerably and, whereas in 1992 there were very few domestic advocates and non-governmental organisations experienced in the ways of the European Court of Human Rights and human rights campaigning, now there were literally hundreds. The development of new media, as well as the training programmes of the KHRP and institutions like the International Bar Association, BHRC, EU and Council of Europe, had borne fruit. More importantly, the old secular nationalist political elites in Turkey, with their slavish adherence to Kemalism, had lost power to an emboldened reform-minded moderate Islamic political movement, the AKP, led by the charismatic Tayyip Erdoğan. Many taboos concerning the Kurdish issue began to dissolve after Erdoğan announced in August 2006 that there was a 'Kurdish reality' in Turkey. His subsequent 2009 democratic initiative to replace the 1982 Military Constitution with a new democratic constitution finally broke the Kemalist and nationalist paradigm. All of this helped create space and fuel the Oslo peace talks that took place between the government and the PKK between 2009 and 2011.

In the summer of 2011 Kerim and I finally closed the KHRP operations after deciding there were more than enough indigenous human rights organisations operating in Turkey. I helped him replace it with the Democratic Progress Institute (DPI), a new organisation dedicated to promoting democratic dialogue within Turkey. This occurred after Kerim and I wrote a position paper about how Turkish and international civil society might help to broaden the base for dialogue and peace within Turkey. This was particularly important after the PKK and Turkish government reverted to armed conflict in July 2011 after the collapse of the Oslo peace process. During the course of 2011 DPI, with the assistance of Sir Kieran Prendergast, built a board of Turkish and international peace and dialogue experts which went on to bring together a remarkable set of Turkish parliamentarians from across the political divide to learn the lessons of peace-making elsewhere in the world. These included high-ranking members of the AKP, the deputy president of the secular opposition Republican People's Party (CHP) and members of the BDP Kurdish party. They were joined by some of Turkey's most influential opinion formers, including journalists and academics. Together they travelled to Northern Ireland, Wales and Scotland to learn lessons from the peace process in Northern Ireland and to see how constitutional change and devolution was achieved non-violently in Scotland. They met with the principal architects of the peace process and devolution, including Jonathan Powell, Gerry Adams and Peter Robinson, as well as leading Scottish MSPs. The visit produced over 4,000 positive articles which helped break many of the remaining taboos in Turkey about talking to alleged terrorists and embarking on a process of societal reconciliation.

This visit was accompanied by a series of conferences in Turkey throughout 2012 that examined reform to the constitution, the media and certain transitional justice and other security issues. All of this helped create conditions for a renewed cease-fire and peace talks between Abdullah Ocalan and the Turkish state between 2013 and 2015. Kerim would go on to take Turkish delegations to South Africa in May 2013 with the help of Tim Phillips and Roelf Meyer. South Africa had a profound effect on the thinking of different parliamentarians from widely different parties. The methodology of DPI was to let the delegation learn from the experiences of others but without expressly requiring them to apply those experiences or lessons to the Turkish context while the trip went ahead. Accompanying the parliamentarians were some of Turkey's top journalists, academics and commentators. These journalists went on to write articles about the South African experience and how it was relevant to the Turkish peace process. These articles, blogs and media interviews helped steady Turkish public opinion and create a momentum in civil society in favour of talks. Huge credit should go to Kerim Yildiz and his deputy director, Catriona Vine, for this work. DPI provided yet another perfect example of how small, innovative, bespoke civil society dialogue organisations could have a huge impact on the search for peace and democratic reform processes if given the right financial and political support.

Further important conferences were held in Mardin and Van in Turkey in June and September 2013 on how the media could support peace. DPI delegations also visited Germany and Dublin in 2014 to better understand how to deal with political transition. One AKP member of a women's delegation to Belfast in September 2013 told Erdoğan how it was one of the most transformative experiences of her life, which had encapsulated twenty years of internal thought and feelings. She had met Monica Williams, former human rights ombudsman and peace campaigner, to learn how her women's coalition had a fundamental impact on the Northern Irish peace process. Further trips to the Philippines and Colombia involving AKP policymakers occurred in 2015 and 2016. For veteran human rights campaigners, like Kerim and me, who had spent long years confronting the Turkish authorities both in court and in numerous international fora about human rights abuses, these were truly inspirational moments. The most impressive aspect was how Kerim had won the trust of a number of AKP influential policymakers close to Erdoğan even after the peace process between the Turkish state and Abdullah Ocalan fell apart in the summer of 2015. Today DPI stands ready to assist both sides to come back to the negotiating table, despite the dramatic decline in relations between Turks and Kurds as a result of the civil war in Syria and the rise of Kurdish influence along the border.

The work of the KHRP and DPI provides a good illustration of what can be achieved when peoples from different cultures, from East and West, come together to protect universal values, and share the load of that struggle over a sustained period of time. But it is not the legal submissions or the eloquent judgments handed down by the great and the good in the courtrooms of Strasbourg that I remember now. No, what is burnt onto my memory is hearing the news that our first applicant was shot dead by the authorities; witnessing my Kurdish driver being forced to kneel down as an automatic rifle was placed in his mouth by soldiers in search of information at a desolate checkpoint; seeing a military colonel drive over a small Kurdish boy without so much as a look back; meeting twelve-year-old paper boys who had their arms cut off for selling opposition papers; and recalling the utter fear of our legal colleagues in Diyarbakir in 1994, who refused to even look at me as they were dragged into the dock of the Turkish State Security Courts, after enduring days of gruesome detention for merely filing human rights claims to the European Court.

These are the images that I retain in my mind's eye. They have a photographic quality about them. But there are other less haunting images. I cannot forget the simple but gracious hospitality of Kurdish villagers I came across soon after their isolated and poverty-stricken homes had been burnt by the Turkish military in the summer of 1994. They had just lost some of their young menfolk, who were run over by a passing tank, and were awaiting others who had fled to hide in the fields. Yet as dusk fell and their loved ones returned, it was we, not they, who were fed with what meagre rations they had left. 'Tell the world what is happening here,' they said. 'It is a miracle you have come,' said another.

These types of first-hand experiences change one's perspective about law, conflict and the protection of human rights. They bind you to a region and people in ways that are scarcely imaginable at the outset. I can still recall the time I met young dissident journalists from the newspaper *Ozgur Gundem* in the back streets of Sultanahmet in old Istanbul, in November 1994, for a late-night meal, after they had got the morning edition out. We had just missed the bombing of *Ozgur Gundem*'s building by some thirty minutes. *Ozgur Gundem* was a Kurdish nationalist newspaper, whose prosecution I was observing. At least twenty-two journalists had gone missing over the previous two years. Some of their bullet-ridden bodies were later found on lonely roadsides in the south-east of Turkey. All my present companions chain-smoked and looked nervously at the door as they ate, conscious that the knock on the door and the midnight run to the security cell could happen at any time. But what I also recall was the laughter, the stolen glances of tenderness between them. There was a collective recognition that they should live in the moment, as any of their number may not be dining with them the next night. In a strange and very real sense, they all seemed so totally alive. They were caught up in a history of their own making. They felt proud to be involved in the fight to convey their version of the truth which, in a normal, pluralist society, would have been permitted.

It was this type of solidarity and commitment that I later experienced in Benghazi, but it was in Turkey during the 1990s where I realised that there was more to human rights campaigning than collecting evidence, drafting, report writing and court advocacy. In the end it was about establishing a sense of human solidarity and shared experience with those experiencing oppression and fighting injustice – a solidarity in which each other's cultures and identities are experienced, tasted and assimilated into one's own existence. None of this work could have been achieved were it not for the active participation of a host of patrons and advisors, who gave us cover in the early days of the KHRP's work. People like Lord Avebury, Harold Pinter, Arthur Miller, Helena Bonner, Madame Mitterand, Gareth Peirce, Helena Kennedy QC, Michael Mansfield QC and many more, as well as young lawyers like Tim Otty, Michael Ivers, Edward Grieves, Ajanta Kaza, Raj Rai, Michelle Butler, Sudhanshu Swaroop, Ben Emmerson and Kirsty Brimelowe, many of whom would go on to take silk.

In his autobiography entitled *Memoirs of a Radical Lawyer* (London: Bloomsbury, 2009), in a chapter called 'Yes We Can', Michael Mansfield cites the work of the KHRP as a shining example of what can be achieved when civil rights people make an enduring commitment. He describes how the BHRC held a lecture for the KHRP, with Harold Pinter and Noam Chomsky at St Paul's Cathedral, where both he and I spoke. Over 3,000 people came to hear about the KHRP and Chomsky's work with the Kurds. A further 500 people listened intently outside the cathedral. It was this sort of integrated legal, political and moral solidarity amongst civil societies from different continents that was lost during the 'war on terror' years. It is precisely this type of solidarity and enduring commitment that is arguably needed now, if like-minded people in the MENA region are to win their struggle to transform their societies and provide a better future for everyone.

18.   Terrorism, Democracy and the Right to Resist Oppression

The trip to Benghazi also made me reflect on how Cameron's support of rebels in Libya (and his advocacy of democratic regime change more generally) impacted on the security and counter-terror paradigm put in place by the Bush and Blair administrations. The Libyan rebel fighters I encountered near Ajdabiya were both secular and religious in nature. They were prepared to come together to use force to rid Libya from the yoke of Gaddafi no matter how the UK government labelled them. The UK's intervention raised interesting questions about how counter-terror strategies interacted with the evolving right to democratic governance in international law and the internationally recognised right to self-determination. Cameron's political recognition of these rebel movements certainly had consequences for how UK authorities applied the definition of terrorism under the Terrorism Act 2000 to movements that sought to resist state oppression and effect political change through armed struggle. Up until a few weeks earlier, the UK authorities would have had no difficulty in labelling these Libyan rebel fighters 'terrorists' for their use of violence towards a political end. The fact that they were fighting against an oppressive regime in support of democratic reform and greater freedom would have been irrelevant.

That this would have been their likely stance is made clear by the 2007 English Court of Appeal case of R v F.[1] In that case, the celebrated human rights lawyer Geoffrey Robertson QC sought to test the definition of terrorism under the Terrorism Act 2000. Section 1(1) of that Act defines terrorism as the use or threat of action falling within s1(2), which is designed to influence the government or to intimidate the public or a section of the public for the purpose of advancing a political, religious or ideological cause. Robertson tried to convince the court that the definition of 'government' in s1 must relate in some measure to 'democratic' government, or at least to a government that had some representative legitimacy. Up until then the UK Labour government had used the wide discretion afforded to it under the Terrorism Act to ban a whole host of rebel movements. The Crown rejected the submission in its entirety. The Court of Appeal later held that the Terrorism Act 2000 provides no legal cover to those who took up arms for political ends even against oppressive tyrannical regimes. The word 'government' in s1(1)(b), as explained in s1(4)(d) in relation to foreign governments, is not limited to those countries which were governed by what might broadly be described as democratic or representative principles but included a dictatorship, or a military junta or a usurping or invading power.

It follows that the range of foreign organisations capable of falling within the definition of terrorism under the Terrorism Act 2000 is extremely wide. In theory it encompasses almost all individuals or organisations engaged in armed conflict around the world, whatever the circumstances. It is certainly wide enough to include organisations which have received the political support of the United Kingdom in the past, such as the Northern Alliance in Afghanistan or the Kurdish Peshmerga in northern Iraq. It also potentially includes organisations otherwise engaged in lawful armed conflict[2] in the exercise of the internationally recognised right to self-determination of peoples. The rejection of Robertson's submission had and continues to have important consequences for all groups who took up arms to resist oppression or effect democratic regime change. Cameron's recognition of the right of Libyan rebels to rebel by using force, however, opens up a whole new can of legal worms. It is now difficult to see how the authorities can legitimately differentiate Libya's ragtag bunch of revolutionary militias from groups that the Blair and Bush administrations proscribed or labelled terrorist in nature. All of this not only impacts upon the credibility of the UK's counter-terror strategies going forward, it also has important consequences for the search for peace in the MENA region more generally.

The Right to Self-Determination

Yet even before the Arab Spring occurred, many liberal commentators criticised the UK's attitude towards peoples and groups seeking to exercise the right to self-determination. They pointed out that international law recognised that liberation movements representing peoples and organised racial groups have the right, in certain circumstances, to engage in armed conflict in order to realise their right to self-determination. Articles 1 of the International Covenant on Civil and Political Rights and the International Covenant on Economic, Social and Cultural Rights both state: '[A]ll peoples have the right to self-determination. By virtue of that right they freely determine their political status and freely pursue their economic, social and cultural development [. . .]'

By the 1990s it was generally accepted that such a right pertained in three distinct situations, namely: where they were under colonial domination; where they were subject to alien military occupation; and where they were a distinct racial group denied equal access to government (so-called 'racist regimes'). It was also accepted that states were bound to refrain from offering material support to states engaged in the suppression of the exercise of this right by military or other coercive means. Such developments were reflected in two key UN resolutions: the 1970 UN General Assembly Declaration on Principles of International Law concerning Friendly Relations and Co-operation among States in accordance with the Charter of the United Nations (Resolution 2625); and the 1974 UN General Assembly Definition of Aggression (Resolution 3314), as well as in the UN International Law Commission's Draft Articles on Responsibility of States for Internationally Wrongful Acts.[3]

In fact, international (if not domestic) practice regarding the right to self-determination had developed to such an extent, that by 2001 Professor Antonio Cassese, the former president of the International Criminal Tribunal for the Former Yugoslavia, was able to summarise the position of international law in relation to the right of self-determination and the use of violence in the following terms:

The importance of these normative developments should not be underestimated: the international community has gone so far in its protection of self-determination as to prohibit not only the use of military force by the oppressive state, but also what could be termed 'institutionalised violence', namely all those measures, mechanisms, and devices destined to prevent peoples or racial groups from exercising their right to self-determination [. . .]

The UN Charter neither authorises nor bans the use of force by dependent peoples (or rather, by liberation movements representative of those peoples) for the realisation of external self-determination [. . .] Although no legal right proper was thus bestowed on liberation movements to resort to force, gradually the view emerged among states that nevertheless resort to force by these movements was not in violation of the general ban on force that had meanwhile emerged in the world community [. . .] However, the attitude of the world community was qualified by a basic condition: that resort to force by liberation movements should only be effected as a response to the forcible denial of self-determination by the oppressive Power, that is by the refusal of the latter State, backed up by armed force, or even coercive measures short of military violence, to grant self-determination to colonial peoples (or to peoples subjected to foreign military occupation or to organised racial groups denied equal access to government). Furthermore, the world community did not go to the lengths of conferring a legal right proper on liberation movements, but only granted a licence to use force [. . .]

On the other hand, third states must refrain from assisting a state that forcibly opposes self-determination. Any substantial help to the oppressive state, be it military or economic in nature, is regarded as illegal under current international law.'[4]

It follows that the rules of international law: forbid a state in such circum-stances from taking military or other coercive action to suppress the lawful exercise of the right to self-determination; recognise that peoples exercising the right to self-determination have, in the last resort, a licence to engage in armed conflict to protect themselves, and to prevent the violent suppression of the exercise of the right to self-determination by the oppressor state; and forbid third states from affording support to oppressive states so as to assist them in suppressing the exercise of the right to self-determination. Yet despite these important normative developments, Western states, like the UK, remain disinclined to encourage any further application of the principle of self-determination.

Self-Determination and Terrorism

This disinclination is due to the international community's longstanding ambivalence towards the principle of self-determination, which essentially arises out of its uneasy relationship to concepts of resistance and terrorism more generally. It is why the Ad Hoc Committee on International Terrorism, established by the UN General Assembly, and which met from 1972 to 1979, singularly failed to reach any consensus on a mutually acceptable definition of the term 'terrorism'. According to Kalliopi K. Koufa, the former UN Special Rapporteur on Terrorism and Human Rights, 109 definitions were put forward between 1936 and 1981, none of which was accepted.[5] On the one hand, formerly colonised states were adamant that the legitimate actions of national liberation movements should not be confused with terrorism. On the other, Western states were deeply suspicious of extending the principle to situations unrelated to the decolonisation process.[6] Quite simply, the right of self-determination – with its suggestion that peoples of a territory can determine by a free and genuine vote the political status of their homeland either through independence, autonomy or integration with another state – presented too much of a threat to the West and their client states, including those that made up the post First World War division of the MENA region.

Why is all of this important? Because underlying many of the conflicts that continue to plague the world today remains the failure of the international community to come to a consensus about what constitutes terrorism and how it relates to the right of self-determination or the evolving right to democratic governance. As Helena Kennedy QC, the former chair of the British Council, perceptively notes, '[U]ntil there is an internationally recognised and sufficiently restrictive definition, it will be hard to have confidence that struggles for self-determination and other political activities will not be wrapped up in accusations of "terrorism".' Kennedy is surely right when she warns of the danger of 'the passing of anti-terrorist legislation against the backdrop of principle'.

The United Nations Human Rights Committee has repeatedly expressed concern about the legislative measures taken by some countries, and has urged states to ensure that measures undertaken pursuant to Security Council Resolution 1373 comply with the UN International Covenant on Civil and Political Rights. Both the UN General Assembly and the UN Commission on Human Rights describe terrorism as being essentially aimed at the destruction of democracy or the destabilising of 'legitimately constituted Governments' and 'pluralistic civil society'; other international resolutions state that terrorism 'poses a severe challenge to democracy, civil society and the rule of law'. The 2002 EU Framework Decision, the 2002 Inter-American Convention, and the Draft Comprehensive Convention are all based on the premise that terrorism jeopardises democracy, and the EU Note that accompanied the draft of the European Framework decision, circulated after 11 September 2001, states that the definition of terrorism did not include 'those who have acted in the interests of preserving or restoring democratic values'.

However, little attempt has been made to expressly embed such democratic principles in counter-terror legislative frameworks. Thus, while the jurisprudence of the European Court of Human Rights consistently upheld the principles of democracy and pluralism as constituting the cornerstone of the Convention, few, if any, member states sought to legally entrench any of the ideas about democratic rights that had begun to be taken seriously by the international community following the end of the Cold War. All of this is important because there is a growing recognition within the international community that mediation should play the primary role in the resolution of conflict, particularly after the failure of military interventions in Iraq, Afghanistan and Libya to produce any long-term peace or stability in those countries. Special Envoy Cowper-Coles's earlier observations on this point remain telling. The failure to properly recognise international rights, including the licence to use force as a last resort, merely encourages the adoption of more violent strategies.

Certainly many peoples and movements pursuing claims of self-determination, such as the Kurds and the Tamils, regularly complain about being unfairly disenfranchised by an unresponsive international community. Many of these conflicts might have been prevented or at least ameliorated had other political and legal avenues of redress been made available to these communities. As my colleague Raji Sourani, head of the Palestinian Human Rights Centre in Gaza, remarked to me: 'The right to self-determination is not a gift but a right of a free people. People should recall that Al-Qaeda does not exist in Palestine. I'm proud of how my people restrain themselves despite the never-ending poverty, bombings and sieges. But no one should expect Palestinians to be good victims.'

The Effect of 9/11 on the Definition of Terrorism

The refusal of the Blair administration to recognise any use of violence for political ends by non-state entities received a massive boost following 9/11, when President George W. Bush warned the United Nations 'either you are with us, or you are with the terrorists. From this day forward, any nation that continues to harbour or support terrorism will be regarded by the United States as a hostile regime.' This declaration went on to frame many state policies towards 'terrorism' and those movements which sought to use armed struggle to effect political change. Seven days after 9/11, on 28 September 2001, Security Council Resolution 1373 imposed extensive obligations on states to prevent terrorism, including its financing. Up until then, not much turned on the definition of terrorism, as few states had taken it upon themselves to define it domestically. The lack of any internationally agreed definition of terrorism meant that it was legally inconsequential, since no international rights or duties hinged on the general term 'terrorism'. Instead the failure of the international community to agree an international definition led to the development of eleven 'act' specific international conventions concerning terrorism since 1963.

President Bush's clarion call to combat terrorism domestically changed all of that and had an immediate impact on state practice towards countering terrorism. This was because Resolution 1373 effectively outsourced the definition of terrorism from the international community to member states, as it required member states to define terrorism and then decide which dissident groups and armed struggles were legitimate and which were not. A legislative frenzy ensued. Within two months, the Bush administration had rushed through the USA Patriot Act, while the UK enacted the Crime and Security Act 2001. On 13 June 2002 the EU adopted its own Framework Decision that required member states to take legislative steps to implement its terms. Australia, Belarus, China, Egypt, India, Israel, Jordan, Kyrgyzstan,

Macedonia, Malaysia, Russia, Syria, Uzbekistan and Zimbabwe all quickly followed suit. Much of the legislation enacted reinforced the sovereignty and supremacy of the state at the expense of rights to self-determination and the evolving right to democracy. Few states recognised any right or licence to resort to armed resistance even for those peoples struggling against vicious and oppressive regimes. Instead, states elected to define terrorism in its broadest sense, so as to give themselves the widest possible discretion to proscribe any group involved in armed struggle, just as the UK authorities had done a couple of years earlier.

Unsurprisingly, many of these states used newly enacted domestic powers to proscribe groups that were an anathema to the United States and themselves. There was a demonstrable international effort not to give succour to any liberation or resistance movement that advocated or used force to further a right to self-determination or resist an oppressive state. Henceforth the use of force for political ends was to be the exclusive preserve of states. Non-state movements who sought to invoke such principles to justify use of force found themselves criminalised through proscription. These provisions were used to delegitimise not only groups, but also their struggles. It was within this context that Blair's government proscribed many of the radical groups referred to earlier. This after friendly regimes, like Libya, invoked the Terrorism Act 2000 to demand that Britain take action against exiled dissidents in exchange for co-operation in the war on terror.

The PMOI

Some movements were proscribed even though their physical presence in the UK was negligible and did not constitute a direct threat to the UK national interest. Such proscriptions occurred as much because of foreign policy considerations as of any strict application of the law. Whether a group found itself on or off a list often had more to do with diplomatic relations between states than with strict threats to domestic national security. Bush's demand for member states to co-operate in countering terrorism had the effect of entwining a whole set of wider foreign, military and strategic objectives that governed relations between states. The temptation to offset any strict application of the law in favour of achieving other desirable foreign policy goals was huge. As a result, little consideration was given to the type of armed struggle in which these groups were actually engaged.

Take, for example, the UK authorities' proscription of the People's Mujahedin of Iran (PMOI), an Iranian resistance movement dedicated to the overthrow of the regime in Tehran. In refusing an application to de-proscribe the PMOI in 2006, Jack Straw, the then UK Home Secretary, stated that he had: 'taken full account of the [. . .] assertion that *Mujahedin e Khalq* is involved in a legitimate struggle against a repressive regime and has no choice but to resort to armed resistance. He notes too the claim that armed resistance is concentrated against military and security targets within Iran only. The Home Secretary does not, accept, however, *any* right to resort to acts of terrorism, whatever the motivation'.[7] The reference to acts of terrorism means any use of force. In Straw's view it is simply impermissible for any non-state movement to deploy force against a state in any circumstances, including those provided for under international law. One might have reminded the then Home Secretary of the preamble to the Universal Declaration of Human Rights (1948) (and its recognition of the rebellion as a last resort), which reads: 'It is essential, if man is not to be compelled to have recourse, as a last resort, to rebellion against tyranny and oppression, that human rights should be protected by the rule of law.' And it did not matter much that the former Prime Minister, Tony Blair, admitted on 8 February 2005 that Iran 'certainly does sponsor terrorism' and was a deeply repressive regime.

What is striking about this case is the desire to proscribe an organisation that did not have as its target any UK interests, and which, in the words of Mr Blair, was fighting a repressive state that sponsored terrorism. The important point is not whether it was legally possible to proscribe it, but the apparent determination of the government to impose a total prohibition on the use of violence whatever the circumstances. The discretion afforded to the Home Secretary under the Act is plainly broad enough for him or her to have had regard for the principles of international law, including the right to self-determination and the evolving right to democracy, when deciding whether to proscribe an organisation that technically fell within the statutory criteria. Yet Jack Straw chose not to, even in relation to a regime that allegedly threatened Western interests. Why? The answer is that the Blair and Brown administrations used proscription as a naked political, ideological and foreign policy tool rather than as a nuanced counter-terror measure.

All of this led a group of prominent UK Members of Parliament to challenge in the courts the decision of the Home Secretary. By the time the application was filed the PMOI had given up its armed struggle for five years, voluntarily disarmed its cadres in Iraq, and publicly pledged itself to overthrow the regime in Tehran through peaceful non-violent means. Certain official papers suggested that the PMOI was proscribed by the Clinton administration and the European Union as a 'good will gesture' toward Iran and its newly elected and moderate President Mohammad Khatami. On 30 November 2007 the Proscribed Organisation Appeals Commission (POAC) gave judgment, and declared the PMOI's continued proscription 'unlawful', characterising the position of the Home Secretary as legally 'perverse'.[8] It held, as a fact, after evaluating open and closed evidence, that the PMOI had abandoned the use of political violence, unilaterally disarmed its cadres in Iraq, and effectively dismantled any current capacity elsewhere to carrying out terrorist acts. Yet the Home Secretary maintained that it was still 'concerned in terrorism' because he could not rule out a contingent intention of its leaders to return to terrorism in the future if it suited them. In April 2008, the Court of Appeal finally upheld the POAC ruling, holding that the Home Secretary had indeed acted perversely, and stating that such a contingent intention was far too remote. What was needed was to evidentially demonstrate that the PMOI was currently engaged in terrorism and/or continued to maintain its organisation for that specific intended purpose. There was no evidence to this effect.[9]

This case, in which I acted, illustrates the hard-nosed ideological position that the Blair and Brown administrations took towards proscription and the use of force for political ends by non-state actors. The terms of Cameron's intervention in Libya seemingly drove a coach and horses through this carefully constructed counter-terrorism paradigm. How, for example, could he champion the right of rebels to use force to institute democratic regime change against Gaddafi in Libya but not in Tehran, while at the same time proscribing groups who used force as a last resort to defend their right to self-determination against an oppressive racist regime? It was difficult to see how UK authorities could continue to maintain a policy of rejecting the use of violence for political ends by all rebel movements with any consistency in the future.

Proscription and the Seach for Peace

To my mind the outsourcing of the definition of terrorism from the United Nations to member states was and remains a dangerous development. Too many states have a vested interest in downplaying the right to self-determination and any evolving right to democratic governance. Many governments used the opportunity presented by the upsurge in terrorism post 9/11 to proscribe groups for purely political reasons. While the tactics deployed by the Bush and Blair administrations might have been necessary in terms of realpolitik, there should be no illusion about how the infusion of politics into law affected the integrity of many proscription regimes and actively hindered the ability of the international community to resolve conflicts through peaceful means. The contamination of legal principle with politics in this way is deeply disturbing.

The hackneyed dictum 'one man's terrorist is another man's freedom fighter' has effectively been replaced with 'one state's terrorist is another state's freedom fighter'. Whether a person or group is considered a terrorist is no longer a matter of political opinion but of national law according to the state in which one finds oneself. Rosalyn Higgins's pre 9/11 observation that terrorism is 'a term without any legal significance' but 'merely a convenient way of alluding to activities which States or individuals widely disapproved of', is no longer strictly accurate. National law has given the term 'terrorism' real legal significance.

Yet it is instructive to note that under the Terrorism Act 2000 the Secretary of State is not required to proscribe an organisation simply because it meets the statutory test. The definition of terrorism in s1 is intentionally over-broad so as to delegate to him or her the judgment as to which organisations should and should not be proscribed. That judgment is a political one, but one guided also by principle, fairness and a proper examination of the surrounding context. Labour Home Secretaries used this almost unfettered discretion to proscribe or refuse to de-proscribe *any* group that used force in support of democratic struggle anywhere in the world. Yet such a policy artificially ossifies the global legal and political order and provides government and the courts with little room to manoeuvre when radical political change happens, as was the case regarding the Arab Spring. Whether such an un-nuanced approach towards proscription is sustainable in the light of the UK's support of rebel movements effecting democratic regime change in places like Libya and Syria needs to be examined.

The continuing refusal of UK authorities to have any domestic regard to rights enshrined in international law undermines the efficacy of its counter-terror strategies, particularly in the minds of many ordinary people who are obliged to live under unrepresentative regimes and regard such proscription regimes as having double standards. Far from crushing terrorism, President Bush's ultimatum simply limited the political space through which these peoples and movements could steer a middle course. All of this has political consequences for the UK's future relationship with the people of the MENA region, and for our security more generally. This is because most sources of violence around the world occur where there is no democratic outlet or protection for indigenous peoples, ethnic and religious minorities, and the like. Take for example what happened to the Sri Lankan Tamils in 2009 when the Sri Lankan government corralled both retreating Tamil Tigers and thousands of civilians into a killing zone. Is it surprising that such communities turn to violence to defend themselves, when rights ostensibly granted to them under international law are trampled upon with seeming impunity? The failure to recognise international rights too often creates a political and human rights lacuna in which stateless peoples, persecuted minorities and societies living under authoritarian regimes are dangerously cut adrift from the international legal system.

The Role of the UK and European Union in Peace-making

UK policymakers should therefore reflect upon how proscription regimes can hinder the UK's capacity to mediate conflict. The UK underestimates the crucial role it can play in such mediation, particularly given its experience of peace-making in Northern Ireland, as well as initiating democratic reform and devolution in Scotland and Wales. Many secular broad-based opposition and liberation groups I have dealt with, including some in Libya, have expressed a real interest in the UK's asymmetrical constitutional arrangements. Furthermore, the UK has built up a unique range of advisors, diplomats, retired statesmen and private sector mediators, who have helped resolve some of the most intractable conflicts in the world. Regional organisations, states and private mediators should be able to utilise and draw upon these vital resources without the fear of being criminalised by a proscription regime that is neither nuanced nor proportionate in its application. In short it is important for the UK's proscription regime not to have a 'chilling effect' on the work of mediators who wish to capitalise on the UK experience.

The European Union should also think carefully about how it deploys its proscription regime, now that it has decided to enhance its mediation capacity and foreign policy role under the Lisbon Treaty. Some argue that its supranational status and ability to transcend individual state interests puts it in a unique position to take advantage of the growth in mediation. An enhanced EU mediation capacity might strengthen its foreign policy capacity. If the EU does choose to go down this path, however, it too will have to take a second look at the operation of its own proscription regime.

EU policymakers should ask themselves these crucial questions. Firstly, how successful have proscription regimes been in actually combating terrorism rather than just delegitimising certain struggles? Secondly, do current proscription regimes help or hinder the work of mediators in their work to resolve conflict and build peace? Thirdly, if they hinder, how can these regimes be improved so as create incentives to armed groups to give up violence once and for all?

I believe the picture is mixed. It is notable that a decade and a half on from the declaration of the war on terror, virtually all armed groups and terror organisations are still in business. That is with the single exception of the Tamil Tigers, who were wiped out in a brutal assault by the Sinhalese-dominated Sri Lankan government in 2009, which allegedly breached norms of humanitarian law. In practically all other circumstances involving proscribed groups, violence continues unabated to this day, save for the Basque conflict, after the Centre for Humanitarian Dialogue convinced the Basque separatist group ETA to give up its armed struggle in 2012. Yet even here proscription continued to hamper ETA's ability to voluntarily disarm and demobilise, or institute a process of reconciliation with the government and victims of the conflict.

In 2013 I appeared before the Grand Chamber of the European Court in the case of Del Rio Prada v Spain, on behalf of an ETA detainee convicted of multiple murders, who had her prison term extended after a parole rule limiting prison sentences to thirty years was redefined unlawfully by the Spanish Supreme Court, in an attempt to stop ETA members convicted in the 1990s from being released. She won the case on a rule of law point, but what was interesting was how the government sought to use the law to deal with this issue, when it could have obtained a better deal under a mediated peace process, which could have provided for the gradual release of ETA prisoners into the community. Over 200,000 people crammed onto the streets of Madrid to protest against the European Court judgment, while a further 80,000 celebrated on the streets of San Sebastian. In the event the judiciary ordered the release of seventy-five ETA prisoners, despite coming under huge pressure from the Spanish government. One could only wonder what might have happened had Spain been a little more flexible with its attitude towards proscription, so as to enable ETA to give up armed struggle in a more structured and definitive manner.

That is not to deny that proscription is a useful tool in disrupting terrorist networks, delegitimising certain types of violent struggles, or building security co-operation between different states and regional organisations. As a lawyer, I have witnessed first-hand how proscription has disrupted the activities of some radical groups by placing curbs on their ability to fundraise, associate and advocate violence, or travel freely across borders. Yet, when not deployed judiciously, proscription, and other un-nuanced counter-terror legal strategies, can have the opposite effect, as in the case of Spain. Some proscription orders can in fact boost the profile of organisations, which often use these as a badge of honour. In Somalia, Al Shabab enhanced its power and prestige as a result of being proscribed. Other groups, such as the PMOI, expertly use proscription to build new coalitions of political support for their cause, despite concerns about their own human rights record. Proscription can send out powerful behavioural messages to give up violence, but when deployed too widely or arbitrarily, it can also spread dissent within communities, and act as a disincentive, particularly when groups become convinced it is impossible to be delisted.

The importance of having, clear, transparent, rational and proportionate criteria concerning proscription and deproscription procedures cannot be overestimated. This was nowhere better illustrated than in the 2004 proscription order made by the EU European Council against the PKK, which had fought a thirty-year war with Turkey over its failure to recognise

Kurdish identity and rights. In April 2004 the PKK found itself proscribed by the EU despite having observed a six-year cease-fire during which virtually no acts of violence occurred. Interestingly, the Council failed to proscribe the PKK in its first proscription list of November 2001, issued just after 9/11, despite conducting a comprehensive review of all organisations potentially caught by EU terror provisions. Six months later, in April 2002, it proscribed the PKK, but only after the latter had voluntarily dissolved itself and created a successor organisation, the Kurdistan Freedom and Democracy Congress (KADEK), whose alleged purpose was to foster a democratic settlement to the Kurdish Question. Quite remarkably, however, the Council elected not to proscribe the successor organisation, despite expressly regarding KADEK as an alias of the PKK. When the Council did finally proscribe both the PKK and its successor organisation in 2004 it provided no reason for doing so. It is extremely hard to understand the legal logic involved in this.

I was instructed to help overturn the order, and in March 2008 the European Court of Justice annulled both the original and 2004 proscriptions of the PKK[10] for breach of procedural rights and a failure to state reasons.[11] It should not have taken four years of highly contested litigation for the European Council to concede that it should provide reasons to justify a proscription. The Council never did explain why, even if the PKK technically came within EU terror provisions, it was necessary to ban it when it had ostensibly given up armed conflict and was in search of a non-violent solution. By 2004 the PKK had honoured a cease-fire for six years, a state of affairs that had substantially assisted the EU accession and reform process within Turkey. Many suspected that the proscription had more to do with the need to politically appease Turkey than to do with the strict application of law. The PKK returned to violence after its allied organisations were proscribed by the European Union and its offer to solve the conflict non-violently through talks was once again rejected by Turkey.

Whether the EU proscription regime helped or hindered the international fight against terrorism remains a matter of real debate. What is clear is that the lack of respect for procedural and substantive rights hardly strengthened the rule of law or the perception that such procedures were being applied impartially or fairly. As counsel in this case, I saw how the lack of legal transparency impacted on the Kurdish Nationalist Movement. The failure to apply any clear-cut criteria reinforced perceptions within the Kurdish community that EU proscription decisions were politically motivated and instituted without regard to principles of natural justice. This helped fuel the PKK's eventual return to violence, as all avenues for dialogue were gradually closed off. The question was not so much whether the PKK was capable of coming within the legal definition of a proscribed organisation, particularly after 2004, but whether in the relevant circumstances it was prudent to proscribe it given the circumstances pertaining at that time.

Material Support and the Search for Peace

UK and EU policymakers should therefore recognise that proscription can sometimes inhibit the search for peace, albeit unintentionally. Certainly the continuing proscription of the Tamil Tigers by the UK and US, after the Sri Lankan government deproscribed the organisation domestically in 2001 to kick-start a cease-fire and a Norwegian-sponsored peace process, did not assist that process. Tamil Tiger peace negotiators were unable to attend donor conferences in the US and Japan or receive funds directly for the purposes of peace-making. This was because proscription acts as a pre-condition to the operation of a range of criminal offences that fundamentally restricts the rights to freedom of expression, association and movement of such organisations. Sections 11–18 of the Terrorism Act 2000 restrict the ability of other individuals or groups to organise any meeting or provide any resources to a proscribed organisation, if it supported that organisation or its activities. These sections can have draconian effects. In one case before the English courts in which I acted in 2009, such restrictions were said to extend even to the giving of humanitarian aid to any humanitarian entity operating in the Tamil Tiger designated area under the cease-fire agreement, even though such funds were going to victims of the 2005 tsunami.

A recent US Supreme Court case ruled that 'material support' to a proscribed organisation under the Patriot Act includes the giving of advice as to how to give up violence and adopt non-violent strategies in order to resolve conflict. I was told how veteran diplomat Tom Pickering was forced to pull out of a dialogue event in Egypt in which Hamas officials were present, because of the ruling. Yet what constitutes 'support' or 'activities' remains a grey and difficult area. A meeting with a proscribed organisation does not contravene the Terrorism Act 2000, if it is a benign meeting. But what constitutes a benign meeting is the subject of considerable uncertainty. All of this can have that 'chilling effect' on the ability of civil society and non-state actors and mediators to engage with proscribed groups or their supporters. It is no coincidence that Norway felt impelled to declare that it was not bound by the EU proscription list. Had it not done so, it would have been unable to support a range of dialogue initiatives involving different radical groups from around the globe.

Policymakers should recognise that the current legislative framework and practice can sometimes bode ill for conflict resolution efforts. While humanitarian organisations should be obliged to ensure that their activities do not contravene criminal and charity laws, there is an urgent need to give greater legal cover to humanitarian and mediation bodies, whether through the tightening of legal definitions concerning what constitutes 'material support' or by providing a humanitarian defence in law to the charge of providing material support to a terrorist organisation. UK and EU policy-makers should give specific consideration to the granting of exemptions or immunity certificates to mediators and humanitarians who engage with proscribed organisations for peace-making or humanitarian reasons. Again this would provide groups with a tangible incentive to work with, rather than against, the current system, including those radical groups in Libya who took control of Tripoli and other areas after Gaddafi fell.

Reforming Delisting Procedures

It is a serious concern that in 2017 there remains a lack of transparent, published delisting criteria in relation to both the UK and EU proscription regimes. Under the EU regime it requires only one competent authority from a single member state to put an organisation on the list, but the agreement of all twenty-eight member states to get it off. The lack of transparent criteria reduces the chances of establishing unanimity. The failure to publish guidance regarding delisting reinforces the perception among many proscribed groups and their supporters that there is no way back once proscription has occurred. All of this acts as a disincentive to groups to give up violence. If proscription is to be used as a nuanced counter-terrorism tool, capable of helping mediators wean armed groups off violence, then both UK and EU policymakers need to review criteria governing the proper exercise of the discretion to delist.

Greater weight should be given to the potential benefits of non-military engagement, and the provision of explicit incentives to proscribed organisations to give up violence. This might include setting out a calibrated set of delisting conditions and staging posts, which broadly indicate what needs to be done. These criteria might include Mitchell-like non-violent principles (these were principles that US Senator Mitchell laid down in the Northern Ireland peace process), such as the voluntary assumption of humanitarian obligations; acts of disarmament; the decommissioning of terror capacity; the creation of non-violent democratic political wings, and so on. It is precisely this type of approach that should have been applied to the militias in Libya in the post-conflict environment.

Another reason why reform to current proscription regimes and the 'material support' provisions is so desperately needed is because of the increasing role now played by non-state mediators and human rights actors in the resolution of conflict and international political issues. The UK government should recognise the pivotal role that civil society is increasingly playing in helping to reduce international conflict and in weaning groups off violence.

Finally, officials must examine the type of proscription orders that ministers should be able to make. For example, listing might be time-limited or capable of partial suspension. And perhaps some consideration should be given as to whether a greater distinction should be made between broad-based liberation movements whose political demands, although unacceptable, are rationally couched and susceptible to negotiations, and jihadist terrorist movements, whose demands are not. A more nuanced approach to proscription will be required if the UK begins to differentiate, as Cameron did, between political groups in the MENA region who use violence for different political ends.

Likewise, some consideration should be given to whether a political or legal distinction should be made between the use of indiscriminate violence as a political weapon, as in the case of Al-Qaeda, and the use of targeted violence or deployment of armed struggle by a rebel movement, when used as a defensive measure against an oppressive regime intent on crushing the right to self-determination or the democratic will of the people. While it is extremely unlikely that either the UK or the United Nations will take up such a debate any time soon, it is important to note that the current inconsistent counter-terror paradigm is unlikely to lead to a reduction in conflict or provide incentives to groups involved in armed struggle to mitigate their use of violence. At the very least, policymakers should review their policy towards those seeking to exercise the right of self-determination against a fascist or racist regime that forcibly denies them such a right. This should be done not only out of respect for international law, but also for solid conflict resolution reasons.

In conclusion, proscription regimes in the UK and EU have too often been used for political purposes, without proper regard to the rule of law or their potential effect in fostering conflict further afield. UK and EU policymakers must understand the complexity of Islam and its various political offshoots, and make careful distinctions between the nature and purposes of Islamic organisations in the MENA region. On a wider level, proscription regimes should incentivise armed groups, whether Islamic or otherwise, to adopt non-violent means to pursue their political objectives. They also need to provide mediators and appropriate civil society actors with enough legal cover for them to be able to enter into dialogue and peace talks with rebel groups without the fear of criminalisation.

19.   The Rise of Non-State Mediation

There can be little doubt that the legal architecture of the war on terror had profound effects on state efforts to mediate conflicts involving liberation and terrorist movements during the first decade of the twenty-first century. The pursuance of security-orientated approaches by the Bush administration, together with the growing need to protect diplomats from terrorist attack, curtailed the inclination of major Western states to undertake mediation work. Apart, that is, from countries like Norway and Switzerland, which continued their quiet peace-making work. This meant that few, if any, UK diplomats developed direct contact with groups like Hamas, Hezbollah, the Muslim Brotherhood, the PKK, or their supporters, even though the influence of these groups continued to grow during this period. Even fewer acquired in-depth knowledge of the security and foreign policy positions of these movements in relation to a range of important issues. Most diplomats stationed in places like Tripoli dealt primarily with other state officials, high-ranking business people or international institutions dominated by state-driven diplomacy. As such they worked with foreign ministries, international multilateral agencies like the UN, the World Bank, or larger development agencies, rather than with fledgling civil society or emerging opposition groups. Accordingly, their experience was of government rather than society, and it is probably why most conspicuously failed to spot the drivers of political change that produced the Arab Spring. This 'statist' disposition was reinforced by the cosy conspiracy alluded to earlier between MENA regimes and Western counter-terror officials, who tended to bundle all Islamic movements together as irredeemably subversive.

The Decline of State-Driven Diplomacy

Yet the political landscape in which these diplomats are now obliged to operate is radically different from that which prevailed before the Arab Spring. Ageing autocratic leaders are slowly being replaced by more populist leaders, whose authority derives not so much from their relationship with the West, but from the masses. All of this requires new approaches in diplomacy if the UK is to retain influence within the region. Security approaches need to be supplemented with different types of overt and covert dialogue and mediation strategies and processes. In short, the UK must develop a full spectrum approach to the stabilisation and resolution of conflict.

This throws up considerable challenges for the UK's foreign policy establishment. As a P5 member of the UN Security Council, the UK retains a responsibility to help stabilise geo-politically sensitive regions and countries caught up in conflict and transition. It will be interesting to see whether it has the will and capacity to develop new approaches to deal with the huge transformations taking place across the MENA region. It was fascinating to glimpse the UK government's COBRA nerve centre on Libya at work in the Cabinet Office, back in April of 2011. I did not appreciate just how small the response room was in reality. The decision to back rebel attempts to remove Gaddafi from power in 2011 manifestly placed strain on the government's diplomatic resources, given the need to respond to the other momentous political events that were unfolding across the region at the same time. In the end I have no doubt this affected the FCO's capacity to deliver on a number of fronts.

There is a popular misconception, fuelled by Hollywood, that Western powers have banks of experts at the ready in times of unexpected crisis. In reality there are only a few desk officers concentrating on non-priority countries at any one time. Although the FCO has seasoned officials well versed in the ways of the Middle East, its so-called Camel Corps probably numbers fewer than a dozen men and women. Many of the young desk officers at FCO in King Charles Street today have next to no first-hand experience of the new political groupings emerging across the Middle East. This lack of capacity must be addressed, although it is hardly a new phenomenon. Jonathan Powell once told me of how he was forced to rush out to a bookshop in London on the afternoon of 9/11, to buy Ahmed Rashid's book *Taliban: Militant Islam, Oil and Fundamentalism in Central Asia* (2000) in order to get some sort of take on the nature of the regime in Afghanistan in 2001. This was because virtually no officials were able to give him a any sort of briefing on the movement. Overnight Jonathan became No. 10's expert on the Taliban.

I have little doubt that similar advisors in No. 10 found themselves rushing out to the very same bookshop in the spring of 2011 after the UN no-fly zone was declared, to devour what little information there was on Libya's peculiar political and social structure. As Rory Stewart eloquently argues, the gradual reduction of seasoned diplomats with real experience of the culture and people of the Middle East, beyond embassy life, is likely to have a profound impact on the ability of the UK government to pursue its interests in the region. Unless, that is, the FCO begins to draw upon the wider pool of diplomatic expertise in the non-state sector that emerged after leading Western governments retreated into the safe confines of multilateral state diplomacy, post 9/11.

The Emergence of New Mediators

Looking at the mounting problems of the MENA region today, it would be utterly self-defeating for the UK government not to take advantage of the rise of non-state diplomatic expertise that has developed since 9/11. A number of innovative civil society organisations have now established themselves in the field of conflict resolution and peace building. These range from larger bodies like the Centre for Humanitarian Dialogue (CHD) in Geneva, International Crisis Group, the Centre for Transitional Justice, the European Institute of Peace in Brussels, the Carter Centre and the Search for Common Ground in the US, to smaller, bespoke, non-profit organisations like Conciliation Resources, Forward Thinking, the Democratic Progress Institute and Inter Mediate in London, the Berghof Foundation in Berlin, the Toledo Centre in Oslo, Beyond Conflict in Boston, Transformative Initiative in South Africa, and Beyond Borders in Scotland. Then there are the more community-based CSOs in Northern Ireland and South Africa. These organisations have been joined by other groups which have likewise become involved in private diplomacy initiatives as a result of their more specialist interests in legal and cultural affairs, such as the BHRC, the British Museum, the Tate and the Delfina Foundation.

The most successful of the mediation organisations is the Centre for Humanitarian Dialogue based in Geneva. Martin Griffiths set up the CHD not simply to take advantage of the gap that had opened up in the international mediation and dialogue market. It was also as a consequence of widespread criticism of the United Nations for its lack of response in a timely and adequate way to a number of conflict situations. Griffiths deliberately sought out former state and UN diplomats, lawyers and humanitarian experts, as well as ex-military personnel and spooks who had either brokered peace deals in the past or currently had a range of contacts and connections with armed groups and crucial elements within civil society in conflict areas around the world. The early twenty-first century, therefore, witnessed the coming together of a remarkable set of private mediators from very different professional backgrounds. These non-state experts exercised a great deal more entrepreneurial flair than their state or UN counterparts, who were invariably required to stay within a strictly agreed policy framework hammered out by their political masters.

I became involved with CHD in 2005, principally because of my human rights and terror-related litigation work, which often involved dealing with opposition groups from some of the most geo-politically sensitive parts of the globe. Some later found themselves in government in places like Turkey, Iraq, Pakistan and Zimbabwe, while others continued their political struggle for power on the streets. For the next few years I swapped the comfortable confines of my legal chambers in Chancery Lane, London, for the streets of the Middle East, under the tutelage of men like Sir Kieran Prendergast, the former head of the UNDPA, who could give any High Court Judge a run for their money in terms of probity and wisdom. Through him, and others like him, such as Jonathan Powell, Martin Griffiths, Roelf Meyer, David Harland who took over from Griffiths, David Gorman, James Leymone, Priscilla Hayner, David Coltart and former combatants like Jerry Kelly, I learnt how back channels were created, cease-fires negotiated, and confidence-building measures sequenced. I witnessed up-close the dexterity of independent negotiators like Griffiths and Powell, as non-state actors elicited the release of hostages, helped mediate elections that had turned to violence, and constructed roadmaps relating to democratic reform in a number of conflicts.

Griffiths had an uncanny ability to instil trust and a sense of empathy within warring parties, while all the time remaining loyal to the core principles of mediation, namely neutrality, integrity and humanitarian commitment. These personal qualities were particularly important for a mediator working in the Middle East, where personal relations, trust, loyalty, empathy and longevity counted for a lot when it came to the business of establishing political and diplomatic relations. I realised then that you couldn't just take a degree in conflict studies or attend an FCO-sponsored course to acquire these skills – you had to develop them in the field. This work was some of the most challenging but rewarding I have ever done. The lack of pretension and pomposity of these mediators, compared to some practitioners I encountered in the legal world, was deeply refreshing. We undoubtedly owe these men and women a debt of gratitude for the work they do in the shadows of our lives. The confidential nature of their work precludes them from being given the type of human rights awards that are routinely showered on lawyers. Yet this should not stop us from occasionally recognising their quiet contribution towards the restoration of stability, peace and the rule of law around the world. Certainly President Obama was right to publicly note Chris Stevens's contribution and support of this work in the field.

Few accounts of this type of work have emerged in the public domain. Jonathan Powell tells a few stories in his book *Talking to Terrorists: How to End Armed Conflicts* (2014), including one in which Griffiths, and particularly James LeMoyne, convinced the Basque separatist organisation ETA to finally give up its armed struggle. In the book, Powell details the painstaking work that can be involved in creating a back channel and then encouraging mortal enemies to sit down together to talk. Teresa Whitfield's account of the ETA process in her book *Endgame for ETA* (2014) is also instructive concerning what it takes to get a mediation process up and running; from dead letter drops to clandestine meetings and swaps in underground car-parks. No doubt new books will be written about how Powell and Bill Ury from the Harvard Negotiating School helped President Santos of Colombia make peace with the FARC rebel movement between 2011 and 2016.

The gravitation of senior ex-diplomats like Martin Griffiths, Sir Kieran Prendergast and Jonathan Powell to organisations like CHD has undoubtedly increased the capacity of the private sector to engage in useful non-state diplomacy in the twenty-first century, in innovative ways. Jonathan Powell went on to set up Inter Mediate with the help of Martin Griffiths, and some assistance from Andrew Marshall, veteran UN and EU mediator, Frances Vendrell and me, in early 2011. It was within this context that Jonathan and I approached UK officials in April 2011 to warn about the need to enter into a NTC and inter-militia dialogue before the Libyan conflict ended. By then Jonathan and I were both individually working to support dialogue in Bahrain with the knowledge of the FCO. Thus, by the start of the Arab Spring, non-state actors were already playing important roles within an increasingly well-connected global community, whether other bureaucrats in the system liked it or not.

The timidity of some of those bureaucrats in not drawing upon the non-state sector during the early part of the Libyan uprising certainly rebounded on the UK government and attempts of the fledgling NTC to stabilise new Libya. But the time has surely come for all concerned to recognise the distinct advantages of using non-state actors in these types of conflict situations. Firstly, non-state mediators have the ability to transcend individual state interests and to concentrate on dialogue issues without regard to countervailing political factors. Secondly, private mediators can often avoid the horse-trading and political intrigue that beset state and mandate-based institutions like the United Nations or the European Union, when it comes to conflict resolution and peacekeeping. Thirdly, 'soft power' or 'weak' mediators can afford to fail in dialogue efforts with rebel movements or pariah states, without encountering the political fallout that often accompanies a state or regional organisation's attempts to open talks with sometimes dubious movements without a proper mandate. Fourthly, non-state mediators can often reach out to rebel movements well before a conflict explodes. They therefore fulfil a preventative diplomacy role by providing states and international organisations with track II type back channels (supporting tracks of mediation involving non-state mediators), once a conflict has ripened.

The FCO should have recognised the growing utility and benefit of deploying non-state mediators like Powell or Griffiths in difficult and fast-moving conflict situations, in the service of the international community, particularly after the Arab Spring exploded.

The Dynamism of Non-State Dialogue Initiatives

One need only look at how non-state actors interfaced with Hamas and the Muslim Brotherhood before the Arab Spring to appreciate the dynamism of the private sector. The failure of Western states to accept the election victory of Hamas in Palestine in 2006 was deeply corrosive and raises acute issues about how democracy is supposed to operate in Muslim societies. But the failure to pursue any 'behind the scenes' dialogue was even more corrosive to the wider search for peace in the region. Both Forward Thinking and CHD managed to establish relations with these organisations during this period, in a way that few states, or regional or international organisations were either willing or able to do. Oliver McTernan, former Catholic priest and executive director of Forward Thinking, spent years in the diplomatic wilderness, quietly working to establish relations with Hamas when no one else was willing to talk to them. In so doing he opened up a channel of crucial private communications at a critical time, creating a platform for future dialogue and, arguably, stopping the organisation from veering even further in a radical direction as a result of sheer diplomatic isolation.

Interestingly, CHD brought the Muslim Brotherhood to Geneva to meet with EU officials and national directors from Paris, Madrid and Berlin with responsibility for the MENA two years before the Arab Spring even occurred. Somewhat predictably the UK government declined to send its officials to these meetings. This dialogue became invaluable after the Arab Spring. I recall David Cameron's Private Secretary pulling me aside at a private dinner in April of 2011 given at the home of Ayman Asfari, the head of Petrofac, to ask about the CHD dialogue with the Muslim Brotherhood. Two weeks later FCO officials started to attend these talks in order to better understand the range of issues that divided the parties.

These quarterly meetings enabled European officials to obtain a more informed view of the Brotherhood's position on constitutional reform, the role of women, and the treatment of Christian minorities. It led the German government to draft a 'non-paper' on engagement with the Muslim Brotherhood. Daniel L. Byman, a professor at Georgetown University's School of Foreign Service, got it about right when he made the following observation in his book *The Arab Awakening* (2012): '[F]rom the US perspective, ignoring the Muslim Brotherhood and other Islamist movements seemed prudent when they had little chance of gaining power. Now, the tables have turned, and the United States needs to catch up. In particular, it should make it clear that it does not want these movements excluded from a democratic system of government.'

These observations remain valid despite the demise of the Muslim Brotherhood in Egypt after June 2013, as it continues to exercise massive influence over civil society and has the ability to act as a spoiler in many MENA countries. CHD would later use this regional dialogue to launch a series of national dialogues with chapters of the Muslim Brotherhood in countries like Yemen, Morocco, Libya and Egypt. In Tunisia it was able to get all parties to sign up to a voluntary charter that helped promote a free and fair election. Thus it is sometimes better for government to let non-state-directed discussions take place without creating too much fuss, whatever its final policy position might be. In the end, knowledge is always better than ignorance.

The Need for a Civil Society Rapid Response Fund

Yet if the non-state sector is to be utilised in this way it needs to have better and immediate access to funds in times of sudden conflict. The BHRC experience of trying to get funds out of the British government in order to do immediate conflict work in Libya suggests a need for a new type of dedicated non-state rapid-response internationally funded mechanism. Such a fund would enable credible non-state actors to deploy quickly when emergency conflict situations flare up, such as the one that occurred in Libya.

Rory Stewart tells the story of a friend who became an expert in writing and analysing development and humanitarian proposals for the international community. He routinely wrote reports for governments and international institutions, like the ISRT report on Libya. These reports were littered with global governance and development terminology, but made little reference to the history or culture of the place that was being 'stabilised'. But when it came to 'assessing' non-state civil society applications he could explain what was wrong with every conceivable project. He disclosed that there is 'a standard global catechism' that can undermine almost any proposal by asking 'Is this project sustainable?' 'Is it replicable?' 'What are your sources of funding?' 'How does it relate to the national strategy?' 'What kind of community consultation have you conducted?' 'How have you sought to involve the [host] government in the project?' 'What is the role of women?' 'How transparent, predictable and accountable are your financial processes?'[1] This is probably what happened to the BHRC bid.

If the UK intervention in Libya has taught us anything, then it is that the time has surely come for the UK government to place a little more trust in the expertise and track record of recognised non-state actors, without having to make them go through such artificial impact assessments. The South Africa and Northern Ireland experiences manifestly demonstrate how civil society can act as a vital catalyst for social, political and economic change when harnessed properly. It can also play a key role in advocating measures to bring an end to ongoing violence and humanitarian suffering. This is because civil society organisations have the moral legitimacy to act as custodians of peace and to help oversee government accountability and legitimacy, particularly where the capacity to deliver essential services to citizens has become weak due to poor governance and a democratic deficit.

As Akram al-Turk, a senior researcher with the Project on US Relations with the Islamic World at the Saban Centre for Middle East Policy at the Brookings Institution, rightly observes: 'A vibrant civil society will be critical to the long-term socio-economic and political health of Libya. Not only does it guard against the potential excesses of the new government institutions and the emergence of a new autocracy, it helps instil and strengthen a democratic political culture in Libyan society.' He pointed to the numerous new non-governmental organisations that have emerged since the February protests of 2012, and which have 'ignited a sense of volunteerism and civil duty' among ordinary Libyans.

According to al-Turk, 'The trick is to ensure that international organisations and development agencies work with local activists to channel that civic duty into building civil society organisations and potentially, into political parties.'[2] Such an approach inevitably requires the assistance of both the international community and the global civil society, since Libya's fledgling civil societies do not have the monetary and human resources to finance or run such programmes at present or in the immediate future.

It was clear from the outset that the NTC needed all the help it could get and as early as possible. ISRT officials need to explain why the above approach was not adopted in respect of New Libya. The early 'buy in' of local civil society and tribal groups was plainly essential to gain any traction. Laying the foundations for lasting peace and security in any country emerging from internal conflict is a complex process, involving many opposing factions. But it is clear that reconciliation and reconstruction programmes must involve all parties at an early point. That is why the NTC Justice Minister was right to try to draw upon the expertise of organisations like the Bar Council. The BHRC was well versed in the ways of the Middle East, had the requisite legitimacy on the ground, and enjoyed good relations with many of the emerging actors that had come to the fore during the Arab Spring.

Thus, if Western leaders are to help Libyan democrats and other conflict-affected countries experiencing violent change to build a viable future, then they have to develop a full spectrum approach to stabilisation. This requires them to partner and provide non-state actors with sustained support, not just when a conflict ends, but while it is going on. This can be achieved by the international donor community coming together to set up a dedicated rapid response fund, which non-state mediators and civil society can tap into as soon as a conflict gets under way, so that soft-power mediation and crucial dialogue work can start in respect of the rule of law, national societal dialogue, political and constitutional reform, as well as in relation to the development of transitional justice approaches and measures. As a senior mediator advisor to the Mediation Support Unit of the United Nations Department of Political Affairs, I have seen up close how valuable its standby team of experts is. These experts are ready to deploy within seventy-two and sometimes twenty-four hours to support the work of a UN political mission or Special Envoy involved in crucial peace-making efforts around the world. Set up in 2008 by the Department of Political Affairs it was designed to remedy some of the shortfall in experience, expertise and lack of flexibility in the international system to which I have drawn attention in this book. It provides a classic example of what can be achieved when you apply disruptive and innovative thinking to help solve old problems. Today its experts are working in one way or another on virtually all the major peace-making processes in the world.

The Importance of Sharing Experience

Finally, in a world where international advisors, experts and consultants proliferate, personal experience is key when it comes to helping leaders resolve conflict. Those who have successfully managed or mediated similar conflict situations elsewhere have the best chance of gaining the trust of leaders. The non-state sector has produced a range of organisations and a class of experienced professionals capable of helping others to think through how to handle and facilitate change in even the most entrenched of conflicts. The international community should draw upon the past experiences of political leaders who have made the difficult transition from dictatorship to democracy. It must harness this type of real experience if it is to properly respond to crises in leadership across the world.

Tim Phillips's and Roelf Meyer's work with Beyond Conflict is a case in point. Both hold an almost elemental belief in the universal power of shared experiences, insisting that these experiences can and do transcend national boundaries. While all conflicts have their unique features there are underlying themes that are common to all. Beyond Conflict has used leaders from a broad spectrum of countries in over fifty-eight initiatives to help share their experiences about how to end conflict, build civil society, and foster effective governance and peaceful co-existence. In doing so it has made a significant contribution to ending conflict in El Salvador, Nicaragua, Kosovo, Colombia and South Africa.

One almost forgets how intractable the apartheid problem was in South Africa. Yet through dialogue a rainbow nation was born. South Africa's inspiring story subsequently helped other countries affected by conflict to overcome their differences. Nelson Mandela later wrote about Beyond Conflict's first trip:

> After decades of isolation in the world community, South Africa was no longer alone. Individuals who struggled through their own national transitions were eager to assist us confront our difficult past and to help us think how we might achieve justice for apartheid's victims. On the eve of the 1994 elections, Beyond Conflict in partnership with the South African NGO, Idasa, brought a number of leaders from Latin America, Eastern Europe and the Middle East to Cape Town to share their experiences from repression and violence to peace and democracy. These international leaders, with their first hand understanding of the challenges of transition and personal experiences of trauma, brought South Africa a powerful message of hope. They showed us that other countries had triumphed over violence, hatred and deep-seated divisions, to find their way to peace and the beginning of reconciliation. If others could do this, so could we.[3]

The leaders in the South African transition, such as Roelf Meyer and Mohammed Bhabha, shared their own experiences with leaders facing similar challenges in Northern Ireland, Latin America, the Balkans and now in the Middle East, while Tim Phillips went on to co-found the Club de Madrid with the help of President Clinton. Its members were all former presidents and prime ministers who had stood down from power either through retirement or by accepting the verdict of the ballot box. Clinton recognised how important this was as an example to other leaders. It is a testament to his values that he spent time helping to sustain the Club as a vehicle for shared experience.

In 2013 I was fortunate to act as Master of Ceremonies for the Club in Little Rock, Arkansas, at the Clinton Presidential Library. That weekend I learned how politics was local and commitment counted for everything. Clinton opened up his home town to world leaders. But instead of being cosseted behind security details, these leaders were invited to local community and music events. The experience touched all our hearts, and it reaffirmed in me the sheer power of shared experience and unencumbered international cultural dialogue. I realised then that an enormous amount of untapped good will and experience exists out there amongst the world's former leaders, many of whom are ready to deploy their skills in the service of the public good. Our foreign policy establishment should overcome the desire to defend its own turf and harness this great gift. It is time for it to fully utilise these new resources if, that is, it is serious about not repeating the mistakes of the UK's intervention and non-intervention in Libya. As a consequence of recent

UN mediation Libya at last has a chance to form another unity government, while the UK has an opportunity to redeem some of the promises its leaders made to the people of Benghazi and the wider regime. This time we should grasp this opportunity with both hands.

20. The Power of Cultural Dialogue and Small Nation Diplomacy

The rise of non-state mediation in the first decade of the twenty-first century did not happen in isolation. It was part of a much wider globalisation of civil society. Since the end of the Cold War in the 1990s the world has witnessed the emergence of all sorts of new global civil society organisations within the field of international relations. They include not only international humanitarian, human rights and environmental NGOs, but also innovative cultural and arts institutions, business organisations and private intelligence services, as well as grass-roots bodies that lobby on behalf of the world's dispossessed and disadvantaged.

The globalisation of civil society means that the conduct of international relations is no longer the exclusive preserve of states or state-based multilateral organisations. Today, civil society organisations from different continents regularly come together to talk about a whole range of political, environmental, cultural and development issues affecting the world. These include elite business forums such as the Davos World Economic Forum, gatherings of social entrepreneurs at the Clinton Global Initiative, the activist gatherings held around the margins of the G8, G20, UN environmental and climate change summits, and the global campaigns against poverty, developing world debt and bad governance led by Bob Geldof and Bono of U2 and the Occupy Now Movement. All of them in their own way seek to harness the power of the private sector and civil society to help solve global political, economic and social problems.

I believe the UK government needs to connect up and tap into this extraordinary new energy when developing new diplomatic strategies. The emergence of these actors onto the diplomatic stage points toward the possibility of an altogether more radical, all-inclusive, multi-layered approach to diplomatic relations in the twenty-first century. An approach in which both state and non-state institutions work together in independent but cross-cutting ways, to improve relations not just between states but also societies, in order to reduce regional conflict and cultural misunderstanding. The type of broad-based, multi-layered approach articulated here should have been incorporated into the international stabilisation plan for New Libya, particularly with regard to the development of Libyan civil society and new political institutions, as well as in relation to good governance, transitional justice, wider constitutional reform and national reconciliation measures.

The Power of Cultural Diplomacy

But let me add one final reflection about the role that cultural diplomacy can play in the resolution of conflict in Libya and around the world. Throughout the war on terror years, institutions like the British Museum (BM), British Council and even the Tate launched a number of innovative initiatives in the field of international relations, to promote greater understanding between cultures and societies around the world. These initiatives occurred within the context of an increasingly fractured world, and it can be no coincidence that the BM, for example, developed greater cultural relations with countries like Iraq, China and Iran.

One person who witnessed this development was my sister, Maria Muller, the then director of development at the BM. She was instrumental in finding much of the private sector funding for the BM. She traces the Museum's entry into global cultural diplomacy to the invasion of Iraq in 2003 and the looting of Baghdad's Museum of Antiquities. Neil MacGregor, the British Museum's director, was horrified by the accidental destruction of Iraq's ancient sites by coalition forces, so he called Tony Blair and took to the airwaves to launch a public campaign to save what was left of Iraq's antiquities. Blair eventually arranged for a column of troops to take up position outside the Baghdad Museum to stop further looting. The incident led MacGregor to start a worldwide campaign to persuade states to have greater regard for the protection of cultural monuments during times of conflict. This in turn helped generate debate about how states had obligations to protect and promote the world's cultural heritage for future generations during times of conflict.

MacGregor used this debate to forge a global coalition in favour of the preservation of cultural objects in places of danger. In doing so he placed the British Museum at the centre of a new form of international dialogue and diplomacy. He was so successful that he even managed to get the US military to distribute playing cards with significant protected monuments on them to soldiers in Iraq. This happened after a helicopter landed on a priceless ancient statute in Babylon without realising its significance. This type of diplomacy helped mend fences with many of Iraq's intellectual leaders. Indeed, the BM's attempt to create a new regional museum in

British-held Basra probably did more to restore trust with the local leaders than the British army ever did through its 'hearts and minds' initiative. As one former diplomat put it, MacGregor did more in twelve months to restore relations with Iraqi leaders than any human rights lawyer did in years of litigation in the UK courts.

No one was too surprised, then, when Tony Blair asked MacGregor to join him on a diplomatic mission to China in 2005. But while the BM's diplomatic interests dovetailed neatly with that of the Labour government, it was in no way directed by it. MacGregor had no desire to be seen simply as an append- age to the UK government. He agreed to join the mission only in order to secure an exhibition of the First Emperor in London. The mission turned out to be another huge success. It resulted in an exhibition that not only brought the two countries closer together, but also opened up Chinese culture to the rest of the world. He followed this up by concluding a series of Memoranda of Understanding with various other museums around the world, particu- larly in Africa. All of this required the utmost diplomacy to get collections moved to and from London, since many pieces were acutely connected to those countries' sense of national identity. New exhibitions followed about other rulers from around the world, from Emperor Hadrian to ancient Mexican leaders. This in turn sparked further debate about the nature of imperial conquest and national identity.

Through these initiatives MacGregor repositioned the BM as the 'lending library of the world', to coin a phrase first used by Maria Muller. The BM's team of curators now infused the BM's collection with a sense of world history by developing wider narratives around individual pieces held by the Museum. This would eventually lead to MacGregor's extraordinary series 'The History of the World in 100 Objects'. In this way the BM became notably more successful than the FCO in smoothing diplomatic and cultural relations with a succession of countries with which the UK had difficult relations.

Within a few years, MacGregor's entrepreneurial spirit had turned the British Museum from an old-fashioned institution into a centre of world debate, and not only about culture but also politics, development and human rights. The BM went on to play a huge role in raising the profile of the Africa Commission, along with the BHRC, which helped Bob Geldof launch the Commission at its biennial lecture at St Paul's Cathedral in 2006. MacGregor regularly held dinners at the Museum, including one I attended in honour of the UN human rights supremo, Sergio Vieira del Mello, who would trag- ically die just a few months later, when insurgents blew up the UN headquarters in Iraq. More insights into the state of international affairs could be gleaned at these dinners than in the official corridors of FCO power at King Charles Street. The BM's use of cultural diplomacy should serve as an instructive note to the UK's foreign policy establishment.

Perhaps MacGregor's greatest coup came in relation to Iran, when in a diplomatic chess move of sheer brilliance, he decided to loan, unsecured, the Cyrus Cylinder in exchange for Iran lending the British Museum pieces from Isfahan. This did more to resurrect some element of trust and respect for the rule of law between Iran and the UK than state-driven diplomatic initiatives during this period. At this time state diplomats were scratching their heads about how to handle Iran and reach out towards it. All of this demonstrates the important role that cultural diplomacy can play in overcoming deep tensions between different countries and their societies in the twenty-first century.

The British Museum was by no means the only cultural organisation engaged in this new type of diplomacy. Its high-level initiatives were replicated on a lower level by the likes of the British Council and smaller private bodies such as the Delfina Foundation, Beyond Borders and the BHRC, which all used cultural exchange in innovative ways to help reconnect the West to the Middle East during the war on terror years. For example, the Delfina Foundation established numerous relationships with art houses in Tehran and elsewhere. It was, of course, much easier for such organisations to operate in places like Syria, Iraq and Iran than for human rights groups, but this does not fully account for such a phenomenon. These bodies, and the people who staffed them, unlike some of the human rights lawyers I referred to earlier, understood the growing sense of cultural polarisation and alienation that was occurring between the Middle East and the West, precisely because of their long-term interest in and commitment to the ancient and modern cultures of the Middle East.

I visited Syria nine times in under three years, between 2006 and 2010, with the Tate, BHRC and the Delfina Foundation, to work with Paul Doubleday of the British Council and leading Syrian cultural, intellectual, legal and youth leaders, on a range of cultural and legal projects. On a visit to Damascus and Aleppo in 2007 with Jon Snow, patron of the Delfina Foundation, and Helena Kennedy QC, the former chair of the British Council, the three of us met a host of civil society leaders, both young and old, who all confessed to feeling utterly isolated from the wider world as a consequence of Bush's war on terror rhetoric. They were overjoyed at the prospect of us initiating a new and benign form of discourse. We even received an impromptu delegation of Kurdish leaders who sought us out at a local restaurant in Aleppo for the human rights work that the KHRP had done with the Kurds.

We were all struck by the value they placed on our physical presence in the country and by how human interaction was the very essence of real diplomacy. It was evident even back then that if freedom were ever to blossom in places like Syria, it would be through the efforts of civil society and resilient communities, rather than through the machinations of big power state diplomacy, whose only approach towards countries like Syria appeared to be one of isolation. It is impossible to underestimate the impact of this kind of face-to-face dialogue between different cultures. If the West is really serious about promoting greater democratic and cultural freedom in places in the MENA region, it must support the work of its own cultural institutions in this area.

The cultural sensitivity of the British Council officials and curators of the British Museum stand in marked contrast to some of the bright young things who now inhabit the FCO and are too often just looking towards their next promotion. UK policymakers need to recognise the value of the painstaking work undertaken over many years by British Council country directors like Paul Doubleday. The British Council remains one of the few UK government-funded institutions that routinely foster dialogue with civil society and intellectual leaders in places like Syria, Egypt, Bahrain and Palestine. Over the course of a decade I have been lucky enough to witness first-hand how these men and women helped create new and exciting relationships between different cultures, regions and competing states, at a time when both the British and US governments were retiring seasoned and culturally sensitive diplomats and replacing them with counter-terrorism experts who knew little of the countries they were ostensibly seeking to deradicalise. We all owe a deep debt of gratitude to cultural leaders for lessening misunderstanding between nations during crucial moments of world conflict.

This is why I believe strongly that cultural diplomacy should form part of any new concordat with the MENA region. The last decade has demonstrated that it can act as a powerful medium of exchange in effecting societal transformation and reconciliation. UK policymakers should be slow to cut the budgets of these cultural institutions, notwithstanding austerity. They need to recognise international cultural discourse as another powerful lever in the toolbox of twenty-first-century diplomacy. Too often diplomatic elites pay lip service to this form of exchange, but rarely lobby strongly enough for more funds to be devoted to it.

Yet policymakers must also let these organisations support government in the right manner. A US State Department official, at a meeting of museum heads in Washington, once waxed lyrical about the British Museum and how cultural diplomacy could play a significant role in furthering US government objectives in the region. MacGregor, I was told, physically squirmed as the diplomat heaped yet more praise on his endeavours. The official had misunderstood the most basic point about what MacGregor was doing, namely using diplomacy to support world culture and not to use culture to support the policies of a particular government. What was important was to bring different civilisations together to begin new conversations, and to make the language of dialogue the primary medium of exchange between nations. The diplomat simply didn't get that it was societal rather than governmental exchange that was important in the long run.

International Fellowship Programmes

This leads me to comment on one other form of cultural diplomacy that is increasingly making its mark and that is the development of bespoke international fellowship programmes. I have seen first-hand how valuable these programmes are, and not only for the fellows who go on them but also for the countries that host and pay for them. As a trustee of the John Smith Memorial Trust (JSMT) I helped develop the FCO-sponsored MENA Rule of Law Fellowship Programme. By then the JSMT Former Soviet Union (FSU) fellowship programme had been running for some twenty years, thanks to the dedicated work of Professor Brian Brivati and long-term trustees such as Elizabeth Smith, David Charters, Roger Munnings and General Sir Mike Jackson. The new MENA Rule of Law programme gave (and continues to give) emerging leaders from the region a unique insight into UK best practice regarding good governance, public administration and the rule of law. Their placements with top practitioners in the UK not only expose them to the realities of governance, but also help build enduring international associations and a sense of fellowship and shared values between the fellows themselves. This gives the UK access to an unparalleled set of interlocutors likely to continue their association with the UK as they rise up the institutional ladder back home.

Iraq

I witnessed first hand how the MENA programme could be useful to the UK in relation to conflict resolution and reconciliation work in places like Iraq where Profession Brian Brivati and I had developed relationships with both the Kurdistan Regional Government (KRG) in northern Iraq and the central government in Baghdad. Brivati and I were both advisors to the KRG and the UK parliament on human rights and genocide issues. We would later work with a number of JSMT fellows to help them develop local reconciliation and accountability projects including one relating to sexual violence through the development of mobile accountability units in Kirkuk which Beyond Borders would later help develop and support.

But perhaps the most important insight as to how these networks could help foster peace came in mid-January 2014 when I was asked by a former fellow, who was the Iraqi Prime Minister Nouri al-Maliki's special advisor, to come to Baghdad to advise him on reconciliation approaches within the context of his counter-terror strategy. At the time the US had pulled out of

Iraq some two years earlier, including literally yanking out its physical intelligence capacity, and a former MI6 official told me that the advice from the service was that it was too dangerous to go there after jihadists took a prominent town just 40 kilometres away from Baghdad. I can still recall the tension as I travelled with Brian Brivati and another former Iraqi MENA fellow into Baghdad along the notorious airport road to the Prime Minister's visitors' residence in the Green Zone, in a high-speed but somewhat ineffectual armoured convoy from the airport. That day seven separate but coordinated bombs went off across Baghdad killing 179 and injuring hundreds more in the largest attack ever on the capital, though we heard none of it in our hermetically sealed diplomatic universe.

At this time Maliki was facing crucial elections in April 2014. We briefed him on how he needed to reach out beyond his comfort zone to reconcile with those Sunni political tribal leaders in the regions who felt his de-Baathification and lustration policies had gone too far. What was needed was a full spectrum approach to countering extremism that included drawing upon the resources of civil society to connect with disaffected youth who had few options to go anywhere other than to the extremists if they wanted to resist. As it turned out, Maliki was more interested in holding an international conference on countering terrorism to help him with his election prospects than with 'reconciliation initiatives'. However, he did set up useful links with some ministries for us.

In late February 2014 I attended the counter-terror conference, which turned out to be a deeply depressing international talking shop packed full of Western diplomats and counter-terror experts who all strikingly failed to tell the Iraqis just how perilous their situation was becoming. It is instructive to note that not a single Western expert I met mentioned the term Islamic State in the two days I was there. Four months later Islamic State took Mosul, to the astonishment of the world. Maliki was later forced to resign but Brian Brivati went on to use the links we established to develop a set of counter-extremism fellowship programmes in 2016 funded by the Cabinet Office with the assistance of former JSMT MENA fellows in Iraq as director of the Stabilisation and Recovery Network which he set up after leaving JSMT.

Ukraine

The utility of the fellowship network as a vehicle for diplomacy and conflict resolution was also graphically brought home to me in relation to the JSMT Former Soviet Union (FSU) fellowship programme after protests erupted on the streets of Kiev in the Ukraine in early 2014. The FSU programme had built up a cadre of some 400 fellows, many of whom had become prominent politicians and policymakers in government and opposition, as well as leaders of civil society and media organisations. As a trustee I would meet these fellows for a weekend retreat at Traquair House every year. When the Ukrainian crisis exploded I was able to allow other conflict resolvers to tap into this network with real effect.

Throughout 2013 the European Union, supported by the UK, courted the Ukrainian government to sign up to an EU Economic Association Agreement. The EU regarded its actions as benign and expressive of European values but anyone with knowledge of the region knew its expansion eastwards was a red rag to a Russian bull, which considered Ukraine part of its historical and geo-political backyard. Few were surprised when President Putin offered the Moscow-friendly government in Kiev an alternative customs union within a group of former Russian Commonwealth and Soviet states, and gave it only a few months to make a decision one way or another.

For six months the government of Ukraine was pulled this way and that, before it rejected the EU bid in late 2013, to the consternation of pro-EU elements in Kiev and the west of Ukraine. As executive director of Beyond Borders, I hosted members of the Ukrainian government at Traquair House in the Scottish Borders in October 2013, as part of a study tour of Westminster and Scottish parliamentary institutions. The delegation included a number of strategic thinkers, including former fellows of JSMT, who were trying to find the most advantageous way out of what was fast becoming a massive geo-political dilemma for the country and the region as a whole. Despite obvious loyalties to Moscow, the delegation recognised what the EU had to offer, but they bitterly resented its lack of understanding of Ukraine's delicate political position in the region.

According to them the EU appeared to be caught up in its own sense of self, as a successful, ever-expanding multilateral state entity. It failed to appreciate why its economic expansion eastward fundamentally threatened the fragile post-Cold-War political balance, in which Russia had ceded control over Ukraine, including over its nuclear arsenal in Crimea, in exchange for a tacit undertaking from the West not to offer Ukraine NATO membership or otherwise encroach upon its back yard. During the Traquair conversations, Alexander Yefremov, the powerful parliamentary chief of the governing Party of the Regions and effective Baron of Luhansk, detailed the nature of EU diplomatic exchanges. The EU appeared more concerned about how to achieve the release of former President Yulia Tymoshenko, who had helped lead the Orange Revolution a decade earlier, than with other more important policy considerations. The Ukranian government had been asked to feign her release on spurious medical grounds. Yefremov was offended by the EU's so-called 'rule of law' agenda as the price for inclusion in the 'European Club', which only served to increase fears that this was, in effect, a political as well as economic takeover of Ukraine. One month later the Ukrainian government rejected the EU offer, sparking widespread protests in Kiev. The protests took EU and UK officials by surprise, just as the Arab Spring protests had done some two years earlier. During this period I was receiving regular updates from former fellows such as Andriy Chevchenko MP, who ended up saving many lives in Maidan Square in central Kiev, as well as from Yefremov's chief of staff, who gave equally compelling accounts of the protests from the other side's perspective. Throughout February 2014, the situation became tenser as more protesters barricaded themselves into Maidan Square. Then on 20 February over 100 protesters were killed in the square by unknown snipers, who appeared to be stationed on the hill behind police lines near the Hotel Ukraine. This was the spark that lit the revolution. Within twenty-four hours the President of Ukraine had fled to Russia and a new political dawn had broken over Kiev. It was like the Arab Spring all over again, but this time the counter-revolution would not take two years to organise. Anyone who knew the region understood that Putin's Russia would not just sit back and allow these upstarts from the west of Ukraine to take control of the whole country, especially of the east.

Almost immediately the Party of the Regions and other pro-Russian elements began to agitate against the Maidan revolution, characterising it as a right-wing Nazi takeover. They claimed the new Western-leaning government in Kiev neither respected nor represented the people and values of the eastern Donbass region, which looked to Russia as both a friend and a strategic partner. With the Party of the Regions in disarray, following the ejection of its top leadership from parliament and the country, a motley crew of new street leaders emerged in the east, who quickly proceeded to barricade themselves into a few central administrative buildings in Donetsk and Luhansk in protest against the revolution in Kiev. Back in Brussels, EU commissioners watched helplessly as Putin began to unceremoniously seize and then annex Crimea.

This was the situation on the ground some three weeks after the Ukrainian revolution, when I took a call from David Gorman of CHD. He had just completed thirty-four rounds of peace talks that led to the 2014 Philippine peace accord between armed rebel groups and the government. He was the CHD official who had also followed me to Benghazi to help set up CHD's operations in that country. Gorman now wanted some help in relation to the Ukrainian crisis, knowing that I had dealt with both sides previously. He had been to Kharkiv to try to make contact with opposition elements on the ground and create some form of back channel, but only managed to make contact with elements of civil society. So on a bitterly cold night in mid-March 2014 we flew from Kiev to the eastern town of Luhansk to meet with Alexander Yefremov and his chief of staff. It turned out that a Scottish steel engineer had founded the town. The last time I had seen Yefremov was at

Traquair House, where we talked politics late into the night over a glass of whisky. In Luhansk we drank something stronger, but the personal and cultural bonds were not lost on us.

Together David Gorman and I sat down and discussed the prospect of forming a dialogue channel in case the conflict deepened. Yefremov was extremely cautious from the outset and in a private moment asked me about Gorman's standing. 'He could be extremely useful,' I explained. 'His record speaks for itself.' We finally got an amber light from a number of players from the east. Over the next twelve weeks, David and I flew back and forth to the Ukraine to establish a contact group of political and parliamentary figures committed to securing a settlement to the conflict emerging in the east through political means, which included JSMT fellows. The experience demonstrated just how valuable international fellowship programmes could be. During this period we did not come across any other government or non-state actors operating on the ground, who had managed to bridge the divide, other than monitors from the Organisation of Security and Co-operation in Europe (OSCE).

The emergence of Russian-backed elements in the East should not have come as any surprise to the EU given that similar elements had managed to control and then freeze conflicts in Abkhazia and South Ossetia in Georgia, as well as in Moldova. What was frightening to see, however, was the EU's total lack of policy response to what was unfolding in the East. It preferred to concentrate its diplomatic fire on offering the new government in Kiev yet more promises of integration, something which may have relieved the worried residents of western Ukraine, but said nothing to the East or the wounded bear next door that was now beginning to sharpen and extend its claws. The EU's diplomatic and military impotence was there for all to see. The promise and prospect of EU economic association in eastern Ukraine seemed almost comical as more and more Chechens, Cossacks and men in unmarked military fatigues began to be appear on the streets of Donetsk.

It was during this period that contact was made with rebel leaders such as Denis Pushilin, who had taken control of the administrative building in Donetsk and who were considered beyond the pale by the EU. These rebels were intent on holding a referendum on 11 May 2014 with a view to declaring independence from Kiev thereafter. With the help of JSMT fellows we met the rebels clandestinely along desolate riverbanks and then in their makeshift redoubt in mid-April 2014. I will always remember climbing the eleven floors of the central administrative building in Donetsk, barricaded and surrounded by tyres and barbed wire, to meet the rebel leadership, and passing the sixth floor door with an image of President Obama with a Yulia Tymoshenko plaited hairstyle and Hitler moustache nailed to it, behind which critics alleged a secret detention centre was located where torture took place. For our part we heard no screams, and the meeting led to the passing on of contact details to the OSCE monitoring mission to help enable successful negotiations to proceed in respect of the release of OSCE monitors who at that time were being detained by other pro-Russian rebels in Slovansk. On 4 May 2014 an offer of a 'pause' in the conflict was elicited from the leaders of the Donetsk People's Republic, which was then transmitted to the EU. This occurred on the same day that President Putin offered an olive branch to the head of the OSCE in Moscow ahead of celebrations of the Soviet victory over the Nazis on 9 May and the all-important referendum date of 11 May. This was an important weekend in the Ukraine crisis since the formal annexation of Crimea was nearly upon us. Tensions were likely to rise further with the anniversary of the Russian victory over the Nazis. The rebel Donetsk referendum was just a few days away and would probably kick start an irreversible process towards either annexation or some form of military escalation ending in yet another frozen conflict. Whether the offer was just a disruption tactic was beside the point – it needed to be stress-tested. We waited for hours for a response from the EU but heard nothing back. Later I learnt that the offer had sparked emergency discussions, much of which focused on how it had come about. 'Who are these guys?' asked one old EU diplomat, clearly unable to countenance how non-state mediators could operate in twenty-first century conflict environments at little cost to anyone. Had the diplomat travelled to the East he would have found that any semblance of the rule of law had disappeared and that irregular forces and groups were now fighting for the spoils of war with little or no respect for the sovereign rights of states. The incident not only laid bare the perennial difficulties in getting instructions from twenty-eight states in real time, it graphically illustrated the need for the EU to respond more effectively as a possible conflict resolver to fast-moving political developments on the ground.

By the time EU policymakers came to consider how to respond, the train had left the track. Certain events were now in play that would come to define the emerging conflict in the East for the next two years. On 11 May 2014 the DPR held its referendum and thereafter declared a form of independence. Within days Donetsk descended into total war as more Cossacks and Chechens flooded into the city and the criminal elements began to run amok. I watched as curfews began to be imposed, leafy suburbs began to be shelled, and the light in the eyes of ordinary working-class Dombass people slowly went out. They had it tough enough already. I remember the pride that local people had had in their gleaming new airport in Donetsk. Within weeks it had been reduced to rubble as both sides fought for control of this strategic asset. The EU push for economic expansion had left the region devastated.

David Gorman would go on to spend the next two years working with elements from both sides of the conflict to help reduce the incidence of violence. This included helping Yefremov's former chief of staff, who set up a non-partisan humanitarian aid organisation that became instrumental in negotiating humanitarian access, aid and assistance in and out of Donetsk with rebel leaders from the so-called Donetsk People's Republic. This alliance was only possible because of the initial trust built up through the JSMT fellowship programme. While in Ukraine I also came across Erik Berglof, the new Director of the LSE Institute of Global Affairs (IGA) and formerly the Special Advisor to the President of the European Bank for Reconstruction and Development. He was one of just a handful of innovators in Kiev bringing together a broad spectrum of policymakers from across the political divide to promote meaningful economic and political reform in the country. His vision and commitment restored my faith in the LSE and the ability of its new leadership to once again add real value to countries experiencing political transition.

The Ukrainian crisis provided yet another graphic illustration of the limits of traditional state-based diplomacy and of how non-state mediators working with civil society can help fill the diplomatic gap when given the opportunity to do so. I know how much British ambassadors in the region value these non-state circles of British influence. This message needs to be heard by policymakers at the centre, and happily in 2016 it was, after the Cabinet Office decided to provide further substantial funding to the JSMT to enable it to run more MENA and FSU fellowship programmes during what on any view is a critical time for the UK's relationship to both regions.

Scotland's Emerging Role in International Affairs

All of this leads me to the role that small nations like Scotland can play within this new diplomatic landscape. I have been constantly struck by how emerging leaders from around the world enjoy and are ready to embrace Scotland as a small but vibrant, soft-power nation with an extraordinary historical brand and important constitutional story to tell. I remember reflecting on Scotland's potential role in the field of conflict resolution in June 2014, just after I returned from Ukraine for the last time, as seventy countries walked out at Hampden Park in Glasgow to celebrate the start of the Commonwealth Games. The last time that happened was in 1986, when Scotland was a very different country with no devolved parliament or government. Since then it has undertaken one of the most radical constitutional journeys of any modern nation in Europe this century. That constitutional journey is likely to continue even though independence was rejected in September 2014, particularly after more reserved and tax-raising powers were given to Holyrood in 2015.

Whether Scotland becomes independent or remains within an enduring political union in the UK as a consequence of the Brexit vote of 23 June 2016, the time has surely come to ask how Scotland can play a greater role in international affairs.

In a recent article the columnist Neal Ascherson was moved to observe that Scots tended to be more progressive, egalitarian and democratic than the rest of Britain, and should break the bond of dependency. He implied those national values needed to be reflected in a foreign policy of Scotland's own making. Whether Ascherson is right or not about how Scots differ from the other parts of the UK remains a matter of debate. What is true is that most people from small northern European states tend to support the use of soft rather than hard power to resolve conflict in international affairs. The Scottish people certainly made their feelings felt about the UK's military invasion and occupation of Afghanistan and Iraq. Why shouldn't that disposition be more clearly reflected within policymaking processes, whether within the UK or not? I confess that when I attended the Scottish debate on the Iraq war in 2003, I found the idea of a different Scottish foreign position within a devolved setting counter-intuitive. I have since changed my mind. My experiences as an international human rights advocate and mediator convince me Scotland has a real and unique contribution to make in the field of conflict resolution, and in the promoting of mutual understanding between nations and cultures.

Firstly, Scotland has a strong separate identity, which exercises a powerful hold over the world's collective imagination. It is perceived as a proud, independent, small nation which has managed to preserve its culture and identity despite the presence of a much more powerful neighbour. This gives it traction, particularly with other small nations and those fighting for national recognition or statehood or some form of autonomy. I experienced a demonstration of the extraordinary affinity people have for Scotland in 1989, when a friend wandered through Prague in a kilt, during the Czech revolution. The crowd treated him as if he had liberated the place. Despite Scotland's role in the British Empire, the bald truth is that it is viewed very differently from its bigger neighbour. In short, certain nations and groups are much more receptive to its advances.

Secondly, Scotland has a phenomenal story to tell. Its devolved settlement is one of the best examples of how smaller nations within larger states can transition towards greater democracy in a peaceful and consensual manner. The decentralisation of power within the UK provides a template for other countries confronted by the need for change, as does the 2012 Edinburgh Agreement, which is a conflict resolution agreement in all but name. These templates have real relevance for those seeking to resolve conflicts peacefully. I will always remember the retort of the rebel PKK Kurdish leader, Abdullah

Ocalan, to me after I met him in his one-man island cell in Turkey in my capacity as his legal counsel just after 9/11. Before turning to his human rights and death penalty appeal before the European Court, I referred to the recent terror attack on America, imagining he would not have heard about it: 'Two things Mr Muller. First I'm not Robinson Crusoe. Second, tell me about the Scottish Parliament.'

Despite winning his appeal Ocalan remains incarcerated in Turkey, but has intermittently entered into talks with the Turkish government to resolve the Kurdish conflict through a democratic reform process. Elsewhere, other Kurdish leaders in Iraq and Syria have achieved a degree of devolved power and remain fascinated by Scotland's constitutional journey. They are not alone. Since 2005 I have worked in Iraq, Syria, Libya, Turkey, Sri Lanka, Zimbabwe, Spain, the Caucasus and Ukraine, all of which have internal conflicts that touch upon cultural autonomy and the devolution of power. International interest in Scotland is therefore unlikely to dissipate any time soon. That is to say nothing of the interest shown in the referendum process and decision itself. As senior advisor to many international humanitarian organisations, I have regularly taken groups to South Africa and Northern Ireland to learn lessons about political transition, so why not to Scotland too? After all, Scotland has elder statesmen and women who have experience not just of government and devolved power, but of multilateral diplomacy within the EU, NATO and the UN Security Council at the highest level, in contrast to some Scandinavian countries involved in conflict resolution.

Elsewhere, Scots lead the field in international cultural diplomacy: Helena Kennedy QC and Neil MacGregor's work cited earlier are just two examples. This, together with the power of Edinburgh's unique cultural festivals, and Scotland's world-class universities, research centres and legal institutions, gives Scotland a commanding platform from which to promote peace and mutual understanding amongst nations, cultures and religions.

Beyond Borders

That is why in 2010 I established Beyond Borders Scotland, with the help of patrons from across the political divide. Apart from its festivals, Beyond Borders has hosted delegations from Georgia, Moldova, Turkey, Kurdistan, Bahrain, Oman, the Basque Country, Ukraine, Iraq and Sri Lanka, all of whom were interested in learning more about Scotland's devolved settlement, parliamentary procedures and referendum process.

None of this would have been possible without the Scottish government and parliament supporting Beyond Borders in this important endeavour. In 2014 the then First Minister, Alex Salmond, helped launch our summer programme celebrating 'The World in Scotland and Scotland in the World', which focused attention on Scotland's international role. One year later, in August 2015, the new Scottish First Minister, Nicola Sturgeon, helped Beyond Borders and the European Institute of Peace launch Scotland's first Women in Conflict Initiative and Peace and Recovery Fellowship Programme in support of UN Security Council Resolution 1325 which seeks to promote women's participation in peace-making processes. The initiative brought together women peacemakers from Syria, Iraq and Yemen in Scotland to meet with other peacemakers, to help devise Scotland's first long-term peace fellowship programme.

This in turn influenced the decision of the UN Special Envoy to Syria, Staffan de Mistura, to let Scotland host the Envoy's Women's Advisory Body for internal discussions and training in relation to the Syria peace talks being rolled out in Geneva. This occurred after I accompanied him to Scotland in my capacity as his co-lead mediation advisor to the talks to meet with Nicola Sturgeon. After touring the Scottish parliament de Mistura immediately understood the significance of having Syrian female peacemakers meet under the patronage of three female party leaders, as well as a female speaker of parliament, and in a parliament that had been created through a political transition without a shot being fired. So one day after the general election of 5 May 2016, all party leaders of Scotland came together to welcome Syrian female peacemakers to the Scottish parliament, which kindly gave over its space for their deliberation. This event demonstrates Scotland's growing standing, commitment and capacity to act in the service of peace-making.

It was partly as a result of this successful collaboration that the First Minister went on to commit the SNP and the Scottish government to provide funding to train fifty female peacemakers and activists every year for the next five years. The first batch of those female peacemakers came to the Beyond Borders Festival in 2016, where Nicola Sturgeon was interviewed by the BBC's international editor Lyse Doucet about women in peace-making and politics. They included Dr Lamia Abusedra, the former member of the NTC's Executive Office of Cultural Relations and Civil Society, who featured in the Mercy report referred to earlier.

As I watched both Nicola and Lamia being interviewed by Lyse my mind returned to Benghazi and to the belief its people expressed in New Libya's ability to create a democratic state based upon the rule of law. Suddenly the image of Salwa al-Dighaili, the Libyan human rights lawyer and NTC official responsible for evacuations from Misrata, came back to me, as she made her impassioned statement to the world's media in 2011 from the NTC's improvised media centre just off Freedom Square, flanked by drooping flowers on a couple of shabby pedestals. How I would have liked her to have been here. But it was not to be. Salwa was assassinated by jihadists not long after Chris Stevens was murdered. This after Libya descended into further chaos when its parliamentary institutions split into two factions in 2013, following the international community's failure to find common ground on how to build a viable government and stable state. If countries like Libya are to find solutions to their problems, they will need the services of women like Salwa, Lamia and Hana el-Gallal, as well as the assistance of well-meaning neutral countries like Scotland, which could help share experience and provide a neutral platform for dialogue.

All of these experiences have convinced me that Scotland has a profound contribution to make in the field of peace building, conflict resolution and wider cultural exchange between nations, cultures and religions. The time has surely come for UK policymakers to consider whether these islands should adopt a more innovative, asymmetrical, full-spectrum approach to conflict resolution. How this is achieved is a matter for further debate. But as the utility of hard power and Security Council diplomacy declines, and that of soft power increases, it ill-behoves any policymaker serious about improving the peace-making record of the UK not to recognise Scotland's growing capacity to act in this area. The positive values that underpin Scotland's current civic nationalism and humanitarianism can only make it a greater force for good in the world.

Epilogue: Benghazi or Bust

Let me end my reflections with a few words about David Cameron's 2011 speech at the UN General Assembly and whether civil society should embrace his R2P doctrine in favour of democratic regime change, given the chequered history of interventions in countries such as Iraq and Afghanistan and now Libya. On the question of principle, Cameron is probably right in pointing to the evolving right to democracy as a potential new driver of international security and stabilisation policy. Certainly the range of R2P measures identified in the UN 2001 report is aimed not simply at stopping but also preventing humanitarian catastrophes from happening again. The UN report did not therefore prohibit military and diplomatic action in support of democratic reform, where that reform probably averted further catastrophes. The inexorable logic of Cameron's position on R2P is that where the humanitarian case is met, and democratic reform is possible, the international community should support democratic regime change rather than allow a despotic regime to return to terrorise its own population.

Cameron's doctrine of democratic regime change might appear superficially attractive to those who support democratic reform in the MENA region, just as Tony Blair's interventionist doctrine did to those seeking to protect fundamental rights in Bosnia a decade earlier. But on a closer analysis it constitutes a dangerous assault on many of the trusty concepts of state sovereignty that still underpin much of the international diplomatic and legal order, and which have served the international community relatively well. Proponents of this traditional view, like Sir Kieran Prendergast, are right to note that, in practice, it is extremely difficult to decouple the pursuit of democratic reform for humanitarian and good governance reasons from the wider geo-political objectives and interests of intervening states, particularly those of the West.

The application of Cameron's doctrine to the MENA region is a potential recipe for international diplomatic disorder and deadlock in the UN Security Council, especially when one has regard to the historical tensions between the West, Russia and post-colonial states, concerning the use of democracy as an ideological weapon to effect regime change during the Cold War. At the very least his advocacy of such a doctrine raises a whole series of questions, not only about the legitimate role of the UN Security Council, but also the efficacy of current definitions of terrorism, the ambit of the rights of self-determination and the scope of any licence to resist oppression through force in international law. It also raises issues about whether states that intervene in an R2P situation to back democratic regime change remain under a continuing obligation to ensure agents comply with international norms and standards regarding the treatment of civilians and enemy combatants. Certainly, Cameron's actions in support of democratic intervention in Libya have opened up a Pandora's Box of legal and political issues for UK policymakers and the courts.

Perhaps the question civil society should therefore ask itself is not whether it supports such a doctrine in principle, but who should be tasked with intervening and ensuring the implementation of R2P objectives in any given situation. For unless civil society is allowed to play a critical role in such interventions I remain deeply sceptical about the potential benefits of such a doctrine, particularly given the less than successful history of state building by the West in Afghanistan, Iraq and Libya. In the case of Libya, there was a discernible attempt to limit the role of non-aligned civil society and non-state mediators during the early phase of the intervention. This starved the NTC and local civic groups of crucial moral, financial and expert support. Whatever the reason for this, the UK's intervention in Libya demonstrates why such interventions should never be left to military coalitions and/or state-driven stabilisation bodies. Civil society should play a role in the design and implementation of R2P measures from the outset, particularly in relation to the building of new democratic institutions. In the end it is society rather than government that makes peace and rebuilds shattered communities.

The crisis in Libya presented the UK with an unprecedented existential dilemma as to where its loyalties ultimately lay. Cameron had to decide whether to support the rebels and back their campaign for greater democracy, social justice and human dignity with all that it entailed, or leave them to a very uncertain fate. Those who argue that the UK could have intervened militarily to avert a humanitarian catastrophe but then leave a few weeks later do not understand what transpired in Benghazi in the spring of 2011. There was simply no prospect of the people of Benghazi or Tripoli accepting another decade of rule by Gaddafi. Whether the UK government could have mediated Gaddafi leaving the country is another matter that probably should have been explored more readily.

Despite all the twists and turns of the Arab Spring and the Libyan revolution, it is clear that the desire for proper governance and respect for human dignity remains undiminished. I know the road to greater freedom and democratic governance in the Middle East will not be easy and that many political obstacles and spoilers will need to be overcome along the way. But let us not kid ourselves about the choice we in the West faced and continue to face. We still stand at a crucial fork in the road, just as the Libyan people did in February 2011. Either we try to construct a better, more inclusive collective future for all, or we elect to continue to support unrepresentative regimes, intent on blocking reform for nefarious ends, in the vain hope they can shield us from further chaos. To my mind the direction to take is obvious. Let us choose the path with at least some light on the horizon – the light of human solidarity. It is better to be guided and illuminated by hope and a belief in the future than by the dark sentiments of suspicion and fear of the other. In choosing this path we might also sow the seeds of the West's rehabilitation by making reparation for some of the past misdeeds we have visited upon the region – from the Sykes–Picot Agreement in 1917 through to the UK's alleged complicity in the abuse of human rights.

After experiencing those few unforgettable days in the spring of 2011, I am left in no doubt why the ordinary people of Benghazi rose up so resolutely and continue to deserve our long-term support. As a multitude of political interests, corporate profit hunters and radical groups descend upon New Libya to devour its uprising, let us resolve to once more come to the aid of those who remain true to the early ideals of that uprising. We in civil society need to bolster its fledgling civil society before it is too late. It is trite to recall that evil prospers while the good do nothing, but it nonetheless remains true. We can no longer afford to leave the future of the MENA region to the machinations of aged political and diplomatic elites, whether in the region or in the West. We live in an increasingly interdependent and globalised world where we can no longer ignore the pain of other people. Donald Trump can put up all the walls he likes, but he cannot pretend that people will stop trying to get over them.

The time has surely come to give up some of our obsessions about the war on terror and let dialogue between cultures and nations move on to more fertile pastures. The infusion of Islam into the politics of the Middle East is not necessarily an anathema to democracy or our freedom. Democracy is messy and its results are not always to our taste, but it remains the only game in town capable of giving ordinary people a sense of empowerment and hope in the future. Tunisia has witnessed the first free and fair election in its history, and the Islamist Ennahda party subsequently ceded power to the secular block in new elections in 2014. The Muslim Brotherhood in Egypt may not have been to everyone's liking, but there can be no doubting it won the December parliamentary elections of 2011 and the presidential election of 2012 convincingly. The West should acknowledge that result for what it was rather than continuing to demonise all Islamic movements irrespective of their character. Nor should it abandon those young people who protested in the squares of the Near East, and whose vision of democracy is closer to its own, simply because they failed to win this time round or build a viable electoral movement. If the West wants to establish long-term stability in the MENA region then it needs to adopt a long-term, more patient approach to the historical events that make up the Arab Spring in which counter-terror strategies run alongside greater societal investment through the deployment of some sort of Marshall plan hinted at by President Obama in his Cairo speech.

What we need then is a full spectrum approach towards the resolution of conflict, which draws upon all the resources and dynamism of the state, including civil society, NGOs, small nation capacities as well as cultural diplomacy. The dichotomy between supporting our immediate interests and known allies as opposed to supporting the longer-term needs and aspirations of the MENA people and the dispossessed is a false one. The history of Iraq and Libya has taught us that botched interventions and disengagement are no longer options open for us to take. We have to get it right next time round. So whether you are on the counter-insurgency side of the spectrum or part of the liberal civil interventionist fraternity matters little. Both sides need to work together if we are to avoid the tragedies and excesses of the past. What is required in the twenty-first century is a new multi-dimensional approach to diplomacy and the resolution of conflict in which some of the more outdated conventions of traditional state-based diplomacy give way to an altogether more dynamic and exciting partnership between state and non-state actors, government and society, leaders and the led, in which humility rather than hubris prevails.

For a brief moment in 2011 a sense of democratic hope arced out across the MENA region. The essence of this arc was inclusivity. It enabled people from different cultures to come together in a global act of political solidarity that for a short time brought our warring world closer together. Such solidarity was exemplified in the way that NGOs, like the Bar Human Rights Committee and the CHD, sought to help Libyans reconstruct and reconcile their country for the better. Such solidarity is the best riposte the West can give to the debilitating, alienating and self-defeating security doctrines that underpinned much of its earlier war on terror. Although Al-Qaeda and Islamic State moved into the vacuum created by the downfall of Gaddafi in places like Mali and Sirte, they have not captured the majority of the hearts and minds of those who rose up in the MENA region in the spring of 2011. That should be an informative lesson for policymakers and future policymaking.

The people of the MENA region retain their dream of living an ordinary life free from fear, oppression and state corruption. It is a dream that most of us in the West live every day. Some sceptics, like J. R. Bradley, say it is an impossible dream for a place like the Middle East. Sixty years ago that same dream seemed impossible for the people of Europe after they emerged from the ashes of the Holocaust and the Second World War. Yet with the help of America, and by co-operating with each other, the people of Europe made their dream real. They did so through investing in democracy and society. The Arab Spring presents us with a similar opportunity: an opportunity to replace a decade of hate and suspicion with one of hope and solidarity. We should have grabbed that opportunity with both hands. Instead we let it slip through our hands.

Despite all the depravities of life in Libya, the people of Benghazi never lost sight of or belief in the principles of good governance. They were made to endure the antics of a tyrannical mad dog dictator for some forty-two years without any help from the West, whose institutions became complicit in a deeply unethical search for profit, all in the name of Western security and stability. It is remarkable fact that after all these trials and tribulations the people of New Libya chose to hold out the hand of friendship towards Britain when it came to their aid. We should salute Cameron for making the case for the no-fly zone against conventional diplomatic wisdom, when the outcome of such an enterprise was far from certain and the impact on our national interests was still unknown. His failure lay not in intervening but failing to see the task through to the bitter end. On 18 March 2011, on the occasion of the passing of Security Council Resolution 1973, the British-Libyan *Guardian* correspondent Alaa al-Ameri wrote this:

> There is a genuine opportunity to cleanse the reputation of humanitarian military intervention. There is clear mandate, credible counterparts, and a well-defined mission with an obvious exit strategy. The Libyan Interim National Transitional Council has made it clear there is no need or desire for troops on the ground [. . .] Libya even has the means to pay for the cost of the intervention upon victory. Those who don't want to be involved should stay out of the way. Disruption of the process will cost lives. Turkey and others should be aware of their short-sightedness and remember that Libya will soon have a new government, freely elected and representative of people who fought tooth and nail for their freedom, no thanks to them. Just as we will not forget those who stand against us, we will owe a great debt to those who have chosen to stand with us. The UK and France, regardless of previous dealings with the Gaddafi Regime, have made an honourable stand [. . .] It is now the job of Libyans to live up to the confidence of those who have come to their aid, and to the aspirations of those who have died fighting for a future that many of us believed we wouldn't see in our lifetimes.[1]

In early 2016 UN mediators finally managed to establish the framework for a new unity government in Libya with the help of non-state mediators like Jonathan Powell as well as advice from the Mediation Support Unit of the UN Department of Political Affairs, including myself. Libya and the international community have both been given a second chance. The opportunity to make something of that chance is fleeting. It will need political resolve and a clear eye about what is at stake. It is time for you to make your own judgment about the wisdom of Cameron's intervention and whether Britain was right to become once again embroiled in the internal affairs of another nation. Whatever your view, be in no doubt about the abiding affection and gratitude that the ordinary people of Benghazi showed towards Britain for a few magical days in the spring of 2011. After decades of opaque political and economic dealing, the UK government finally acted rightly to save the lives of a distant but awe-inspiring people, to the total amazement of everyone who was there.

Perhaps we should not dwell too much upon the erudite doubts of professional diplomats and officials in high office who questioned the wisdom of such an intervention, because of its potential impact on the future conduct of international affairs and diplomacy, both in the Security Council and elsewhere. International diplomacy has always been fraught with difficulty, and the debates of the Security Council have rarely proceeded upon the basis of humanitarian imperatives cut loose from national interests. To expect otherwise is to delude oneself in a way that only helps foster impunity and inaction in those who hold power and should know better.

Let us dwell instead upon the bravery of ordinary people like Qais and diplomats like Chris Stevens. They sacrificed their lives in order to free Libya from the yoke of tyranny and to give the Libyan people a chance to build a new democratic future. They were part of a titanic societal struggle within Libya, which, but for a miraculous international intervention, might never have happened. Let us also reflect upon the work, commitment and gripping images of Tim Hetherington, Chris Hondros and Guy Martin – as well as upon the brave dispatches of Martin Fletcher, Hala Jaber, Chris McGreal, Marie Colvin and the other brave citizen journalists whose work features in this book. Without their contribution the truth about the Libyan uprising and the Arab Spring could not be told. They risked their lives so that we in the West might better understand the suffering of the people of Cairo, Benghazi and Misrata. They went there to report on why the struggle for greater freedom, democracy and human dignity remained and remains so unyielding. Sceptics like Donald Trump may question why such men and women go to distant lands and risk their lives to make these reports and bring back these images for us to read and look at. The answer is because in the end it is not just a case of 'Benghazi or Bust' for the people of Libya, or for those leaders who put their physical and political necks on the line to support uprising, but for all of us, collectively, wherever we live. The struggle for greater human dignity and freedom is one that ultimately affects us all in some way or another, and we ignore that struggle at our own peril.

As Ernest Hemingway, quoting John Donne, once remarked about another faraway conflict that came to prefigure an entire world war, '[N]ever send to know for whom the bell tolls; it tolls for thee.' Let us not stand by, as some nations did during the Spanish Civil War, only for history to teach us what we know already when nations try to ignore the suffering of others in an attempt to avoid a similar fate. Far better to look this struggle right in the eye, rather than hope that it might somehow pass us by without our needing to fight. So, notwithstanding all the chaos, misunderstanding and uncertainty in the MENA region, let us resolve to choose light rather than darkness, hope rather than fear, commitment over disengagement, solidarity over individualism, and the hand of friendship rather than a wall of hate. And if we should occasionally fall short in this common endeavour let us not immediately reject our better values, but redouble our efforts to build a world based on human dignity, respect for the other and the right of all peoples and societies to pursue some civilised form of life, liberty and a chance of happiness wherever they happen to be situated.

Appendix: Report of the Northern Ireland Affairs Committee

HM Government Support for UK Victims of IRA Attacks that used Gaddafi-Supplied Semtex and Weapons

Conclusions and recommendations

Colonel Gaddafi and the IRA

1. There is no doubt that the weapons, funding, training, and explosives that Colonel Gaddafi provided to the Provisional IRA over the course of 25 years both extended and exacerbated the Northern Ireland Troubles, and caused enormous human suffering. Whilst other countries have sought compensation from the Libyan Government for its role in fostering terror, the UK Government has not done so, instead leaving the matter for victims themselves to resolve. We pay warm tribute to the quiet dignity and determination of those individuals and organisations who have campaigned tirelessly over the years to rectify this injustice. As they grow older, time is running out for many of the victims, and so we hope this Report will encourage the next Government to adopt a fresh approach which secures the compensation these people deserve. We hope also that our successor Committee will continue to campaign on this issue in the 2017 Parliament, until there is a satisfactory resolution for the victims. (Paragraph 9)

The Government's relationship with the Gaddafi regime

2. It is not clear how far the Tony Blair Government was aware of the campaign to seek compensation for the victims of Gaddafi-sponsored terrorism, and how far that Government pursued the matter with the Libyan authorities. Whatever the reality of the situation was, we believe the UK Government missed a vital opportunity, during the period in which Libya was seeking a rapprochement with the west, to act on behalf of IRA victims by placing this issue firmly on the negotiating table to secure a compensation package. (Paragraph 21)

3. We should emphasise that the conclusions and recommendations in this Report encompass all UK victims of Gaddafi-sponsored terrorism by the Provisional IRA, and not just those victims who were named in the McDonald writ. (Paragraph 23)

4. The exclusion of the UK victims of Gaddafi-sponsored terrorism from the terms of the US-Libya Claims Settlement Agreement 2008 was another missed opportunity to resolve the issue of compensation. Although the then UK Government claimed it had made representations to the US for the victims' inclusion, we received no evidence of the level they were made, and with what force. That said, even assuming that the UK Government had put its full weight behind the victims' cause, it cannot be known now, almost 10 years later, whether it would have affected the US Administration's position. Whatever its reasons were, it is deeply regrettable that, in 2008, the US appears not to have been willing to assist the UK in delivering justice for its victims. However, this does not absolve the former Labour Government for having failed to pursue the issue of compensation itself bilaterally with Libya with the same determination and vigour demonstrated by the Governments of France, Germany and the US. Had it done so, it might well have been equally successful. (Paragraph 33)

5. We have already deprecated the then UK Government's failure to pursue the issue of compensation when Libya was brought in from the cold in the early 2000s. However, it is not clear that Mr Blair's influence after leaving office was such that he could have made a material difference to the outcome of the US-Libya Claims Settlement Agreement 2008. Besides, he had ceased to be Prime Minister in June 2007. Negotiations between the US and Libya in 2008 took place on a bilateral basis, and whilst Sir Vincent Fean's email suggests that Mr Blair played some role in encouraging an agreement, it also suggests that it was not pivotal. We have already noted that the US Administration declined to include the UK victims in the terms of the LCSA. (Paragraph 36)

6. The establishment of the FCO's Libya Reconciliation Unit represented an acknowledgement by the then UK Government that it could not continue to ignore the campaign for compensation by the UK victims of Gaddafi-sponsored IRA terrorism. However, its support for the parliamentary delegation which visited Libya in 2009 underlined the fact that only direct government-to-government negotiations would have carried sufficient weight in pressing the victims' case. With the complete collapse of the Gaddafi regime in 2011, an eight-year window of opportunity, during which successive UK Governments could have sought to resolve this issue, had closed. (Paragraph 42)

The Government's relationship with Libya after Gaddafi

7. Whilst there was initial optimism that the Coalition Government would take a different approach on the issue of compensation after the fall of Gaddafi, that Government's rhetoric did not translate into any tangible progress. This was, yet again, a missed opportunity. The fact that lawyers acting on behalf the UK victims were able to have the then Chairman of the National Transitional Council of Libya sign a statement in support of providing compensation early in 2011, suggests to us that, if the Coalition Government itself had taken up this issue at that time, it would have had a good chance of reaching an agreement. (Paragraph 52)

8. Over the next few years, the UK Government may well play a key role in the reconstruction of Libya, both in terms of financial and political support. If so, this would present an ideal opportunity for the Government to leverage a response in kind from the Libyans by finally resolving the issue of compensation for the UK victims of Gaddafi-sponsored IRA terrorism. This can only be achieved through direct government-to-government negotiations. Statements made by the Libyan Deputy Prime Minister acknowledge this is an issue that the Government of National Accord needs to consider. We believe that, with sufficient determination, the UK Government should be able to reach an agreement. But, as one of our witnesses said: "it requires somebody to bang on their door, not with a wet sponge, but [with a] bang". (Paragraph 57)

Notes

Chapter 2   The Libyan Uprising

1 Daniel Kawczynski, *Seeking Gaddafi* (London: Biteback, 2010).

2 George Tremlett, *Gaddafi: The Desert Mystic* (New York: Carroll & Graf, 1993).

3 Deborah Haynes, 'Exclusive: spy game that halted Gaddafi WMDs', *The Times*, 1 November 2011.

4 David Kirkpatrick and Mona el-Naggar, 'Qaddafi's grip falters as his forces take on protesters', *The New York Times*, 21 February 2011.

5 See Peter Bartu, 'The Corridor of Uncertainty', in P. Cole and B. McQuinn (eds), *The Libyan Revolution and Its Aftermath* (Hurst, 2015), p. 35.

6 Fred Halliday, *Political Journeys: The Open Democracy Essays* (London: Saqi Books, 2011), p. 225.

7 Amartya Sen, *The Idea of Justice* (Cambridge, MA: Harvard University Press, 2009), p. 335.

8 *The Woolf Inquiry: An Inquiry into the LSE's Links with Libya and Lessons to be Learned*, October 2011. Available at: www.woolflse.com

9 Jack Doyle, 'Blair government tried to get Saif a place at Oxford . . . but he wasn't bright enough', *Daily Mail*, 1 December 2011.

10 Ethan Chorin, *Exit Gaddafi: The Hidden History of the Libyan Revolution* (London: Saqi, 2012).

Chapter 3   Memorandum of Misunderstandings

1 Ethan Chorin, *Exit Gaddafi: The Hidden History of the Libyan Revolution* (London: Saqi, 2012), p. 143.

2 Gareth Peirce, 'The Framing of Al-Megrahi', *London Review of Books*, vol. 31, no. 18, p. 24, September 2009.

3 Foreign Affairs Select Committee of Inquiry, 'Oral evidence: Libya:

Examination of intervention and collapse and the UK's future policy options', HC 119. Third Report of Session 2016–17. Col. 53, p. 19, Q159. Available at: https://www.publications.parliament.uk/pa/cm201617/cmselect/cmfaff/119/119.pdf

Chapter 4   Libya, Bahrain and the 'Responsibility to Protect'

1   John Pilger, 'Westminster warriors untouched by Libya's suffering and bloodshed', *New Statesman*, 8 April 2011.
2   Rory Stewart, 'The gentle art of not intruding', *New Statesman*, 14 April 2011.
3   Foreign Affairs Select Committee of Inquiry, 'Oral evidence: Libya: Examination of intervention and collapse and the UK's future policy options', HC 520. Tuesday 27 October 2015, Q88.
4   Foreign Affairs Select Committee of Inquiry, 'Oral evidence: Libya: Examination of intervention and collapse and the UK's future policy options', HC 520. Tuesday 1 December 2015, Q153.
5   'Libya: David Cameron Statement on UN Resolution', *BBC News*, 18 March 2011. Available at: http://www.bbc.co.uk/news/uk-politics-12786225.
6   House of Commons Official Report, 21 March 2011, col. 703.
7   Muhammad min Libya, 'Libya is united in popular revolution – please don't intervene', *The Guardian*, 1 March 2011.

Chapter 5   Passing through the Egyptian Revolution

1   Khedive Ismail was in charge of Egypt and Sudan until he was removed by the Ottoman Sultan Abdulhamid II at the behest of the British in 1879 after supporting the nationalist Urabi revolt. He was replaced by his son Tewfik Pasha. Tewfik Pasha remained Khedive of Egypt and Sudan until 1892 when he died and was succeeded by the last Ottoman Khedive Abbas II Hilmi Bey, who served until he was removed by the British in 1914.
2   Jean-Pierre Filiu, *The Arab Revolution* (Oxford: Oxford University Press, 2011), p. 76.
3   Quoted by Vijay Prashad in *Arab Spring, Libyan Winter* (Chico, CA: AK Press, 2012), p. 120.

Chapter 6   Entering Rebel-Held Libya

1   Mark Urban, 'Inside story of the UK's secret mission to beat Gaddafi', *BBC News Magazine*, 19 January 2012.
2   Notes taken by MMS.

Chapter 7   Experiencing Rebel-Held Benghazi

1 Martin Fletcher, 'Gaddafi's war victims sail on ship of horrors', *The Times*, 4 April 2011.

2 Xan Rice, 'Radio Free Libya shakes up Gaddafi regime from Misrata', *The Guardian*, 29 April 2011.

Chapter 8   Misrata and Negotiating with the NTC

1 Hala Jaber, 'Revealed: The full horror of Misrata', *The Sunday Times*, 10 April 2011.

2 'Q&A interview with Tim Hetherington, director of Restrepo', *Tree Pony*, 20 March 2011.

3 Marie Colvin, 'We were just told to kill, says Libyan teen soldier', *The Times*. 25 May 2011.

4 Contemporaneous note of author, 5 April 2011.

Chapter 9   Leaving Rebel-Held Libya

1 Peter Bartu, 'The Corridor of Uncertainty', in P. Cole and B. McQuinn (eds), *The Libyan Revolution and Its Aftermath* (Hurst, 2015), p. 48.

2 Chris McGreal, 'Libyan rebels deny offering Lockerbie compensation', *The Guardian*, 5 April 2011.

3 Martin Fletcher, 'Rebels offer to compensate Gaddafi terror victims', *The Times*, 5 April 2011.

4 Chris McGreal, 'Libya rebels vent frustration on Nato and a silent leadership', *The Observer*, 9 April 2011.

5 Chris McGreal, 'Torture and killing in Kenya – Britain's double standards', *The Guardian*, 8 April 2011.

6 Chris McGreal, 'Libya and Middle East uprising – Saturday 9 April', *The Guardian News Blog*, 9 April 2011.

7 Chris McGreal, 'Dispatch from Libya: The courage of ordinary people standing up to Gaddafi', *The Guardian*, 23 April 2011.

Chapter 10   Towards a New MENA Policy

1 In the event Cameron's administration failed to give the MDC any of the support that David Coltart pleaded for in London in 2010, despite it endorsing the Global Political Agreement. Without such support, the MDC could do little to improve the lot of the ordinary Zimbabwean or provide an incentive to the Zimbabwe African National Union Patriotic Front (Zanu-PF) to toe the line. Three years later Mugabe secured an

emphatic victory in presidential and parliamentary elections, thereby consigning a peace-loving people to another decade of poverty. While William Hague talked of 'grave concerns' about the conduct of the election, such protestations were all too little and much too late. I remember calling David Coltart on the day after the election. He had lost by a mere twenty-nine votes. It was a dreadful and depressing phone call to a good man, who had been badly let down by the West.

2 See Ian Martin, 'The United Nation's Role in the First Year of Transition', in P. Cole and B. McQuinn (eds), *The Libyan Revolution and Its Aftermath* (Hurst, 2015), p. 128.

3 See SC/7295 (2002) where Brahimi advocates an integrated mission with 'a light footprint' when discussing the future United Nations mission in Afghanistan.

4 See Peter Cole with Umar Khan, 'The Fall of Tripoli: Part 1', in P. Cole and B. McQuinn (eds), *The Libyan Revolution and Its Aftermath* (Hurst, 2015), p. 67.

5 Quoted by Vijay Prashad in *Arab Spring, Libyan Winter* (Chico, CA: AK Press, 2012), p. 115.

6 Foreign Affairs Select Committee of Inquiry, 'Oral evidence: Libya: Examination of intervention and collapse and the UK's future policy options', HC 520. Friday 11 December 2015, Q212.

7 Robert Fisk, 'President's fine words may not address the Middle East's real needs', *The Independent*, 18 May 2011.

8 Barack Obama and David Cameron, 'Not just special, but an essential relationship', *The Times*, 24 May 2011.

Chapter 11   Bahrain

1 Andy McSmith, 'Bahrain visit: Cameron embraces tyranny', *The Independent*, 19 May 2011.

Chapter 12   Stabilising Libya

1 Rory Stewart and Gerald Knaus, *Can Intervention Work?* (New York: Norton, 2011), p. xxii.

2 Stephen R. Grand, 'Democratization 101: Historical Lessons of the Arab Spring', in K. M. Pollack et al. (eds), *The Arab Awakening: America and the Transformation of the Middle East* (Washington, DC: The Brookings Institution, 2011), pp. 21–9.

3 Rory Stewart and Gerald Knaus, *Can Intervention Work?* (New York: Norton, 2011) p. 16.

4 Stephen R. Grand, 'Democratization 101: Historical Lessons of the Arab Spring', in K. M. Pollack et al. (eds), *The Arab Awakening: America and*

the Transformation of the Middle East (Washington, DC: The Brookings Institution, 2011) p. 26.

Chapter 13   Endgame in Libya

1 Peter Bartu, 'The Corridors of Uncertainty', in P. Cole and B. McQuinn (eds), *The Libyan Revolution and Its Aftermath* (Hurst, 2015), pp. 50–3.
2 Marina Hyde, 'Gaddafi has crossed the line between murderous tyrant and plonker', *The Guardian*, 26 August 2011.
3 Bobby Ghosh, 'The Gaddafi regime is broken. What will take its place?', *Time Magazine*, 5 September 2011.
4 Stephen R. Grand, 'Democratization 101: Historical Lessons of the Arab Spring', in K. M. Pollack et al. (eds), *The Arab Awakening: America and the Transformation of the Middle East* (Washington DC: The Brookings Institution, 2011) p. 27.
5 Marie Colvin, 'Final dispatch from Homs, the battered city', *The Sunday Times*, 19 February 2012.

Chapter 14   Whither the Revolution?

1 See Ian Martin, 'The United Nation's Role in the First Year of Transition', in P. Cole and B. McQuinn (eds), *The Libyan Revolution and Its Aftermath* (Hurst, 2015), p. 131.
2 Vaclav Havel and Desmond Tutu, 'Introduction', in Jared Genser and Irwin Cotler (eds), *The Responsibility to Protect: The Promise of Stopping Mass Atrocities in Our Time* (Oxford: Oxford University Press, 2011) p. xxv.
3 Barack Obama and David Cameron, 'Not just special, but an essential relationship', *The Times*, 24 May 2011.
4 See page 73.
5 Ian Cobain, 'Special report: Rendition ordeal that raises new questions about secret trials', *The Guardian*, 8 April 2012.
6 Ian Cobain, 'Special report: Rendition ordeal that raises new questions about secret trials', *The Guardian*, 8 April 2012.

Chapter 15   The Fall of the House of Gaddafi

1 Kareem Fahim, 'In his last days, Qaddafi wearied of fugitive's life', *The New York Times*, 22 October 2011.
2 'Clues to Gaddafi's death concealed from public view', *Reuters*, 22 October 2011.
3 Con Coughlin, 'The West should not have allowed Muammar Gaddafi to be murdered in cold blood', *The Telegraph*, 27 October 2011.

4 See Dirk Vandewalle, 'Libya's Uncertain Revolution', in P. Cole and B. McQuinn (eds), *The Libyan Revolution and Its Aftermath* (Hurst, 2015), p. 23.

5 Patrick Cockburn, 'This was always a civil war, and the victors are not merciful', *The Independent*, 24 November 2011.

6 See Ian Martin, 'The United Nation's Role in the First Year of Transition', in P. Cole and B. McQuinn (eds), *The Libyan Revolution and Its Aftermath* (Hurst, 2015), p. 142.

7 Amnesty International Libya, ' "Out of control" militias commit widespread abuses, a year on from uprising', *Amnesty International Website*, 15 February 2012.

8 Human Rights Watch *World Report 2013: Events of 2012* (2013). Available at: https://www.hrw.org/sites/default/files/wr2013_web.pdf

9 See Ian Martin, 'The United Nation's Role in the First Year of Transition', in P. Cole and B. McQuinn (eds), *The Libyan Revolution and Its Aftermath* (Hurst, 2015).

Chapter 16   Ambassador Stevens

1 See Ian Martin, 'The United Nation's Role in the First Year of Transition', in P. Cole and B. McQuinn (eds), *The Libyan Revolution and Its Aftermath* (Hurst, 2015), p. 148.

2 Fred Burton and Samuel L. Katz, '40 Minutes in Benghazi', *Vanity Fair*, August 2013.

3 Fred Burton and Samuel L. Katz, '40 Minutes in Benghazi', *Vanity Fair*, August 2013.

4 Raf Sanchez, 'Britain hid secret MI6 plan to break up Libya from US, Hillary Clinton told by confidant', *The Telegraph*, 21 May 2015.

5 Foreign Affairs Select Committee Inquiry, 'Libya: Examination of intervention and collapse and the UK's future policy options'. FCO (LIB0012), para 10 of submissions.

6 Foreign Affairs Select Committee Inquiry, 'Oral Evidence: Libya: Examination of intervention and collapse and the UK's future policy options', HC 520. Tuesday 19 January 2016.

7 Patrick Wintour and Nicholas Watt, 'David Cameron's Libyan war: Why the PM felt Gaddafi had to be stopped', *The Guardian*, 2 October 2011.

8 Foreign Affairs Select Committee Inquiry, 'Oral Evidence: Libya: Examination of intervention and collapse and the UK's future policy options', HC 520. Tuesday 1 December 2015. Answer to Q157.

9 Foreign Affairs Select Committee Inquiry, 'Oral Evidence: Libya: Examination of intervention and collapse and the UK's future policy options', HC 520. Tuesday 19 January 2016. Answer to Q293.

10 Foreign Affairs Select Committee Inquiry, 'Oral Evidence: Libya: Examination of intervention and collapse and the UK's future policy options', HC 520. Tuesday 27 October 2015. Answer to Q104.

11 Peter Cole and Brian McQuinn (eds), *The Libyan Revolution and its Aftermath* (London: Hurst and Co, 2013) p. 150.

12 See Ian Martin, 'The United Nation's Role in the First Year of Transition', in P. Cole and B. McQuinn (eds), *The Libyan Revolution and Its Aftermath* (Hurst, 2015), p. 150.

13 Foreign Affairs Select Committee Inquiry, 'Oral Evidence: Libya: Examination of intervention and collapse and the UK's future policy options', HC 520. Tuesday 19 January 2016. Answer to Q290.

14 See note 1 of Chapter 10 as to the British government's reluctance to offer any meaningful assistance to the MDC in Zimbabwe.

15 Foreign Affairs Select Committee of Inquiry, 'Oral evidence: Libya: Examination of intervention and collapse and the UK's future policy options', HC 520. Tuesday 19 January 2016. Answer to Q371.

16 Foreign Affairs Select Committee of Inquiry, 'Oral evidence: Libya: Examination of intervention and collapse and the UK's future policy options', HC 520. Tuesday 13 October 2015. Answer to Q3.

17 'Hillary Clinton's WMD moment: US intelligence saw false narrative in Libya', *The Washington Times*, 29 January 2015.

18 Daniel Boffey, 'Britain made same mistakes in Libya as it did in Iraq', *The Guardian*, 24 January 2016.

19 Foreign Affairs Select Committee of Inquiry, 'Oral evidence: Libya: Examination of intervention and collapse and the UK's future policy options', HC 520. Tuesday 9 February 2016, Qs 491–2.

20 Jody Harrison, 'UK government spent 13 times more bombing Libya than on rebuilding post war', *The Herald*, 26 July 2015.

21 Jeffrey Goldberg, 'The Obama doctrine: The US President talks through his hardest decisions about America's role in the world', *The Atlantic*, April 2016.

22 Muhammad min Libya, 'Libya is united in popular revolution – please don't intervene', *The Guardian*, 1 March 2011.

Chapter 17   Reflections for the Future

1 Ethan Chorin, *Exit Gaddafi: The Hidden History of the Libyan Revolution* (London: Saqi, 2012), p. 310.

2 David Leppard, 'Libya to give IRA victims £450m', *The Sunday Times*, 23 October 2011.

3 Lucy Clarke-Billings, 'Tony Blair apologises for Iraq War mistakes and accepts invasion had part to play in rise of Islamic State', *The Telegraph*, 24 October 2015.

4 'GOL still bristling over victims of terrorism legislation, UTA judgment', *WikiLeaks*, 12 March 2008.

5 Eric Lipton 'Libya seeks exemption for its debt to victims', *The New York Times*, 22 April 2008.

6 Robert Mendick and Edward Malnick, 'Tony Blair helped Colonel Gaddafi in £1bn legal row', *The Sunday Telegraph*, 4 August 2013.

7 House of Commons Northern Ireland Affairs Committee Fourth Report of Session 2016–17: HM Government Support for UK Victims of IRA Attacks that used Gaddafi-Suppplied Semtex and Weapons, 2 May 2017.

Chapter 18   Terrorism and the Right to Resist Oppression

1 See Court of Appeal judgment dated 16/02/07, in R v F. Case No: 2007/00579/B5. [2007] EWCA Crim 243.

2 See 'The Right to Self-Determination' on page 316.

3 UN International Law Commission Draft: Responsibility of State for Internationally Wrongful Acts 2001.

4 A. Cassese, *Self-Determination of Peoples: A Legal Reappraisal* (Cambridge: Cambridge University Press, 1998) p. 200.

5 Kalliopi K Koufa 'Terrorism and Human Rights Working Paper submitted by Ms K K Koufa in accordance with Sub-Commission Resolution 1996/20 E/CN.4.Sub.2/1997/2826', 26 June 1997.

6 The ICJ has virtually denuded the right of practical effect by (1) equating the term 'peoples' with the 'government of a whole territory'; and (2) through (the '*uti possidetis*') rule that the exercise of self-determination must not involve changes to existing frontiers except where relevant nation states consent. This conflated territorial constraint has effectively disenfranchised minority peoples in a majority in a province or part of a state from invoking the right of external self-determination. (One need only take a cursory glance at the Namibia case to understand just how far the principle has been neutered.)

7 Mark Muller, 'Right to resist oppressive regimes must be recognised in terrorism legislation', International Conference of Parliamentarians & Jurists. Available at: www.scribd.com/document/71836573

8 POAC judgment dated 30/11/07 in Lord Alton of Liverpool & Others (in the Matter of the People's Mojahadeen Organisation of Iran) v Secretary of State for the Home Department. Appeal no: PC/02/2006.

9 Times Law Report dated 13/05/08. Court of Appeal judgment dated 07/05/08 in Secretary of State for Home Department v Lord Alton & Others. Case no: 2007/9516.

10 Judgment dated 15/02/05 of the European Court of Justice and 03/04/08

of the Court of First Instance of the European Communities, in PKK and KNK v Council of the European Community. Case T-229/02.

11 Judgment dated 03/04/08 of the Court of First Instance of the European Communities, in Kongra-Gel and Others v Council of the European Union, United Kingdom of Great Britain and Northern Ireland. Case T-253/04.

Chapter 19   The Rise of Non-State Mediation

1 Rory Stewart and Gerald Knaus, *Can Intervention Work?* (New York: Norton, 2011), p. 20.

2 K. M. Pollack et al. (eds), *The Arab Awakening: America and the Transformation of the Middle East* (Washington DC: The Brookings Institution, 2011), p. 126.

3 Timothy Phillips et al. (eds), *Beyond Conflict: 20 Years of Putting Experience to Work for Peace* (Brideswell Books, 2013).

Epilogue

1 Alaa al-Ameri, 'Libya will not forget this help', *The Guardian*, 18 March 2011.

Index